A HISTORY OF MONEY

Everyone is familiar with money. Yet few realise that currently contentious issues and financial difficulties are not new. On the contrary, most are firmly rooted in the past and when examined help to put current economic problems into historical context.

This book presents a detailed history of money from Charlemagne's reform in approximately AD 800 to the end of the Silver Wars in 1896. It also offers a summary of twentieth century events and an analysis of how the past relates to present problems. The book examines how virtually all modern difficulties associated with money have precedents in the past. It discusses how a mercantile system developed alongside simple, metallic, medieval coinage, in a way which has important lessons for the countries now emerging from central planning. It covers the great periods of monetary disputes, Henry VIII and Sir Thomas Gresham, Isaac Newton's Great Recoinage of 1696, Ricardo and the Bullion Committee Report, the battle between the Banking and Currency schools, and the much neglected but increasingly relevant, issues of bemetallism and European monetary union in the late nineteenth century. The monetary theories of such diverse characters as Locke, Defoe, Swift and Sir Walter Scott are discussed as well as those of many economists. The coverage is international, and includes the controversial private banking period in the early United States between Independence and the Civil War.

John Chown founded J. F. Chown & Company in 1962. His firm specialises in international tax. He is also co-founder and Executive Committee member of the Institute for Fiscal Studies. He has previously been editor of the *Journal of Strategy in International Taxation* and for some years was a contributor to a regular column in the *Financial Times*. He has written and lectured extensively on taxation and finance in the United Kingdom, the United States, Canada, Europe, Australasia and the Far East. He is currently on the editorial board of *Treasury Today* published by the Institute of Chartered Accountants.

A HISTORY OF MONEY

From AD 800

John Chown

London and New York

First published 1994
by Routledge and the Institute of Economic Affairs
11 New Fetter Lane, London EC4P 4EE

Simultaneously published in the USA and Canada
by Routledge
29 West 35th Street, New York, NY 10001

Reprinted 1995, 1996
First published in paperback 1996

Routledge is an International Thomson Publishing company

© 1994, 1996 John F. Chown

Typeset in Garamond by J & L Composition Ltd, Filey, North Yorkshire

Printed and bound in Great Britain by T J Press, Padstow, Cornwall

British Library Cataloguing in Publication Data
A catologue record for this book is available from the British Library

Library of Congress Cataloguing in Publication Data
A catalogue record for this book has been requested

ISBN 0–415–10279–0 (hbk)
ISBN 0–415–13729–2 (pbk)

CONTENTS

CONTENTS

LIST OF TABLES

FOREWORD

The history of money in all its facets impinges on almost every aspect of social and economic history. At one end of the spectrum it touches on the discovery of metals and mining technology, and the production of coin (and later paper) and the technological changes involved in these. It ranges over the means of circulation of money and to the institutions that emerge – different kinds of banks according to theories and circumstances – to facilitate its transmission. The story does not get far before public finance enters; in fact the needs of public finance frequently come first, and so the risks of inflation and of its effects in the economy arise. A popular notion that has appeared at many times is that purchasing power can, by a monetary innovation, somehow be increased to improve the lot of the poor. This last lies behind some of the many schemes promoting land banks and the like, where the reserves are long-term assets. In more modern times monetary policy enters the story, and its relationship with other policies and its impact on the real economy have extended the historian further.

Interestingly, in the early days of academic economic history in the first part of the twentieth century money was at the very centre of the discipline, generated a lot of excitement, and featured regularly in the academic journals. It faded somewhat after that as issues of economic growth and development became dominant. But in the closing years of the twentieth century discussion of money is returning to a more central role. This is not surprising since the great debates currently are about inflation, exchange rate regimes, the proper conduct of bankers, European central banking, and what is necessary to establish market economies in the former Soviet Union and in eastern Europe.

John Chown's book will be of interest to a wide readership for he introduces these subjects in monetary history, dealing with a host of topics of current interest and at a level accessible to a wide range of students and practitioners and policy makers. The book opens up the world of monetary history ranging over the use of coin in early medieval Europe, through its role in the commercial revolution, the great debasement of Henry VIII's reign and the Locke–Lowndes debate in the financial revolution of the late

FOREWORD

seventeenth century. There is extensive discussion of that difficult subject bimetallism in Europe, the USA and in India. The development of modern banking is a major subject in itself, and Chown devotes Part II to this story taking the reader through from the earliest forms in Europe to the emergence of modern banking. This story touches upon all the difficulties encountered in the creation and transmission of money, the sometimes resulting crises, and so introduces the possibility of the need for supervision or regulation, and the numerous debates to which that leads.

This book will serve as an excellent introduction to the many topics in monetary economics that concern us today; and it shows that there is both insight and instruction to be gained from discovering that they have almost all been around before. The book will have great appeal to those approaching the subject for the first time; but there is also much of interest for those who are familiar with the subject. This is a grand sweep across several centuries covering some of the most fascinating experiences in monetary history.

Forrest Capie
City University Business School

1

INTRODUCTION

Since 1914 the world has been bedevilled by inflation, depression, devaluation, unstable exchange rates and other 'diseases of money'. In 1923–4 hyper-inflation wiped out the currencies of Germany, Hungary, Poland and Russia. Greece went the same way in 1944, and Hungary (again) in 1946. The depression of the 1930s had, some would argue, led directly to the Second World War. In the 1970s, nearly all countries suffered from double digit inflation or worse.

The proposals for European Monetary Union produced some unexpected turns: this is a saga which will run and run. Proud and prosperous Germany ran into economic problems from which they thought they were exempt. Who would have thought that Germany's inflation rate would exceed that of France? This happened because of a serious technical error in setting the terms of the monetary union between the two Germanies (in 1990, following the collapse of East Germany) which had its perhaps inevitable repercussions in 1992 with the expensive partial collapse of the Exchange Rate Mechanism (ERM). The president of the Bundesbank, asked to comment on the rate chosen, said 'it was a political decision', and he was not being polite. The ERM was again in serious difficulty in the summer of 1993.

It would be unfair, unrealistic and narrow to blame all our ills on, and give all the credit for our prosperous times to, the failure or success of monetary management. No one can really understand the history of this century, or hope to prescribe for the problems of the next, without some understanding of how money and its management can affect, and affect profoundly, broader, economic, political and social affairs. The successful statesman, businessman, investor or trader sees this crisis, that stock market boom, the other free fall or rise in the dollar or the oil price in perspective. He knows what has happened before and can better judge what can happen this time than those who, ignorant of the past, are condemned to repeat its mistakes.

Even those who make it their business to remember last time and who are familiar with what happened in 1929, are tempted to believe that there was, before 1914, a golden age of the gold standard when prices were stable,

1

employment was full and the intending traveller could pull down from his father's bookshelf a dusty but still accurate ready reckoner which told him how many francs, marks, or lire he would receive for his pounds or his dollars. There was such a golden age, but it had lasted for all of eighteen years, since 1896. Economists, and those whose business it is to comment on, or react to, economic affairs, have to understand money. History helps a great deal. This book is not so much a history for economists as an economist's view of history. Rather to his surprise the author discovered how many of the world's apparently modern problems have their precedents in the past.

THE PLAN OF THE BOOK

The book has been divided into three main sections, which to some extent overlap chronologically. Part I deals with coinage, and Part II with banking and credit as it developed to supplement what was basically a gold, silver or bimetallic standard. Part III deals with experiments, beginning (in the West) in 1720 with the type of inconvertible paper money we have today.

The main story in this book begins in about 800 AD when Charlemagne reintroduced silver money to the West with the concepts of pounds, shillings and pence. The history of *coinage* actually begins in about 800 BC when the first coins were struck from electrum, a naturally occurring alloy of silver and gold, bearing the sign of a half lion as a guarantee of their weight.

The history of *money* goes back even further. Primitive societies must soon have found the need to progress from simple barter such as 'two horses for that field' to finding the need for a standard item which could be used as a medium of exchange to facilitate triangular or more complex barters or in some cases, more subtly, simply as a unit of account by which values could be compared without the unit of money necessarily changing hands. Mrs Quiggin (1949) describes the wide range of expedients adopted by primitive societies in her book *Primitive Money*, a labour of love which she began to write when she was already 70 years old. Only one society, that of the Incas of Peru, appears to have developed an organised civilisation without the invention of money (Hemming: 1970).

Eventually, societies developed the idea of coined metal. Its natural advantages tended to supplant rival forms of money, and a sophisticated monetary economy developed in the ancient world. It is quite clear, from even a cursory reading of the sources, that many of the problems and events we shall discuss had their parallels in earlier centuries. I can offer only a tantalising glance at a few of these earlier events. There were certainly monetary crises under Solon of Athens, Cleopatra of Egypt and the Emperor Nero which seem, from a brief study, just as interesting as the later ones we shall be studying.

During the early period, money meant coins. Charlemagne divided a pound weight of silver into 240 deniers or pennies, and this efficient and sound system was imposed on the territories he conquered. Various English kingdoms (which were to be united in 973) were never conquered, but chose to adopt the system. Later, though, it was England alone who preserved the Carolingian system with only modest, but technically interesting, deprecia-tions for many centuries. In the rest of Europe, the coinage became very sick indeed (not long after the death of Charlemagne) and soon all that circulated were grubby pieces of base metal with just a taint of silver. On the Continent, sound money had effectively to be reinvented to meet the needs of the dramatic revival of trade in the thirteenth century. At this stage, the Italian city states become the main centre of interest.

The whole mechanism of government-induced inflation, which we now associate with 'turning on the printing press', can be seen at work within the framework of a simple silver coinage. The Navy has always argued that even for those whose destiny is to navigate a nuclear submarine, there is no training like sail training. Get back to first principles, learn to face the elements with few mechanical aids and you really will understand the weather and what going to sea in ships is all about. Really understanding how money works in a 'simple' system with only one type of money – silver coins – is remarkably illuminating and greatly helps to put modern monetary theory into perspective. The principles are discussed in Chapter 2 and the history, to about 1250, in Chapter 3.

The reintroduction of gold coins alongside the silver created a new set of problems, those associated with foreign exchange and 'money of account'. The sophistication of the money markets proves to have been quite remarkable: after the end of the fourteenth century no really original type of foreign exchange instrument or problem remained to be invented.

The commercial revolution of the thirteenth and fourteenth centuries also involved the development of credit instruments and the early beginnings of means of payment not involving metal coins. During this period there was a battle between the Church, which wanted to stamp out usury, and the merchants, who needed to borrow money on terms which gave both an acceptable rate of interest to the lender while leaving a margin of profit to the borrower. The story has many of the features of the battle between those who invent tax loopholes and those who draw up anti-avoidance legislation and has its modern applications in the concepts of Islamic banking. Fortunately, the Arabs could still exploit loopholes that the Christians closed centuries ago. This is discussed at the beginning of Part II.

Generally, though, the emphasis would still remain on coined money for a few more centuries. Henry VIII's Great Debasement produced a rate of inflation in England which was to remain unsurpassed until the days of Harold Wilson. The idea that a gold standard ensures price stability was proven false at about this time. South American gold discoveries forced major price rises throughout Europe; and, incidentally, ruined the Spanish economy. Some of the problems of the coinage were settled, in what was by then the United Kingdom, in 1696 after a major public discussion involving men as eminent as the philosopher John Locke and the most distinguished Master the mint has ever had – Isaac Newton.

Banks and bank notes

By this time the role of gold and silver were already being supplemented by banks and bank notes, again discussed in Part II. These new inventions very soon had their own excesses, in parallel but rather different events. The South Sea Bubble in the United Kingdom and the activities of John Law in France both came to a head in 1720 and are, with the Dutch tulip mania, the original models of financial booms and busts. These events set back the development of paper money for half a century, although banks and financial instruments continued to grow apace. In some ways the mid-eighteenth century was perhaps another short golden age with few financial crises, but a lot of very intelligent philosophising about economic theory. Sound metal currencies caused few problems, while alternatives were quietly developing.

This period ended in 1776, the year of publication of *The Wealth of Nations* and of the American revolution. Much of the Part III material, on inconvertible paper currencies has its origins here. Both the American and the French revolutions were largely financed by the issue of paper money which subsequently became worthless. As a direct result of the Napoleonic wars and the 'suspension of payments' of 1797 the United Kingdom, too, developed a paper currency inconvertible into gold or silver, but, unlike the other two cases, eventually restored to its full value. These three parallel but very contrasting stories represent the birth of the system of paper money and banking as we know them. It is also a classic period of debate and pamphleteering on monetary theory, focused largely on the Bullion Report of 1810.

Nineteenth century developments

The United Kingdom then began the attempt to develop an adequate system of bank and credit regulation (back to Part II). The Bank Charter Act of 1844, was preceded and followed by a series of financial crises as the country learnt to master the system.

The United States was by now an economically important nation in its own right, and provides an excellent case study of the problems of creating a monetary system in a newly emerging independent country. It had its own financial crises which related to, but did not always parallel, those in the United Kingdom and the rest of Europe. There is the story of the attempts to set up a Bank of the United States and the conflict between its head,

Nicholas Biddle, and President Andrew Jackson. The Bank Wars soured the American political attitude to banking, and explain what can seem to Europeans the parochialism and backwardness of American retail banking.

At this time, the 1830s, small private note issuing banks formed under State law were, to mix similes, springing up like mushrooms and dying off like flies. The concepts both of free banking and 'deposit insurance' in the form of the 'safety fund' have their origins in this period. These events proved to be inadequately covered in the general literature, and a study of contemporary sources has proved particularly rewarding.

During the American Civil War, there was another attempt at printing press finance in the form of the greenbacks: the different histories of the winning and losing sides both have their lessons. After that war, American monetary history is very well covered in the modern literature, and indeed the United States began to develop its role as the world's leading financial power.

Silver, gold, exchange rates and monetary unions

Although the emphasis seemed by now to have switched to banking and paper money, the problems of gold and silver became a major monetary issue in the late nineteenth century: indeed the last few chapters of Part I cover this highly instructive period. The problems of bimetallism go back to medieval Italy. There is no law of nature that says an ounce of gold must at all times be worth exactly fifteen times as much as an ounce of silver although this was broadly true for a very long period, including much of the nineteenth century.

Early in the nineteenth century the United Kingdom had introduced a formal gold standard, using silver only as a subsidiary coinage, while British India operated a silver standard. Some countries, notably France and the United States, attempted a bi-metallic standard: both gold and silver were legal tender and were exchangeable into each other at a legally determined rate of exchange. This worked fine so long as the ratio did not vary too much.

Indeed, as with the Bretton Woods system of fixed exchange rates, the system could itself absorb and take in its stride quite substantial fluctuations. Neither system could, by its nature, deal with a material change in the fundamental equilibrium: in this case when the relative price of silver collapsed. It is a period of monetary history usually buried in obscurity, but has again become particularly topical. Bimetallism itself raises all the problems of fixed versus floating exchange rates. Whatever arguments, good and bad, which have come up in the post war period prove already to have been deployed, probably at far greater length, by some nineteenth century pamphleteer.

Even more topical was the closely related subject of the Latin Monetary

Union and the abortive attempts to create a universal world currency in the mid- nineteenth century. This was preceded by more local monetary unions between the multitude of small states which now form Germany and Italy and between the cantons of Switzerland. There are good precedents both for European Monetary Union and for the problems of the Eastern European countries returning to a market economy.

A natural, although arbitrary ending to the main part of the book comes with William Jennings Bryan, his unsuccessful 1896 Presidential campaign and his famous 'cross of gold' speech. This was a final but doomed attempt to preserve the central monetary role of silver. There is a final chapter giving a quick overview of the twentieth century, a period already covered adequately in the literature.

Note Chapter 2 sets out some fairly abstract economic concepts in what is intended to be a reasonably digestible form. It is by way of being an introduction to Part I, and those reading the book as part of an economics course, or with some background knowledge of the subject, should certainly begin with it. Other readers may prefer to omit Chapter 2 for the moment, returning to it only when they have read the more narrative treatment in the rest of Part I.

Part I
MONEY AS COIN

2

SOME CONCEPTS OF MONEY

INTRODUCTION

Coin struck from precious metals such as gold or silver was the earliest form of organised money. Only much later was this to be supplemented or replaced by bank notes, bank deposits and other means of payment or stores of value. Part I of this book discusses the history of coin, and shows how many apparently modern problems of monetary theory have their roots in a simple coinage system. This chapter discusses the specific analytical points, which are then illustrated in later chapters in Part I.

It costs money to manufacture coins from silver or gold, and the mint authority charges a turn (usually including a profit) known as 'seigniorage'. Issuers can cheat, and make an extra profit by debasing the coinage. If this is detected, as it usually is, the public may value coins 'in specie' (i.e. by their bullion content) rather than 'in tale' (their official legal value). The purchasing power of coins may change without any debasement; the value in trade of the coinage metal itself may change. The monetary system may be threatened by clipping and counterfeiting and, even if rulers and citizens are scrupulously honest, the coinage has to contend with fair wear and tear.

All these factors are relevant even with a simple coinage system based on a single metal, usually silver but sometimes gold, and are discussed in the first part of the chapter. There are further complications when two or three metals circulate side by side. Moneys of account and ghost moneys mean that the monetary historian must study the exact meaning of the data very carefully indeed. Bimetallism has been one of the great subjects for debate, persisting into the late nineteenth century long after the development of modern banking. There were corresponding small change problems, while Gresham's Law, properly understood, helps make sense of it all.

Seigniorage

A coin was, in concept, simply a piece of precious metal (usually gold or silver) the weight and fineness of which was guaranteed by the ruler whose name, portrait or symbol was stamped on the coin. The ruler might have been be a king or queen as in England or Scotland, a duke or count of one of the many small independent states which made up Germany or Italy, an ecclesiastical authority, bishop or abbot, or an Italian city state. In France both the king himself and his feudal underlings had coinage rights.

In principle, and for a long period of history, a mint operated on the basis of a laundry. Private citizens would bring bullion to the mint. It would then be assayed, refined and struck into coins, and the citizen would receive in return coins equal to the value of the metal brought in less a deduction known as seigniorage. Mint practices obviously varied from country to country and at different periods of history: even when this principle operated, the citizen would not typically expect to receive the coins struck with his own metal. He would usually be paid with already minted coins as soon as the weight and fineness of his gold or silver had been agreed. Sometimes, too, the mint would buy bullion in the market in exchange for its coins, on its own initiative. In all cases, the principle is the same – the mint exchanges coins for gold or silver, and retains a small proportion for its trouble.

Coins were more convenient than bullion and therefore you would expect them to have an economical value of a small premium over the bullion content. Even today, sovereigns and specially minted coins such as Kruger Rands command a market premium over their gold content. The mint adds value, and the public accepted that it would exact a reasonable charge for its services, and that the weight of coins handed over by the mint in exchange for a pound weight of silver or gold would be something less than one pound.[1]

Seigniorage, the charge made by the mint for turning bullion into coins, can be defined in two ways (and spelt in rather more). The mint's total charge included the actual cost of making coins plus the profit made by the government. Some writers define seigniorage as the profit element only. However, using the term to mean the total gross margin has the practical advantage that it can be derived from facts which will typically be known accurately to the historian, who may have more limited evidence on the division between cost and profit. This preferred usage is supported by the Oxford English Dictionary:

> A duty levied on the coining of money for the purpose of covering the expenses of minting, and a source of revenue to the crown, claimed by the sovereign by virtue of his prerogative.

Moneying, as an activity, needs to be under strict royal or equivalent control. There is therefore a wealth of documentary evidence to show how at different times and places the seigniorage was calculated. These sources often, but not always, show how it was divided between costs, and the profit respectively of the moneyer, the ruler and (sometimes) the intermediate authorities.[2]

At some time in early modern history, coins began to be minted as a public service without seigniorage. In England, for example, this reform dates from 1666. The costs of the mint were thereafter borne out of taxation. For instance, in 1793, (immediately before the French Wars upset British monetary arrangements) the citizen could formally require the Mint to coin gold bullion for him at the rate of 44½ guineas per troy pound of standard (22 carat fine) gold – that is at a value of £3 17s.10½d. would get back the exact weight of gold: the mint made no charge for its services. He would, however, have to wait for his guineas until they were coined. As a practical alternative, he could, and generally would, go to the Bank of England's Bullion Office which would buy his gold bullion for coins, paying £3 17s.6d. on the spot – a discount of less than 0.5 per cent.

Debasement

It is a modern fallacy that monetary debasement is exclusively a disease of paper money. The history of coined money is a history of an intermittent and from time to time dramatic fall in value. The reason is not hard to find. There is an interesting example in the famous Thalers or 'Pieces of Eight' of the Spanish Main, so called because they were designed to be divided into eight pie-shaped slices (reals). This is the origin of the American slang expression 'two bits' for a quarter dollar. It was said at the time 'he who could divide it into nine and escape detection profited, dishonestly but accordingly'. More generally, anyone who could put into circulation a coin purporting to have a higher metal content than it actually had (and provided that the coin continued to be accepted at its face value – that is in tale – was potentially capable of pocketing the difference. Who was this 'anyone'? Both the public sector, and private enterprise, had their part to play.

Debasement, as generally understood, is the practice of rulers gradually to reduce the precious metal content of the coins they issued under their so-called guarantee. There was thus created a widening premium to be made on issuing the coinage. This might be achieved relatively honestly, by increasing the seigniorage, or by deception. The trick could be achieved in one of three ways. The simplest but easiest to detect, was to reduce the weight of the coins. More subtly, the ruler could keep the weight the same but increase the proportion of non-precious alloy, thereby reducing the fineness. This could be detected only by assay. The goldsmiths and merchants, but only they, would quickly spot what was going on. A third method (only possible when the concept of fiat money is firmly established), is to 'cry up' the value of an existing coin – decreeing that it would henceforth pass for a higher value. These three techniques were referred to in late medieval France as *'mutacion du poid'* (change of weight) *'mutacion de la matiere'* (change of quality) and *'mutacion de l'appelation'* (change of name).[3]

These methods were effective provided that the public at large did not immediately notice the change. Merchants, who did, would pass on the debased coins, or when they became too numerous, accepted them at a discount, refused to accept them at all, or accepted them only at their assayed value, i.e. as bullion. It was often in the interest of the merchants to let the general public remain misinformed. They could then profit by collecting and culling better quality coins from general circulation. This particular opportunity for profit was one factor which was later to encourage goldsmiths to diversify into banking (see Chapter 15), and it also illustrates one aspect of the operation of Gresham's Law.

Tale or Specie?

Debasement usually became obvious fairly quickly. Indeed, if the ruler was successful first time round, he would invariably go on repeating the exercise until he was found out. Success depended on whether coins were in fact accepted 'in tale', i.e. at face value, or 'fiat value'.

Suppose that a particular coin has a nominal face value of 10 pence, but that the actual silver content is worth rather less – say 9 pence or 8 pence. At what value will it be accepted in trade? It may be accepted at nominal value, in tale, or at its bullion value, in specie. A sound currency will normally circulate in tale particularly if the issuing authority is politically strong, as in Anglo-Saxon England, but a debased or heavily clipped coinage will cease to be trusted and the coins will be accepted, at least by the sophisticated, only in specie. Modern token coins have of course to be accepted in tale. The pound in your pocket is worth little as a piece of brass. Where coins, particularly the higher value gold or fine silver coins, were taken in specie instead of in tale, it was less necessary to control the actual weights. Lane and Mueller (1985: 45) quote the extreme example of the tari of Naples and Sicily. The heaviest were struck eight times the weight of the lightest. The *oncia* (ounce), a unit of weight became the currency of account. This was divided for convenience in 30 tari of account: a debt of 60 tari (of account) was settled by delivering coins to the weight of two ounces, not by counting out 60 coins. Such coins were regarded as guaranteeing the fineness, but not necessarily the weight, of the gold and silver. Elsewhere, as in England, weights were effectively controlled. The Venetian grosso was struck to a uniform weight, but until 1321 settlement was often by weighing. In 1321 payment in tale was made obligatory, and creditors had to accept at face value any that were no more than 10 per cent under weight.

Changes in the value of metal

Changes in the silver content of the penny, were not the only cause of price movements. Silver itself does not necessarily have a stable relationship to the price of commodities. Neither does gold, of which more later. Prices of individual commodities (or of a basket of commodities – what we would today call a price index) depended both on the relative value of the commodity with respect to silver and on the actual silver content of the unit of currency. An Anglo-Saxon silver penny would be worth about 12 pence today as silver, but its purchasing power in Anglo-Saxon times was perhaps fifty times greater. Over the centuries, the purchasing power of silver has fallen, sometimes steadily, but with more dramatic falls in the seventeenth century and in the late nineteenth century

Short-weighting, clipping and counterfeiting

Apart from the official monetary authority there were three other groups who could profit from passing underweight or debased coins. The moneyers themselves (false moneyers) could, contrary to their instructions, make short weight coins and make an extra profit which was not shared with the ruler. The tight system of control used in England was designed to prevent this, but there is substantial documentary evidence that it did not always succeed. The practice was commoner elsewhere.

Counterfeiting, the making of false money having apparently 'honest' inscriptions but usually with a considerably reduced weight or (more commonly) fineness was widespread in England and elsewhere. Such coins might be made of base metal with a silver plating. The counterfeiter took the whole of the profit after costs of manufacture, including the cost of the metal.

Clipping was a third form of private enterprise. A private citizen would receive coins in payment, clip as much as he thought he could get away with from the edge and pass it on in payment. In due course he would collect a useful store of gold or silver bullion. The milled edge on coins introduced experimentally by Elizabeth I and permanently adopted in England in 1696 was designed to prevent this practice. A variant was 'sweating': silver or gold coins were put into a leather bag which was then shaken violently. The coins would emerge showing the type of wear normally associated with a couple of years circulation and rattling in people's pockets and purses, and after regular repeats of the process, a small but useful amount of gold or silver dust would accumulate in the bag. This was one of the perquisites of being a money changer: there was, in this and other ways an extra profit to be made from handling large amounts of coin.

Fair wear and tear and the breakdown of the coinage

Coins lose some of their weight by wear over the years and the quality of the coins actually circulating would decline. The activities of false moneyers, counterfeiters and clippers would speed up this process. Assume that coins were newly minted to a 20 grain standard, while worn coins actually in circulation averaged only 18 grains. It would not then be worth anyone's while, private citizen or ruler, to melt down 20 old coins and issue 18 new ones. There comes a point when new coins would cease to be struck, while any full weight old ones which remain in circulation would be culled by merchants to be melted down as bullion or, where this is illegal, exchanged abroad by weight. The coinage system then breaks down, to the detriment of trade. This has happened several times in English experience, as explained in Chapter 3.

COINAGE SYSTEMS WITH TWO OR THREE METALS

All the phenomena discussed so far can be observed with a simple coinage metal. By the end of the fourteenth century nearly every country in Europe was using three coinage metals – gold, silver and a base metal such as copper or nickel – often known in contemporary literature as 'yellow' 'white' and 'black' money, and this created a further set of complications. In substance this system has continued to the present day except that gold coins have (in this century) been totally replaced by paper while white money has lost even the pretence of being worth its weight in silver.

In medieval and early modern times coins were expected (although in some places and times only by the credulous) to contain the appropriate weight of metal. The use of more than one metal raised problems. These are sometimes referred to collectively as 'tri-metallism', but are more conveniently divided into the two separate problems of 'bi-metallism' (the relationship between silver and gold) and 'small change' (the role of the black coins). The new and more complicated coinages also caused problems of definition – 'ghost money' and 'money of account'. These related concepts, are vital for an understanding of the history of coined money. They all have their roots in the early middle ages, but they help illuminate the monetary problems of today.

Bimetallism

At least since the thirteenth century, gold and silver coins have circulated side by side in most European countries. For most of this period governments have tried to set a simple relationship between the two. It is obviously convenient for trade if, for instance, a gold sovereign of stated weight can be exactly equal to 20 silver shillings, also of a stated weight. Unfortunately, the relative value of the two metals as bullion was not consistent, and they were not necessarily the same in different countries. Table 2.1 gives some examples of the ratio and shows that, until the later 1600s, when transaction costs fell and arbitrage became more organised, significant differences could exist between countries. Thereafter, only one figure is given: the last, and most striking will be discussed in more detail at the end of Part I.

Table 2.1 Bimetallic ratios in Europe 1300 to 1900

Date	England	France	Venice	Germany	Spain	Mean
1300	9.29		10.84	10.00		10.04
1350	11.57	11.11	14.44	11.33		12.11
1400	11.15	10.74	11.69	11.37		11.24
1450	10.33	11.44	12.10	11.12	5.82	10.16
1500	11.15	11.83	10.97	11.12	10.01	11.02
1550	12.23	12.07	11.07	11.38	10.76	11.50
1600	10.90	11.68	12.34	11.50	12.29	11.74
1650	13.34	13.50	15.37	11.64	13.52	13.47
1700				14.81		14.81
1750				14.53		14.53
1800	*1815 : 15.26*			15.68		15.68
1850	*1895: 30.6* 15.70					1570
1900	26.49					26.49

Arbitrage and bimetallism

If gold was valued eleven times as highly as silver in France and nearly ten times in England, an entrepreneur could bring ten pounds of silver to England, convert it into one pound of gold, ship it over to France convert it into eleven pounds of silver and repeat the operation at a 9 per cent profit. This may seem an enormous margin for a simple transaction by the standards of modern arbitrage, but we have to remember that the costs and risks of physically transporting the metals were high. Before the invention of the electric telegraph (the classic example, in the economic text-books, of a capital saving invention) he also had to take the risk of a price movement while his bullion was in transit. Even without systematic arbitrage, any sensible merchant would settle debts from England to France in gold and from France to England in silver until either one country was completely denuded of one of the precious metals, or the ratios came into line.

The silver standard

During the late medieval and early modern period Europe was on a *de facto* silver standard. In practice the value of gold coins fluctuated with changes in the ratio, that is with market conditions. Various attempts to enforce a fixed ratio on the gold coinage were ineffective and short lived. There was in practice no particular difficulty in having the standard based on silver (as in England) and accepting that gold coins such as the noble (or later the guinea) might fluctuate in value against the silver denomination. In those days, the only people who used gold were, after all, sophisticated merchants who could look after themselves. In England official values were put on the gold coins, but these were frequently amended or, if they diverged from reality, simply ignored.

Bimetallism was an issue during three periods of special interest: the rise and fall of gold during the fourteenth century; the seventeenth century changes arising from New World gold discoveries and the bitterly fought triumph of gold at the expense of silver in the late nineteenth century (Chapters 8–11). The wider use of gold coinage in Italy resulted, not surprisingly, in an increase in the relative price of gold. From a traditional 10, the bimetallic ratio (the price of gold in terms of silver) rose, in Venice to 14.2. After that it fell sharply to 9.6 in 1353, before recovering to 11 by the end of the century. The fall had a dramatic impact on what were by then established monetary systems.

Gresham's Law

Sir Thomas Gresham (1519–71) was Queen Elizabeth's financial adviser, responsible for clearing up the mess of her father's 'Great Debasement', and founder of the Royal Exchange. He is known for Gresham's Law: 'Bad money drives out good'. Properly understood, this simple statement can offer a deep insight into monetary policy and numismatic history. No definitive statement of Gresham's Law by him seems to have survived[4], and in any case the point had been made, much earlier, by Nicholas Oresme (c. 1360) and Aristophanes (445–383 BC) (see Chapter 12). Braudel quotes the Gonzaga agent writing, in June 1472 'che la cativa cazara via la nona'(Braudel 1972: 388).

In Gresham's day, money meant 'coin'. In concept a coin is a piece of gold or silver, the weight and fineness of which is guaranteed by the ruler by whose authority it was issued. (Of course as we have seen, rulers, and not only Henry VIII, could and did cheat.) Coins have to be minted, and mints charge seigniorage. Minted coins, being more convenient, would command a small premium over their bullion value. In some times, and at some places, coins may be accepted in trade at nominal value, in tale, which may be more than its bullion or specie value. A sound currency will normally circulate in tale particularly if the issuing authority is politically strong, as in Anglo-Saxon England, but a debased or heavily clipped coinage will cease to be trusted and the coins will be accepted, by the wise, only in specie.

Gresham's Law, as usually stated, applies only if coins are widely accepted in tale. Suppose that the circulation consists mostly of worn, clipped or debased coins worth 20 per cent less than their bullion value, (bad money) but that some full weight ones remain in circulation (good money). If you are lucky enough to be paid in a good coin, you hold onto it; it is no better than the bad one as a means of payment but far better as a store of value. The early goldsmith bankers regarded the opportunity to 'cull' good coins from a high turnover as a major source of profit.

During the late medieval and early modern period Europe had been on a *de facto* silver standard. In practice, the value of gold coins fluctuated with changes in the ratio: various attempts to enforce a fixed ratio on the gold coinage were ineffective and short lived. We shall see later that during the eighteenth century, after Newton's reform, the United Kingdom moved towards a *de facto* gold standard, formalised in 1816. Thereafter, silver coins were deliberately struck underweight, i.e. with a fiat value below their bullion value. During the latter half of the nineteenth century the problems of bimetallism, created by the operations of Gresham's Law, were a major preoccupation and source of dispute in much of Europe, particularly France, the United States and India.

Gresham's Law applies only if the bad money has *effective* fiat value. Economists use a more precise statement of Gresham's Law. This is one:

> Where by legal enactment a government assigns the same nominal value to two or more forms of circulatory medium whose intrinsic values differ, payment will always, as far as possible, be made in that medium of which the cost of production is least, and the more valuable medium will tend to disappear from circulation
>
> (Palgrave's Dictionary 1926 edition)

If the bad money becomes discredited, merchants and others may prefer to use a sound money, even if it is foreign. In this case 'good money drives out bad' and there are many examples. Charlemagne introduced the denier or penny, struck 240 to the pound of silver or 24 grains, and this standard, was for a time, current throughout the West. Two centuries later this sound currency, having survived only in England, spread again to Scandinavia, Viking Ireland and Bohemia. The Edwardian sterling and its imitations, as a good money was widely used beyond the king's dominions. The Venetian gold ducat and silver grosso, the gold florin, the Maria Theresa dollar and the gold sovereign have all, in their time, enjoyed wide circulation as intrinsically sound, respected and preferred coins for international trade. The US dollar was, for a time after the war, a preferred alternative currency, and is still used as such (not always successfully) in high inflation countries such as Brazil and Israel (Friedman 1992).

Money of account and ghost money

For much of the late medieval period, there would be more than one coinage type in circulation in a country. This creates a serious problem for the modern historian, as it presumably did for the contemporary accountant. Cipolla (1967) discusses the problem of what he calls 'ghost money', units of account which have names based on actual coins which have disappeared from circulation. It arose, of course, from depreciation and the phenomena of bimetallism and petty coins. The Carolingian system of pounds shillings and pence had survived the ravages of depreciation only in England and, rather less successfully, in Scotland: in the rest of Europe the system had disappeared in terms of actual coins. Its ghosts persisted.

Pounds and shillings were themselves originally ghosts. Charlemagne had decreed that the pound weight of silver be struck into 240 pennies, while the term shilling, referring to 12 pennies, linked the system in with the then familiar Byzantine gold solidus. As the weight of the penny fell, it remained convenient to use the term pound (money) to refer to 240 pennies of the type then current, even though they would no longer contain a pound (weight) of silver. Even at this level there can be some confusion. As already explained coins can change hands in tale (nominal legal value) or in specie (according to the weight of silver or gold): the distinction can be of practical importance whenever the circulating coinage contains a high proportion of clipped or below-weight coins.

Money is used as a 'unit of account' as well as a medium of exchange and store of value. Some system was needed by which debts could be recorded and settled, and in which merchants could keep their accounts. It was convenient to have a money of account for this purpose. This could be based on a silver or a gold standard, or very occasionally on black money. Two systems often existed side by side. The value of actual real coins could fluctuate in terms of the appropriate money of account and this was often based on a ghost from the past.

In England, at least, it can be assumed that the term pound either refers to a weight of bullion, or to the value of 240 pennies, as the context requires. Gold coins, when they were introduced, were valued with reference to the silver pound shilling pence system. In Continental Europe any pretence of a relationship between the pound (money) and pound (weight) had long disappeared. New gold and large silver coins had been introduced to supplement the old debased ones. This led to a wide and confusing variety of practices in describing monetary amounts. Initially, the weight of these coins was designed to relate in a simple way to the small coins. When Louis IX introduced the gros tournois in 1266 it had a value of 12 (then current French) pence (i.e. one shilling), while his gold ecu was intended to have a value of 120 pence or half a pound. The pound, previously a ghost now became the basis of a real coinage, but it had long lost all relationship to a pound weight of silver.

In Florence, the gold florin was originally a 'lira' of 240 pence. The silver coinage continued to depreciate, so that the gold florin, which maintained its weight standard, was by the year 1500 not the original 240 but 1,680 much debased pennies. By the year 1700 it was worth 3,192 pennies. Debts due could be expressed in terms of either silver or gold. The silver accounting pound (ghost pound) was simply worth 240 current pennies. To begin with, the Florentine silver money of account was simple enough. If the value of the gold florin was 750 pennies, it would be expressed in the system (translating the terms into English) as 3 pounds 2 shillings and 6 pence. However, in the course of time, and in various Italian states, different and more complicated patterns were followed.

In Milan the florin was originally rated, in 1252, at 120 pennies, but the depreciation of the base penny, meant that by 1340 the undebased florin was worth 384 pennies. This rate was then to remain stable for the next sixty years, and during this period stability may well have been taken for granted, much as later generations have regarded any period of exchange rate stability of more than a couple of decades as normal and permanent – in spite of the lessons of history. During this period, the term florin could be used to mean 384 pence without ambiguity either as real money or as a money of account. From 1340–1400 Milan therefore had four units: the florin (384 pence, and a real coin); the pound (ghost) of 240 pence; the shilling (ghost) of 12 pence; and the (real) penny itself. Debts could be denominated in pounds shillings and pence or (in practice more commonly) in florins shillings and pence. There was, at this stage, only one money of account, but two of its four units were ghosts. In about 1400 the silver coinage again began to depreciate. Thereafter, debts were commonly, but not universally, expressed in terms of the 'real' florin which retained its gold content. Such debts would have to be settled either in gold, or in pennies at the current valuation: perhaps 800 or more. For some purposes, though, a ghost florin worth 384 (real) pennies persisted as a money of account. Its value was now a fraction of the real gold florin. Great care is needed in interpreting documents to see whether the reference is to real or ghost florins. The ghost florin, although using the name of a gold coin, was actually based on a silver standard.[5]

The Milan example (and others) is of a silver standard based on the name of gold coins. It was possible to reverse the procedure and to express shillings and pence in terms of a real gold coin: the smaller units then become ghosts. For instance the silver coinage of Florence was for a time stable at 348 pence to the gold florin. Later, as in Milan, the petty coins depreciated, but the Florentine merchants (in contrast to those of Milan) kept to the real florin as the basis of their accounts. A (ghost) shilling was one twenty-ninth of a real florin, and a ghost penny was a twelfth of this. This was more (and eventually, with silver debasement, very much more) than the value of the real pence. Retailers and ordinary citizens continued to use the pound shilling and pence system. There was no such coin as a shilling (solidus) but the term could mean a quite different sum according to whether it was a ghost in the merchants' system based on a fraction (one twenty ninth) of the real florin, or a ghost in the citizens' system based on a multiple (twelve times) of the real penny. Fortunately for historians, Florence (unlike Milan) never adopted a ghost florin! (Cipolla 1967: 38–51; Braudel 1972: 14–8). Venice was even more complicated and interesting and is discussed in the Appendix to Chapter 3.

Small change and the petty coins

A separate but related problem was that of small change. In 1393 'many worthy persons that would give alms to poor beggars could not, for scarcity of halfpence and farthings, to the great withdrawing of the sustenance of these poor beggars' (Craig 1953: 82). Modern travellers to Italy and the Middle East can experience similar problems. Typically, by the nineteenth century the small coins were not, and did not pretend to be, worth their weight in the metal from which they were struck. This would not matter so long as the coins were convertible at a stated rate of exchange – they would then in effect become 'bank notes struck on metal', (passing in tale) as virtually all modern coinages are.

The difficulty was that the medieval citizen (in spite of ample evidence to the contrary) assumed and expected that the coin should be worth its weight in metal. This was reasonable enough for the gold and silver, but really could not apply equally to the petty coins. From a practical point of view the cost of manufacturing a base metal coin is much the same as the cost of making a silver coin of twenty times the value. Queen Elizabeth had been (rightly) advised against reintroducing the silver farthing which would have weighed 2 grains (0.13 grams) as minting would have cost 2s. 8d. a pound or nearly 5 per cent of face value. Sir Richard Martin (sensibly) recommended a copper coinage but 'The Queen refused to have base metal for royal coins in England' (Craig 1953: 128).

Coinage rights, royal, municipal, ecclesiastical or private, were seen as a source of profit rather than a service to the public. Because the petty coins were used mainly by the uneducated, the scope for gradual, and sometimes not so gradual, debasement was greater and was totally at the expense of workers and peasants. 'Honest' petty coinage was unprofitable: the tradition of honest money in countries such as England was, from most other points of view, beneficial, but this very honesty caused a shortage of petty coins for trade. The gap was filled partly by the issue of trade tokens. The antiquary Akerman (1849) has described those 'current in London 1648–1672' and they were a feature of English coinage until they were prohibited in 1817. Towards the end of the period the variety of designs attracted the interest of collectors: some seem to have been struck specifically for that market.

The situation was particularly bad in Ireland.

> The country was flooded with unregulated brass token of the basest sort. They purported indeed to be issued by tradespeople with promises of ultimate redemption: one issuer of the sort acknowledged that he put out, in the ratio of ten to one, forgeries of his tokens, which forgeries he refused to accept again.
>
> (Craig 1953: 369)

In 1720 the Irish government petitioned Parliament to authorise the issue of a reliable copper coinage. A contract was awarded to William Wood on 12 July 1722. He proceeded to produce halfpennies weighing 116.5 grains, and farthings. The value of the copper was materially less than the price value, but Craig (1953: 370–1) doubts whether the operation was particularly profitable, even ignoring the £10,000 bribe Wood is said to have paid to the Duchess of Grafton, the King's mistress. The proposal was, by the standards of the time, not unsound. It would have created a supply of small coins at a fairly reasonable cost. Nevertheless, they were not popular. In 1724 (following, rather than leading the public outcry) a series of letters 'To the shop-keepers, Tradesman, Farmers, and Common People of Ireland' was published denouncing 'Wood's Halfpence'. The Lord Lieutenant issued a proclamation offering three hundred pounds reward 'to such person or persons as shall . . . discover the author of the said pamphlet, so as he be apprehended and convicted thereby'. Jonathan Swift, Dean of St Patrick's Cathedral and the author of Gulliver's Travels, admitted authorship and successfully defied arrest. Swift's 'Drapier's Letters' are a masterpiece of invective, but add little to economic science. The decision to withdraw the coins had been made before Swift's campaign. The coins were subsequently reissued in the American Colonies, who were to defer their revolt against British financial management for another half century.

Irish suspicions were in part due to their earlier experience. James II had issued vast quantities of gun money and pewter 'crowns and halfcrowns' to pay his Irish troops in his war against William of Orange. After William became King in 1689, these base coins were called down to 1 penny or less.

In France, Italy and elsewhere the process of debasement had by the time of the commercial revolution reduced the intrinsic value of the penny to a small fraction of its original figure. These coins were typically made of billon – an alloy of copper and silver. However far the debasement went, there was always some silver in the mix to give it a limited degree of credibility. Most countries (other than England), which reacted to the needs of trade by devising completely new sound silver and gold coinages already had petty coins in the form of the old debased pennies. (In many places debasement had gone so far that the petty coin was the shilling – the penny had sunk below the level of visibility.) The problem here was that these petty (black) coins still nominally kept their relationship with bullion value and there was a fluctuating relationship between the petty (billon) and the sound (gold and silver) coins.

The Continental aspect of the problem is discussed by Cipolla:

While the workers were paid with small coins the big merchants and entrepreneurs selling their products usually wanted to be paid with gold coins. In such a condition, given the usual lag of nominal wages behind the deterioration of the petty coins, and the consequent rise of

21

gold coins and commodity prices, any debasement of the petty coins provoking the depreciation of petty black coins in terms of the gold ones and in terms of commodities resulted, in the short run at least, in (1) a decrease of real wages and (2) an inflation of the profits of the entrepreneurs even if the selling prices of the products on the market did not increase in terms of the big gold coins. It was natural therefore that the two classes of entrepreneurs and workers strongly opposed each other on the monetary question, the first backing a policy of debasement of the petty coins the second a policy of stabilisation.

(Cipolla 1967: 34–5)

There is a fascinating example of an attempted currency reconstruction in Florence in 1378. The gold florin had been worth 20 shillings of black money when it was introduced in 1252. By the beginning of the fourteenth century the petty money had depreciated to the point at which there were 260 shillings to the gold florin. In 1378 a popular revolt overthrew a government of businessmen and replaced it with one drawn largely from wage earners. The Popular Party immediately set about trying to prevent any further depreciation of the petty coins, and proposed a radical plan, approved on 24 October 1380. This required the government to withdraw from circulation and melt down black coins to the value of 2,000 gold florins on 1 January in 1381 and for each of the next eight years. The aim was to cause the value of the petty coins actually to appreciate and to increase real wages without modifying nominal wages. This, said Cipolla, 'certainly remains one of the earliest conscious and logical attempts to control the value of money through the control of its quantity'. However, 'it does not seem that these people had even a vague idea of the unemployment which their measures could create'. Unfortunately for students (whether enthusiasts, or opponents) of monetarism, the Popular Party was defeated the following year and the measures were never implemented. The laboratory was destroyed before the experiment had really begun.

3

MONEY IN EUROPE TO 1250

THE CAROLINGIAN REFORM

Twelve pence make one shilling
Twenty shillings make one pound.

Every British schoolboy knew this – until 1971. This system went back a long, long way, to the effective founder of the Western European monetary system, King Pepin the Short of France (751–68), the father of Charlemagne. He introduced a new standard for silver coinage. He decreed that a livre (pound) weight of silver should be divided into 240 denarii (pennies). The penny (apart from the occasional half-penny or obol) was the only coin in circulation in the West for some centuries. As the then current Byzantine gold solidus was worth about twelve of the new coins, a sum of twelve denarii (one-twentieth of a pound) was referred to as a 'solidus' (sou or shilling) although this was at first simply a unit of account. No actual shilling coin was struck in England until 1508, in the reign of Henry VII, and the coin only entered general circulation under his grandson, Edward VI.

Under Charlemagne, the Carolingian system of pounds, (livre, lira) shillings (sou, solidus) and pence (denier, denarius) spread into most of Western Europe including the several Anglo-Saxon Kingdoms which now constitute England. The prolific and attractive coinage of King Offa of Mercia (757–96) is a significant early example. This relationship between the pound as a weight of silver and the pound as a unit of money did not last long although it survived rather better in England than elsewhere. During the Anglo-Saxon period of sound money, the weight of the penny fluctuated between 18 and 27 grains, (with no apparent ulterior motive) and, after the Norman Conquest, was formalised by William I at 22.5 grains of silver, rather less than the 24 grains that the strict relationship would have required.

During the centuries that followed there was a gradual, though not steady fall in the weight standard until the 1696 re-coinage when coins to the value of 66 shillings (instead of 20) were struck from a pound of silver. The pound (money) lost two-thirds of its silver content over eight centuries, an average rate of depreciation of only 0.13 per cent per annum. (This 'average' involved several quite specific changes, some of which are discussed later, while Henry VIII's great debasement was a dramatic interruption in the pattern.) After 1696 the silver content remained constant until the United Kingdom formally adopted the gold standard with a silver subsidiary coinage, in 1817. The pound shilling penny relationship continued until 1971.

Other countries were less lucky. After the break-up of the Carolingian Empire there was no centralised monetary authority in Western Europe. Coins were struck by various feudal lords and ecclesiastical authorities. A standard reference book describes the coins of no less than 136 different French feudal and ecclesiastical issuers for this period, with another 247 for 'Germany', a loose geographical term which also included what are now Austria, Switzerland and the Low Countries (Engel and Serrure 1890 vol. 3). The designs of the coins became degraded. Copies of copies became increasingly barbarous. Depreciation was rapid, and by 1200 the 'denarius' was little more than a grubby piece of base metal. Even the French royal coinages lost two-thirds of their silver value within a century. The situation was much the same in Italy, where coinage rights typically vested in the trading cities. It was very important, in drawing up contracts, to indicate clearly which currency was meant. The quality of coinage survived rather longer in the Ottonian Empire (very roughly modern Germany), while some countries in Eastern Europe continued to regard coinage as a royal prerogative. Stefan I (997–1088) of Hungary, for instance, established a sound silver currency.

Scotland (at this time an independent Kingdom) was an intermediate case. The Scottish coins were, until about 1300, very similar to the English in general appearance (except that they were distinguished by having the King's head in profile instead of full face) and deliberately identical in silver content. From then onwards the silver content depreciated more rapidly than the English for the next 300 years. The Scottish penny became a base metal coin in about 1484. It sunk without a trace (as a separate coin) in about 1513, to be replaced by the bawbee (6 pence Scottish) as the standard small change coin. In 1605, after the Union of the Crowns, it was decreed that one shilling Scottish was to pass as the equivalent of one penny English. Over the period 1300–1605 the Scottish currency was on average depreciating at about 12 per cent every ten years, three times the then English rate, but nevertheless an enviable record of stability by post 1945 standards.

ENGLISH AND SCOTTISH COINAGE

In about 760 King Offa of Mercia introduced a silver penny based on that of Pepen of France which was to form the basis of the Carolingian reform. Both Craig (1953: 7) and Oman (1967: 18) comment on its superior workmanship and design. While Charlemagne imposed the new currency by conquest, it spread to neighbouring kingdoms within England: an illustration of how 'good money can drive out bad' in appropriate circumstances.

Although the various kingdoms (including the parts of the North East which were for a time under Viking rule) had their own coinages, they seem to have been of much the same weight and standard. There is little evidence of whether there was a formal attempt at anything approaching a monetary union before the political union, largely achieved by Alfred the Great and finally consummated in 959 when Edwy, the last independent king, died and Eadgar became the first king of a United England. In 973 Eadgar introduced a centrally controlled system of coinage. Although coins were struck at as many as eighty mint towns, control of the dies from which the coins were struck was centralised. Each coin bore the name of the responsible moneyer and of the mint town. The design on the coins was changed every six years. A wealth of historic information can be deduced from the study of these coins and their inscriptions. It was a classic period of coinage: they were produced in quantity under Aethelred II (978–1016) (to pay the Danegeld) and the English system of coinage spread to Scandinavia, to Viking occupied Ireland, and for a time, to Bohemia. A high proportion of the English coins of the late Anglo-Saxon period still existing today were discovered in Scandinavian hoards.

The Danish rulers of England, Cnut (1016–35) and Harthacnut (1035–42) continued the system with the same Anglo-Saxon moniers. After the Conquest, William I was quick to appoint his Norman followers to these and other offices of profit, but the system, as such, continued virtually unchanged. It was, after all, the best in Europe. It ensured that the responsibility for a below weight coin could be traced to the moneyer, and explains why England was exceptional in that the weight standard (22.5 grains of fine silver) was not only still intact in 1066 but persisted for a further couple of centuries. It even emerged unscathed from the anarchy during the (nominal) reign of Stephen.

The short cross coinage (1180–1247)

Compared with the abundance of late Anglo-Saxon and early Norman coinage, relatively little English coinage was struck between 1100 and 1180. Indeed, during this period, money declined in use throughout Europe, which reverted towards a subsistence and barter economy. In 1180 Henry II ordered a major recoinage under the technical direction of a Frenchman, Philip Emery, from the famous mint city of Tours, which, in 1203, was to become important in the history of French coinage. This was the first of the three designs which were to be used for the coins of England for three and a half centuries: the short cross issue bearing on the obverse a full faced bearded portrait of the King wearing a crown with his hand holding a sceptre. These coins were to remain unchanged in general type for sixty-seven years. Even through the reigns of Richard and John, the King's name continued to appear as Henricus. There was no attempt at a realistic portrait.

After twenty-five years, a high proportion of the circulating coinage had become worn or clipped. It was not worth bringing in the old coins to be reminted as the bringer would lose money: a phenomenon explained in Chapter 2. There was a shortage of coins, and if nothing had been done the monetary system would have broken down. Coins might, at best, have been accepted only by weight. King John therefore ordered another general recoinage in 1205 without any change in the weight standard or the design. Clipped money was called in. That which had lost no more than one-eighth of its proper weight was recoined and the bringer was given 234 pence for 240 pence brought in. Silver more heavily clipped was accepted only as bullion, and there were penalties for continued ownership of clipped coins. This operation, to restore the effects of clipping and wear, was at a heavy cost to public funds: 240 pence of the minimum acceptable weight would have a silver content of only 210 pence, and in this, extreme but probably not uncommon case the issue of 234 pence would have resulted in a loss to the King of 24 pence. The lesson was learnt: future recoinages were handled differently and to the profit of the King.

Silver pennies were introduced into Scotland by David I (1124–53). These were deliberately minted to the same weight and fineness as their English contemporaries. The first coins to circulate widely are those of the third coinage (1195) of William the Lion. These were based on the short cross type introduced in England fifteen years earlier but with two differences, both of which were to persist through the next two types. The king's head appeared in profile (usually, but not always, to the left) instead of full face, and stars appeared, instead of the groups of three pellets, between the angles of the reverse cross.

The voided long cross Coinage (1247–79)

Henry III succeeded John in 1218. History had once more caught up with the title Henricus on the coins. The short cross type continued until the next major recoinage, that of 1247. A new coin type, the voided long cross, was introduced. The obverse type remained much the same (a stylised facing portrait of the King) but the reverse cross now extended through the legend. This still gave the name of the mint and the moneyer. Henry had learnt from his father's expensive mistake but went to the other extreme. This time the operation was a source of profit to his brother, Richard of Cornwall. Richard had acquired a stock of 10,000 marks of silver and could in effect 'prime the pump' by having this coined into long cross coins. These were then available to provide an instant exchange to those who brought short cross coins to the mint. This time coins were accepted only by weight and the mint charged a very high seigniorage of 13 pence out of 240. There was again no change in the weight standard and the whole loss fell on those who were left holding clipped or otherwise below weight coins. Many new country mints were opened: Richard and the King shared the substantial profits.

Scotland followed this change three years later. The first coinage of Alexander III (1250) also adopted the voided long cross, but retained the Scottish characteristics of having the king's head in profile with stars or mullets in the reverse angles. As in England, the reverse legend still gave the name of the moneyer and mint town.

Henry III died in 1272. His son, now Edward I, returned from his crusade in Palestine to find the currency in a bad state. He authorised a substantial issue of new coins, but continued his father's design and (again) name. This did not suffice. Clipping was rife (many accused of clipping were hanged) and in any case many of the coins in circulation were old and had suffered badly from fair wear and tear. The periodical recoinage to take account of this was five or ten years overdue.

The long cross coinage (1279–1544)

This took place in 1279. The two previous recoinages had maintained the *de jure*, and restored the *de facto*, weight standards, but at a substantial cost to the King (in 1205) or the public (in 1247). This time the official weight of the penny was reduced slightly from 22.5 to 22.2 grains: this was certainly more than the actual weight of the old coins in circulation but was a tentative move to the perhaps obvious solution of simply bringing the *de jure* standard into line with the *de facto* bullion content of the worn coins actually circulating. There was also a change of type. The formalised bust of the King was now represented beardless and with a five pointed crown. There was still no attempt at portraiture – indeed Edward himself did have a beard. On the reverse the voided double cross gave way to a broad simple cross and, perhaps more significantly, the reverse inscription no longer gave the name of the responsible monier but simply the name of the mint town, e.g. CIVITAS LONDON or VILLA NOVICASTRIA (for Newcastle). There were still three pellets in each of the four quarters of the cross. This general design was to persist for over two centuries (until the Tudor debasement) although during this period the royal name did change with that of the reigning monarch. During the Wars of the Roses in particular, with its alternation of Lancastrian Henrys and Yorkist Edwards, this was politically important – no time was lost in making the change. There were thus only three main coin types in three and a half centuries, a striking contrast with the deliberate six-yearly design changes of the Anglo-Saxons.

Edward I's coinage was the first to introduce denominations other than the penny. The rare Edward 1 groats were not at this stage readily accepted as money. Most of the surviving specimens have been mounted as brooches. Round silver halfpennies and farthings (rather than just pennies cut into two or four parts) did however become a normal part of the currency. The first issue of farthings, (with the reverse legend LONDONIENSIS instead of CIVITAS LONDON found on the other coins), contained the full five and a half grains of silver which proportion required, but to make them slightly larger and easier to handle an extra grain of copper was added. This well intentioned departure from the use of fine silver was not popular: the public was suspicious. Later issues omitted the extra alloy, and reverted to the CIVITAS LONDON type legend.

Although the design of the English penny remained unchanged until the Tudors, future recoinages were accompanied by reductions in the weight standard. These adjustments were partly to recognise the actual fall in weight of the *de facto* circulating medium, but also reflected the problems discussed in Chapter 2 arising from introduction of a gold coinage.

Scotland

In Scotland Alexander III's second coinage of 1280 closely followed (this time only a year later) Edward I's long cross recoinage. While English reverses showed the name of the mint town, dropping that of the moneyer, the Scottish reverses merely read REX SCOTORUM without the name of the mint. However each of the four stars or mullets in the angles could have 5, 6 or 7 points, in an apparently systematic code, giving totals of between 20 and 28 points. This code is believed to have been used to indicate the mint. Ian Stewart (1955 and 1967) (now Lord Stewartby, once Financial Secretary to the Treasury, who wrote a standard work on the Scottish coinage while still a schoolboy), suggested that, of the commoner varieties, four mullets of 6 points (a total of 24) indicated Berwick, four mullets of 5 points (20) was for Edinburgh and two mullets of 5 points, two of 6 (22), St Andrews. All the other total combinations (21,23,25,26,27 and 28 points) exist but specimens are less common, and are presumed to be from the smaller mints such as Aberdeen and Dundee. As in England, round halfpennies and farthings were introduced at this time.

MONEY IN CONTINENTAL EUROPE

England was unique in preserving the spirit of the Carolingian reform. Most of the feudal coinages of Europe quickly degenerated into grubby pieces of base metal, with an apology for a silver content. Amidst this confusion some standard coinages began to develop. The Abbey of St Martin of Tours (called after the Soldier-Saint who cut his cloak in half with his sword to share it with a beggar) had operated a mint under ecclesiastical authority since the seventh century – just before the Carolingian reform, and was a leading

French feudal mint when, in 1203 Philip Augustus of France (1180–1223) confiscated the county of Touraine from King John of England, and with it the mint. The 'denier tournois' intended as the standard French royal coin only for the west of France, actually became more popular than the rather earlier 'denier parisis', of Paris. The latter was 25 per cent more valuable, and the two units managed to keep this stable relationship for some centuries. Both were used as moneys of account, important in the assessment and collection of royal revenues. Some other coins such as the deniers of the major trade towns of Champagne and Poitou became more widely used than others. Their respective standard types of coin, ('type immobilise') continued without change in design, for over a century.

Other countries introduced or re-established sound silver coinages by the simple expedient of copying contemporary English coins. The earliest example is perhaps the least well known. Boleslas II of Bohemia (967–99) married Emma, sister of Aethelred II of England (978–1016) and struck an extensive coinage, many of which were closely copied from an English prototype (Aethelred's 'hand' type of 979–85), which has a hand of providence, surrounded by a legend, on the reverse). These were unusual in one respect. The king's name and title on English coins is, with one minor exception under Edward VI on the same side as his portrait. The moneyer and mint name, later just the mint name was on the reverse. The Bohemian coins have the title BOLESLAUS DUX on the hand side, with the mint name and moneyer e.g. OMER IN PRAGA CIVI on the portrait side. This causes some confusion to numismatists: which is the obverse and which the reverse? (Bohemian cricketers, had the game been invented would have had no problem, and would presumably have called heads or hands.) Bohemian coins also copied Byzantine and Carolingian prototypes. One unusual specimen is based on a French design (the temple type) with a Bohemian mint signature and, for some inexplicable reason, the name of the English king Aethelred on the obverse!

A few years after Boleslas II (about 995) Ireland, then occupied by the Danes developed a splendid coinage, ('Phase I' of the Hiberno Norse coinage) based on well- struck copies of the last four types of Aethelred II (the first of these immediately following the hand type copied in Bohemia) and the first ('helmet') of Cnut. Most of these were 'honestly' inscribed, with the name of the ruler (Sitrick) the moneyer and the mint town (Dublin). Some carry Aethelred's name, or an English mint signature. These probably resulted from slavish copying by illiterate die cutters rather than an attempt to deceive the public. They certainly deceived earlier generations of numismatists! For the next two centuries 'imitations of imitations' continued with a steady deterioration of weight, fineness and workmanship.

In Scandinavia for a time foreign coins circulated extensively, passing by weight. Many were English coins – since found in Scandinavian hoards (Danegeld payments) – having characteristic peck-marks where the fineness of the silver was tested. When the demand for local coins grew, the obvious expedient was again to copy foreign coins. Most of these imitations are based on Anglo-Saxon types (with Aethelred's long cross type predominating) but with a healthy mixture of Byzantine, Carolingian and other styles. The early coins were typically actually rather heavier than the English equivalent.

Later still, imitation sterlings based on Edward I's long cross type, became widely used in the Low Countries and elsewhere. This, though belongs to the period of the 'commercial revolution' and Chapter 4.

4

MONEY IN THE COMMERCIAL REVOLUTION

INTRODUCTION

For much of the twelfth century, up to about 1180, the European economy, based on the feudal system, was essentially a self-sufficient agricultural community. Landlords received their rent, and the church its tithes, in the form of produce. Everyday transactions were, as often as not, settled by barter. There were a few travelling merchants, and a small part of the population lived in towns, but the real growth revival of international trade had hardly begun. Money had a relatively minor role, and had actually declined in importance over the previous two centuries. In most of Continental Europe the only coin, and the only form of money in circulation, was the denarius, a base coin of little value. Exceptionally the English penny continued to be struck in fine silver and at full weight. But it was the only coin circulating: nothing larger, and nothing (apart from cut halfpennies and 'fourthings') smaller.

By 1250 the situation had changed out of all recognition. After the upheavals of the twelfth century, Europe was at peace, and citizens could travel freely.

> It was a momentous period for medieval civilisation when the furs of Smolensk and the dried whale of Greenland reached Bruges in Hanseatic ships, when the cloths of Flanders were exchanged in Africa for Guinean gold and the linens of Rheims were bought for the silks of China in the heart of Asia.
>
> (Bautier 1971: 146)

The great trade fairs of Champagne grew up and 'suddenly, in a generation at the most, currency and credit became vital over a large part of the West' (Bautier 1971: 147). Europe was now ready for a more substantial and stable coinage to serve the needs of expanding trade. This was to take the form both of large pure and stable silver coins, and of gold. (Expanding trade also required the development of credit instruments and the means of settling, or at least clearing, debts without transporting bullion. Trade provided the

31

opportunity, and the need, for lending and borrowing money at interest, in conflict with the church's prohibition of usury. This is discussed in Part II Chapter 14, which covers much the same period as the present chapter.)

The first attempt to produce a coin larger than the base denarius had been made by Frederick Barbarosa who, around 1160, began issuing denarii imperialii of double the normal weight. The idea spread, being adopted by both Guelph and Ghibelline states, but as even the double denarius was worth only about a sixth of the then contemporary English penny, the initiative was quite inadequate. The key step was taken by Venice, which in 1202 introduced a new, large and pure silver coin, the 'grosso' or matapan, worth 26 denarii or about two of the then current English pence. Other Italian City states introduced similar coins, and in France the Gros Tournois issued by Louis IX in 1266 was in the same tradition. The Byzantine Empire, had, in spite of its own ups and downs, continued to operate on a gold standard, and at this time gold coinage began to return to the West. Italian merchants were used to handling the coins of the empire, and its final decline left a gap which had to be filled.

The first European gold coin, the Augustale, was struck by Frederick II of Brindisi in 1231, but serious gold coinage really begins in 1252, when the city state of Florence began to strike the hugely successful 'Fiorino' or florin. The initiative was quickly followed, or, Robert Lopez (1986) would argue preceded, by Genoa, and the idea quickly spread across Europe.

The development of a coinage suited to the needs of trade created its own problems. Two of the concepts discussed in Chapter 2, seigniorage and debasement had their roots in the simple mono-metallic coinage of Chapter 3. The introduction of gold adds two more, money of account and bimetallism, which were to have their repercussions at least until the end of the nineteenth century.

In the thirteenth century, the typical European money issuing authority was a feudal mint under the control of a baron, count, or sometimes a bishop, serving the needs of a mainly rural population. The main object of monetary policy of such a ruler was to raise revenue, whether honestly by seigniorage or dishonestly by debasement. Although he might be constrained 'by the teaching of the churchmen and lawyers about his obligation to do justice or by powerful subjects' opposition to change,' (Lane and Mueller 1985: 91) the needs of trade, or the benefits of stable prices, would not concern him.

Italy

Italy was different. Several cities, with their relatively dense populations dominated by merchants, had already become independent, self-governing City States. Venice, at the crossroads of the Carolingian and Byzantine empires, had become independent of both and, with superb diplomacy, negotiated favourable trade treaties with them. For two centuries Venice prospered and grew under a hereditary (but partly constitutional) dukedom. In 1172, following the failure of the last such Doge to renew a key treaty with the Comneni rulers of Constantinople, there was a revolution. Sebastiano Ziani, (1172–8) a rich merchant, became the first elected Doge. Election was in practice indirect: the populace elected the Ducal Council, which nominated the Doge subject to (formal) popular confirmation. Political power was in fact in the hands of the rich, mercantile families, and a century later the powerful 'serrata' of the Great Council was to become closed and hereditary. Some 1200 adult male nobles (out of a population of 120,000) thereafter formally dominated the state. These were traders, bullion merchants and bankers rather than the traditional landowning aristocrats,

> they were all in a position to see that debasement or devaluation, or the raising of the seigniorage on a particular coinage might in the long run do less to increase the government revenue than would Venice's reputation as an international trade center ... the loss or gain in general revenue from the turnover on the Rialto, consumption of wine in the taverns, and other incidentals of being a world market weighed against a variety of other considerations in determining policy.
>
> (Lane and Mueller 1985: 92)

Other Italian cities, such as Pisa, Genoa, Florence and Bologna had also become independent and financially important. Their political structures were rather different: in Florence and Bologna power was more diffused amongst the guilds. These other cities were serious challengers as banking and trading centres, but Venice remained pre-eminent as a centre for the bullion trade.

Sebastiano Ziani had presided at a peace conference in Venice at which Pope and Holy Roman Emperor met and embraced: this led to the Peace of Constance. Under one clause of this treaty the Emperor renounced claims (which had never been effectively enforced) to control minting rights in Italy: this encouraged the development of coinage by the City States. Ziani launched Venice's long career as an independent monetary authority, and was the first Doge to strike an extensive coinage of denarii. They weighed 0.36 grams of 0.270 fine silver. Although fifteen of them would be needed to equal the bullion value of the then current English penny, they were as good as, or better than, the typical coinage of the rest of Europe.

Such a coin was far too small for the trading nation Venice was becoming. Something better was needed and the key step was taken by Ziani's successor Enrico Dandolo (1192–1205) who introduced a larger silver coin, called first a ducat but later a grosso or matapan. The source of the silver was 40,000 marks of silver paid by the French Crusaders for services rendered to the Fourth Crusade. This new coin became a principal coin of commerce, retained its stability for centuries and was used in trade far beyond Venice. The coin itself was copied often, but not always honestly, throughout Venice's trading area. Other City states, Verona, Florence and Genoa introduced similar coins, and the idea spread to France in (1266) and elsewhere. England was a late starter (effectively 1346) perhaps because the undebased English penny was in any case half the weight of the new large coins, and there was no really urgent problem.

GOLD

The groat revolution resulted in new silver coins having the purchasing power of (typically) thirty of the debased denarii which was the sole coin in most of Europe, but only twice that of the stable English silver penny. The needs of the expanding trade required an even more substantial means of payment, and this could only be provided by gold.

The Byzantine empire had retained a gold coinage, based on the solidus. Seventy two soldii were struck from a Roman pound of 327.4 grams, giving a theoretical weight of 4.55 grams but a practical weight of 4.4 grams. These coins were also known as nomisma (plural nomismata) or hyperperon (hyperpera). This coin was introduced by Constantine the Great in AD 309, and maintained its standard until the reign of Michael IV (1034–41). It was then debased, but the old nomisma continued as a money of account. Alexius I Comnenus repaired some of the ravages of Michael's debasement in 1092, introducing a new nomisma (hyperperon or perpero) seven-eighths of the value of the original. As we shall see, this became used as a (gold) money of account in Venice, alongside the Carolingian libra.

There had also been occasional issues of gold coinage in Sicily and Spain under Byzantine or Islamic influence. The first gold coin of the new era was the Augustale struck in 1231 by Frederick II in Brindisi. This weighed one fifth of an oncia – about 18 grams, and related to a 'tari' (Moslem) system. It had limited success outside its own region.

Florence had introduced its own heavier silver coin in 1232. This was smaller than the Venetian grosso and had a value of one soldo or twelve denarii. It bore the familiar Florentine punning device of the lily (fiori) and was generally known as the fiorino or florin. In 1252, Florence added a gold coin valued at a lira (twenty soldi or 240 denarii) so that for the first time after 452 years, the Carolingian accounting system of the pound, shilling and penny was actually represented by circulating coins respectively of gold of silver and base metal, in a form familiar in nineteenth and early twentieth century Britain. The new gold coin was (originally) known as the fiorino duro to distinguish it from the silver florins but soon the name florin was to become exclusively associated with the gold coin.

Robert Lopez, in 'Back to Gold 1252' argues that the genovino of Genoa was actually struck early in 1252, giving that city priority over Florence. 'As we shall see later, this is not merely a question of retroactive municipal pride.

The whole interpretation of the return to gold hinges on it'. An important point, he claims, is that Genoa, believing in minimum state intervention, did not attempt to fix a value in terms of silver. In both cases the weight was designed to make the coins of a value familiar to Sicilian and Syrian trading partners. These two cities, whose merchants handled much of Europe's exports, had accumulated substantial gold reserves which formed the basis both of their coinage and of their subsequent success in banking. Lucca (1273) was the third Italian city to have a successful gold coinage.

Venetian merchants, in contrast, specialised in imports from the Orient. Venice already had a circulation of (Byzantine) gold coins and the merchants accounted in gold perpera (as the new nomismata were now called) as well as in silver. The need for a new coin was less urgent, and it was not until 1284 that Venice, using Hungarian mined gold, began to strike its own gold ducats. The then Doge was Giovanni Dandolo: the Dandolo family produced several doges, and four of them were responsible for monetary innovations. These were quickly accepted by suppliers, with the result that the Venetian gold ducat and to a lesser extent the silver gros or matapan became internationally recognised currencies throughout the eastern Mediterranean. These coins have sometimes been referred to as 'the dollars of the Middle Ages', a reference to the use, after the last war of the dollar as a universal second currency.

The wider use of gold coinage in Italy resulted, not surprisingly, in an increase in the relative price of gold. From a traditional 10, the bimetallic ratio rose, in Venice to 14.2. After that it fell sharply to 9.6 in 1353, before recovering to 11 by the end of the century. The fall had a dramatic impact on what were by then established monetary systems. Silver (or gold) content is, not the only factor affecting prices. Lane and Mueller, in their excellent and detailed study of Venetian monetary history, have to conclude (pages 32) that 'no student of Venice has so far succeeded in producing a study of prices, much less than of wages, for the centuries preceding 1550'. This is 'in sharp contrast to that of Florence' where data has been compiled by Richard Goldthwaite and others.

France

By this time the concept of large silver and gold coins had spread beyond Italy. In France, Louis IX the Pious, subsequently canonised as St Louis, and later giving his name to an American city with a high reputation for sound monetary thought, instituted a general monetary reform. He began by strengthening the 'royal' status of the denier tournois which was rapidly superseding the many feudal issues. He achieved this by providing that while the royal coins were legal tender throughout France, the feudal issues would be valid only in their area of issue. Many of the feudal issuers had actually imitated the denier tournois, a practice successive kings had been unable to prevent. In 1266, Louis issued a new large silver coin, the gros tournois worth 12 pennies or 1 sou, or shilling. This was immediately popular and was widely imitated in Northern Europe, often by issuers who had already been copying the English sterlings. The livre tournois became established as the standard accounting unit in France although the parallel Parisis system (with a stable accounting ratio – 5 tournois equal to 4 parisis) was not finally abolished until 1667.

In 1265 Louis also tried to institute a gold coinage, but repeated the mistake made a decade earlier by Henry III: see below. His new coin, the denier d'or, or ecu, (the first, but not the last, time the name was used for a coin) was the same weight as the gros but ten times its value. This was the same, and wrong, bimetallic ratio of ten adopted by Henry, and the coin never became established. A possible explanation is that both rulers took a more authoritarian view of economic affairs than did the Italians (where political power was in the hands of the rich merchants) and thought they could impose an artificial value on the gold coins.

Philip IV (1285–1314) did eventually introduce a successful gold coinage into France but, like Edward III of England, he needed several tries before the right ratio was reached. Unfortunately Philip is also notorious for his repeated debasements of the silver coinage, mainly the denier but also, on a couple of occasions, the gros, as part of an attempt to finance his war against England. This general structure of coinage spread throughout Europe and persisted through the various misfortunes of the fourteenth century. There were plenty of examples of debasements.

The concept of the florin as a gold coin spread northward, being introduced into Germany in 1328 by the Emperor Louis IV the Bavarian, generally keeping the same weight but adopting an appropriate local design. It eventually became, in the Germanic countries, the gulden. Many of these became debased, and there was an interesting language switch. As the Venetian ducat was never debased, the term ducat became synonymous with a sound coin, while the term florin implied a debased one. Although the Florentine original was never itself debased or devalued, its image suffered from the 'devaluation' abroad of its original name: it, too, became known as a ducat.

England

Unlike the rest of Europe, England entered the new age with a sound, undebased coinage. As in Continental Europe, there was still only one denomination of coin in circulation; the silver penny but this still weighed a virtually full 22.5 grains. These pennies were occasionally cut into halves and quarters to make half pennies and fourthings (farthings). Round silver halfpennies and farthings, struck as such, only became a regular feature of the coinage from 1279. Such a coinage was now quite inadequate. At one level merchants did not want to settle their transactions in thousands of small silver coins – for them gold was obviously more convenient. At another, the silver penny (or even its quarter) was too large a unit for the everyday transactions of paid workmen. (The Edward I penny contained silver worth about 12 UK pence or 20 US cents at 1992 prices – and the relative purchasing power of silver has fallen dramatically since those days. In modern terms, it was as if the smallest available coin was worth about two pounds or three dollars.) Continental countries had reacted to the 'commercial revolution' and the needs of trade by introducing gold and large silver coins alongside the heavily debased pennies or denarii. England's problem was less urgent, and early attempts to introduce the larger coins proved premature and unsuccessful. In 1257 Henry III made the first attempt to introduce an English gold coin: the gold penny of 1257 was derived from the Florentine florin of five years earlier, although the design, by the king's goldsmith, William de Gloucester, was quite different. It had the weight of two silver pence and a value equivalent to 20 pence. This was its downfall. The market value of gold in terms was more than ten times that of silver. This attempt to fix the bimetallic ratio at 10 had its inevitable consequence. The gold coins were melted down: very few have survived but as these were from four different pairs of dies there must have been a fairly extensive circulation. Oman (1967: 153) describes a meeting between the King and the Mayor and Mayoress of London. The latter 'considered the gold penny a pernicious invention, and especially likely to be a snare to the poor'. Oman comments that as the 'poor' 'whose whole chattels in many cases are not worth one piece of gold' were highly unlikely ever to meet with such a coin, they were concealing their real objection: they feared that it would bring down the market price of gold.

There also survive two or three specimens of what appears to be a pattern for a Henry III silver double penny, comparable in weight to the new Italian silver coins.[6] There is no documentary or other evidence that this was intended for circulation. The first attempt to introduce a large silver coin, a fourpenny groat, was part of the 1279 recoinage of Edward I. This also included the first round silver halfpennies and farthings. These groats were never really accepted in trade, but caught the eye of the ladies: most of those which survive had been gilded and mounted as brooches.

Both attempts to introduce new coins were abortive thanks perhaps to 'stupid conservatism or interested intrigues on the part of the money dealers' (Oman 1967: 170) or possibly because the need was less urgent. The undebased English pennies were in any case about half the value of the new large coins being introduced elsewhere. Indeed the English 'sterling' of the time had (at least since Edward's recoinage of 1279) become synonymous with a sound currency, and was extensively copied, particularly in the Low Countries. To begin with, most of these imitation sterlings were an honest attempt by rulers to provide their subjects with a sound currency on an accepted model: soon though, many of them cheated by issuing below-weight or debased coins in the vain hope that no one would notice. Such imitations, known as pollards, crockards and lushbournes (i.e. from Luxembourg), circulated back into England, polluting the purity (well, more or less) of our coinage with a wide variety of deceptively similar looking, but often debased pieces.

There was another recoinage in 1299, mainly to replace these below-weight imitation sterlings. The latter were called down to half their face value for a year, and then banned from circulation permanently. Many of them did contain rather more silver than half the face value would require, and were therefore offered and accepted at full weight as bullion for recoinage. There was no general calling in of the English issue of 1279, and it appears that most of the substantial issue of new coins in that year must have been struck from imported silver or the proceeds of melting down old plate. It was not until 1344, following the Black Death, that larger coins were effectively introduced into England. Edward III was in financial trouble: he could borrow no more from the Florentine bankers and indeed defaulted on his debts. There was a temporary lull in the war with France. In Parliament, attention had been drawn in 1343 to the disastrous effects of the premium on gold current in Flanders and the need for an English gold coinage (Oman 1967: 170).

The 1344 recoinage involved only a small weight adjustment in the silver. A second attempt to introduce a gold coinage, the beautiful but rare florin with its half ('leopard') and quarter ('helm'), failed because the bimetallic ratio (14.81:1) was this time set too high. The weight was 108 grains, and the value 6 shillings, equal to exactly 1,600 grains of silver. These coins were replaced in the same year with a noble, weighing 138.9 grains and valued at 6 shillings and 8 pence. The ratio was now a little too low at 11.90:1 and was fine tuned in 1346, by reducing the weight to 128.6 grains. At the same time the weight of the penny was reduced to 20 grains, giving a ratio of 12.44:1. After a couple of adjustments, the right ratio was found and from 1346, the gold noble, (6 shillings and 8 pence, or a third of a pound) half noble (3 shillings and 4 pence) and quarter noble (1 shilling and 8 pence) were an important part of the English coinage. In 1351 though there were reductions in the weight standard of the gold noble to 120 grains and of the silver penny to 18 grains, a ratio of 12.0. This was the first time that there was a major reduction in the weight standard of the English penny. The motive again seems to have been to adjust the bimetallic ratio. Whatever the motive, this ratio, persisted for another half-century, by historical standards a remarkably long period.

The fourpenny groat was also now effectively introduced and simply represented four sound sterlings. In contrast with most European countries, where the large coins were the foundation of a new system, in England the new coin reflected the need of trade for larger denominations rather than any reconstruction of the monetary system as such. Groats and half groats (two pence) were at once accepted as a normal and continuing part of the English coinage. Still larger denominations of silver were not to be introduced for another two centuries.

There were two further reductions in the weight standards during the Wars of the Roses: to 15 grains in 1412 (Henry IV) and to 12 grains in 1464 (Edward IV). This was half the original weight of nearly 700 years previously, but the rate of depreciation had speeded up. There had been a loss of weight of 33 per cent over a century, but still less than 0.4 per cent per annum. The 12 grain standard continued until the reign of Henry VIII, when the history of English coinage becomes rather more sensational, as discussed in Chapter 5.

Scotland

The Scottish coinage had followed the English in standard, but not in design, until Robert the Bruce (1306–29) reduced the weight of the coinage rather below the English standard. His successor David II (1329–71) quickly followed the example of his contemporary, Edward III, in introducing the silver groat and the gold noble. The documents suggest he had intended to follow Edward's example exactly, e.g. by reducing the weight of the penny to 18 grains. However in 1356 Edward III issued a proclamation that Scottish coinage should no longer be current in England: that this was necessary suggests that the Scottish coinage was regarded (rightly or wrongly) as having fallen below the English standard. From then on there was a steady fall in the silver content of Scottish coinage until, in 1805, after the Union of the Crowns two years earlier, the coinages were united on the basis of one shilling Scottish being worth one penny English, a factor of 12:1. The correct ratio, based on the silver content of recent coins was about 13, giving a small bonus to the Scottish money owners. After that Scotland no longer had an independent coinage system, although separate coins were in fact struck until 1709. It continued to have its own, and significant, banking history.

APPENDIX

MONIES OF ACCOUNT IN VENICE

After the introduction of the grosso, the term lira (libra in Latin) could have two meanings. The traditional Venetian lira ('lib ven' in documents) continued to mean 240 actual current denarii parvi (or piccoli) and was described more precisely as the 'libra denariorum parvorum' or 'lira di piccoli'. For large transactions, it became convenient to use a new money of account, the 'libra grossorum' or 'lira di grossi' which was simply 240 of the new grossi. (There was a similar usage in the Burgundian Netherlands, where the term 'pound groat' meant simply 240 groats.)

So far, so good, but a new and confusing 'ghost' was added in 1282. The grosso had originally been worth 26 denarii, and a debt of one lira di piccoli would typically be settled by handing over 9 grossi and 6 parvi. ($9 \times 26 + 6 = 240$). By about 1254, the accepted legal relationship become 9 grossi and 5 parvi (239 pence) implying that the grossi and therefore the lira di grossi was worth 26⅑ times the denarius and the corresponding lira di piccoli. This became a conventional relationship, which survived further debasement of the piccolo. This resulted in a ghost money of account, the libra ad grossos (occasionally 'libra parvorum ad grossos' which, say Lane and Mueller, might be translated as 'the pound of pennies paid in groats') or lira a grossi. This called for payment of 240 old pennies, conventionally valued at 26⅑ to the grosso.

The lira di grossi (240 grossi) was thus valued at 26⅑ times the lira a grossi, regardless of the actual silver content of the piccoli. The value of the lira di piccoli would depend on the relative value of the piccolo, giving the relationships for 1282 shown in Table 4.1.

Table 4.1 The value of the *lira di piccoli*: 1282

		Value of coin expressed in	
Coin	*Lira di piccoli (Libra parvorum)*	*Lira di grossi (Libra grossorum)*	*Lira a grossi (Libra ad grossorum)*
Grosso	32 denarii	1 denari	26 ⅑ denarii
Piccolo	1 denario	1/32 denaro	0.816 denarii

The lira di piccoli was used within the city for retail trade.

There was yet another complication. For some purposes the original relationship of 1 grosso to 26 denarii persisted. On this basis the lira di grossi manca, perhaps translated as 'short pound' was worth 239 grossi instead of 240. All three (or four, if we include the manca) were based on a silver standard. Later (from around 1328) further moneys of account became based on gold (see Lane and Mueller: 333).

5

THE GREAT DEBASEMENT OF HENRY VIII'S REIGN

The average rate of depreciation of England's currency between Eadgar's reform of 973 and Charles II's recoinage of 1696 was remarkably low, about 0.4 per cent per annum. This average conceals one of the most extraordinary interludes in English monetary history – the Great Debasement of Henry VIII and Edward VI. The Tudor period as a whole (1485–1603) actually shows the same averages: 0.37 per cent for the silver and 0.35 per cent for the gold. However, to quote Oman's summary:

> . . . from 1526 onwards we are in the midst of financial crises which do not end till 1562 . . . Henry VIII tried all manner of expedients . . . Chaos supervened: he had taken over from his father the finest, the best executed, and the most handsome coinage in Europe. He left to his son the most disreputable money that had ever been seen since the days of Stephen – the gold heavily alloyed, the so called silver ill-struck and turning black or brown as the base metal came to the surface. The problem which was left to the ministers of his son Edward VI was the rehabilitation of the currency. Protector Somerset made nothing of the problem, and continued in his old master's evil ways. Protector Northumberland, a very bad man but a good financier, made a serious and partly successful attempt to put things right.
>
> (Oman 1967: 244)

There were other factors at work. During the Tudor period, the purchasing power of silver and gold were falling. Prices were rising considerably faster than the change in the composition of the coins would suggest.

THE EARLY YEARS

Henry VIII came to the throne in 1509 and for his first seventeen years (his 'first coinage') made no changes in the coinage system. Not only were the designs and weights unchanged; the coins actually continued to show a portrait of his father, Henry VII. The only change was in the figure 'VIII'. Henry VIII was not as frugal as his father, his military successes had been dearly bought, and substantial sums had to be remitted to Flanders. English money was not being accepted there at the usual 30 shillings Flemish to the pound sterling: Henry disputed the lower tariff but after assays at the Goldsmiths Hall confirmed the lower rating, he had to accept it (Challis 1978: 87).

There had to be a recoinage (the 'second coinage') in 1526, and this did involve a change of design and of weight. After various experiments, Cardinal Wolsey recommended and superintended a reform. The gold coinage was correspondingly 'enhanced' or 'cried up', one of the three methods of debasement discussed earlier. Gold sovereigns and angels continued to be struck at the old weight and fineness, but the angel was increased in value from 6s.8d. to 7s.6d. and the sovereign from 20s. to 22s.6d. A new gold coin, the George noble of 6s.8d., was introduced, while the Crown of the Double Rose (5s.) and its half (2s.6d.) were struck from crown gold, only 22 carats, instead of 23 carats 3.5 grains fine but with values corresponding to the fine gold content. As yet there were none of the features of the debasement which was to follow.

The mint changed the basis of its operations from the Tower Pound of 5400 grains to the Troy Pound of 5760 grains. This did not affect the substance of any of the coinage changes discussed here, (weights are given in grains) but care may be needed to check which unit is referred to in contemporary documents. The relationships are shown in Table 5.1.

Table 5.1 Units of weight in the Tower and Troy systems

| Unit of weight | grains in system | |
	Troy	Tower
Pennyweight (dwt)	24	22.5
Ounce (oz)	480	450
Pound (lb)	5760	5400

Neither is to be confused with the avoirdupois pound of 7000 grains, divided into 16 ounces of 437.5 grains, still used in Britain and America for normal commercial purposes.

Silver coins bearing Henry VIII's own profile portrait were struck at a reduced weight, 10 grains of silver, instead of 12, to the penny. This was an open move, clearly associated with a new design. The motives were much the same as previous weight adjustments: there had not been one since 1464. The overall effect of the changes was to bring a plentiful supply of silver to the mint. The retariffing of gold was in two stages, in August and November: there was an unusually heavy coinage of gold. A proclamation was issued 'forbidding any person to raise the price of any goods or merchandise under the colour of the money being enhanced'. This was an early attempt at price control, and no more successful than those which were to follow in future centuries.

This second coinage, taken alone, could be seen as simply another of the periodical adjustments needed to take account of normal wear and tear on the actual circulating coins and of changes in the relative prices of gold and silver. Wear and tear has been estimated at between 2 per cent and 2.75 per cent per decade, and it was probably better, and indeed more honest, simply to adjust the legal weights of the coinage downwards from time to time at something like this rate (Challis 1978: 211; Jevons 1875: 134).

THE GREAT DEBASEMENT

The Great Debasement, 1542–51, was another matter. During this period, the weight of the silver penny fell by one-third but more significantly the coins, instead of being virtually pure silver, were at one point only one-quarter silver and three-quarters copper. The actual fine silver content of the penny fell to one-sixth of its previous value: an average rate of depreciation of 22 per cent per annum. This went far beyond the necessary adjustment to the 'fair wear and tear' problem which accounted for earlier debasements. Clearly totally different forces were at work. Challis (1978: 251) distinguishes between 'normal currency depreciation' which was 'part of a general European phenomenon over which England had no control' and 'fiscal exploitation of the coinage' which was 'arbitrary, particular and fraudulent'.

The gold content of the pound was also reduced, but only by about a third. Something decidedly odd must have happened to the bimetallic ratio, which must surely be out of kilter – indeed based on the metal content of the circulating coins it fell from the fairly normal 11 or 12 to below 5. This had no parallels on the Continent: what was happening? There are two other obvious questions.

First, what did the government expect to gain by these changes? Second, how did they get away with it? One way in which the government could, and most European rulers in earlier centuries did, profit from debasement was by using debased coins to pay their suppliers or pay off their debts. This was not the main factor at work here.

Debasement in Ireland – A trial run?

The first debased coins were, in fact, struck for Ireland, probably in 1536. These 'harp' groats (and much rarer half harps and pennies) were first struck, only slightly debased, from silver 10 ounces fine or 83.3 per cent pure. This change seems to have been accepted by the public and in the 1540 there was another issue, this time only 9 ounces fine and the quality was to fall rapidly to 3 ounces. A feature of this coinage is that successive issues can be dated by the initials on either side of the harp. The earliest issue had the letters 'H' for Henry and 'I' for Jane (Seymour) who was then Queen, but as every schoolboy knows Henry changed his queens as often as his coinages.

Was this a deliberate experiment preceding the English debasement? Certainly on 3 March 1542 John Bowes, master of the mint, was instructed to experiment with coins of different fineness (Challis 1978: 82–4). Challis suggests that Thomas Wriothesly was the master mind behind the scheme, the concepts of which are discussed below. In 1556–8 substantial quantities of English base silver were reminted on government account into Irish coinage. No mint accounts survive from that period (Gould 1970: 67).

The stages of the Debasement

The Appendix to this chapter reconciles the information with modern numismatic usage and includes some key statistical information. Table 5.2 shows, for the various coinages, the weight and fineness of the silver coins, and the face value of coins actually struck from one pound of pure silver: the mint equivalent. In decimal rather than £. s.d. terms this rose from £2.43 to £14.40 at the peak of the debasement. It was a little more complicated than that. As explained in Chapter 2 the mint charged a percentage, seigniorage for its services. This had traditionally been of the order of two or three per cent, enough to cover costs and leave a small profit for the king. There is another concept, that of the mint price which is value of coins that would be given to the citizen who tendered a pound of silver to the mint. The difference between the two was the gross profit to the mint, and these figures can be seen in the right hand columns of Table 5.2. For instance, with the 1526 coinage the penny weighed 10.67 grains, 0.925 fine, and 584 pennies (£2.8s.8d. or £2.43 in decimal) could be struck from one pound of pure silver. This was the mint equivalent. The mint price though was only 573 pence (£2.7s.7d. or £2.38) the odd 11 pence being retained as seigniorage – a perfectly normal 2.2 per cent.

Under a secret indenture of 16 May 1542, coins were struck at the same weight as before, but the metal was debased – the gold from 23 and three-quarter carats to 23 carats and the silver from the traditional 11 ounces 2 pennyweights fine to only 10 ounces fine. This is known to numismatists as the third coinage. One effect, possibly unintentional, was to change the bimetallic ratio between gold and silver to 1:10, whereas in the rest of Europe the ratio was still around the traditional 1:12.

This first stage of the debasement was also clearly associated with a change in the design of the coins – in the case of the groat it changed to the facing bust – but no publicity was given to the (initially fairly slight) debasement of the metal. A new coin, the testoon or shilling was introduced at this time. Apart from a small issue under Henry VII, this was the first shilling coin to be struck in England. (There had already been a pound sovereign, but this had been revalued to 22s.6d.) Some authorities suggest that the ten ounce coins actually struck were never issued, but were eventually remelted. Mint records show silver with a face value of £52,927 to have been struck. Some coins may well have passed into circulation; being obvious candidates for the melting-pots of the day it is unlikely that many would have survived, and no 10 ounce coins have been positively identified. They could probably not be picked out by eye: systematic non-destructive analysis might produce a few specimens.

The fourth coinage of 9 ounce silver was, as the accounts show, struck in much larger quantities, under the terms of the indenture of 28 May 1544. This coinage also included the testoon. There was this time a big increase in the seigniorage to 22 per cent (11s.7d). £149,287 was coined, at a profit of some £32,500. As subsequent practitioners of debasement or inflation as a method of Government finance have discovered, the first small step is profitable, but the profits come less easily once people notice what is going on. (Unanticipated versus anticipated inflation.) Successive steps have to be larger and larger, and the profits smaller and smaller. A year later Henry, by the indenture of 27 March 1545, (the fifth coinage) reduced the fineness of the silver to 6 ounces and the gold to 22 carats. (Although the relative change in the gold was much less, the absolute profit was greater.) No testoons appear to have been struck during this period. An interesting feature was that coinage was resumed in Southwark, Canterbury and York (the latter two probably to coin confiscated monastic plate) while a second mint under Thomas Knight was opened at the Tower. The change in seigniorage was now dramatic: £2.00 out of a mint equivalent of £4.80 (£4.16s.) or 41.7 per cent. Silver to the face value of £440,213 was struck. This would imply a maximum profit (assuming all minting was on private account) of £183,000. The margins on gold were smaller (8.3 per cent): the £372,120 struck would have produced a maximum profit of £31,000.

A sixth coinage was ushered in by indenture of 1 April 1546, the fineness of the gold being reduced to 20 carats and that of the silver to 4 ounces or only one-third fine. Seigniorage was again up. This coinage probably did include testoons. A feature was the opening of a seventh Mint in Bristol under William Sharington. Gould estimates output at £451,811, silver and £263,130 for the gold. Henry died on 28 January 1547/8 (old and new style) but coins of his sixth coinage continued to be struck during the first couple of months of the reign of his young son, Edward VI.

Edward's first coinage was under the indenture of 5 April 1547. There was no change in the quality of either metal although there was a small increase in mint price, a modest reduction in seigniorage. Some of the groats and smaller coins were struck bearing the portrait of Edward VI himself. Others, bearing Henry's portrait, can also be associated with this coinage as can some of the testoons struck at the Tower. His second coinage was struck to the same standard for the silver but some further depreciation of gold. (Indenture of 16 February 1547/8 i.e. 1548 new style). No testoons appear to have been struck in this period, but for the first time the York Mint was empowered to and did strike groats.

Edward's third coinage (indenture of 24 January 1548/9) represented an unsuccessful attempt to improve matters. The quality of the gold was restored to 22 carats but the weight of the sovereign was reduced proportionately. Another new mint, Durham House, near the Strand, was opened. Little gold seems to have been struck. A more remarkable experiment was tried with silver. A new shilling (the name testoon being in bad odour) was struck of 8 ounces fine silver, but weighing only 60 grains, with the portrait of Edward VI himself. Groats and smaller coins continued to be struck on the 4 ounce standard, but, with his father's portrait. As a groat weighed 40 grains, it will be seen that the new shilling was very little larger although the proportion, in terms of fine silver content, (mint equivalent £7.4s.0d.) was strictly maintained. These are the fairly rare shillings with 'legends transposed', i.e. with the King's name and title on the reverse, an unusual arrangement, possibly designed to ensure that they could be distinguished from the Edward portrait groats of the first coinage. The intention was obvious – to place the odium for the really debased coins on the shoulder of the dead father rather than on the living son – or in practice, given the son's age, on the Protector, Somerset.

The experiment lasted less than three months and then, under the indenture of 12 April 1549 the fourth coinage was introduced. This included the new shilling with the weight raised to 80 grains (twice as large as and easily distinguishable from, the groats) but with the fineness reduced to 6 ounces, leaving the actual silver content as before. There was no change in the gold or the small silver. There was some experimentation with the mint price. It appears to have started at £3.8s.0d. (the relationship then ruling on the coins) but to have been increased successively to £3.12s.0d. and £4.0s.0d. presumably to attract more silver to the mint. Towards the end, there was perhaps felt to have been unnecessary generosity, and there was a reduction to £3.18s.0d. No corresponding changes are noted in the 4 ounce groats and smaller coins, and it is not clear whether any were in fact struck.

The fifth coinage (indenture of 8 December 1550) represents the last phase of the debasement. The fineness of the shillings was reduced to 3 ounces, even below that of the groats which continued to be struck, with Henry VIII's portrait (Bust 6) on the 4 ounce standard.

ANALYSIS OF THE GREAT DEBASEMENT

Over the period the mint equivalent rose sharply but the mint price changed much less. Before April 1544 a citizen bringing a pound of silver to the mint would receive 584 good quality pennies. After that date, he would have received 629 slightly lighter ones. If he assumed that the quality of silver was unchanged there was little real change in the deal he was being offered.

In fact the silver content had been reduced from 0.925 to 0.75 fine. The mint equivalent was 768 pence. 139 pence, about 22 per cent, had been kept by the mint. This was nearly all profit, but a modest skim compared with what was to come.

In spite of this bad bargain the activity of the mints rose dramatically, as shown in Table 5.4, which actually needs treating with some reserve. Multiply the output by the percentage: the potential profits for the King were, by the standards of the day, enormous. This figure, though, is a theoretical upper limit and in practice of little relevance. This answers the first question. There was plenty of gain for King Henry. What of the second question? How did he get away with it? How was the citizen persuaded, or conned, into using the mints on such unfavourable terms?

In the earlier stages, undoubtedly, many ordinary citizens simply failed to recognise the deception, but there were plenty of goldsmiths capable of analysing coins, and international merchants very quickly recognised and took account of the true trading value of the coins. Economists do not necessarily have to believe that all economic behaviour is rational, but it is obviously unsatisfactory to have to rely on any theory which assumes that most of the people can be fooled for most of the time. It is better to assume that, generally, economic agents at least try to behave in their own self interest. A more sophisticated theory is needed and the most convincing is that given by Gould. His theory:

> ... undertakes to explain certain economic data (in this instance figures of mint output) by assuming that light will be thrown on the matter when we can demonstrate how such and such lines of action can be explained in terms of the economic self interests of those pursuing them. It postulates, that is, the pursuit of gain as the only behavioral assumption and shows how, given that the particular economic restraints and opportunities of the time led to the actions in question.

> (Gould 1970: 32)

Gould's analytical approach has in fact wider applications and has indeed been reflected to some extent in Chapters 3 and 4. 'The theory of mint affairs ... should therefore prove useful to economic historians who wish to concern themselves with monetary and allied topics in any part of the medieval and early modern periods' (Gould 1970: 5–6).

It can be seen at once that mint output was substantial – so apparently were the profits, although the 'maximum profit' figure in the last column of our table is not explicitly given by Gould on the sound enough grounds that there is one important piece of data missing. This would be the profit figure if, and only if, all the mint output were on private account, i.e. by citizens bringing silver or gold coins or bullion to the mint, suffering the full seigniorage charge and taking away the advertised number of coins.

A HISTORY OF MONEY

Another and less profitable method of keeping the mints at work would be by minting on 'public account'. The government could, and indeed did, buy metal on the open market, have it minted, and pay its suppliers in the resulting debased coins. This was profitable so long as the fiat value of coins produced exceeded, even by a small margin, the cost of buying the silver plus the actual cost of minting. This would typically be a far smaller profit than the full seigniorage and the actual profit from the operation would be considerably less than the maximum profit figure.

Minting on private account there undoubtedly was, in spite of the poor terms offered and therefore profits certainly bore some relation to the figures given. Gould asks:

> ... what would induce private citizens to sell silver, either coined or in the form of bullion, to the Mint? Or more specifically, what would induce them to offer more when the mint price was increased? It is sometimes suggested that debasing the coinage is akin to trickery, the subject being 'deceived' into selling coin or bullion by an increase in the mint price which, the fact of an adulteration of the fineness of the coin being unknown to the seller, conceals from him that in reality he may be receiving not more, but less, intrinsic value in return.
>
> (Gould 1970: 13)

With the help of his table he analyses and dismisses it as a jejune theory of debasement. He distinguishes three potential sources of gold and silver; newly mined metal, gold and silver, plate and ornament which can be melted down for coining and coins themselves (Gould 1970: 15). The owner of silver plate for example or someone contemplating buying it had to compare the utility of the plate as such with the utility that could be derived from the purchasing power of the coins the Mint would give in exchange for the silver content of the plate. To the extent to which prices in general did not rise to reflect the full extent of the debasement, the alternative purchasing power of plate actually rose, the temptation to melt down was increased.

Why was coin presented for reminting? At first sight, it seems counter-productive. As the Tables show clearly, anyone presenting coins to the mint would receive back coins containing materially less silver or gold than those offered, the rest having disappeared in seigniorage. Gould answers this one very ingeniously, making full use of the distinction between mint equivalent and mint price. Supposing a Tudor citizen owns 146 pre-debasement groats with a face value of £2.8s.8d.(£2.43), and containing exactly one pound of pure silver. In the year 1545–6 he knows that the mint *price* is £2.16s.0d. (£2.80). He does not know, but may be able to infer, that the mint *equivalent* is £4.16s.0d. (£4.80). If he takes his coins to the mint he will hand over coins with a face value of £2.8s.8d., and containing one pound troy, or 12 ounces of fine silver. He will receive in return coins containing only 7 ounces of fine silver, the other five having, in effect, been confiscated by the mint. That is the bad news. The good news is that he now has 168 groats with a face value of £2.16s.0d. (£2.80). In terms of silver, he has lost, but having no use for silver as such he is from a practical point of view, (given the institutional structure and trade customs of the times, the spending power of coins depends on their face, or fiat, value) better off by £0.37. The king has made £2.00: who has lost? The answer of course is those holding the debased coins when the music stops.

The profits of the debasement resulted from the dramatic increase in the mint equivalent as the silver content of the coins was reduced. Citizens were induced to bring coins to the mint by a steady increase in the mint price. As Gould shows, at every stage of the debasement the mint price offered in newly minted coins exceeded the mint equivalent of some earlier issue, thereby encouraging the older and finer coins to be brought to the mint for recoining. This is shown schematically in Gould's Table 6. The overall pattern was thus very ingenious. The clever scheme for generating a non-parliamentary profit to the King appears to have been devised by Thomas Wriothesly.

Modern students will detect a possible flaw in the reasoning. Why should 158 new groats with a silver content of only seven ounces have more purchasing power than a 146 old groats with a silver content of twelve ounces? How did the coins maintain their fiat value when their intrinsic value had been so much debased? Why did not some entrepreneur offer the holder of pre-debasement groats a premium over the mint price, and export them for the bullion content, splitting the difference between the mint price (£2.16s.0d.) and the mint equivalent (£4.16s.0d.) and the vendor? Gould suggests legal tender constraints and convenience. Convenience was probably the more important influence at work. In certain circumstances though, coins would change hands at something approaching intrinsic value. This was particularly true of the gold coins where the debasement proceeded less rapidly. At some stages indeed, the figures only make sense on the assumption that at certain periods certain gold coins did change hands at a premium suggesting a new concept of '*de facto* mint equivalent' based, not on the face value, but on the value at which such coins did in fact change hands between merchants.

Gold

So far, the analysis has referred only to the silver coins. A glance at Table 5.3 reveals a quite different pattern for gold. First, the debasement, as such, did not go nearly as far. Whereas the silver content of the worst silver coins fell to 25 per cent, losing three-quarters of their value, that of the most debased gold coins (the April 1546 issue) fell only to 83 per cent losing only a sixth, resulting, in a decidedly odd bimetallic ratio of under 5 on a mint equivalent basis. Table 5.5 summarises the key figures for gold, with the bimetallic ratio calculated on three bases. The highest rate of seigniorage, on the same gold issue, was 15 per cent compared with a maximum of 55 per cent on the silver. One reason the changes had to be so much more modest was that gold coins were handled by more sophisticated merchants, who could and did arbitrage. The depreciation of the gold coins mainly took the form of a crying up or enhancement in their value.

Obviously the dramatic debasement of the silver coins coupled with a more modest debasement of the gold coins totally distorted the bimetallic ratio, as traditionally defined on the basis of mint equivalent or actual bullion content. This figure is simply a statistic. As always in economic analysis, we have to ask what real people would actually have done. It is no good a merchant knowing that gold was undervalued in England unless he can find a way of making a profit from this fact. How, if at all, can he arbitrage the anomaly? He could acquire gold coins at their face value (mint equivalent) or at some period the enhanced value at which they were actually exchanged (the *de facto* mint equivalent). He could then export these to Flanders and exchange them for silver. In Flanders though the fiat value of the coins would be irrelevant. Merchants there would 'buy' the coins on the basis of their bullion value, and the merchant could exchange them for silver bullion only at the more normal ratio ruling there.

> This silver . . . he then imported to be coined, or to be put to some other use. If the Mint was enjoying an ample supply of silver bullion, we may take this fact as demonstrating that the value of silver in other uses was, at the most, not appreciably higher than its value of silver brought to the Mint. The values, then, appropriate in computing the silver/gold ratio would be, not the mint equivalents in both cases, but the mint equivalent of the exported metal (in this case gold) and the mint price of that imported (in this case silver).
>
> (Gould 1970: 29–30)

In fact the ratio on a 'mint equivalent' basis fell below 10 in only two cases. More strictly, we should use the *de facto* mint equivalent of the best gold coins. These have been calculated by Gould and are shown in the last column of Table 5.5. These revised figures explain the mystery of why gold continued to be coined in 1546 when the ratio (5) appeared to be extremely low. Only after 1549 was there a real outflow of gold. We do not have to explain away the December 1550 and April 1551 figures: as Table 5.4 shows, virtually no gold was struck.

Prices

What happened to prices? If international purchasing power of bullion had remained unchanged one would expect that coins with one-quarter of the precious metal content would *eventually* come to have only one-quarter of the purchasing power. Prices would rise fourfold. Similarly exchange rates would eventually reflect the relative bullion contents of the circulating media in two countries. In the nature of markets though, they would not adjust very quickly to changed circumstances, especially to such a sharp unprecedented and unanticipated shock. Prices are likely to be affected more directly by the actual quantity of money in circulation. The two factors would be the same if, and only if, the amount of bullion in circulation remained the same. The reduction to a quarter in the silver content of the penny does not necessarily mean that four times as many pennies were in circulation. Some part of the mint's profit could be exported in the form of bullion, economising on the silver content of the coinage.

In testing 'quantity theory' concepts there are two problems. First, although we have precise (if incomplete) information on mint output and can infer the gaps, we cannot simply add up the total of coins produced over a period and assume that they are still all in circulation at the end of that period. This procedure is of limited value even in normal times, and in this case there was a special factor at work. A large part of the mint output comprised a recoinage of earlier issues: indeed this was Henry's principal source of profit. The figures given in Gould are estimates and subject to his own very detailed reservations. In his words:

> . . . at several points the assumptions made have an element of the heroic . . . the author cannot condone or support other scholars who choose to borrow these estimates without hedging them about with the substantial warnings and qualifications which, it is insisted, ought to accompany them.
>
> (Gould 1970: 72)

This warning must be duly noted. Similarly, price data are at best unreliable and for this period 'have usually been very heavily weighted on grain prices'. Good harvests in the later 1540s followed by the harvest failures of 1555 and 1556 seriously distort the figures, masking inflationary effects of the earlier part of the debasement, while misleading 'those who place their trust in index numbers into looking for evidence of monetary instability in the middle of Mary's reign'.

In summary, money supply rose from £850,000 in 1542 to a maximum of £2.17 million in July 1551, implying an actual fall in the bullion content of the circulating medium. It was then instantly halved following Edward's 'calling down' but grew again to £1.39 million after Elizabeth's successful recoinage in 1562. This was an increase of 64 per cent. The price index also shows an increase of 64 per cent from which 'quantity theorists will doubtless take encouragement'. However, 'closer scrutiny . . . makes one a little more cautious about claiming this as a signal victory for quantity theory' (Gould 1970: 84).

THE RESTORATION OF THE COINAGE

In 1551 Edward resumed striking coins in standard gold and in sterling silver, but the value of the 240 grain sovereign was called up (or enhanced) to 30 shillings and the weight of the silver coinage was reduced to 8 grains per penny. There was an extensive issue of shillings and four new denominations, the silver crown (five shillings) and half-crown, the sixpence and the threepence were introduced. No more groats were struck until the reign of Mary, but there is an extremely rare fine silver penny. Although the story ends with the reintroduction of fine silver in 1551, some base pennies, half-pennies and farthings (a unique example of the latter has survived) with Edward's name but without a portrait appear to be contemporary. This base issue continued into the reign of Mary, which reduced the standard to 3 ounces. They continued to form an active part of the circulation until Elizabeth's reform of 1560. In the meantime base pennies, halfpennies and farthings, significantly not bearing the royal portrait, continued to be struck, possibly for Ireland, and possibly as a first attempt to introduce to England the concept of base token coins for small change, a practice which had long been common in Scotland and on the Continent.

Elizabeth I, assisted by Sir Thomas Gresham succeeded in restoring the sound coinage which continued, with few incidents, for a century until Newton's recoinage of 1696. There were in fact three occasions during Elizabeth's reign where consideration was given to fraudulent profits from coinage: Dandyprats (Challis 1978: 251); the rose noble exercise (Challis: 263 ff) and the late Irish debasement (Challis: 268). (Sir Thomas Gresham (1519–71) was Queen Elizabeth's financial adviser, responsible for clearing up the mess of her father's Great Debasement, and founder of the Royal Exchange. He is known for Gresham's Law: 'Bad money drives out good', which has been discussed in Chapter 2 and which will become a major topic in the chapters dealing with bimetallism. In Gresham's day, money meant 'coin'. In concept a coin is a piece of gold or silver, the weight and fineness of which is guaranteed by the ruler by whose authority it was issued. Rulers, including Henry VIII, could and did cheat.)

PRIVATE ENTERPRISE

The Debasement generated a substantial profit from coinage. The King could effectively double his money by buying bullion and turning it into coins: so, in principle, could anyone else. Whereas in earlier periods, the counterfeiter could only make a profit by producing coins to a lower standard and escaping detection, it was in this case quite profitable enough to produce coins to the official, debased standard, in effect collecting the high seigniorage charged by the official mints. It seems in fact that the main source of unofficial coinage derived from unrecorded mint activity (profiting the mint masters) rather than forgery as such. This is a major source of distortion in the statistics, and Gould cautions his readers 'against placing unbounded trust even . . . [where] the figures *are* calculated from surviving Mint accounts' (Gould 1970: 37). He points out that 'Officials who made coins which they did not account for could pocket the inflated sum which the King levied on each pound of metal struck' and draws attention to the well-known case of Sir William Sharington at Bristol who worked in the mint illegally to finance the rebellion by Lord Seymour. In the climate of the time he might have got away with it if his motive had been the more acceptable one of self-enrichment (Gould 1970: 39–41; Challis 1978: 274–99).

LONGER PERIOD PRICE TRENDS

Peter Ramsey (1963) refers to the Phelps-Brown figures, but over a longer period. He is remarkably reluctant to accept a monetary explanation of a phenomenon he describes briefly in the course of a more general book. He describes the Tudor inflation as beginning about 1510, the index having hovered around its (1451–75) base of 100 for some time. It then rises to 167 by 1521, and stabilises at around 150 in the early 1540s. This was before the debasement, and other factors must have been at work. There is then a rise to over 200 in the late 1540s, and to 409 in 1557. This is the debasement: there is a fall to 230 in 1558 (restoration of the coinage) but the rise then resumes. Prices rose to 459 by 1600.

The monetary explanation of the sharp rise is obvious. The general trend over the century reflects a number of factors, the main one being the influence of American silver imports. Ramsey disputes the classic Hamilton (1934) thesis. Some of the comments are interesting in that they show how, not so long ago, economic historians could be so out of touch with modern economic theory. He regards it as 'a very dangerous and misleading argument when applied to sixteenth century England. In the first place, silver imports to Spain reach a significant volume only after 1545' (the Potosi discoveries). 'We have [he says] to explain how Spanish silver got to England, or how rising prices abroad forced up those at home' (Ramsay 1963: 117).

Do we? An increase in money supply will have forced down the relative price of silver, and forced up the prices of commodities as measured in silver. The effect would surely spread quickly across frontiers by trade arbitrage, without any major change in the trade flows. There is no need to assume that 'the price of silver at the Mint would have fallen', nor does it matter that 'the import trade dealt largely in luxuries or near luxuries'. He does have an interesting analysis of the social consequences: the difference between those on fixed or custom dominated income and those who could take a more entrepreneurial role. There were big movements (not, he suggests peculiar to this period) of those moving up and down the social scale.

APPENDIX

THE COINS OF THE DEBASEMENT

Readers wanting more information on the actual (English) coins in circulation at most periods can turn to standard numismatic catalogues such as Seaby (annual) and North (3rd edn, 1992). These give too little detail to be helpful for the debasement period, lumping all the debased coins under a 'third period'. Some of their attributions are misleading. For instance there is no evidence that their so-called 'First Period' portrait shilling of Edward VI ever existed as a currency coin. A 'pattern shilling in the style of the first period shilling' is certainly known (Spink Numismatic Circular December 1992). The 'Second Period' (sic) of Edward VI includes, remarkably, full shillings weighing 60 grains made of 8 ounces fine silver, and shillings weighing 80 grains, 6 ounces fine. Neither standard work gives any clue as to which coins are which. Their 'Third Period' included both those struck during the last stages of debasement and also the fine silver coins which replaced them. Excusably, they do not attempt to classify the coins of the Bristol mint, simply saying that it is impossible to tell which were struck during Henry's, and which during Edward's, reign. The present author did at least once make an attempt (Chown, 1976).

The series is in fact well documented if one is prepared to track down back numbers of journals dating back to Sir John Evans' classic article (1886). (Even if it surprisingly often turns out that many attributions subsequently accepted as fact on the authority of an earlier writer were put forward by the first writer only in the form of a tentative hypothesis.)

The documentary evidence for the coinage of the period is reasonably good, although the Mint accounts are by no means complete. One can identify from the indentures six separate coinages of Henry VIII and five, or possibly six, base coinages of Edward VI. Most of the coins can be identified with one or other of the indentures, but the evidence for this information is widely scattered. A particularly intriguing source is a series of articles by Raymond Carlyon- Britton in Spinks Numismatic Circular in 1949 and 1950. For the period covered (the silver coins struck during the reign of Edward VI whether bearing his own or his father's portrait) the attributions seem virtually complete and detailed. Unfortunately the illustrations are poor, thanks to post-war austerity printing standards.

Even more unfortunately, this was the work of a dying man, and the evidence he may have had for his attributions seems to have died with him. They are convincing in the negative sense that I have not been able, after fairly close study, either to fault the attributions, (or to find any published articles attempting to do so) but in most cases there appears to be no positive evidence, either in the literature or by inspection of the coins, actually to support them. In particular I am intrigued to know how he convinced himself that a particular coin was struck at one rather than another of the two and sometimes three mints operating at the Tower. Mr Carlyon-Britton deviates from the pattern deduced from the indentures and listed in the body of the chapter. He dates his 'fifth' coinage of Edward VI from an undetermined date in 1549. He then had a 'sixth coinage' consisting entirely of groats distinguished by the 'rose mantle clasp' variation of what is usually known as Bust 5. Most writers prefer to treat these two issues as being a continuation of the fourth coinage. Mr Carlyon-Britton then lists as his 'seventh coinage' what is generally described as the fifth.

Table 5.2 The coinages of Henry VIII and Edward VI: Silver

| Coinage issued | Date | Silver pennies | | | | | | |
		Weight in grains	Fineness	Grains fine silver	Mint[1] equivalent	Seigniorage	Mint[1] price	Seigniorage (percentage of mint equivalent)
Henry VIII								
second coinage	1526	10.67	0.925	9.87	2.43	0.05	2.38	2.2
third coinage	May 1542	10.00	0.833	8.33	2.88	0.48	2.40	16.6
fourth coinage	Apr 1544	10.00	0.750	7.50	3.20	0.58	2.62	18.1
fifth coinage	Apr 1545	10.00	0.500	5.00	4.80	2.00	2.80	41.7
sixth coinage	Apr 1546	10.00	0.333	3.33	7.21	4.40	2.81	61.1
Edward VI								
first coinage	Apr 1547	10.00	0.333	3.33	7.21	4.00	3.21	55.5
second coinage	Jan 1549	10.00	0.333	3.33	7.21	4.00	3.21	55.5
third coinage	Apr 1549	6.67	0.500	3.33	7.20	3.80	3.40	52.8
fourth coinage	Jul 1550	6.67	0.500	3.33	7.20	3.80	3.40	52.8
	Dec 1550	6.67	0.500	3.33	7.20	3.80	3.40	52.8
fifth coinage	Apr 1551	6.67	0.250	1.67	14.40	8.40	6.00	58.3
sixth coinage	Oct 1551	8.00	0.924	7.39	3.25	0.05	3.19	1.7
Mary								
	Aug 1553	8.00	0.917	7.34	3.27	0.08	3.19	2.4
	Aug 1557	8.00	0.917	7.33	3.27	0.08	3.19	2.5
Elizabeth								
	Jan 1559	8.00	0.917	7.33	3.27	0.08	3.19	2.5
	Nov 1560	8.00	0.931	7.44	3.22	0.08	3.14	2.5

Source: Gould Table I
Note: [1] Expressed in modern decimal £

Table 5.3 The coinages of Henry VIII and Edward VI: Gold

Coinage issued	Date		Coin value (p)	Weight in grains	Fineness	Grains of fine gold	Mint[1] equivalent	Bimetallic ratio on mint equivalent	Seigniorage	Mint[1] price	Bimetallic ratio on mint price	Seigniorage (percentage of mint equivalent)
Henry VIII												
second coinage	1526	(6/8)	80	71.10	0.970	69.00	27.83	11.44	0.14	27.68	11.64	0.5
third coinage	May 1542	(8/0)	96	80.00	0.958	76.67	30.05	10.43	0.16	29.89	12.44	0.5
fourth coinage	Apr 1544	(8/0)	96	80.00	0.958	76.67	30.05	9.39	1.25	28.80	10.99	4.2
fifth coinage	Apr 1545	(£1)	240	192.00	0.917	176.00	32.73	6.82	2.73	30.00	10.71	8.3
sixth coinage	Apr 1546	(£1)	240	192.00	0.833	160.00	36.00	5.00	5.40	30.60	10.90	15.0
Edward VI												
first coinage	Apr 1547	(£1)	240	192.00	0.833	160.00	36.00	5.00	1.20	34.80	10.85	3.3
second coinage	Jan 1549	(£1)	240	169.41	0.917	155.29	37.09	5.15	1.09	36.00	11.22	2.9
third coinage	Apr 1549	(£1)	240	169.41	0.917	155.29	37.09	5.15	1.09	36.00	10.59	2.9
fourth coinage	Jul 1550	(£1)	240	169.41	0.917	155.29	37.09	5.15	1.09	36.00	10.59	2.9
	Dec 1550	(24/–)	288	240.00	0.970	232.92	29.68	4.12	1.70	27.98	8.23	5.7
fifth coinage	Apr 1551	(24/–)	288	240.00	0.970	232.92	29.68	2.06	1.70	27.98	4.66	5.7
sixth coinage	Oct 1551	(30/–)	360	240.00	0.995	238.75	36.19	11.14	0.16	36.02	11.28	0.5
Mary												
	Aug 1553	(30/–)	360	240.00	0.995	238.75	36.19	11.06	0.20	35.99	11.27	0.6
	Aug 1557	(10/–)	120	80.00	0.995	79.58	36.19	11.06	0.20	35.99	11.28	0.6
Elizabeth												
	Jan 1559	(30/–)	360	240.00	0.995	238.75	36.19	11.06	0.20	35.99	11.28	0.6
	Nov 1560	(£1)	240	160.00	0.970	155.28	37.09	11.51	0.22	36.88	11.73	0.6

Source: Gould Table II
Note: [1] Expressed in modern decimal £

Table 5.4 Quantities of silver and gold coins issued during the reigns of Henry VIII and Edward VI

Coinage used	Date	Mint output (£ face value)				
		Silver	Gold	Total value	Gold (%)	Maximum profit[1]
Henry VIII						
second coinage	1526					
third coinage	May 1542	52,927	15,581	68,508	22.7	8,888
fourth coinage	Apr 1544	149,287	165,917	315,204	52.6	33,921
fifth coinage	Apr 1545	440,213	372,120	812,333	45.8	214,430
sixth coinage	Apr 1546	451,811	263,130	714,941	36.8	315,300
Edward VI						
first coinage	Apr 1547	397,572	434,160	831,732	52.2	235,124
second coinage	Jan 1549	401,072	76,772	477,844	16.1	224,855
third coinage	Apr 1549					
fourth coinage	Jul 1550	102,272		102,272	0.0	53,971
	Dec 1550					
fifth coinage	Apr 1551	252,955	2,765	255,720	1.1	147,701
sixth coinage	Oct 1551	41,640		41,640	0.0	694
Totals (not given by Gould)		2,289,749	1,330,445	3,620,194	36.8	1,234,884

Source: Gould table V.
Note: The table needs to be read with Gould's qualifications. He gives information by mint. [1] The profit figures may not be reliable (see text)

Table 5.5 The coinages of Henry VIII and Edward VI: bimetallic ratios

Coinage used	Date	Silver		Gold		Bimetallic ratio			
		Mint equivalent	Mint price	Mint equivalent	Mint price	Mint equivalent	Mint price	Mint equivalent gold/mint price silver	Gould
Henry VIII									
second coinage	1526	2.43	2.38	27.83	27.68	11.4	11.6	11.7	11.7
third coinage	May 1542	2.88	2.40	30.05	29.89	10.4	12.4	12.5	12.0
fourth coinage	Apr 1544	3.20	2.62	30.05	28.80	9.4	11.0	11.5	11.6
fifth coinage	Apr 1545	4.80	2.80	32.73	30.00	6.8	10.7	11.7	11.3
sixth coinage	Apr 1546	7.21	2.81	36.00	30.60	5.0	10.9	12.8	11.7
Edward VI									
first coinage	Apr 1547	7.21	3.21	36.00	34.80	5.0	10.9	11.2	10.7
second coinage	Jan 1549	7.21	3.21	37.09	36.00	5.1	11.2	11.6	10.3
third coinage	Apr 1549	7.20	3.40	37.09	36.00	5.2	10.6	10.9	
fourth coinage	Jul 1550	7.20	3.40	37.09	36.00	5.2	10.6	10.9	9.3
	Dec 1550	7.20	3.40	29.68	27.98	4.1	8.2	8.7	9.5
fifth coinage	Apr 1551	14.40	6.00	29.68	27.98	2.1	4.7	4.9	
sixth coinage	Oct 1551	3.25	3.19	36.19	36.02	11.1	11.3	11.3	11.4
Mary									
	Aug 1553	3.27	3.19	36.19	35.99	11.1	11.3	11.3	
	Aug 1557	3.27	3.19	36.19	35.99	11.1	11.3	11.3	
Elizabeth									
	Jan 1559	3.27	3.19	36.19	35.99	11.1	11.3	11.3	
	Nov 1560	3.22	3.14	37.09	36.88	11.5	11.7	11.8	

Sources: Gould, Table IV and some calculations from Tables 5.2 and 5.3. Gould's figures (his Table IV) are based on *de facto* mint equivalent of best gold coins.

6

THE RECOINAGE OF 1696
– LOCKE, LOWNDES AND
NEWTON

BACKGROUND

In the century after Elizabeth I and Sir Thomas Gresham had engineered the restoration of the coinage following Henry VIII's debasements, there were no formal changes in the weight standards of English coins. The country was preoccupied with politics and religion, rather than with money. Following the death of Elizabeth in 1603 James VI of Scotland became James I of England, making a single kingdom whose currencies were unified on the basis of the shilling Scottish equalling the penny English. This tells us something about previous monetary policy, but there is little to guide us about modern problems of monetary union. The actual ratio was about 13, and the convenient rounding gave a very small benefit to the smaller partner. The Civil War between Charles I and Parliament led to the reign of the Stuarts being interrupted by Cromwell's 'Commonwealth' (1649–60).

The restoration of Charles II and the end of the Puritan dictatorship ushered in a lively period of literature, theatre and music. After his death the nation's stability was again threatened as James II tried to bring it back within the fold of the Catholic church: the traditional Tory (and Anglican) doctrine of 'divine right' collapsed under the strain. James's staunchly Protestant daughter, Mary, was married to her cousin, William of Orange, a grandson of Charles I and in 1688 he landed in England and quickly defeated James, who fled the country. William and Mary were proclaimed co-sovereigns on 13 February 1689. In 1690 James landed in Ireland, with French support, but was defeated at the Battle of the Boyne. The death of the Queen from smallpox in December 1694 weakened the position of the surviving co-sovereign, and led to fears that James II might be restored to the throne. William was already at war with Louis XIV of France, regarded, after the decline of Spain, as the greatest threat to Protestant Europe.

Money once more became an issue again at the end of the century. From 1660 until about 1688, prices actually fell and there is some evidence that there was a trade recession caused by the shortage of coins. Certainly the coinage was in a bad state, and the exchange rate deteriorated in 1695. On the Gresham principle, good silver coins were melted down and exported. There was an expensive war with France which marks the beginning of the national debt (not recognised as such) and, in 1699, a run on the recently founded Bank of England. William Lowndes, newly appointed Secretary to the Treasury, published his famous 'Essay for the amendment of the silver coin' on 12 September 1695. It was rebutted by John Locke, in what is perhaps the most famous currency dispute in history. All the great and the good joined in the battle: the spate of pamphlets and proposals included one by Sir Christopher Wren, while the practical problems with recoinage were such that Sir Isaac Newton himself was called in first as Warden, and later as Master, of the Mint.

THE STATE OF THE COINAGE

There was definitely a shortage of silver as a circulating medium and the arguments about the reasons were to some extent a rehearsal of those that were to be deployed before the Bullion Committee of 1810. The main opinion was that it was either a balance of trade deficit arising from the war or the activities of wicked speculators. There was surprisingly little discussion about what seems to us to be the obvious explanation: simply that the bimetallic ratio in the United Kingdom was out of line. If an ounce of gold was worth 11.5 ounces of silver in Antwerp and 11 ounces in London there was obviously a profit to be made, even allowing for the then high cost of transportation and risk.

In 1662 the Roelters mill and screw press replaced the earlier 'hammered' process for manufacturing coins. These were (fairly) proof against clipping and the edge of the larger coins carried the inscription 'DECUS ET TUTAMEN' reintroduced in 1983 on the first of the modern pound coins. The 'milled' coins circulated (or not as the case may be) alongside the old hammered coinage. Examining the figures of the silver shortage, Li (1963: 29) draws a striking comparison between the periods before and after the establishment of the Commonwealth in 1649.

Table 6.1 Annual average coinage: 1558 to 1694 (£)

Period	Silver	Gold
1558–1649	171,961	86,299
1649–1694	83,886	155,853

The total silver coined in the period was £19.7 million, of which Hopton Haynes, Assay Master of the Mint, reckoned that about £10 million was still in circulation in 1695, most of the balance having been melted down or exported. Of the total of £15 million gold coined in the period, only between £3 million and £5 million was still in circulation. Two problems follow from these figures. First, there was a shortage of coins in circulation. Second, £7 million out of the £10 million of silver coins were pre-1649, and were badly worn and clipped.

Fleetwood's attack on clipping

William Fleetwood, the Royal chaplain, preached his 'Sermon against Clipping' in the Guildhall chapel on 16 December 1694. He took his text from Genesis 23:16 – the passage where Abraham weighed out the silver to pay for a burial field. The first part of the sermon reads as a lecture in monetary economics. Money, he said, should be portable, durable and beautiful. In the days of Abraham, silver

> . . . was valued both by Buyer and Seller according to its weight . . . but because it was too troublesome, and took up too much time, to carry Scales . . . Men found it convenient to have a Stamp or Mark set upon every piece, to signify its weight and value. . . . Yet something was still needed to secure the truth of Payments: Men might be fraudulent and false . . .
>
> (Fleetwood 1694)

The second part is more in the good old hell-fire sermon tradition, and denounced the sin and evil of clipping. Several times did he deny the argument 'Who is hereby wronged?' – just because the clipper did not know by name who he was defrauding. The convicted 'can be sorry for their great misfortune, but they know not how to repent . . . the sense of these offences affects them little or nothing'.

He described the punishments of former times – cutting off the right hand, or – a man of the cloth must choose his words carefully – some 'who were found to Adulterate the King's Coin, were so punished as if the Laws intended to prevent Adultery itself'. With a rather wistful glance backward at the good old days, he concluded that his age was merciful in letting clippers off lightly with a Modern Execution – 'a short and easy Death'.

Shortly afterwards, on 3 May 1695 Parliament passed the 'Act for Preventing, Counterfeiting and Clipping' (text bound in with my copy of the Sermon) but had little effect.

> But did this prohibition, tho by Act of Parliament, cure the evil? Alas no. The forbidden Fruit was of too luscious a relish to be so easily relinquished. It was not in the power of any Paper-spell to stop the spreading Gangrene.
>
> (Anon 'Universal Remedy' 1696: 18–19)

Certainly Newton was second to none in his determination to catch and hang counterfeiters.

The Lowndes proposals

Against this background, Lowndes proposed a formal devaluation which would have left the clipped old coins substantially at par with full weight new ones: the obvious, civilised and honest solution adopted in every century or so in the past. Specifically he suggested that a new piece having the same weight and fineness as the old crown (five shillings) would be called the Sceptre, or silver Unite, which would pass for six shillings and three pence. In the case of the shilling the old name would be kept but the weight of the new shilling would be 80 per cent of that of the old. He began by examining the historical evidence looking, as we have already done, at the experiences of Henry II, Edward I and Queen Elizabeth. He concluded, correctly, that there were precedents in other reigns, and put forward nine specific arguments.

1. The market price of silver had risen to 6s. 5d. per ounce and the value suggested would defend the coins from being melted down.
2. Unless the value of silver was raised by 25 per cent none of the silver would have been brought to them for coinage.
3. The higher the denominative value of the coins, the greater would be the amount of money in tale, which would then be sufficient to satisfy the needs of trade.
4. The market value of the unclipped coins was already at least 25 per cent higher than the clipped ones, so the coins of equal quantities of silver should have the same denominative value.
5. The proposed value of 6s. 3d. (i.e. 75 pennies) for the crown was divisible into a great number of integral parts.
6. Although new names would be given to new coins, the denominations of Pound, Shilling and Penny would remain, so that there would be no confusion in computing accounts.
7. The raising of the denominative value had to be sufficient to bring out the hoarded milled coins and to make it unnecessary to recoin them.
8. The cost of recoinage would be much less if the denominative value of the new coins were raised by 25 per cent.
9. Unless the devaluation was sufficient it might be necessary to devalue again should the price of silver continue to rise.

(Li 1963: 96–7)

Locke's views

John Locke the greatest philosopher of his age but perhaps a rather muddled economist, took up the cudgels against Lowndes. He argued that it was a mistake to assume that 'standard silver can be priced in respect of itself' and 'that standard bullion is now for whatever it was worth sold to the traders in it for 6s. 5d. of lawful money of England'. (Silver was no more valuable than it had ever been – it was simply that the coins passing 'in tail' were lighter.) He argued in effect that the denominative value of the coins was irrelevant. What mattered was the quantity of silver in circulation.

> Whether you call the piece coyn'd a 12d. or 15d., or 60d. or 75d., a Crown or a Ducatoon, it will buy no more Silk, Salt or Bread than it would before, that therefore cannot Tempt the people to bring it to the Mint. . . . For bullion cannot [be] bought hither to stay here, whilst the Balance of Our Trade require all the Bullion to be Exported again and more Silver out of the former Stock with it to answer our Exigencies beyond the Seas.
>
> (Locke 1691)

Newton argued that 'it seems reasonable that an ounce of bullion should be by Parliament enacted of the same value with the crown piece of milled money'. There were no penalties and this he argued was 'the only sure means to make milled money constantly of the same intrinsic and extrinsic value there ought to be and thereby to prevent them melting or exporting of it'. Of the two ways of achieving this end Newton appears in 1696 to have favoured devaluation.

> It seems more reasonable to alter the Extrinsick rather than the Intrinsick Value of Milled Money, that is, to raise a Crown Piece to the Value of an Ounce of Bullion which at present is at least 6s. 3d. than to Depress Bullion to the present Value of Milled Money.
>
> (Li 1963: 217)

His third argument in favour was that this would lessen the cost of recoining all the unmilled money. On the 'contract' point, he argued:–

> If it be said that by raising the Extrinsick value of Milled Money the King in receiving Excise, Customs and Taxes, and all persons in receiving Annuitys, Rents and other debts must be content with the Crown-Piece instead of 6s. 3d. and so lose 1s. 3d. which is one fifth of his Money: I answer that if the Loss be computed in the Extrinsick value of the Money, it will be none at all because a Crown-Piece after it is raised, will be of the same Extrinsick value with 6s. 3d., and go just as far in a Market or in buying land. But if it be Computed in the Intrinsick Value it will be no New Loss because Taxes, Rents, Annuitys & all other Debts are payable by law in Unmilled Money which has already lost at least 2/5 parts of its Intrinsick value by Clipping and Adulteration.
>
> (Li 1963: 218)

Newton (1696) also made a point about the gold/silver ratio.

> . . . care should be taken that they bear nearly the same proportion to one another at home and abroad, and this Affords another reason for

64

raising the value of Milled Money to that of Bullion. For if Gold in proportion to Silver be of much more value at home than abroad the Bullion and Milled money will be Exported to buy up Foreign Gold, and the contrary would happen by raising the Value of Milled Money and Bullion too much without raising Gold in due proportion.

(Li 1963: 218)

This is exactly what happened.

The issues

It seems to us nowadays that much of the argument was about names rather than realities. Locke was in error in assuming that silver was the only measure of value. In any case, given that the crown pieces actually in circulation contained only 4 shillings worth of silver the necessary recoinage could be carried out in one of two ways. The first, which Lowndes proposed, would have been to recoin to the lighter standard. Old full weight coins would have emerged from hoards and could have circulated at a stated premium, or be accepted by the mint by weight as bullion. The second alternative, in fact adopted, was to recoin to substantially the old standards and to call in the old coins.

The two strategies would have very different effects on the level of prices. If coins circulate in tale, that is at face value, and the silver content of a coin falls then the debtor will have to deliver to the creditor a smaller amount of silver to settle an existing debt. It does not matter whether the reduction in the weight of the coin was the result of clipping or by devaluation (which Locke described as 'a clipping done by public authority, a public crime'). The Lowndes proposal would recognise a *fait accompli*, but looked at from another point of view would perpetuate the 'robbery'.

Political action

Parliament passed an 'Act for Remedying the Ill State of the Crown of the Kingdom', on 17 January 1696, omitting three extra clauses inserted by the Lords, but deferred for later consideration by the Commons. This was the first formal act of the recoinage. For reasons obvious with hindsight guineas rose in price in terms of the silver coinage. One problem was the now familiar one of the cost of uncertainty. This profited the goldsmiths and indeed anyone who chose to make a speciality of currency markets at the expense of the ordinary trader or citizen. These definitely lost out: they had, typically, to accept guineas at 30 shillings and part with them to the bankers for only 29 shillings. On 15 February Parliament voted (by 164 to 129) to reduce the price of guineas to 28s. This was soon found to be still too high.

On 24 February 1696, Parliament passed the 'Act for taking off the Obligation and Incouragement for Coining Guineas for a certain time therein mentioned'. Members complained about the substantial imports of gold and the abundance of guineas which was, it was said, indebting the country to foreigners. (It was of course caused by an inevitable and predictable bimetallic flow.) From 2 March 1696 until 1 January 1697 the mints would have no obligation to coin gold and it would be illegal to import guineas or half guineas into the country. This was a kind of reverse exchange control, designed to keep money out. An exception was made for The Royal Africa Company of England, whose main trade was gold mining in West Africa. The Act also provided that certain import taxes should be applied to the encouragement of the silver coinage. On 26 February 1696, Parliament resolved that the value of the guinea be reduced to 26 shillings (a compromise – it was hoped to reduce it to 24 shillings) and the penalties for passing guineas at higher rates were included in an Act passed on 7 March. On 26 March a clause was inserted into another bill providing that guineas should not pass at more than 22 shillings after 10 April 1696 with a penalty of double the value plus £20. By October the guinea had in fact come down to 22 shillings (not thanks to any efforts of Parliament) the prohibition on gold imports was repealed ahead of time and the Mint was instructed to commence coining guineas from 10 November.

Meanwhile Newton had been appointed Warden of the Mint on 25 March 1696. In 1698 the Commissioners of the Council of Credit, which included John Pollexfen and John Locke, (Li 1963: 126–8) argued that at 22 shillings the price was at least 6 per cent higher than that fixed by the Mint in neighbouring countries – hence the small coinage of silver and the export of silver bullion. A reduction to 21 shillings and 6 pence would make the ratio 15.5 compared with 15 in neighbouring countries. On 16 February 1699, Parliament resolved that no-one was obliged to take guineas at 22 shillings. At that time they were in fact accepted in payment of taxes at no more than 21 shillings and 6 pence. The effort proved in vain. Although nearly £7 million pounds worth of silver was coined, the new coin disappeared almost immediately as the market price of silver remained higher than the mint price.

The question of the gold ratio was not effectively settled until 1717. The guinea then became worth a maximum of 21 shillings. The bimetallic flow continued to favour the influx of gold. Guineas became the main component of the circulating medium, supplemented by foreign (mainly Portuguese) gold coins. The recoinage of 1774 was the *de facto* acceptance of a gold standard which was formalised in 1817. Meanwhile, though, the United Kingdom was, during and after the Napoleonic Wars, to go through a long period of inconvertible paper money, discussed in Part III.

7

FORMALISING THE UNITED KINGDOM GOLD STANDARD

TOWARDS A GOLD STANDARD

The important point to remember about the international gold standard, as a method for regulating monetary arrangements between nations, is that it lasted such an extraordinarily short time. The United Kingdom adopted gold in 1821, after the Napoleonic Wars. Portugal adopted the UK-style standard in 1854, even making British sovereigns legal tender, (Del Mar 1895: 487) and Canada acceded in 1867. The 'system' only really came into being as such between Germany's accession in 1873 and that of the United States in 1879 (Chapter 9). Austria-Hungary adopted the gold standard in 1892 (by when Portugal had abandoned it) followed by Russia and Japan in 1897. The system broke apart in 1914 with a short lived revival between the wars.

For most of the nineteenth century there was no internationally accepted standard: Germany, the Netherlands, Scandinavia, India, China and most of Latin America were on silver. The United States together with France and, eventually, her Latin Monetary Union partners, were bimetallic, while some countries, Russia, Austria-Hungary and Greece (Chapter 28) had inconvertible paper money for much of the century (Panic 1992: 20).

The United Kingdom had officially been on a silver standard at least since Newton's recoinage of 1696. With the growth of trade, the country had been on a *de facto* gold standard for many years. In any case the problems of the coinage had not really been resolved. There was a recoinage in 1733, when the old hammered gold coins were demonetised, and after 1750 little silver was minted (Oman 1967: 352). Indeed for much of the century mint output was low, and there continued to be problems with clipping and illegal coining. A circular 'issued casually in 1769 by the Mint solicitor to remind the populace that clipping . . . was a crime . . . set off the latent mistrust' of the guinea, and bank notes actually went to a premium (Craig 1953: ch. xiv). Bank notes, and foreign gold coins, formed an increasing part of the circulating medium, and the period saw the introduction of an official copper coinage and of private 'token' coinages.

An Act of 1773 required below weight coins to be cut and defaced, and in effect to be surrendered to the Bank of England at bullion value. The small customary charge was waived. The official weight of a newly minted guinea was 129.438 grains: coins were acceptable at face value down to a weight of 128 for recent coins; 126 or 123 for older ones. The stimulus for this came from Charles Jenkinson, first Earl of Liverpool and a keen amateur of money. Later he was to write the classic 'Coins of the Realm' (1805) which was to influence later events.

It can be argued that the system was bimetallic, and that the defects in the coinage can be attributed to variations in the ratio. Liverpool said that until 1717

> . . . the people in their payments never conformed [to the rule making the guinea current at 20 shillings. In 1717] the rate or value of the Guinea in currency was fixed at 21 Shillings by proclamation. It was then evident that the Government meant to enforce this regulation; and the Guinea . . . became from thenceforth at that rate legal tender.
>
> (Liverpool 1805: 128)

This statement, if correct, is a classic definition of the circumstances in which Gresham's Law applies. He goes on to say that a Bill of 1774 limited the legal tender of silver coins to £25, but that in 1783 'by neglect, it was suffered to expire'.

The solution adopted was not the only one discussed: 'now had been the chance, if men so desired, to return to the silver standard' (Craig 1953: 242). Adam Smith suggested that silver money should be deliberately over-rated and be legal tender for payments up to a guinea, but

> . . . no one seems to have entertained for one moment the idea of giving the mint the right to buy silver as required at market price, to issue the coins definitely as tokens in just sufficient quantities to meet the demands of the public . . .
>
> (Feaveryear 1931: 159)

The government, he goes on were content with instructing customs officers to search for and confiscate light or base silver coin.

A Committee on Coin was set up in 1787 to continue the discussion (which had continued for most of the century) on the proper weight of the silver coin. Certainly the mint price of 62 shillings per pound was for most of the period slightly below world market price, which discouraged coining. The mint advised the Committee that the UK bimetallic ratio was 15.21 (based on 22 carat gold) whereas it was 14.47 in France and 14.79 in Holland, and suggested that the weight of the silver should be reduced (65 shillings being struck from a pound of 0.925 fine silver) or that the fineness be reduced to 0.883 leaving the weight unchanged. Before the Committee reached any conclusion, the Napoleonic Wars intervened, and the Suspension of Payments in 1797 (see Chapter 26) meant that the British now had an inconvertible paper currency: reform of the coinage had to wait. A great deal of nonsense was talked, by bankers in particular, about 'real' reasons for the 'high price of gold bullion', but David Ricardo and others put them right. After the Suspension of Payments the United Kingdom restored convertibility, at the old parity, in 1821. Bank notes, the use of which had become well established, were again convertible, but convertible into what? Gold or silver? The United Kingdom was lucky enough to find a simple answer, but there were major problems in France, America, India and elsewhere.

The gold standard was now to become formalised, under the leadership of the second Earl of Liverpool, son of the first Earl who had taken a prominent role in the earlier debates. As Lord Hawksebury, he had served as Master of the Mint in 1799–1801. His predecessors had received a salary of £500 plus a share of coinage fees, but he agreed to commute the latter for a straight salary of £3,000. On the historical figures, this looked like a sound wartime economy to public funds, but with the decline in coinage activity it proved a wise (or lucky) move for him. Later in 1816, having become Prime Minister, he resolved to move on to a gold standard replacing the 21 shilling guinea with a £1 coin (the gold sovereign) of pro rata value. Action was taken in advance of the 1821 Resumption, and the United Kingdom introduced a formal gold standard in 1816.

Lord Liverpool's Act of 22 June 1816 (56 Geo III c. 68) 'to provide for a New Silver Coinage, and to regulate the currency of the gold and silver coin of the Realm' was to be the basis of the currency for a century. The sovereign was defined as 123.27447 grains of standard 22 carat (11 ounces or 91.67 per cent fine) gold, i.e. 113.0016 grains of fine gold. A key point was that silver was given a subservient status. Silver coins, legal tender for no more than £2, were deliberately struck underweight and the standard silver content of the shilling was reduced from 92 to 87.27 grains, equal to 80.73 grains of fine silver. At market prices a pound of silver was worth 61 shillings (a ratio of 15.46) but was struck into coins worth 66 shillings. The object of this slight undervaluation was to prevent silver coinage leaving the country. Their value in specie (the bullion value of the silver content) was at a 7.5 per cent discount to their value in tale (i.e. as legal tender). This gave some margin against a fall in the ratio which was, in the event, enough, but only just, to survive a period of rising silver prices which lasted until about 1870. The public no longer had the right to bring silver to the mint, which would coin silver only on government account. This discount allowed for what was probably then regarded as a reasonable fluctuation in the ratio. There would in fact have been a problem had the value of silver risen above 66 shillings in relation to gold: that is if the market ratio had fallen below 14.29. The relative value of silver actually did rise following the enormous gold discoveries in the 1840s. The ratio rose to 15.19 by 1859 and this, as we shall see, resulted in silver coins disappearing from circulation and into the melting pot in the United States and in much of Europe. Britain, fortunately, had a wider margin.

The gold standard thus became official with the gold 'sovereign' as the basis of the currency. These began to be struck in 1817, with the same weight and general design as those still produced by the Mint. Bank notes were of course still inconvertible, but as the new gold coins came into circulation, the Bank of England began to test the waters. In April 1817 it announced that it would cash all notes under £5 dated before 1 January 1816. There was little demand for gold. The public found the small notes convenient and stuck to them at least until the new sovereigns and half sovereigns became available. Even then, they were in demand 'at first only as objects of curiosity' (Clapham 1970 vol. ii: 63). There were in any case only about £1 million of eligible notes in circulation. The lesson was mis-read: the much more important fact that the gold price, at £4, was still at a premium over mint price was ignored. In October 1817, the offer was extended to all notes issued before 1 January 1817. This was less successful: there was a sharp fall in the Bank's reserve of treasure as high denomination notes were cashed. Although the Bank paid out some 6.75 million sovereigns between 1 January 1817 and 25 March 1819 few actually got into circulation. They were nearly all lost to export.

The gold standard, with a subsidiary silver coinage, worked well and survived until, and indeed after, the 1914–18 War. Its triumph was not universally accepted. The main monetary dispute in the immediate post-war period was between the banking and currency schools, and the main issues concerned 'money other than coin', bank notes and bank deposits, discussed in Part II. Coin itself, though, was still discussed. Tooke said that the banking principle held

> . . . that the purposes of a mixed circulation of coin and paper were sufficiently answered, *as long as the coin were perfect*, and the paper constantly convertible into coin and that the only evils to be guarded against . . . were those attending insolvency of the banks.
>
> (Tooke 1844)

Most of the arguments in the mid-nineteenth century were on the latter part of this statement: how to regulate the banks. But what about his qualification: 'as long as the coin were perfect'? With hindsight, we know that it was, and that the gold standard would continue to ensure that it remained perfect (in England) unamended and without serious problems, for over a century.

This was not self-evident to contemporaries, and there continued to be disputes over the coinage as such, even though this was no longer (in England) the central issue. Fetter and Gregory (1973: 16) summarize these disputes over the thirty years following the resumption of cash payments in 1821. They distinguish between three main forms of criticism:

1. The resumption of 1821 should have been with smaller gold content of the pound i.e. a higher gold price. (This argument was to be repeated in 1931.)
2. Resumption should have been either on the basis of an outright silver standard, or bimetallism at the legal rate ruling in 1797. This would have meant a pound was about 5 per cent less valuable in terms of gold, assuming that the action itself did not change the market ratio of the two metals.
3. Inconvertible paper money should have been continued. This third issue is rarely presented in pure form. The closest approach to a consistent support of inconvertible paper came between 1816–47 from a Birmingham group of which Thomas Attwood is the most articulate spokesman.

Support for silver was not, in England, necessarily associated, as it was to become in the United States, with political radicalism. Following the crisis of 1825, Alexander Baring won over William Huskisson as a supporter of silver, and in 1828 succeeded in convincing Robert Peel and the Duke of Wellington. However, the case was not pressed. This support for silver had originally been based on the idea that it would result in a higher price level than a gold standard. The Californian and Australian gold discoveries were soon to stand this argument on its head: there were fears that the retention of the gold standard might be as inflationary as the paper money proposals of the Birmingham economists.

Gregory in his introduction to two volumes of collected documents suggests that 'it is characteristic of the period of middle class ascendancy after 1832 that it produced much heat and little light: many massive volumes, but no classic reports; much legislation but . . . no final solution' (Gregory 1929: ix). Nevertheless, he commends the study of the original sources in revealing the tendencies of thought and the temper of the age.

In the United Kingdom the gold standard worked remarkably well but, arguably, for accidental reasons. There would have been problems with the 'subsidiary silver' solution if, as a result of the random pattern of gold and silver discoveries, the price of gold had fallen below a ratio of 14.2 for any length of time. It is also not self evident that the activities of miners will produce just enough 'high powered money' both to meet the needs of trade and to ensure stable prices. The experience of other countries was very different, and there was certainly no rush to follow the British example. After the Napoleonic Wars much of Europe was on a bimetallic standard, while it took the United States most of the century to sort out its monetary arrangements. It took the strains on the bimetallic ratio in the 1860s, and the move to gold by Germany in 1873, to ensure the eventual, but short lived triumph of gold.

THE OPERATION OF THE GOLD STANDARD

A nation is on the gold standard if, and only if, its unit of money is defined as so many grains of fine gold. Citizens must be free to convert any other form of legal tender money into gold, and to import and export gold without restriction. This does not ensure stable prices in the long or the short run. Long run stability would require that money supply more or less kept pace with the needs of trade, unlikely if the monetary base is determined by the activities of mines (and indeed the demand for monetary gold in other countries, notoriously Germany in 1873). In practice, during the relevant period total money supply was augmented by bank notes and deposits. Table 7.1 gives combined figures for the United Kingdom, United States and France (Panic 1992: 27–8 quoting Triffin) showing that over the century an unchanged value of gold or silver would have resulted in a six-fold increase in money supply.

Table 7.1 Components of money supply: 1815 to 1913

Money	Year		
	1815	1872	1913
Gold and silver	66	40	10
Notes and sub coins	28	28	25
Bank deposits	6	32	65
Total as multiple of gold	1.5	2.5	10

The United Kingdom gold standard did not ensure short run stability nor did it prevent trade cycles and financial crises. These arose from fluctuations in size of the credit superstructure built on the gold base, discussed in Part II.

The classical international gold standard, although it lasted for such a short time is still looked back on, nostalgically, as the best way to regulate payment arrangements between countries. Exchange rates could vary only within the 'specie points' outside which it was profitable to import or export gold. The mechanism was described in Hume (1752). The gold standard rules of the game required each country to permit anyone, citizen or foreigner, the right to import and export gold, and to exchange their holdings of its currency into gold at the fixed price. Provided that these rules were followed (and sometimes they were broken) a country with a trade deficit would lose gold, shrinking the monetary base and reducing prices. The change in the purchasing power parity would stimulate exports and reduce imports, restoring the payment balance. The surplus country would receive gold, and should expand its money supply and the burden of adjustment should fall symmetrically on both parties. In practice the 'surplus' country might sterilise the inflow.

This, at least is how it was meant to work and, for a time, it did. Its opponents argue that too much of the adjustment process fell on employment and output, and that, as the 1930s showed, the system would be quite incompatible with modern rigid wage structures. The record is now being re-examined, with special reference to monetary union and related issues in the 1990s (e.g. Panic 1992) and it is arguable that the system was appropriate for a particular period of history rather than being the panacea. It had many good features from which we can learn, but may well have succeeded so well by 'breathing through its loopholes' and by its members not always keeping to the rules of the game. It needs to be studied in the context of the bimetallic disputes which preoccupied much of the century and which form the subject of the next three chapters.

8

BIMETALLISM IN THE NINETEENTH CENTURY

After the Napoleonic Wars, during which Britain had had an inconvertible paper currency convertibility into gold was restored in 1821. As discussed in Chapter 7, a key point of Lord Liverpool's Act of 1816 formalising the gold standard was that silver coins, legal tender for no more than £2, were deliberately struck underweight. The bullion value of the silver content was at a 7.5 per cent discount to their value in tale i.e. as legal tender. This coinage system was to survive until 1914. It had its tribulations but these were trivial compared with the coinage problems suffered elsewhere.

Chapter 2 explained the problem of the bimetallic ratio, and how Gresham's Law can denude a country of gold, or of silver, if the ratio gets out of line. The problem had been around a long time, but now became more acute. With growing prosperity after the wars gold became the more appropriate metal for larger and more widespread transactions. Another factor was the relative ease, economy and speed (compared with medieval times) by which a trader could exchange gold for silver and export it to take profitable advantage of small differences in the ratio in different countries. There were no longer any material mercantilist restrictions ('exchange controls') to be evaded, seigniorage had typically been abolished, transportation was cheaper and safer and information could be exchanged more rapidly. Specie points were much closer together: if the ratio was even only slightly out of line with international markets, the country would quickly lose gold, or silver.

The battle over bimetallism was to be fought for much of the nineteenth century. It gave impetus to, and eventually caused the collapse of, one of the greatest and most exciting initiatives ever taken towards Monetary Union. These two related issues, once regarded as an obscure byway of economic history, have become very topical and relevant at the end of the twentieth century. The Latin Monetary Union was born in response to one bimetallic problem: the 1848– 70 fall in the ratio and the disappearance of small change. It collapsed, quite unnecessarily, as a reaction to another: the post-1870 rise in the ratio and the fall in the price of silver.

Groseclose points out how long the issue has preoccupied mankind:

The development of gold coinage ... on a widespread scale in the thirteenth century, created a factor of extreme disturbance in the reviving money economy of Christendom. The maintenance of a stable relationship, or parity between two precious metals ... now became the perplexing problem of honest governments, and at the same time the opportunity of dishonest ones. Nothing is more vocal of the incapacity of European philosophy and practice to deal with the money mechanism than the absorbtion of attention for the better part of five hundred years in the question of the ratio. ...

(Groseclose 1934)

Lord Liverpool's reduction of the silver content of the silver coins meant that the British now had no real problem. In other countries, notably France, the United States and India the issue of bimetallism was very much alive. However this (British)

... solution was not the result of conscious effort directed by intelligence and governed by far-sighted objectives, but, rather the chance outcome of the play and interplay of mercantile and financial interests. ... In Europe, the history of the ratio is filled with even more blindness, and groping, undirected effort.

(Groseclose 1934: 159)

Similarly, in the United States 'Congress spent so much time discussing silver during these years [the 1870s] as evidenced by the pages of the Congressional record that it is a wonder that any other business was transacted' (Myers 1970: 201).

THE ISSUE STATED

The issue can be re-stated very simply. If a country permits free minting of both gold and silver and affords both the gold and silver coins full legal tender status at pre-determined rates there will be problems. In this context 'free minting' means that any citizen (and in some countries foreigners as well) could bring metal to the mint and receive in exchange coins containing the same amount of the metal less a small deduction for expenses, seigniorage. Full legal tender status meant that the offer of coins of the appropriate value had to be accepted as good legal discharge of a debt of any amount: the creditor was not entitled to demand (although he could agree to accept) payment in any other form.

As explained in Chapter 2, if gold was valued eleven times as highly as silver in France and only ten times in England, an entrepreneur could bring ten pounds of silver to England, exchange it for one pound of gold, ship it over to France convert it into eleven pounds of silver, and repeat the operation at a 9 per cent gross profit. During the period discussed in Chapter

4, this was in fact a quite normal discrepancy. Table 2.1 (p. 15) gives the course of the ratio from 1300–1900 and suggest three periods of special interest: the rise and fall of gold during the fourteenth century; the seventeenth century changes arising from New World gold discoveries; and the present subject, the bitterly fought triumph of gold at the expense of silver in the late nineteenth century.

For much of the earlier period various governments tried, not always very hard, to set a fixed relationship between the two: it is obviously convenient for trade if, for instance, a gold sovereign of stated weight is exactly equal to 20 silver shillings, also of a stated weight. For a long time Europe had been on a *de facto* silver standard, while the value of gold coins in practice fluctuated with changes in the ratio. Attempts to enforce a fixed ratio on the gold coinage were ineffective and short lived. Jevons cites

> . . . the most extreme instance which has ever occurred. At the time of the 1858 treaty, European traders discovered that the ratio in Japan was 4 to 1. Great profits were made – for a short time . . . At the time of the treaty of 1858 between Great Britain, the United States and Japan . . . a very curious system of currency existed in Japan. The most valuable Japanese coin was the kobang . . . a thin oval disc of gold. . . . It was passing currency . . . for four silver itzebus, but was worth in English money 18s.5d., whereas the silver itzebu was equal only to about 1s.4d. Thus the Japanese were estimating their gold money at only about one third of its value as estimated . . . in other parts of the world. Not surprisingly, the early traders made hugh profits before 'the natives' withdrew gold from circulation. A complete reform of the Japanese currency is now [i.e. 1875] being carried out, the English mint at Hong Kong having been purchased by the Japanese government.
>
> (Jevons 1909: 84)

(The story is also told by Walker 1888: 230. He uses the charming spelling of 'Itzi Boo' for the silver coin.)

BIMETALLISM IN THE NINETEENTH CENTURY

During the latter half of the nineteenth century the problems of bimetallism, created by the operations of Gresham's Law, were a major preoccupation and source of dispute in much of Europe, particularly France, the United States and India. Gresham's Law applies only if the bad money has effective fiat value. Economists use various more precise statements of the Law. This is one: 'Where by legal enactment a government assigns the same nominal value to two or more forms of circulatory medium whose intrinsic values differ, payment will always, as far as possible, be made in that medium of which the cost of production is least, and the more valuable medium will tend to disappear from circulation' (Palgrave's Dictionary 1926 edition). If it becomes discredited, merchants and others may prefer to use a sound money, even if it is 'foreign'.

By the late nineteenth century, the transaction costs had greatly reduced, far smaller differentials was needed to make arbitrage worth while, – and the problems became more serious. The experience of other countries is discussed below. Meanwhile the bimetallic ratio had in fact been fairly stable at least since Newton's recoinage in 1696. It had normally been within a range 14.5 to 15.5, fell below in 1751 and 1760, rose above during the Napoleonic Wars – but afterwards traded in the range 15.2 to 15.9.

To begin with the price of silver rose. In those countries which had 'full weight' silver coins the bullion content rose above their face or fiat value: they were therefore melted down or exported, creating a shortage of small change. The United Kingdom was saved by the 'token' element in the silver coins, but a few more per cent and we too would have had problems. The trend then reversed: a dollar shortage, so to speak, became a dollar surplus. The relative price of gold began to rise, at first slowly. The Germans, observing that the British were economically successful, and that the British were on a gold standard, decided, not altogether logically, that they too must have a gold standard. When Germany went on to gold, silver collapsed. The French were furious, there was a vast political campaign in the United States (it was the major issue in the 1896 Presidential election) and monetary arrangements in India broke down.

France

The French experiment with paper money (the assignats) had been less successful than the United Kingdom (Part III, Chapter 25). Paper money became worthless by about 1799: inflation, as a method of war finance, was burnt out, and this may have contributed to Napoleon's successful *coup d'état*. The French were forced, against their political instincts, to revert to honest money. There were complicated and not particularly successful attempts to decide in what currency a debt could be repaid. Gold and silver came back (mainly from hoards) and Calonne's law, originally passed in 1785 but overtaken by the Revolution, came into force in 1803 (Laughlin 1892: Appendix IIIB gives a translation of the main provisions).

Calonne's law provided for a new, and more honest, coinage based on the silver franc of 5 grams 0.900 fine, and a gold 20 franc Napoleon of 6.45 grams. Unlike the old livres the value was stamped on the coin and could not be manipulated. It was a true bimetallic system. The French mints were open to all (foreigners included) for the coinage of both silver and gold, and coins in both metals had full legal tender status. After the Wars, France thus became the bimetallic country *par excellence*. While the system lasted 'any foreigner possessing silver could thus indirectly convert his metal into gold sovereigns at the French rate of 15½ that is to say 60¹³⁄₁₆ pence per ounce,

Table 8.1 Bimetallic ratios, France: 1815 to 1895, and imports (exports) of silver and gold resulting from the operation of Gresham's law

year	Ratio	5 year moving average	France Minimum	France Maximum	France Deviation	¹Gold	US$	¹Silver	US$	Total	Net export of silver (gold)
1815	15.26		15.46	15.74	(0.20)						
1816	15.28		15.46	15.74	(0.18)						
1817	15.11		15.46	15.74	(0.35)						
1818	15.35		15.46	15.74	(0.11)						
1819	15.33	15.27	15.46	15.74	(0.13)						
1820	15.62	15.34	15.46	15.74							
1821	15.95	15.47	15.46	15.74	0.21						
1822	15.80	15.61	15.46	15.74	0.06	4		125		95	
1823	15.84	15.71	15.46	15.74	0.10	(19)		114		161	(19)
1824	15.82	15.81	15.46	15.74	0.08	37		124		0	
1825	15.70	15.82	15.46	15.74						0	
1826	15.76	15.78	15.46	15.74	0.02					0	
1827	15.74	15.77	15.46	15.74						0	
1828	15.78	15.76	15.46	15.74	0.04					0	
1829	15.78	15.75	15.46	15.74	0.04	10		151		161	
1830	15.82	15.78	15.46	15.74	0.08	10		181		191	
1831	15.72	15.77	15.46	15.74		(39)		60		21	
1832	15.73	15.77	15.46	15.74		24		75		99	(39)
1833	15.93	15.80	15.46	15.74	0.19	(7)		101		94	
1834	15.73	15.79	15.46	15.74		(20)		74		54	(7)
1835	15.80	15.78	15.46	15.74	0.06	(14)		27		13	(20)
1836	15.72	15.78	15.46	15.74		(4)		120		116	(14)
1837	15.85	15.81	15.46	15.74	0.11	24		75		99	(4)
1838	15.62	15.74	15.46	15.74		49		96		145	
1839	15.62	15.72	15.46	15.74		(5)		117		112	
1840	15.70	15.70	15.46	15.74		(12)		92		80	(5)
1841	15.87	15.73	15.46	15.74	0.13						(12)

Year											
	15.93										
1842	15.85	15.75	15.46	15.74	0.19	(14)					(14)
1843	15.92	15.79	15.46	15.74	0.11	(6)		103		89	(6)
1844	15.90	15.85	15.46	15.74	0.18	(14)		82		76	(14)
1845	15.80	15.89	15.46	15.74	0.16	(9)		90		76	(9)
1846	15.85	15.88	15.46	15.74	0.06	(13)		47		38	(13)
1847	15.78	15.86	15.46	15.74	0.11	38		53		40	
1848	15.70	15.85	15.46	15.74	0.04	6		214		252	
1849	15.46	15.81	15.46	15.74		17	1.2	244	48.8	250	
1850	15.59	15.72	15.46	15.74		85	3.4	73	14.6	90	
1851	15.33	15.68	15.46	15.74		17	17.0	78	15.6	163	3
1852	15.33	15.57	15.46	15.74	(0.13)	289	3.4	(3)	(0.6)	14	117
1853	15.38	15.48	15.46	15.74	(0.13)	416	57.8	(117)	(23.4)	172	164
1854	15.38	15.42	15.46	15.74	(0.08)	218	83.2	(164)	(32.8)	252	197
1855	15.27	15.40	15.46	15.74	(0.08)	375	43.6	(197)	(39.4)	21	284
1856	15.38	15.34	15.46	15.74	(0.19)	446	75.0	(284)	(56.8)	91	360
1857	15.19	15.35	15.46	15.74	(0.08)	488	89.2	(360)	(72.0)	86	15
1858	15.29	15.32	15.46	15.74	(0.27)	539	97.6	(15)	(3.0)	473	171
1859	15.50	15.30	15.46	15.74	(0.17)	311	107.8	(171)	(34.2)	368	157
1860	15.33	15.33	15.46	15.74		(24)	62.2	(157)	(31.4)	154	
1861	15.35	15.34	15.46	15.74	(0.11)	165	(4.8)	(62)	(12.4)	(86)	
1862	15.37	15.34	15.46	15.74	(0.09)	12	33.0	(86)	(17.2)	79	86
1863	15.37	15.38	15.46	15.74	(0.09)	125	2.4	(68)	(13.6)	(56)	12
1864	15.44	15.41	15.46	15.74	(0.02)	150	25.0	(42)	(8.4)	83	42
1865	15.43	15.39	15.46	15.74	(0.03)	465	30.0	72	14.4	222	
1866	15.57	15.44	15.46	15.74		409	93.0	45	9.0	510	
1867	15.59	15.48	15.46	15.74		212	81.8	189	37.8	598	
1868	15.60	15.53	15.46	15.74		275	42.4	109	21.8	321	
1869	15.57	15.55	15.46	15.74		119	55.0	112	22.4	387	
1870	15.57	15.58	15.46	15.74		(214)	23.8	35	7.0	154	
1871	15.63	15.59	15.46	15.74		(53)	(42.8)	15	3.0	(199)	
1872	15.92	15.66	15.46	15.74	0.18	(108)	(10.6)	102	20.4	49	
1873	16.17	15.77	15.46	15.74	0.43	(21.6)	360	181	791	73	(15)
1874	16.59	15.98	15.46	15.74	0.85	454	86.2	36.2	72.0		(53)
1875	17.88	16.44	15.46	15.74	2.14		90.8	194	38.8	648	(108)

Table 8.1 Continued

year	Ratio	5 year moving average	France			French imports (exports) millions of Francs					Net export of silver (gold)
			Minimum	Maximum	Deviation	¹Gold	US$	¹Silver	US$	Total	
1876	17.22	16.76	15.46	15.74	1.48		100.6		29.8		
1877	17.94	17.16	15.46	15.74	2.20		87.2		20.8		
1878	18.40	17.61	15.46	15.74	2.66		47.2		23.8		
1879	18.05	17.90	15.46	15.74	2.31		(35.0)		15.2		
1880	18.16	17.95	15.46	15.74	2.42		(42.6)		7.8		
1881	18.19	18.15	15.46	15.74	2.45		2.2		10.2		
1882	18.64	18.29	15.46	15.74	2.90		18.4		18.2		
1883	18.57	18.32	15.46	15.74	2.83						
1884	19.41	18.59	15.46	15.74	3.67						
1885	20.78	19.12	15.46	15.74	5.04						
1886	21.13	19.71	15.46	15.74	5.39						
1887	21.99	20.38	15.46	15.74	6.25						
1888	22.10	21.08	15.46	15.74	6.36						
1889	19.76	21.15	15.46	15.74	4.02						
1890	20.92	21.18	15.46	15.74	5.18						
1891	23.72	21.70	15.46	15.74	7.98						
1892	26.49	22.60	15.46	15.74	10.75						
1893	32.56	24.69	15.46	15.74	16.82						
1894	31.60	27.06	15.46	15.74	15.86						
1895	30.66	29.01	15.46	15.74	14.92						

Note: Laughlin (1892: 119)

less the expense involved in the operation' (Cernuschi 1881: 6). The price relates to (92.5 per cent pure) standard silver: fine silver would be 65.77 pence. In effect, allowing for expenses, France was the buffer supporting a fixed bimetallic ratio within an 'intervention band' of 15.46–15.74. As Table 8.1 shows, the actual ratio did not, at first stray far outside the band. Any other country could (and some did) adopt bimetallism at this ratio. As the system's supporters continued to argue, France could absorb quite considerable changes in the relative supply of, or demand for, gold and silver.

Between 1841 and 1847 the gold price was above the range, and France exported gold – to a total of 100 million francs – equivalent to 2,900 kilograms or 93,000 ounces of fine gold. In 1848 the price of gold started to fall as a result of new discoveries, and the flow reversed. Between 1848 and 1870, net imports of gold totalled over 5,000 million francs: about half the world production of newly mined gold. Figures such as these clearly put a strain (but not an intolerable one) on the system: the extra gold could be absorbed as a higher proportion of gold circulating in France.

The period of silver shortage (1848–70)

During this period the ratio was falling: silver was becoming relatively over-valued, and following Gresham's Law was being driven out of circulation in countries where its exchange value was fixed by statute. The side-effects were potentially beneficial: had it continued, without going too far, the world could well have been nudged, without too much fuss, towards a universal currency based on gold, but with a subsidiary silver coinage on the British model.

The first effects were felt in the United States, which had introduced a bimetallic system with a 15:1 ratio in 1792. This figure proved too low. Gold coins disappeared, or traded at a 5 per cent premium. Discussions from 1818 onwards recognised that a change in the ratio was needed. By an Act of 1834, this was established at 16:1. The silver dollar remained at 371.25 grains fine but the gold dollar was effectively devalued from 24.75 grains to 23.22 grains. This was too high and within three months $50 million (nearly 40 million ounces) of silver disappeared from circulation. It was shipped across the Atlantic in exchange for gold, on a scale which caused some alarm at the Bank of England (Clapham 1970 vol. ii: 151).

After the gold discoveries of the 1840s nudged the market ratio towards 15.5, it even became worth while to melt down the small silver coins: quarters and dimes. To prevent this, in 1853 silver was effectively demonetised: the United States went on to a *de facto* gold standard. The content of the subsidiary coins was reduced from 371.25 to 345.6 grains of silver per dollar, once more implying a 'too low' ratio of 14.88. Free minting of silver was abolished and the subsidiary coins were legal tender only for up to five dollars. The silver dollar retained its full value at 371.25 grains and its legal tender status: none were minted, as the value was about $1.04 in terms of gold. It had disappeared from circulation years before. (There is an interesting modern parallel. In Belgium a gold ecu coin was, in 1990, made legal tender; an aspect of monetary union which has exercised some commentators. As its bullion value is higher, legal tender status is irrelevant: it is valued only as a collector's item or souvenir.

The same small-change problem hit Europe a few years later. In 1860 Switzerland had debased, to 0.800 fine, its subsidiary silver coins of 2 francs and less. This was not to cheat the public (the Swiss reputation for financial probity was already long established) but was simply a practical measure to keep them in circulation. The five franc piece, which remained at 0.900, became the standard silver monetary unit but in practice, as with the US silver dollar, none were struck. The smaller silver coins would not have been worth melting down unless silver fell to about 14.5, and at that level the United Kingdom, too, would have had problems. These Swiss coins also circulated in France and Italy which instead of following suit, tried in vain to buy time with an exchange control approach.

Something more fundamental was needed, and a pressing problem was, for a time, matched with an exciting solution: the prospect for a universal world currency.

9

MONETARY UNION IN THE NINETEENTH CENTURY – THE COLLAPSE OF BIMETALLISM IN EUROPE

Bimetallism is closely related to the history of the Latin Monetary Union, and of the more local monetary unions which preceded it. If different nations all issue money convertible into gold (or all into silver) the exchange rates between them can fluctuate only between very narrow limits, the specie points. Why, therefore, need merchants and travellers suffer the inconvenience of different national coinages and the need for ready reckoners to convert one currency to another? Why not adopt a universal coinage with an agreed content of fine gold? Why not indeed – if you are an economist, or even a mere trader or traveller. Politicians, though, can be depended on to create problems where none really exist, and in this they have changed little over the centuries. The Latin Monetary Union was born in response to one bimetallic problem: the 1848–70 fall in the relative price of gold in terms of silver, 'the ratio', and the disappearance of small change. It collapsed, quite unnecessarily, as a reaction to another: the post-1870 rise in the ratio and the fall in the price of silver.

EARLY MONETARY UNIONS

After the Napoleonic Wars Europe was fragmented. Italy was not a nation. Switzerland, although a loose Federation, did not have a single currency. Germany, had had an 'alternative system' (introduced by Frederick the Great after the peace of Hubertsburg, 1763) by which gold and silver could be substituted for each other in making payments. This became a *de facto* silver standard, with gold trade coins circulating at market value.

> In Germany the condition of the currency had been one of the greatest chaos prior to the establishment of the gold standard. Six different systems were legally in force, and in addition an uncounted number and variety of coins were to be found in circulation.
>
> (Groseclose 1934: 149–50)

At the Dresden Convention of 30 July 1838 a number of German states adopted the Prussian 14 thaler or 21 gulden standard. (The members were: Bavaria, Saxony, Hanover, Wurtemburg, Baden, Electoral Hesse, Ducal Hesse, Ducal Saxony, Oldenburg, Saxe-Meiningen, Saxe-Coburg Gotha, Saxe-Anhalt-Bemburg, Schwartzburg-Sondenhausen, Schwartzburg-Rudolstadt, Waldeck, Pyrmont, the Reusses, the Lippes, Landgraviate Hesse and the City of Frankfurt. See Del Mar 1895: 395.)

In pursuance of a provision of the Treaty of Carlsruhe, 19 July 1853, the Vienna Convention united its members with the rival systems of Prussia and Austria. The basis was the 'pound' of 500 grams, with 30 thalers being struck from a pound of fine silver. The Convention thaler was made equal to 1.5 florins Austrian or 1.75 florins (gulden) South German. Although the intention was simply to facilitate regional trade, the question of the gold/silver ratio was already a serious one, even though the market ratio had yet to move outside its customary 15–16 range.

> At this period the commercial world was agitated by a strange disease; the fear that so much gold would be produced in the mines and pass into the form of money, that disastrous rise of prices – that is disastrous to millionaires – will ensue sufficient to shake the foundations of society.
>
> (Del Mar 1895: 393)

The Vienna Convention conferred the right of coinage as to full legal tender silver, and as to gold coins to private individuals – gold coins were forbidden to be made legal tender in any of the states. The silver coins were to be legal tender coins in all the states in the appropriate ratios. Austria could continue to strike ducats until the end of 1865. 'The paper money and banknotes of each state were permitted to circulate in the other states so long as "adequate" provision was made for their redemption in full legal tender silver coins' (Del Mar 1895: he lists ten systems in existence in Germany. He refers to his 'Money and Civilisation' p. 339 and to 'United States Commercial Relations' 1867 p. 447).

The Vienna Convention decided not to establish a fixed ratio but to permit only the coining of gold crowns and half crowns, the crown being valued at 0.50 to the pound of silver. The idea was that the gold content could be adjusted in line with market changes. This rather clumsy expedient appears to have been ineffectual.

Monetary union in Switzerland

The Swiss Cantons also lacked a uniform monetary system. The French-speaking cantons wanted to adopt the French monetary system, while the German-speaking ones wanted to follow Germany. Johann Jakob Speiser of Basle (a German-speaking Canton) was appointed to prepare a report.

'*Rapport et projet de loi sur la monnaie par l'Expert Fédéral des Monnaies M Speiser à Bâle, d.d 6th Octobre, 1849*'. He pointed out that the French had a single coherent system, while the Germans did not. He therefore recommended the adoption of the French system. A few years later, the UK Royal Commission report on decimal currency (1857) took evidence on the experience of other countries, including Switzerland. The evidence includes a letter from William Brown, M.P., to a banker, Augustus Lemonius which ends: 'I believe your partners, Mr Zwilchenbart and Mr Speiser, of Basle, were prime movers in conferring the benefit on Switzerland'. (I am grateful to Professor David Speiser, whose wife and mine are cousins, for information and documents on his great-grandfather.)

The over-valuation of silver

Silver being over-valued on the fixed ratio, France and its neighbours were thus faced with a problem of disappearing silver coinage. Switzerland had responded by debasing coins of two francs and less to 0.800 fine, and the effective circulation of these debased Swiss coins in France and Italy put pressure on these neighbours to re-examine their own currency. There were two solutions: the right one would have been to follow suit, but monetary decisions do tend to get taken by politicians. These worthies favoured an exchange control approach, and France therefore introduced a decree on 14 April 1864 prohibiting the receipt of Swiss coins at public offices. As with exchange controls, before and since, this only bought time, and not much of that.

The conference of 1865

France called a conference in Paris in 1865, which 'had for its object the adoption of a uniform and universal coinage' (Barbour 1885: 14) leading to the formation of the Latin Monetary Union. The four participating countries, France Italy Switzerland and Belgium already had a bimetallic coinage based on the French system, first imposed by conquest, but later reverted to for convenience. France had imposed the system on the Netherlands until 1814, but it was abandoned after independence. When the Belgians revolted against the Dutch in 1830, they reverted to the French system. Switzerland (1848) and Italy (1861) chose to adopt the system in the course of their own monetary and political unions. In all the countries concerned the five franc silver coin had disappeared and the two francs was rapidly following. Henry Russell commented:

... that France should worry over the introduction of a few Swiss coins into her territory displacing national coins and then form a treaty making all coins of three states legal throughout the territory is not easily understood.

but agreed that this:

> ... was the first important monetary meeting on international lines, the only one that ever resulted in a treaty.
>
> (Russell 1898: 28)

Latin monetary union: Stage 1

The treaty on Latin Monetary Union came into effect on 1 August 1866: this was in fact no big deal, as the countries concerned already had, in substance, a common currency. They were soon joined by the States of the Church (in 1866) and Greece and Bulgaria (1867). Under the terms of the treaty (for text see Laughlin 1892 Appendix III D) the four countries agreed that they would coin only gold pieces of 100, 50, 20, 10 and 5 francs, together with silver coins of 5, 2, and 1 franc, and 50 and 20 centimes. Other coinages were to be withdrawn from circulation by 1 January 1869.

Subsidiary silver coins (2 francs and less) were on a 0.835 fineness and free minting of silver was abandoned. This has been described a fictitious double standard but was in fact very close to being the UK model of a gold standard with a subsidiary coinage. Honour was perhaps satisfied by maintaining full value for the 5 franc piece: this apparently innocuous gesture to tradition was to lead to some extraordinary complications at a later stage in the story. The treaty became effective on 1 August 1866, and was to continue until 1 January 1880, unless formally dissolved a year before that date, it would continue in force for further periods of fifteen years.

The Latin Monetary Union did far more than solve the original problem, created by the rise in the relative value of silver against the background of a rigid French bimetallic ratio. It actually created a substantial single currency area to the great convenience of travellers and traders. The survival of this achievement was to depend on whether or not the hoary old problem could finally be laid to rest.

THE CONFERENCE OF 1867

Seeking to extend this initiative, France called a further conference in 1867, to discuss a uniform world monetary system. While the 1865 Conference, and the Latin Monetary Union, had arguably been a technical response to a specific problem, this was a far more ambitious project. As is usual with monetary questions, politics and personalities influenced events more than rational economic analysis although, then as now, plenty of the latter was offered. According to Russell the initiative for the conference was taken by Louis Napoleon, who had been seeking to extend the French name and influence.

> He was quick to see that if the United States adopted for their half eagle the weight and fineness of the English sovereign, as Secretary

Chase was proposing, it would not only be of great advantage to England but would compel France to change her whole coinage system without getting any glory from it.

(Russell 1898: 25)

In Germany, 'Bismarck probably had no disposition at this time to "Frenchify" the coinage of the new empire, even had it been convenient to do so ... he regarded the plan for international coinage as a Napoleonic dream' (Russell 1892: 116–7).

The sovereign was worth a fraction over 25 francs, and there was an obvious technical solution requiring two apparently simple steps:

1. The United Kingdom would devalue the pound (by only 0.83 per cent) to make the relationship exact.
2. The French and their Union partners would replace or augment their basic 20 franc gold napoleon with a 25 franc coin, but making no change in the substance of their monetary arrangements.

The Americans were in the course of reintroducing a gold coinage after the Civil War: the half eagle of 5 dollars was worth 25.85 francs. With an adjustment of about 3.5 per cent, it could have been brought into line with either the sovereign or a 25 franc coin, if only the Europeans would get their act together. The Americans were keen on monetary union, and were prepared to reduce the value of the dollar by the amount needed. They wanted a quick decision: the use of gold coinage was growing rapidly, and in a few years the cost of re-minting would become prohibitive. John E. Kasson, presenting his report to Congress in May 1866, supported a uniform system of coinage:

The only interest of any nation that could possibly be injuriously affected by the establishment of this uniformity is that of the money changers – an interest which contributes little to the public welfare – while by diversity of coinage and of values it adds largely to private accumulations.

(Russell 1898: 35)

He recognised that transaction costs were the real problem.

At the conference, the United States argued for the 25 franc piece, pointing out that:

... such a coin will circulate side by side everywhere and in perfect equality with the half eagle of the United States and the sovereign of Great Britain. These three gold coins, types of the great commercial nations, fraternally united and differing only in emblems, will go hand in hand around the globe freely circulating through both hemispheres without recoinage, brokerage or other impediment. This opportune concession of France to the spirit of unity will complete the work of civilisation she has had so much at heart and will inaugurate that new monetary era the lofty object of the international conference, and the noblest aim of the concourse of nations, as yet without parallel in the history of the world.

(Russell 1898: 76)

The same point had been made in Sherman's letter of 18 May 1867 (see Russell 42–4.)

The French did not rise to this. They feared that a 25 franc coin would compete with their standard gold coin: the napoleon of 20 francs. They would have to bear some of the cost of re-minting, and might lose out on their political objective of being seen to impose a French standard on the world. The conference reassembled on 26 June under the chairmanship of Prince Jerome Napoleon 'whom the Emperor had appointed to preside as a mark of his imperial favour' (Russell 1898: 72) 'but it is doubtful if this mark of approval had quite the effect the Emperor intended or desired'.

Was the time ripe for British membership?

What of the British? With a strong lead, they could probably have forced it all through. The British delegates had said little up to this time, but now intervened. After lengthy courtesies and expressions of goodwill, the UK delegate, Mr Rivers Wilson, expressed a very 'British' point of view:

So long as public opinion has not decided in favour of a change of the present system, which offers no serious inconveniences, either in wholesale or retail trade, until it shall be incontestably demonstrated that a new system offers advantages sufficiently commanding to justify the abandonment of that which is approved by experience and rooted in the habits of the people, the English government could not believe it to be its duty to take the initiative in assimilating its coinage with those of the countries of the continent.

But the English government will always be ready to aid any attempt to enlighten and guide public opinion in the appreciation of the question and facilitate the discussion of the means by which such an assimilation so advantageous in theory may be effected.

Thus while consenting to be represented at this Conference the English government has found it necessary to place the most careful restrictions upon its delegates; their part is simply to listen to the different arguments, to study the situation as developed in discussion and to report to their government ... they cannot vote for any question tending to bind their government or express any opinion to induce the belief that Great Britain would adopt the convention of 1865.

(Russell 1898: 73–4)

The conference ended on 6 July with, in effect, only a resolution to meet again as soon as the different states had reported back. The majority voted for this to be 15 February 1868. Austria, Belgium, Italy, Sweden and Norway wanted an earlier date, only three months ahead. The United States supported 15 May and Great Britain, 1 June. This gave the Royal Commission time to produce its somewhat negative report.

The UK Royal Commission

Following the conference a Royal Commission on International Coinage was appointed in England in 1868 under Goschen to consider and report on the proceedings of the Paris Conference. Substantial evidence on the advantages of an international currency was accepted by the Commission.

> Smaller manufacturers and traders are deterred from engaging in foreign transactions by the complicated difficulties of foreign coins . . .
> by the difficulty in calculating the exchanges, and of remitting small sums from one country to another. Anything tending to simplify these matters would dispose them to extend the sphere of their operations.
> . . . One large dealer . . . said very fairly that the adoption of a common currency would facilitate the competition of other importers . . . from which . . . it is obvious the public would benefit. . . . The convenience
> . . . to persons travelling . . . too obvious to require remark.
>
> (Report 1868: vii–viii)

All that was standing between the United Kingdom and membership was a transitional problem occasioned by the fact that a French 25 franc gold piece, (which the Americans and others were pressing France to introduce) would have had a gold content of 0.83 per cent less than the sovereign. (The US Half Eagle of $5 would have needed an adjustment of 3.5 per cent.)

The report dwelt on the cost saving to the business community, encouraging small business to export and the advantages of 'promoting commercial and social intercourse, and thus drawing closer the friendly relations between different countries'. The Committee agonized over the difficulties of adjusting salaries and rents and whether the change 'would be tantamount to a legal permission for every creditor to rob his debtor of 2 pence in the pound', and in the end caution won the day. (Against this, supporters argued that under existing arrangements, British travellers carrying sovereigns incurred losses because these were often accepted as being equal to 25 francs, when the real value was 25.20.)

WAS BIMETALLISM AN ISSUE?

Bimetallism was still an issue, but not, at this time, the major one. A majority of countries (Holland dissenting) decided in principle to adopt the gold standard, in the rather simplistic belief that this had contributed substantially to British prosperity.

The only other true gold standard country represented was Portugal. Their delegate, Count d'Avilla, thought his government would have no objection to making the change, but naturally England would have to set the example. The true gold standard was supported by Belgium, Switzerland and Italy, but opposed by the Banque de France and the Rothschild interests, both of which were loath to forego lucrative arbitrage opportunities (Groseclose 1934: 164–6). France only supported bimetallism on technical grounds hoping to give way to gold in return for other concessions. Parieu, the vice president and guiding genius, was a convinced gold monometallist but 'his object was to suggest the easiest means for [coordinating] other systems with the French on any standard so long as France was the centre of the unification' (Russell 1898: 55).

Russell suggests that the mention of silver was an afterthought and that a gold standard was taken for granted. Writing in 1898, two years after silver had been a key issue in the presidential election, his pro gold view is clearly and frequently expressed, and his dispute with Walker comes out in the footnote to page 41.

The fall of bimetallism

All this had happened in the 1860s, when silver was the overvalued currency, at risk of being driven out of circulation. The dollar shortage then became a dollar surplus, so to speak: the price of silver began to fall, threatening the very existence of the bimetallic system to which France and the United States were for different reasons, becoming attached. There is nothing in the earlier conference and other discussions to hint at the emotional and political overtones the question was to acquire. Indeed, it has been suggested that, but for the Franco-Prussian War, France might have adopted a gold standard by 1870 (Laughlin 1892: 153).

The Germans, victors in the Franco-Prussian war, observed two facts which were not necessarily related: the British were economically successful; and the British were on a gold standard. They decided that they too must have a gold standard, and the payment of French reparations made this possible. The chief proponent of the gold standard in Germany was Ludwig Bamberger 'virtual founder of the Reichsbank'. He was opposed by Bleichroder, (amongst others) who:

> . . . knew how to appeal to Bismarck on this highly technical issue. In 1874 he warned him that the early introduction of an exclusive gold standard would make Germany dependent on the British gold market, which the British defended by raising rates.
>
> (Stern 1977: 180–1)

This switch by Germany from silver to gold put an intolerable strain on the ratio, and on France's support. 'All of a sudden, in December 1871, the German legislator introduced that famous and pernicious law, the operation of which was destined to introduce derangement and confusion into the monetary affairs of the entire world' (Cernuschi 1878).

Germany adopted the gold standard on 4 December 1871. The mark was redefined as 5.532 English grains of fine gold: this did not quite fit in with anyone else: a 20 mark coin was worth about 2 per cent more than the sovereign. (Had there been a firm British lead, Germany would surely have made this small adjustment.) Germany immediately set about buying up gold. By the end of 1880, 1,080 million marks in silver coins were withdrawn from circulation, of which 383 million were coined into new (subsidiary) coins, and 700 million marks (7.5 million ounces of fine silver) was sold for gold (Shaw 1896: 219). Inevitably, silver collapsed: the ratio went off the chart (Table 8.3). Not everyone believed the change was permanent. Walter Bagehot in December 1876, a few months before his death said

> The rise in price in silver which has just taken place is as local as the fall which preceded it. . . . Indeed such perturbations as a rise of 20 per cent, and then a fall to the old level in a single year . . . would have caused a vast derangement of transactions.
>
> (Bagehot 1877: 112)

It did.

The French were furious, and there was a vast political campaign in the United States. It has been argued, persuasively, that 'The Wizard of Oz' is really an allegory of money (Rockoff 1990: 739–60). France was forced to suspend free mintage of silver. The members of the Latin Union limited the coinage of silver to 6 francs per head of population. Monetary arrangements in India broke down, with consequences discussed in the next chapter. The ratio fell to 16.6 by 1875. The dramatic fall was yet to come, but this change was sufficient to damage bimetallism beyond repair. The debate, however, was to continue for the rest of the century.

End of the Latin Monetary Union

The Latin Monetary Union broke down but not because it was not a 'political union' and not, directly, because of bimetallism. At no stage, not even in 1785, were the French committed intellectually to the principle: what began as a bargaining counter became, inadvertently, a political and emotional commitment. There was a real problem in that the value of the silver coins had become half their fiat value. There was a big seigniorage profit from putting them into circulation, but, given the trend, an even larger loss to the issuer when they were redeemed or used for the payment of taxes. Competition between different issuing authorities obviously caused

problems, but these could surely have been resolved by commercial agreement. Finally, discussions on optimum currency areas seem irrelevant to
gold standard conditions: they are more obviously key to relationships with
the silver-based East.

10

BIMETALLISM – THE UNITED STATES AND INDIA

Two major countries, outside Europe, were concerned in their different ways, with the question of bimetallism. These were the United States and India.

THE UNITED STATES – INTRODUCTION

In the United States bimetallism was a major issue, for reasons other than in France. Silver was the major industry of certain thinly populated states (Arizona, Colorado, Idaho, Montana, Nevada, New Mexico and Utah) and in the US political system, these are over-represented in the Senate. Their allies were the 'soft money' lobby who had tasted blood with the greenbacks, only to see prices falling sharply in the run up to 1879, and continuing through what we used to call the 'Great Depression'. They regarded free coinage of silver as second best (or as General Walker (1888) commented, 'second worst'). For much of the period when Europe was discussing Latin Monetary Union and indeed when the so-called 'Crime of '73' was perpetrated, the issue was not in fact particularly relevant. The Americans had an inconvertible paper currency, the Greenbacks, from 1861, when the Civil War began, until 1879, long after it was over.

Early history

The double standard of gold and silver followed Alexander Hamilton's 'Report on the Establishment of the Mint' (1791). He was concerned with practical issues, and perhaps under-estimated the problem of fixing the ratio.

> There can hardly be a better rule in any country for the legal, than the market proportion, if this can be supposed to have been produced by the free and steady course of commercial principles ... each metal finds its true level, according to its intrinsic utility.
>
> (Doc. Hist. vol. i: 104; Laughlin 1892: 15)

The Mint Act of 1792 authorised the free coinage of silver and gold (Doc. Hist. vol. i: 133 ff). It set the weight of the silver dollar (including alloy),

93

at 416 grains, containing 371.25 grains of fine silver, while the gold eagle ($10) weighted 270 grains (247.5 grains fine) giving a ratio of fifteen. Both had unlimited legal tender, creating the classic 'Gresham' problem. Until 1819, this undervalued gold only slightly, and gold eagles and half eagles were in fact minted from 1795. After the resumption of specie payments in the United Kingdom the gold price rose, and gold disappeared from circulation in the United States. The place of gold coins was taken largely by bank notes, many of them issued by dubious 'wild cat' banks. The main financial story of that period, the 'Bank Wars' and the rise and fall of the two Banks of the United States, is told in Part II.

Laughlin (1892: 56) exonerates the effect of increased paper circulation in the earlier period. True, paper money had become widespread at the time that gold disappeared but in his view it was an effect, or possibly a coincidence, rather than a cause. Paper money 'would have driven out silver equally well with gold'. The Treasury produced a detailed report on the relative value of gold and silver dated 4 May 1830 (Doc. Hist. vol. ii: 99–111). Gallatin recommended a moderate devaluation (Doc. Hist. vol. ii: 112–5.)

The Act of 1834 (Doc. Hist. vol. ii: 119–20) changed the ratio from 1:15 (too low) to 1:16 (too high). Another Act of the same date set the legal value, on the basis of weight, of certain gold coins: (Doc. Hist, ii: 116). The market ratio was 15.625, a figure repeatedly recommended by the Select Committee but 'political considerations triumphed' (Laughlin 1892: 63) and the higher ratio was chosen. This could have been implemented either by increasing the silver content of the silver dollar, or by lessening the weight of the gold dollar. In the event, the pure gold content of the eagle ($10) was reduced from 247.5 grains to 232 grains – a devaluation of 6.26 per cent. According to Laughlin:

> The Coinage Act of 1834, in contradistinction to the policy of Hamilton in 1792, did not show the result of any attempt to select a mint ratio in accord with the market. It was very clearly pointed out in the debates that the ratio of 1:16 would drive out silver.
>
> (Laughlin 1892: 64)

There follows a good explanation of the technical operation of the Gresham mechanism under then current US mint practices.

Another Act, of 1837, (Doc. Hist. vol. ii: 120–8) made minor adjustments, and provided that both the gold and silver coins would be exactly 0.900 fine. The total weight of the silver dollar, including alloy, was reduced from 416 to 412.5 grains, but the fine silver content remained unchanged at 371.25 grains. The total weight of the gold eagle remained unchanged at 258 grains, but the gold content was rounded up very slightly from 232 grains (i.e. 0.899225 fine) to 232.2 grains. These small adjustments changed the ratio from 1:16 to 1:15.98. The implied price of an ounce of gold was $20.67: that of silver was $1.293.

Sure enough silver now disappeared from circulation. Its place was taken by Spanish and other foreign coins which, not having legal tender status, could circulate in accordance with their actual bullion value. 'The Act of 1853 was a practical abandonment of the double standard in the United States. There was virtually no opposition even though its real purpose was openly avowed in the clearest way in the House . . .' (Laughlin 1898: 79). He quotes from Mr Dunham's speech: 'We have had but single standard for the last three or four years. That has been, and now is, gold. We propose to let it remain so, and to adapt silver to it, to regulate it by it'. Laughlin adds

> We have heard a great deal in later years about the surreptitious demonetisation of silver in 1873 . . . the real demonetisation . . . was accomplished in 1853 . . . The Act of 1853 tried and condemned the criminal and after waiting twenty years for a reprieve . . . the execution only took place in 1873.

This was, in substance, the English 'subsidiary coinage' solution, but it was not popular. The pressure for change was to come in part from silver mining interests. The price of silver which had been (and was to revert to) $1.29 per ounce on the bimetallic system fell, in terms of gold, to $1.16 by 1876 and to 78 cents by 1893.

Meanwhile the silver issue was, in the United States, over-shadowed by other events. The crisis of 1857 was closely followed by the Civil War: see Chapter 27. Specie payments were suspended, gold went to a substantial premium in terms of greenbacks, and this wartime emergency measure (like so many of its kind) survived the war, actually remaining in force for nearly seventeen years. One side effect was to drive the subsidiary silver coins out of circulation. The value of the silver dollar was 96.9 cents in terms of gold: when paper fell below this figure it was worth melting down the smaller coins.

In 1869, the war having ended, John Jay Knox, Controller of the Currency was put in charge of a plan to reintroduce metal subsidiary coins, and codify the conflicting laws dealing with the operations of the United States Mint. His recommendations included the effective abolition of the silver dollar (the relevant paragraph was headed in capitals: SILVER DOLLAR – ITS DISCONTINUANCE AS A STANDARD), and these were incorporated in the Coinage Act of 12 February 1873, which was to be described in bimetallist literature, and has been handed down in American folklore, as 'The Crime of '73'. The Treasury was preoccupied with the crisis of that year, while in any case resumption was still six years in the future. So long as the actual circulating medium remained neither gold nor silver, but inconvertible greenbacks, the question was of little practical importance. By the end of the war prices had doubled in terms of greenbacks: if resumption was to be at the old parity, they had to halve. Remarkably, they did.

During the war the gold price rose more or less in line with the GDP deflator. After the war, though, the gold premium fell, distorting purchasing power parity, derived largely by investor expectations of resumption. This was perhaps the last time the expectations trick worked: it certainly did not for Winston Churchill some fifty years later. Walker (1888), at the time, asked: 'Does the premium on gold in a country having Inconvertible Paper Money measure the depreciation? This is perhaps one of the most difficult questions in the theory of money'. Friedman and Schwartz (1963: 70) ask the key question: did investors react to the fact the greenback price was high, or that it was rising?

After much debate, the Resumption Act was passed on 14 January 1875. It provided, that from 1 January 1879, greenbacks were to be redeemable in coin. Senator Sherman (who had replaced Chase as Treasury Secretary) built up his gold reserve to $114 million and by 17 December 1878 the premium on gold, which had been falling, finally disappeared. Resumption Day (2 January) was a non-event: a mere $135,000 was deposited in exchange for new notes. The Resumption Act authorised the coinage of subsidiary silver, but this only became practicable in 1877 when the gold premium fell to 104 (Laughlin 1892: 89–90).

There was in October 1873 what Laughlin (1892: 89) describes as 'a futile and ridiculous attempt of the Secretary of the Treasury' (Richardson) to redeem fractional dollar notes. 'This incident is an evidence of extraordinary ignorance in a finance minister'. For this operation to have worked the gold value of the paper dollar would have had to rise above 96.9 cents.

The Act of 1873

A 'trade dollar' weighing 420 grains 0.900 fine continued to be struck for Eastern and South American trade. As such it would effectively pass at bullion value. It was not a great success. In any case, during the greenback period, and indeed after, paper money and cheques were much more widely used in the United States than they were in Europe.

Recession after 1873

The measures of 1873 were followed by the long recession known (at least to historians writing before 1931) as 'the Great Depression'. The victims were both industrial workers and farmers. The price of wheat fell from $2.95 in 1866 to $1.40 in 1875 and $0.56 in 1894.

> To the farmers and the workers whose incomes were falling . . . it seemed self-evident that what was needed was more money. It is so clearly a matter of common sense that more money is good for the

individual that it seems to follow as a matter of logic that more currency is good for the country.

(Myers 1970: 199)

Laughlin says that, had silver not been legally demonetised in 1873,

... we [i.e. the United States] would have found ourselves in 1876 with a single silver standard, and the resumption of specie payments on 1 January 1879 would have been in silver, not in gold; and 15 per cent of all our contracts would have been repudiated. The Act of 1873 was a piece of good fortune, which saved our financial credit

(Laughlin 1892: 93)

It is not surprising that many measures were put before Congress aimed at increasing the price of silver and the stock of money – two separate but connected aims. A Commission of Enquiry was set up on 15 August 1876 to enquire into various monetary matters. Its terms of reference were to investigate the causes of the change in the relative value of gold and silver, the effects upon trade, and to report on the policy of restoring a double standard. 'It was packed in favor of a report for the remonetization of silver, and its conclusions have never had much weight' (Laughlin 1892: 204). He says that 'the minority report of Prof. Bowen and Mr Gibson is excellently done'. The majority report came down in favour of bimetallism and the remonetization of silver. The minority referred to this view as 'an illusion and an impossibility'.

The Bland-Allison Act

The Bland-Allison Act became law on 28 February 1878. On that day President Hayes vetoed it, but was over-ruled the same day by the necessary two-thirds majorities of both houses (196 to 73 in the House; 46 to 19 in the Senate). It provided that between 2 and 5 million dollars of silver were to be coined each month, at a weight of 412.5 grains. (This implied a ratio of 15.5). Silver was to be legal tender, silver certificates could be issued and silver could not be used to redeem gold certificates. Cernuschi (1881: 145) points out that 'It is not silver that is money, but only coined silver; hence uncoined silver is worth less than coined silver'. The House version of the Bill would have permitted free coinage of silver: this provision was deleted by the Senate, which added a clause by which the administration was instructed to convene an international monetary conference to determine the ratio (Laughlin 1898: 184–5). The coinage policy was said to be a failure. The Sherman Silver Act of 1890 required the Treasury to buy $4 million of silver each month, but not necessarily to coin it.

Silver and gold controversy in the United States

Grover Cleveland was elected President in 1892, and was inaugurated on the day of a Wall Street crash. Brogan says of him: 'There was not much room for ideas in Cleveland's massive head but when one had battered its way in it could never be dislodged. Cleveland became the leading "gold bug"'. His administration coincided with the worst (and in the event final) phase of what was referred to as 'The Great Depression': (see below). The Free Silver movement became a major political issue.

> Unfortunately silver as an issue had no appeal to the industrial workers whatever – rather the reverse, for the gold bugs told them again and again that industry would be ruined unless the threat to dilute the currency with silver coins was beaten back.
>
> (Brogan 1985)

The 1896 election was fought on this issue between the Republican McKinley and William Jennings Bryan of Nebraska. Bryan won the Democratic nomination with his famous speech to the party Convention, presided over by the inappropriately named Governor of Illinois, John Peter Altgeld. He said:

> You came to tell us that the great cities are in favour of the gold standard; we reply that the great cities rest upon our broad and fertile plains. Burn down your cities and leave our farms, and your cities will spring up again as if by magic; but destroy our farms and the grass will grow in every city. . . . If they say bimetallism is good but that we cannot have it until other nations help us, we reply, that instead of having a gold standard because England has, we will restore bimetallism, and then let England have bimetallism . . . we will answer their demand for a gold standard by saying to them: You shall not press down upon the brow of labour this crown of thorns, you shall not crucify mankind upon a cross of gold.
>
> (Democratic Party Convention 1896)

After a vigorous campaign, Bryan lost, and the Democrats were not to regain power for sixteen years. It also marked the end of the Great Depression, and of bimetallism as a serious political issue. The gold standard reigned as the supreme arbiter of a system of convertible paper currency in the United States and most of the civilised world. The year 1896 also brings this story to a close, ushering in as it did a golden age of stability, when the problems of money were finally resolved. It was to last all of eighteen years.

The period of falling prices

During the period 1874–96 prices fell steadily. The period used to be known as 'The Great Depression' although gross national product and real incomes continued to rise. It is a major battle-ground between economic historians who argue about the relative importance of the various factors in operation. Prices fell, it was argued, because this was a great period of cost-saving innovation. This was also true of earlier and later periods. Undoubtedly, effective money supply must have been growing more slowly than output.

The international moves towards a single gold standard were obviously squeezing the monetary base. Nations were competing for gold, an activity which would force up its relative price: given that every other price is measured in terms of gold, the observer would see these other prices falling. (Measured in silver, they would have risen.) Gold production had fallen to £27 million per annum as easily worked known deposits became exhausted. Production was to rise again towards the end of the period with major new discoveries in South Africa and Australia.

France was deliberately seeking gold by aggressive use of the discount rate. The United Kingdom was, nevertheless, a net importer of gold: £25.7 million worth came in during the period, increasing the stock by about 17 per cent. As population grew by 27 per cent, and real national product by even more there was a relative squeeze in the gold base for the currency. The use of alternative means of payment continued to grow; but not by enough to compensate (Saul 1985: 27). Saul also refers to the 'Gibson paradox'. 'If the fall in prices was caused by the supply of money growing more slowly than production, then this relative shortage should have caused rates of interest to rise. In fact they did the opposite.' (p. 16). He says that Alfred Marshall suggested that 'the shortage of money had prevented the rate of interest from falling as quickly as it might' and in a footnote gives Irving Fisher's views which were 'followed by Friedman and Cagan'.

Why was it called a 'Depression'? Rentiers with their money in 'the funds' obviously benefitted. In the United Kingdom money wages had a tendency to fall, but may actually have risen slightly on balance over the period. Real wages probably rose by a third and unemployment was low. Natural debtors, merchants and some manufacturers, will have been squeezed. Agriculture suffered, and although this was part of a necessary structural adjustment the complaints will have been vocal. In the United States both the farmers and the silver miners were loud in their complaints.

INDIA

As Miss Prism said to Cecily (The Importance of Being Earnest: Oscar Wilde): 'The chapter on the fall of the Rupee you may omit. It is somewhat too sensational. Even these metallic problems have their melodramatic side'. Indian monetary questions fascinated British economists, from Sir James Steuart, who, in a 1772 report to the East India Company, recommended paper credit as a method 'for correcting the DEFECTS of the present

CURRENCY', to Maynard Keynes, 'Indian Currency and Finance' (1913).
Lindsay's proposals of 1879 foreshadowed what was to come.

Between 1835 and 1893, The Indian mint was 'open to the free coinage
of silver; the rupee and the half rupee are the only standard coins, and are
legal tender to an unlimited amount. . . . Gold is not legal tender and there
are no gold coins' (Report of the Indian Currency Committee 1892: 28–9)
and the falling value of silver amounted to an unexpected and unwanted
depreciation in the currency. The rupee had a silver content of 165 grains.
For many years, the ratio being 15.5:1 and the price of silver 65.13 pence
per fine ounce, the rupee had a par value of 22.39 pence in terms of the UK
gold system. Allowing for costs and delays, it was only worth shipping
bullion to coin rupees at 23.308 pence – the arbitrage, or specie, point
(Cernuschi 1881: 24–5).

The outcome of the report was the closing of the Indian mints to silver
on private account. The rupee was thereafter effectively on a gold exchange
standard. Rupees, or rupee notes, were supplied, on the tender of gold, at
1s. 4d. per rupee. The British sovereign was subsequently (1899) declared
legal tender at the same rate – that is 15 rupees. Effectively there was a gold
standard but a silver circulating medium. Although the silver rupee was for
practical purposes the circulating coinage of India, it was in substance a
subsidiary token coinage, valued on exactly the same basis as paper rupees.
The concept puzzled contemporaries. Irving Fisher (1920b: 43) quotes Sir
David Barbour's story about the British Commissioner who asked an Indian
merchant about how serious was the fall in the rupee. The merchant said he
had never heard of the fall in the value of the rupee, but his Calcutta agents
were very concerned by the rise in the price of gold.

A. J. Balfour (later British Prime Minister) said at the Mansion House 3
April 1895:

> What is the British system of currency? I fix my attention on those
> parts of our great empire . . . under the rule of the British Parliament
> . . . You go to Hong Kong and the Straits Settlements, and you find
> obligations are measured – in silver; you go to England, and you find
> that obligations are measured – in gold; you stop halfway, in India,
> and you find that obligations are measured – in something which is
> neither gold nor silver – the strangest product of monometallist ingenuity
> which the world has ever seen – a currency which is as arbitrary as any
> forced paper currency which the world has ever heard of, and which is
> as expensive as any metallic currency that the world has ever faced,
> and which, unhappily, combines in itself all the disadvantages of every
> currency which human beings have ever tried to form.
>
> (Rothwell 1897: 246–7)

A few years later, Maynard Keynes was to make his first contribution both
to public policy and to monetary analysis on the questions of Indian
currency. This, though, is beyond our period.

11

SUPPORTERS AND OPPONENTS OF BIMETALLISM

THE NINETEENTH CENTURY

This was one of the classic periods of monetary pamphleteering, comparable to 1696 and 1810. There is an immense literature supporting and opposing bimetallism, and most of the heated views expressed on European Monetary Union in the late twentieth century were already being well rehearsed. In both cases much of the writing is of indifferent quality, but there are some gems. The best books on each side are by authors who were later to play an active role in monetary reform. J. Lawrence Laughlin (1888) an opponent, was to play the major role in the US Monetary Commission of 1897 which led to the formal introduction of the gold standard. Sir David Barbour (1885), perhaps the most readable and coherent of the supporters, was Financial Secretary to the Government of India and was to have the misfortune (given his views) to preside over the 1893 closing of the Indian silver mints.

Laughlin's book is mainly historical and factual, but his summary of the arguments used by supporters is an excellent starting point. Friedman (1992) praises his 'major scholarly contribution . . . cited by proponents and opponents' but suggests that as a leader of the hard money school he 'was dogmatic and demagogic'. Laughlin divides supporters into two groups. He dismisses group (A) National Bimetallism, which he defines as 'The selection of both gold and silver by an individual state as legal payment of debts to any amount without regard to the legal ratios of other states' adding that 'such a system is not upheld by any economic writer of repute' (p. 3–5). He has more sympathy for his group (B), the International Bimetallists who believed that: 'An agreement between the commercial nations of the world on one given ratio (e.g. 15.5:1) would . . . keep the value of silver relative to gold invariable, and so cause the current use of both metals'.

Supporters of National Bimetallism (A) in the United States put forward four main arguments. They fear that without silver there may be a shortage of precious metals for monetary purposes (his point 2); they expect, by example, to induce other countries to adopt bimetallism (3); they wish to sustain the price of silver (4) or they wish to force the cheaper metal into use as a means of relieving debtors of part of their burdens. The first two of these were given a good airing in Europe: his (4) though, is a preoccupation of silver producers (mainly in the US), while (5) was, in Europe usually seen not as an advantage but as an objection to be overcome.

Most of the European supporters were international bimetallists. Laughlin summarises their arguments:

(6) 'The essential part of this theory is that the legal provision for the use of coinage . . . creates a demand for silver; and that [given the same ratio there is no reason] why either gold or silver should leave one country for another.

(7) 'it is urged that the "compensatory action" of a double standard will prevent that extreme fluctuation of the standard of prices

(8) The 'gold famine' argument equivalent to (2) above.

(9) 'the general demonetisation of silver would so increase the value of gold, and the value of the unit in which the enormous public debts of the world must be paid, that it would entail a heavy loss to the taxpayer'

(10) Other writers] 'urge that the two precious metals were designed by a Higher Power as media of exchange, and that it is a mistake arbitrarily to set one of them up . . . and to discard the other'.

(Laughlin 1892)

Barbour's (1888) arguments can be recognised, in a more incoherent form, in earlier authors. He was understandably concerned about the position of those in countries, such as India where he served, where incomes were fixed in silver while their debts were often contracted in gold. He asks the 'interesting question . . . how long a bimetallic country surrounded by monometallic countries can, unaided, sustain the bimetallic system' (page 51). His 'answer is simple' and indeed mainly technically correct. It did not in fact support his case: the passage quoted highlights the fatal flaw.

A single country can sustain the system so long as its currency is actually composed of both metals.

If one metal becomes so abundant in comparison with the other the latter is completely driven out of the country which uses the alternative standard, the principle of compensation ceases to act and the country that was bimetallic becomes practically monometallic.

The market ratio between the two metals will then cease to be constant, and may vary to any extent.

So far so good. Optimism then creeps in.

If the metal which was over-produced ceases to be over-produced, and if over-production begins, the bimetallic country which was denuded of the latter metal will begin to get it back again *as soon as the market returns to the legal ratio* (emphasis added).

Quite so. The French circulating currency, like the Bretton Woods system, the tin buffer stock or the Bundesbank, could readily absorb fluctuations *around* a central market price. Any such system collapses when the pegged price becomes permanently out of line with market realities. Sir David is wrong when he says:

> To contend, in the face of the facts . . . that the legal ratio fixed under the bimetallic system . . . will not control and regulate the market price of the two metals, is simply to abandon reason, argument and experience, and take refuge in assertion.
>
> (Barbour 1885: 63)

Another leading UK bimetallist, Herbert C. Gibbs was to make a similar claim:

> It is claimed for bimetallism that the existence of that system in France maintained the relative value of silver and gold in all the markets of the world and certain it is that the relative value was maintained until 1873.
>
> (Gibbs 1894: 15)

This is the key issue. It is, of course true, as with the Bretton Woods system (and with the US silver price in the 1960s) a fixed rate system can, up to a point, ensure stability. As we have seen, the sheer volume of the French circulating currency could absorb quite substantial fluctuations in industrial and monetary demand. It is significant that in France gold and silver coins formed a larger part of the circulating medium than in other countries. France had two bad experiences with paper currency, John Law (in 1720) and the Assignats, and bank notes were not as acceptable there as elsewhere. Bimetallism worked pretty well for much of the nineteenth century – for any country which adopted the dominant French ratio. No country, as the United States discovered, could effectively adopt strict bimetallism with a different ratio, as this created continuous arbitrage opportunities until one metal disappeared.

In the United States, the two metals never in fact circulated side by side. At any stage, one metal drove out the other, following sound Gresham rules. Indeed the bimetallists explicitly recognised that any extension of the system would have to be on an internationally agreed ratio. It is interesting to speculate what would have happened if the Americans had successfully launched a true bimetallic system on the French ratio after the Civil War, substantially enlarging the size of the buffer.

The system was in any case probably doomed to eventual failure. It had survived fairly substantial (but subsequently reversed) discrepancies, but nothing as great as the challenges of the 1870s when fundamentals were quite out of line. This was partly due to supply factors (silver discoveries exceeded gold discoveries) but it was the spread of the gold standard (monetary demand factors) which finally destroyed bimetallism. Was this inevitable, and could an American initiative have prevented it? The French system had served very well. So, across the Channel, had the gold standard, but the superior economic performance of the United Kingdom, which had so impressed the Germans was not, properly analysed, really due to the choice of monetary metal. Perhaps the real lesson is the folly (and huge expense) of defending a good old system when it has ceased to work. Alfred Marshall put his finger on it:

> It may be admitted that an agreement, entered into by all the commercial countries of the world to keep their mints open to gold and silver at almost any reasonable ratio, would tie the values of metals to that ratio, so long as the agreement lasted. . . . But it seems probable that – as human nature is constituted – such an agreement would not endure very long after changes . . . had made the relative costs . . . differ widely from their relative ratings.

> (Marshall 1923: 63)

Henry Dunning MacLeod also summed it up well:

> Is it the Fixed Legal Ratio . . . which governs the relative Value of Metals in Bullion? Or is it the relative Value of the Metals . . . which governs the Value of the Coin?
> And if it be impossible for any single countries to maintain . . . a Fixed Legal Ratio, is it possible for any number of countries to do so by International Agreement?

> (MacLeod 1894: p. vi.)

Francis A, Walker (1888) discussed the motives of the bimetallists. There were the 'inhabitants of the silver-producing states [whose interest was] of the same nature as the interest of Pennsylvania in the duties on pig-iron', the 'soft money' men those who were in the forefront of the greenback heresy (Schumpeter's 'monetary monomaniacs') and the third group of genuine bimetallists. He opposed unilateral bimetallism, but had some sympathy with the concept internationally.

Gibbs and Grenfell

Two Governors of the Bank of England, Henry Hucks Gibbs[7] and Henry Riversdale Grenfell[8] were pamphleteering bimetallists, and there was some discussion on what evidence should be given to the 1887 Royal Commission on the values of gold and silver. Some key pamphlets are conveniently reprinted in Gibbs and Grenfell 1886. (See also Friedman 1992.)

The views of the bimetallists tend to be repetitive, and it is more interesting to see how they reacted to their opponents. For instance, Gibbs wrote to Goschen in 1882 suggesting that they were in accord on silver, and wondering what was needed to 'restore that white-faced Monarch to his Throne'. He said that 'The allegation of the severer monometallists is that the bimetallist desires unjustly to enable the debtor to pay his debt in a metal the real value of which is less than the legal value' (Gibbs 1883: 4). Earl Grey (son of the Second Earl, of the Reform Act) wrote to Grenfell on 31 May 1881 inspired by Gibbs' pamphlet 'The Double Standard'. 'Mr Gibbs admits the force of the objections to the adoption of a Double standard of value by a single nation which since the days of Locke have been generally recognised as insurmountable'.

Gibbs had argued that these objections do not apply to universal bimetallism. Grey found the arguments 'exceedingly ingenious' but not, to him, 'satisfactory'. He raises the 'Gresham' type arguments and can see nothing in the plan to deal with the problem created by variations in the output and cost of production of silver relative to gold. Gibbs had expected the price of silver to rise to the legal ratio. Grey comments:

> it would be unsafe to rely on the expected rise in the price of silver in consequence of it having the character of money available for paying all debts conferred upon it by most of the commercial nations of the world . . . it is still more uncertain whether such a stimulus might not be given to the production of silver that . . . would . . . bring back its price to the present level.
>
> (Grey 1881: 6)

He is unconvinced by the 'ingenious and elaborate argument' set out, and goes on to discuss production costs, which he regards as key.

Grey then has some constructive suggestions. He agrees with Gibbs that if gold completely supersedes silver as an instrument of exchange, the supply of gold may be inadequate, that 'the price of all commodities in gold will fall, and that great commercial difficulties must ensue'. (These were the early days of the 'Great Depression'.) He agrees that 'it is desirable that silver should be used to a greater extent' and asks 'whether it would not be possible to secure this advantage by some arrangement that would be free from the objections to which the scheme of Mr. Gibbs is open?' (Grey 1882: 9). The Bank of England is permitted to hold part of its reserves in silver, but as 'silver cannot be used in payment of notes it is of little real use'. To validate this silver and encourage it to be held, Grey suggests that the Bank should be permitted to redeem notes for over £500 half in sovereigns, 'half in silver, coined or uncoined, at the market price of the day'. This he regards as a modification of Ricardo's plan for a 'Secure and Economic Currency' (Ricardo 1951 vol. iv: 43 ff). Similar provisions could apply in other countries: 'in France, it is well known that the Bank is encumbered by having a large stock of five-franc pieces which it is at a loss what to do with, since it cannot use them at nominal value to pay its notes without depreciating the currency' (Grey 1882: 12).

In reply, Grenfell repeats (or anticipates) the 'Barbour' type arguments and asserts that 'there could not be any relative price than the legal one'. He misunderstands Grey's suggestion,which, he says, would 'be practically an admission of bimetallism; since, *of course* [sic] this would only be done on condition of France and the United States agreeing to bimetallism'. This is because (he assumes) 'the price of the day would be the mint price of France'.

Grey, when he came to reply, had also read Grenfell's article in the *Nineteenth Century*[9]. He did not think that it 'sufficiently recognises . . . that the relative values of gold and silver currencies will ultimately be determined by the comparative cost of producing the two metals, in spite of any laws which may have been enacted'. (Very true, but those who thought like Grey may have underestimated the significant (but not in the last resort decisive) effect of monetary arrangements on the demand for silver.) He also corrects Grenfell's misunderstanding: his proposal was *not* conditional on action by France:

> I hold that our action on this question ought to be entirely independent . . . Neither this nor any other country can, without imprudence, make the regulation of its currency a matter of negotiation with other nations. Each nation should . . . keep itself free to deal with the subject as it thinks fit.

The *Nineteenth Century* issue for April 1882 carries an article by Viscount Sherbrooke[10] 'What is Money?' (1882, 1884) is very much opposed to 'bimetalism' (as he consistently spells it). Tempers now rise, and he begins scathingly: 'The wisest course which can be taken with popular delusions is, very often found to be treating them like raging waves of the sea, and let them foam out their own shame'. Why, he asks, do these monetary delusions persist? 'Too little allowance has been made for the power of fear and interest to warp and obscure the intelligence'. He is concerned to find 'the Governor of the Bank of England[11] coming forward as a bimetalist and recommending a general committee . . . presided over by a gentleman of the ability and authority of Mr Cazalet' and refers to the *Bullionist* newspaper being enlisted as their organ, putting 'those who adhere to the doctrines of Smith, Ricardo and Mill' on the defensive. Cazalet had written *Bimetallism and its connection with commerce* in 1879).

12

THE EARLIER HISTORY OF MONEY

This chapter is by way of a postscript to Part I, and gives a brief overview of the sixteen centuries or so of earlier history. The history of coinage actually begins not in 800 AD, but in about 800 BC when the first coins, were struck from electrum, a naturally occurring alloy of silver and gold.

ANCIENT GREECE

According to Burns (1927) the first Lydian coins will have been privately made, with a stamp 'guaranteeing' the quality (but not the weight) of the metal. He refers to the obvious 'temptation grounded in a profit motive in conflict with the primary one of simplifying exchange' (p. 318). He suggests that an acceptable stamp may confer political power. Gyges (died c. 645 BC) replaced private minting with a state monopoly, and his 'first imperial currency of the world' lasted for a century, until the reform of Alyattes.

These early coins were made of electrum, a naturally occurring mixture of gold and silver. As the proportions varied 'from 5 to 95 per cent' there were obvious problems (Burns 1927: 321). He suggests that there was a parallel silver coinage with a 10:1 ratio, but this seems implausible. 'The failure of this early experiment in symmetallism might easily have resulted in the abandonment of coining which was saved, however, by the practice of private counter-marking and, most of all, by the abandonment of electrum for gold and silver' (320–1). Alyattes introduced gold coins (staters) alongside the electrum, while his son Croesus (560–546 BC) completed the process by replacing the electrum with silver shekels. After the conquest of Lydia by Cyrus, this system was adopted in the Persian empire. Ridgway (1892) also discusses the Lydian and Persian Systems in Chapter XI.

> Both gold and silver coins were, so far as we know, full-weight coins, but there is now evidence of any legal ratio between the values of the two metals, which were probably not current by tale. Nevertheless, it is quite possible that the Lydians introduced bimetallism.
>
> (Burns 1927: 321)

The text goes on to suggest a 10:1 ratio, based on the apparent logic of the coin weights. (A source quoted suggests that the army was paid in gold coin, the navy in silver, perhaps reflecting the coinage current in their respective sphere of operations.) There is more evidence that the Persians attempted bimetallism at a 13.3:1 ratio, but at one stage this undervalued silver, which disappeared.

An active monetary economy developed in early Greece. This, it seems, created familiar problems of over extended debt, particularly when the then current form of 'chattel mortgage' could result in the debtor being sold into slavery. Solon, a contemporary of, and who visited, Croesus, was elected archon of Athens in 594 BC. He took dramatic steps to stave off, at best a collapse, and at worst an insurrection followed by anarchy. He decreed a debt moratorium, freeing debtors who had been sold into slavery and prohibiting 'personal' security for a loan. This action, undermining the structure of credit, was accompanied by a devaluation, calling up the value of the mina from 73 to 100 drachma. (The silver content of the drachma presumably fell from 92 to 67 grains.) What surprises the modern reader is not that such an event took place, but that it was not, apparently, repeated. Solon was certainly the father of a stable Athenian democracy: were his monetary measures also followed by a long period of prosperity and stability?

Burns contrasts the Greek and Asiatic experience which is remarkably similar to the later experience of Venice and other city states:

> While in the latter monarchical government was the rule and kings controlled the currency, in the former the people were organised in small city-states, and preserved in their own hands the right to issue such money as they thought necessary.
>
> (Burns 1927)

During the fifth and early fourth centuries Greek coins began to circulate by tale. Given the number of independent issuing authorities this must have initially added to the confusion. However Athens was becoming pre-eminent and her familiar silver coins, with the head of Athena and an owl on the reverse, became probably the first of many cases where a superior coin type became widely accepted far beyond its country of issue: 'good money' driving out 'bad' in the right circumstances. The weight standard was, it seems, maintained within a 1 per cent margin. There were political motives, as well as a desire to find an outlet for the production of silver mines. The Athenian coins soon dominated.

> While in 434 BC the treasurer's lists at Athens mention separately the silver coins of other cities, after 418 BC foreign silver was quoted merely by its weight in talents and fractions, indicating that 'owls' were accepted by tale and all other coins by weight.
>
> (Burns 1927: 346)

Athens initially appears to have had an exclusively silver coinage, deliberately distinguished from the Persian gold system based on the daric. Gold coins were reluctantly introduced after the loss of the expedition to Syracuse and was 'a device to relieve financial pressure' by melting down and coining the temple treasures and the golden statues in the Parthenon.

> The Athenians had here one advantage over more modern peoples. Their gold reserve was always in use; any citizen could go to the Parthenon and admire the winged statues of victory. But it is not open to any citizen of England, France ... to call at the national bank and see the reserve, and, if he could, he would not find it in a form likely to appeal to his aesthetic sense,
>
> (Burns 1928: 348)

Burns discusses the possible 'inflationary' effects, and what might have happened had it occurred to them to issue paper money. He draws parallels with gold issues by Rome at the time of the Punic War, and refers to a comment by Ruding (1840 vol. i: 186) on Henry III's gold penny of 1257.

Some time later (early fourth century BC) bronze small change was introduced, but silver remained the standard with no attempt at bimetallism. There was, says Burns, no support for the idea 'because, on the one hand, bimetallism was an Asiatic notion, and, on the other, it did not appear to be capable of enduring in times of change'. Burns is clearly intrigued by the subject but frustrated by lack of information. There must be scope for a modern monetary economist to look at the classical period near 408 BC.

Burns concludes that debasement was extremely rare in Greece, but mentions incidents with plated coins about the time of the fall of Athens (404 BC) He quotes Aristophanes and refers to *The Frogs*, often cited as the earliest statement of Gresham's Law.

> The noble silver drachma, that of old
> We were so proud of, and the recent gold,
> Coins that rang true, clean-stamped and worth their weight
> Throughout the world, have ceased to circulate.
>   Instead, the purses of Athenian shoppers
> Are full of shoddy silver-plated coppers.
>   Just so, when men are needed by the nation,
> The best have been withdrawn from circulation.
>   (Penguin Classics edition, translation by David Barrett)

Burns ends his Greek chapter by praising the general soundness of policy which he attributes in part to the greater interest in economic affairs taken by the rulers of city states as compared with those of military empires. He draws some comparisons with 'modern' times – but in 1927 there was still much to come.

ROME

Numismatists divide the Roman coinage into the Republican and Imperial periods. The Emperor Augustus, (44 BC to 14 AD) introduced a monetary system remarkably similar to that of England before 1914. The coins in circulation were of three metals, gold, silver and copper, and there was no attempt at bimetallism. The basic monetary unit was the silver denarius. The gold Aureus did not have a stated value, but was simply (like the English guinea until 1816) treated as worth its known and guaranteed content of pure gold. The brass and copper coins were valued at a fraction of the denarius. Although there appears to be a close relationship between their 'tale' or 'legal tender' value and their metal value, they had, again as in eighteenth century England, many of the features of a token coinage backed by imperial authority.

The title Augustus, had been conferred on the Emperor in January, 27 BC This date is regarded by numismatists as the commencement of the Roman imperial coinage. Meanwhile coinage in the Greek tradition continued in the eastern parts of the Roman Empire and beyond. Silver drachmas and tetradrachmas continued to be struck in Parthia until the invasion of the Sassanids in 226. In Egypt the Alexandra mint continued to strike very base tetradrachms which traded at par with the (purer but lighter) Roman denarius. There was the inevitable debasement. Robin Porteous refers to the Roman Empire meeting its deficit on defence and administrative costs

> partly by higher taxes and partly by inflation which took the simple form of a debasement of the denarius. For about 200 years this debasement proceeded at a supportable pace. . . . In the third century the process began to get out of hand . . . the denarius contained about 40 per cent silver when in 214 Caracalla replaced it as the standard coin by a double denarius intrinsically worth about one and a half of the current pieces.

He says that the Emperor Gallienus (253–68)

> abandoned all restraint in striking the now wholly debased double denarius. Enormous numbers were issued, the government's credit was destroyed and the currency became worthless. The inflation of Gallienius' reign was almost as intense as that of Germany in 1923 and far more widespread. Nevertheless it may not have been so grievous in its social effects. The Roman Empire was never a monetary economy in the modern sense . . . the enormous hoards of double denarii dating from Gallienius' reign suggest not so much savings lost in the crash as the abandoned hopes of currency speculators.
>
> (Porteous 1969: 11–12)

Diocletian succeeded in restoring the currency, and his reforms were the basis of the early monetary system of the Byzantine, or eastern, empire, which was to survive the fall of Rome.

BYZANTIUM

Diocletian's monetary reform forms the starting point of Michael Hendy's excellent *Studies in the Byzantine Monetary Economy.*

> It took some time for Diocletian (284 to 305) as the leading legislative and administrative force in his tetrarch system of imperial rule, to turn his attention to a radical reconstruction of the coinage system: curiously enough almost exactly the same amount of time as Alexius I took in somewhat similar circumstances 800 years later.
>
> (Hendy 1985: 449)

Diocletian's first step in 286 AD was to restandardise the weight of the gold coin at one-sixtieth of a pound weight (about 5.3 grams). About ten years later he introduced a silver coin 'apparently of high purity' with a weight of one ninety-sixth of a pound. It appears that a pound of gold was worth some 72,000 denarii making the gold solidus worth 1,200 denarii. It does appear that the ratio was 'a perfectly traditional one to twelve'. Therefore 'the Dioclenatic silver coin at one ninety-sixth of a pound should – other things being equal – have been worth 62.5 denarii. But other things were not equal' (p. 451). Hendy quotes documentary sources to suggest that it was worth 100 denarii and offers an explanation for this apparent discrepancy:

> The forms of the entries for gold and silver in the Edictum de Pretiis give a clear implication as to what was happening. Gold is defined in terms of ingots, coins and spun gold and is given a single price; silver is defined in no such terms. Gold in whatever form is therefore being treated entirely as a commodity. Silver only in its bullion form (i.e. ingots etc.) is being so treated. Silver in bullion form was then indeed worth 6,000 denarii to the pound, but silver in monetary form was indeed equally worth 9,600 to the pound: the Dioclenatic argentus worth 100 denarii was therefore overvalued to the tune of some 60 per cent. This is unexpected, and unexpectedly large, but by no means improbable since to tolerate both gold and silver coins circulating at their bullion or near bullion value is to invite complications as their values inevitably fluctuate.
>
> (Hendy 1985: 451)

The subsidiary billon or copper coinages were very important throughout this period. There does seem to be a retariffing of the nomus in 301. Diocletian, for all his virtues, appears to have been preoccupied with price control. 'It was in the subsidiary coinage as represented by the billon nomus that the greatest weakness of the Dioclenatic system lay. There were debasements under Constantine (Jones 1953).

There was another currency reform under Anastasius in two phases, 498 and 512. Thereafter, the gold coinage at least, remained stable until the solidus was debased by Michael IV (1034–41) who is said to have been a money changer before his accession. This is, of course, two centuries after the Carolingian reform in the West: at that time the Byzantine gold solidus or Bezant was the standard stable and respected gold coin of the East. This was worth twelve of Pepin's denarii, hence the term solidus or shilling.[12] Meanwhile the Byzantine empire was under pressure from the Sejluks and other neighbours. By 1071 the solidus was only one-third pure gold. The last great currency reform of the ancient world was undertaken by Alexius 1 Commenus (1081–1118). In 1091 he introduced a gold hyperperon (with a theoretical fineness believed to be 20.5 carats). This was supported by coins deliberately and openly made of alloys: electrum (gold and silver) and billon (silver and base metal). There were also copper coins as small change. After the fall of Constantinople in 1204, the fringe successor states tended to adopt silver for their 'best' coins. After the brief revival of empire there was, in about 1304, a last and intriguing link with 'Western' money. A new sound silver coin was introduced by the co-emperors Andronicus II and Michael IX, copying the design of the then widespread Venetian grosso: another classic example of an internationally trusted coin spreading its influence beyond its country of origin.

Part II

THE DEVELOPMENT OF CREDIT AND BANKING

13

INTRODUCTION

Part I dealt with money as coin and showed that how even that simple concept could create difficult enough problems. At the beginning of the period coin was (more or less) the only real means of payment other than barter. By 1896 and the (temporary) triumph of the gold standard, coin was only a small part of the total money supply. There were highly sophisticated banking systems and capital markets and most payments of any size were made either in bank notes or in cheques drawn on bank deposits. The alternative means of payment were, however, convertible directly or indirectly into gold (or silver) which remained the standard and measure of value. The alternatives could, over-simplifying, be regarded as methods for economising in the use of gold.

The following chapters trace the history of this development while Part III will deal with the early experiments in and eventual triumph of inconvertible paper money. This distinction, though logical, means departing from a chronological sequence and some readers may prefer to take the chapters in a rather different order. For instance, while most of the development of the UK banking system is dealt with here in Part II, the narrative is interrupted by the critically important incident of the 'suspension of payments' during the Napoleonic Wars which is covered in Part III, while certain purely coinage aspects of the reconstruction after that war have already been covered in Part I. Similarly, in the United States both the American Revolution and the Civil War were financed with inconvertible paper money and these important incidents are covered in Part III while the important interesting and much under researched history of pre-Civil War banking in the United States is dealt with here. Even this departs somewhat from a strict logical structure as there were short periods during which the convertible bank notes were suspended. These, though, were defaults by the banking system rather than of the nation and can be regarded as quirks in the development of banking rather than actual attempts to introduce inconvertible fiat money. One more of the experiments with paper money in France in 1720 is covered in Part III. The contemporary events in England, the South Sea Bubble, have many parallels but did not involve any collapse of, or interference with, the general monetary system. It is therefore included in Part II as an important event in the development of banking and finance.

The thirteenth century revival of trade needed more than larger and more valuable coins to oil the wheels. One requirement was simply to avoid the expense and significant risk of transporting bullion from one place to another and to this end merchants devised means of offsetting or 'clearing' balances. Another factor was the church's prohibition of usury interpreted to mean any lending of money at interest and which made some sense in a society where the only borrowers were those who hit on hard times and who looked to their more fortunate neighbours for temporary assistance. It was quite incompatible with a mercantile society where loans at interest benefit both parties and indeed society at large. At the secular level the laws and customs of the feudal system were ill-suited to economic development. Essentially what happened was that a new mercantile system grew up paralleling rather than superseding the old. Beginning in Italy, independent city states came to terms with the feudal system but were essentially governed by and for tradesmen and merchants rather than the feudal aristocracy. In the course of trading with each other they developed a system of 'trade fairs' where, in effect, normal laws were largely suspended during the 'peace of the fair' and replaced by what amounted to a system of self-regulation and arbitration designed and run by the merchants themselves. Bills of Exchange drawn for settlement during these fairs were effectively treated as forward exchange transactions which fell outside the prohibition of usury.

The fairs brought revenue to the feudal lord on whose territory they took place. These Lords were therefore happy to guarantee 'the peace of the fair' and to use their political clout to negotiate with their neighbours to guarantee the merchants safe passage between the various fairs and their home cities. The fairs in this extraordinarily important form lasted for rather more than a century and effectively faded away (in that form) when commerce developed to the point at which merchants could carry on much of their business, and make most of their payments, by correspondence instead of physically having to travel from fair to fair.

The next stage involved primitive banking, originally used mainly for safe custody but also as a method of intermediating loans. Until the end of the seventeenth century there was little concept of banking as we know it, although the foundations had been well and truly laid. Then were laid more or less simultaneously the foundations of the Bank of England and a series of proposals for a new species of money in the form of land banks. Although the mainstream of change was then in the direction of banking based on convertible notes and deposits, John Law's experiments were an early, and in the end unsuccessful attempt to take the world straight into an inconvertible paper regime such as is discussed in Part III. There was the first legislation to deal with options trading and a speculative mania came to its head in the South Sea Bubble of 1720. In the United Kingdom this incident actually set back the development of financial instruments, but left monetary arrangements intact.

> Law carried his consolidation to the extreme point of amalgamating his bank with the trading companies . . . [which] . . . made excessive issues of inconvertible paper. . . . In England, although . . . the South Sea company affected the purchasing power of money, it fortunately happened that the Bank of England stood firmly for convertible paper-money, and the currency was not tampered with.
>
> (Scott 1912 vol. iii: 300)

There was then a period of consolidation and by the end of the eighteenth century a fairly sophisticated banking and financial system was in place.

The events surrounding the French and American revolutions involve inconvertible paper currency and are dealt with in Part III but after the Napoleonic Wars the progress towards a modern sophisticated banking system with actual coins as a relatively minor part of money supply moved fast. In the United Kingdom there were philosophical disputes between the 'banking' and 'currency' schools about the monetary nature of bank notes and bank deposits. The first two crises of the century in 1825 and 1837 were based on an over issue of bank notes. The Bank Charter Act of 1844 was designed to ensure that note issue was properly under control and that such crises could never happen again. Needless to say the problem re-emerged in another form as early as 1847 when it was discovered that the real weakness of the 1844 legislation was that it was assumed that bank notes were the only alternative to coin, ignoring the expansion of bank deposits. By the end of the century, though, a reasonably stable system of banking and bank regulation had been developed.

It was otherwise in the United States when a new nation was, for the first half-century or so of its existence effectively without an agreed Federal banking policy and dependent on state governments for the regulation of banks. A large part of its circulating medium at that period comprised notes issued by banks which had no real substance and which eventually failed. Following the monetary upheavals of the Civil War, the United States developed a workable banking system. It did not have anything even approximating a central bank until the Federal Reserve Bank was set up in 1913, and (a hangover from the earlier political disputes) was remarkably slow to develop what Europeans (or Canadians) would recognise as a national banking system.

The key question which recurs through this Part is 'what is money?' Should we regard a particular financial instrument as a convenient method of making a payment or as something which has all the characteristics of money? The next section, a brief digression on the concept of 'velocity of circulation' suggests that we can perhaps afford to be a little flexible in our approach. The last section in this chapter discusses the concept of usury. This may be important as background for Chapter 14 but not particularly relevant for modern times, except for those concerned with Islamic banking.

MONEY THEORY

The classic Fisher (1911) 'quantity theory' of money is often stated by the formula $MV = PT$. This is a tautology in the sense that it must be true provided that the terms are consistently defined. If M (quantity of money) rises without any change in V (velocity of circulation of that money) and T (volume of transactions) then P (prices) will inevitably rise. This begs the question of the nature and direction of any causal relationship and specifically of whether velocity, V, is independent. It is perfectly possible that, in certain circumstances, an increase in the money supply, M, could simply be met by a fall in velocity, V. Similarly an increase in V would have an effect on prices even if M remained constant. Throughout history, and particularly during the period we are discussing, there is a tendency for the means of payment to be expanded. Coin is supplemented, first by bank notes and bills of exchange, and later by bank deposits, credit cards, and interest bearing current accounts. These become effective money substitutes and (arguably) money itself. Should we look at such a development as a change in the nature of M or a change in V?

In an all-coinage economy the concept is simple. The quantity of money is measured by the number of gold sovereigns (or silver groats, or whatever) in circulation, and velocity is measured by the average number of times those coins change hands, in the literal sense, each year in the course of trade. Assume a gold coin changes hands ten times per annum: this may imply that a typical merchant finds it convenient to hold 10 per cent of his annual turnover (or a customer 10 per cent of his annual expenditure) in the form of coins. The velocity of circulation would be ten.

With the growth of credit and trade bills in the fourteenth century it became possible to transact business between merchants without pieces of metal changing hands. Suppose that credit develops, and that for every transaction settled in coin another of equal value is settled by a credit transaction which is netted off without gold changing hands. Although the velocity of movement of coins remains the same, the effective velocity becomes, for our purposes, twenty. This mechanism works only if (as is probable) merchants now find it necessary only to keep 5 per cent of turnover in the form of coin. The credit mechanism has developed as a means of economising the holding of cash. In these circumstances it is probably still useful to say that the velocity of circulation has doubled. As MV has doubled so must PT. This mechanism is potentially inflationary but (in the fourteenth century) the movement of V was more likely to be a response to the growth of T and would therefore not increase P. The quantity of coin (or uncoined bullion which is not actually the same thing) was little changed, but had to support a growing volume of trade. Merchants handling an increasing volume of trade on the same cash resources had to find ways of raising cash. Had they continued to require 10 per cent of turnover and cash balances, trade could have expanded only with a massive price deflation. (If in the twentieth century, one had continued to define 'money' in terms of the gold reserves of the Bank of England V would be a very high figure indeed.)

It has become more useful to use various broader definitions of money, but we must recognise that for each definition of M there is a corresponding value of V so that at any time (tautologically) MV will be the same whatever definition of M we choose. Traders may respond to a restriction of one particular form of M by switching to substitutes, thereby economising the use on that particular M and increasing the value of V appropriate to the definition. This explains the familiar Goodhart's Law' which states that 'whichever aggregate the monetary authorities attempt to control will prove to be the inappropriate one'. The Cambridge approach may throw light on certain periods of history distinguishing as it does between money held as convenience to trade and money held as a store of value. Historians might find it useful to adopt this approach and also perhaps to distinguish between the monetary transactions of merchants than those of private citizens.

Usury

At the beginning of the period, during the Commercial Revolution itself, the major issue was the concept of usury, the idea that it was unlawful, sinful and un-Christian to take a reward for lending money to others. The growing needs of commerce proved to be in conflict with the traditional doctrines of the Church: this conflict did much to shape the financial institutions and methods which were then developing. Whereas 'the closed economy of the barbarian period allowed only the most unjustifiable form of usury, that practised at the expense of a needy neighbour borrowing the necessaries for the means of work' they continued into

> ... a world in which capital had once again assumed a function essential for the promotion of the major undertakings of trade by sea and land. Shipowners, manufacturers and bankers all required a considerable capital which they could not get from philanthropists content with the choice either of making the fortunes of others without a share themselves or of losing everything without any compensation. The relaxation of the rules might have been expected. It was the contrary which happened.

(Cambridge Economic History of Europe vol. iii: 565)

Ashley (1919: 436–7) takes a more sympathetic view, while Henri Pirenne stresses the role of the Church as 'the indispensable money-lender of the period'. Monasteries supplied credit against land to neighbouring lords. Up to the mid-thirteenth century:

> . . . the loans were all loans for consumption . . . the money received would be spent at once, so that each sum borrowed represented a dead loss. When it prohibited usury for religious reasons, the Church therefore rendered a signal service to the agrarian society. . . . It saved it from the affliction of consumption debts from which the ancient world suffered so severely.

Situations changed and

> . . . the revival of commerce, by discovering the productivity of liquid capital, gave rise to problems to which men sought a satisfactory solution in vain. Right up to the end of the Middle Ages society continued to be torn with anxiety over the terrible question of usury, in which business practice and ecclesiastical morality found themselves directly opposed, . . . it was evaded by means of compromise and expedients.
>
> (Pirenne 1936: 121)

On the whole it does seem that instead of adapting to change, the theological attitude to usury actually hardened. The point is not merely of interest to medieval historians and theologians. The legal and moral system was quite out of line with the needs of commerce. The story of how the business community adapted by inventing 'loopholes' which the canon lawyers then tried to close will sound only too familiar to anyone whose role it has been to guide business through the maze of tax, regulatory exchange control and other laws imposed by twentieth century interventionist states.

The Christian view on usury

The Council of Nicea (325) banned the practice of usury by the clergy and the prohibitions were extended to all church members by Leo I (died 461). The Decretum Gratiani (probably about 1140) which became the standard textbook on canon law, dealt with the point and there were other developments. The basis of the Christian objection to usury is to be found in two texts, whose brevity did not inhibit dogmatic discussions on interpretation. 'Thou shalt not lend upon usury to thy brother: . . . Unto a stranger thou mayest lend upon usury but unto thy brother thou shalt not lend upon usury . . .' (Deut. 23: 19–20). The word brother was interpreted to mean all mankind but on this view, what could the writer have meant by strangers? The other text is found in Exodus: 'If thou lend money to any of my people that is poor by thee, thou shalt not be to him as an usurer neither shalt thou lay upon him usury' (Exodus 22: 25). St Thomas argued that this prohibition applied only to Jews amongst themselves, and that a Jew could exact interest from a gentile.

The loopholes

A number of loopholes were used to permit interest to be charged. Interest was permitted to indemnify the lender from actual loss, *damnum emergens* or opportunity loss, *lucrum cessens* i.e income foregone as a result of making the loan. A loan could be turned into a rent charge, and there were variations on the 'partnership' theme, leading to a rather ingenious form of organisation known as the *Contractus Trinius*.

The Roman legal code of Justinian effectively defined '*inter est*', that which 'is in between' the creditor's actual position and what it would have been if the contract had been fulfilled. It was arguably, therefore, reasonable to demand a penalty if a loan was not repaid on time. This became formalised as a conventional penalty (poena conventionalis), written into the contract. A borrower would borrow, and would in due course be expected to repay exactly the same sum. Meanwhile, on each nominal repayment date he would pay over the penalty (effectively interest) and roll over for another period. Presumably if he actually repaid on the due date the creditor would have no claim for interest. Effectively, borrower and lender could agree a rate of interest provided that there was an initial interest free period, which could be very short. Could it be dispensed with altogether? Theologians could argue for hours on such points.

The 'Deed of Partnership' was frequently used. Every act of financial participation entailed a risk, for which compensation was provided by the eventual profit; and, since the partner retained the ownership of the sum invested there was no question whatever of a 'mutuum'. The Contractus Trinius, which appeared in the late fifteenth century, raised more difficulties: it consisted of three contracts simultaneously entered into between the same parties:

1. A sleeping partnership. The investor brings his money, the merchant his work and they divide the profits.
2. An insurance against all risks whereby the investor is given a guarantee against loss in exchange for a percentage of the eventual profit.
3. The sale by the investor, for a fixed sum to be paid to him each year, of his chances of profit above a certain level.

All three, taken separately, bypass the usury provisions, but the overall effect is simply a loan for interest. The church authorities tried to look through the form to the substance, and over the years kept tightening up the rules. Ashley (1913: 411) suggests that the practice grew up independently of the need to avoid the usury laws.

Another form of transaction was the annuity or rent-charge, a kind of sale and leaseback. This could be achieved by a sale of a property with all its rights, including the right to receive the rent roll, and the near-simultaneous repurchase without this right. Later, this was extended as a common way of obtaining a fixed income. The owner of the property alienated against a perpetual annuity had a title which could be negotiated by its vendor, effectively by first 'buying' (or purporting to buy) a piece of land on this basis and simultaneously 'selling' it to parties who had entered a transaction which in substance amounted to an interest bearing loan on the security of the property.

Pirenne (1936: 137) refers to the creation of house rents as the most general form of medieval credit. He points out the distinction between a 'live' (vif)gage where rents contribute to the payment of principal and a 'dead' (mort)gage where it did not.

An important source of capital for the municipalities was the sale of 'life rents' for one or two lives (annuities certain). These were a popular investment for prosperous citizens. 'Neither municipal accounts nor individual memoranda recoil before the word "usury", but in documents intended for the public the reality was dissimulated' (Pirenne 1936: 129).

It appears that, as loopholes were invented, attitudes hardened (Nelson 1949). Specifically, although it was virtually impossible for the Church to restrict the use of Bills for genuine commercial transactions: i.e. where the Bill was originally drawn to pay for goods purchased and which were in transit, fictitious bills, drawn solely as a cloak for a money lending transaction, were another matter. This was known as dry exchange or *cambio secco*, which the Church tried to outlaw.

> Profits derived by money-changers and bankers presented the moralists with a problem. Transfers from one currency to another . . . were an opportunity for usurious speculations. . . . Nevertheless the cambium was a necessity for the Apostolic Chamber no less than for those who frequented fairs. . . . Theologians . . . in spite of reservations . . . generally admitted a premium which was justified by the money changer's time and trouble and the risks attending carriage.
>
> (Cambridge Economic History of Europe vol. iii 1971: 568–9)

Islam

Moslems today use the *mudaraba*, a simple, but apparently flexible partner-ship between investor and entrepreneur, or the *musharaka*, where profit is distributed pro rata to capital. Islamic banks offer 'deposit account' holders a share in the profit of a pooled fund, with the bank acting as fiduciary agents, charging an agreed management fee. Depositors can apparently share in the profit of the bank itself.

14

CREDIT AND THE TRADE FAIRS

INTRODUCTION

The commercial revolution, the dramatic revival of trade and commerce which began in Western Europe around 1150, was to a large extent the creation of merchants who, starting with the simple concept of a trade fair as a meeting place, developed what was virtually a separate political and legal system. They negotiated rights of trade, passage and protection with rulers whose archaic laws were quite unsuited to the needs of the developing society, and simply put their own system in its place. This, surely, was a quicker and more effective means of creating the framework needed for a market economy than waiting for, or trying to engineer, changes in the complex web of feudal and ecclesiastical law and custom of the time.

Chapter 3 has described how the coinage towards the end of the twelfth century consisted of no coin larger than a penny (in most countries, other than England and Scotland, even that was sadly debased), and Chapter 4 explained how gold and large silver coins were then introduced to meet the needs of trade. There was a parallel development. This period also saw the growth of credit as the means of settling large international transactions without the physical expense and risk of transporting coined or uncoined bullion. In due course various types of bills of exchange would develop into paper money, while the concept of banking also has its roots in this period.

This book is about the history of *money*, which is separate from, though intimately connected with the history of trade, of public finance and financial capitalism, and of banking institutions. This chapter in particular will need to look a little beyond the narrower subject.

THE HISTORY AND PURPOSE OF THE TRADE FAIRS

The medieval trade fairs, in their classic form, grew to prominence as trade revived in the 1100s, reached a peak in about 1250, and had effectively served their main purpose, from the point of view of the history of money, by about 1400. These trade fairs were quite different in purpose from the local fairs and markets which have a far longer history and which are still to be found today (Postan 1973). The trade fairs were meeting places for professional merchants, open to all regardless of nationality or the type of goods they wished to buy and sell. 'They may perhaps be compared with international exhibitions, for they excluded nothing and nobody; every individual, no matter what his country, every article which could be bought and sold, whatever its nature was assured of a welcome' (Pirenne 1936: ch. iv, part ii).

Since the middle of the twelfth century, cloth merchants and others had been coming to trade fairs in Champagne and Flanders. Rulers, notably the Counts of Champagne, set out deliberately to offer *conduits des foires* (safe conducts and protection) to visiting merchants and to encourage their activities. Custodes nundiarum, 'guards of the fairs' maintained order. Treaties with neighbouring potentates, such as the Duke of Burgundy, extended protection for the journey to and from the fair. Bautier (1971 ch. iv) describes how trade between Flanders and the South expanded from 1169, as testified by receipts at the Bapaume toll-house. In 1174 Milanese merchants began attending the Champagne trade fairs, where they bought, for export to the Orient, cloth brought from Flanders and Arras. They were soon joined by others, and by 1180 the pattern was established. In Champagne there was a regular series of six trade fairs staggered over the year in Lagny, Bar, Provins, and Troyes, the last two having two annual fairs each. These are not, and were not, particularly important towns in their own right but became great trading centres. Much of the trade seems to have been between Flanders and Italy and thence East. The Flemish drapers would set up their tents and exhibit their cloth. 'Clerks of the fairs' could travel freely, carrying correspondence, between Champagne and Flanders. Each of the six fairs had a fairly standard pattern:

> to begin with there was a week during which merchandise was exempt from taxes; then there was the cloth fair, then the leather fair and the *avoirs du poids* (goods sold by weight: wax, cotton, spices etc.); finally came the concluding stage when debts incurred during the fair were settled. The complete cycle lasted from fifteen days to two full months for each fair.
>
> (Bautier 1971: 111)

A particular privilege was the 'franchise': exemption from legal action for crimes committed, or debts incurred, outside the trade fair. It also suspended lawsuits and their execution for so long as the peace of the fair lasted. Pirenne says the most precious of all was the suspension of the prohibition of usury, but it may not have been quite as simple as that.

Eventually, contracts made at one trade fair were valid, and could be enforced, anywhere in the system 'sur le corps des foires' or supra corpus nundiarum (Bautier 1971: 113) and the fairs developed their own legal system for the settlement and arbitration of claims. Although merchants were protected from outside claims during the 'peace of the fair' obligations entered into within the trade fair system were strictly enforced by what was effectively a substantial and well staffed private enterprise legal or arbitration system created by the merchants themselves. If a merchant refused to recognise the jurisdiction, the dispute was reported to his own city or state. If they failed to enforce a judgment the fair officials could pronounce the 'interdict of the fairs' against the offending city, all of whose merchants, and not only the offender, would be banned. This sort of lay excommunication was a very powerful deterrent. The general community of merchants had a strong interest in enforcing the system: in a closely knit community self regulation works splendidly. (Some interesting examples of the similar powers of the Hanseatic League are given in Bautier 1971: 126. He refers to them as a 'boycott' in contrast with the 'interdict' of Champagne.)

Groups of merchants from one city or area doing business in a particular foreign market tended to form themselves into a 'hanse' using their collective power to negotiate concessions, and to achieve a certain degree of self-government. Bautier points out that the Italians from independent and often mutually hostile cities assembled as a 'nation', which 'perhaps gave birth to the idea of nationhood' (Bautier 1971: 112–13 and Carus-Wilson 1967: p. xvii ff). There was 'a fantastic rise in the cloth industry of north-western Europe' now sold via Italian merchants into Italy and to the East. In Florence, an expanding industry dyed and prepared the cloth.

The action was not only in Champagne. Other rulers, particularly those controlling alpine passes, sought a share of the potential revenue. The merchants, though competing vigorously between themselves, 'formed a kind of users' syndicate', used collective bargaining to play off rivalries and to secure reductions in tariffs and substantial road improvements, including the effective opening of the St Gotthard pass in 1225 (Bautier 1971: 116–17). Marseilles became an important port and Louis IX of France (St Louis) tried to create an export harbour under his own control at Aiguesmortes.

Northern trade developed along similar lines. From Flanders and Bruges there were connections via Cologne, and a close link developed with the English wool industry via trade fairs in St Ives (Clapham 1957: 151), St Giles, Winchester and St Botolph, Boston. The English monarchy replaced full free trade with a 'system of export licences, associated with personal safe-conducts for the merchants, and levies of "reasonable" taxes' (Bautier 1971: 120).

The German Hanse was an alliance of mercantile cities in the Baltic who came together to safeguard their position in the trade between Bruges and Novgorod. Lübeck was founded in 1150. Its inhabitants were exempt from tolls throughout Saxony. Fur, honey and wax from Russia were exchanged for the ubiquitous Flemish cloth. New towns were founded along the Baltic including Rostock (1200), Wismar (1228), Straslund (1234), Stettin

(Szczecin) (1237) and Danzig (Gdansk) (1238). These, and many other towns, some inland, enjoyed the privileges of Lübeck. In 1251, the Germans founded Stockholm as a base for trading with Sweden (Bautier 1971: 122–4). As with the network of mainly Italian merchants based on the Champagne Fairs, the merchants of these cities obtained a substantial degree of self governance, independent economic power and freedom from political restrictions in their commercial activities. Allied in various leagues, they eventually came together at the end of the thirteenth century in the Hanseatic League. They acquired privileges from, among others, the English crown, and had their own enclave, the Steelyard, in the City of London (Clapham 1967: 150).

> Clearly . . . the political organisation of the free Hanse towns was far more effective than that of the surrounding territorial states. This was the unique objective of Hanseatic external policy, while royal or ducal governments had to play a game complicated by dynastic entanglements, greed for military glory, social privileges and territorial disintegration.
>
> (*Cambridge Economic History* 1971 vol. iii: 389)

Later, the fairs (in this form) began to decline. In part this was because there was less need for the fairs, thanks to the system's very success. Merchants, instead of travelling personally, came to stay more at home and to operate through a network of correspondents. (They could use the credit mechanisms which had developed during the trade fairs.) Goods, which had previously been transported overland across Europe, could now be sent by ship from Italy and the East to England and Flanders.

There was also a sharp decline in actual trade. After a century of peace there started in 1294 the series of conflicts constituting the so called Hundred Years War, while the Black Death of 1348 reduced the population of Europe by 30 or 40 per cent. This brought a serious check to economic development, but not to the development of business and financial techniques. When the concept of the fairs was revived, the aims were different. The towns put on entertainments and facilities, and generally sought to encourage merchants to foregather, in the hope of stirring up lucrative tourist trade.

The role of the fairs in monetary history

A major problem, during the Commercial Revolution, was how to reconcile the attitude of the Church to usury with the need of merchants to borrow (Chapter 13). An important loophole, in terms of the development of the money economy, was to be found at the trade fairs, which thus had a major role in the history of money as well as of trade. Payments between merchants were often settled by promises to pay at a future date. Originally these took the form of notarised contracts, often expressed in foreign currency, but in due course these became formalised and standardised as bills of exchange. Payment was usually expressed to be made at a particular fair, and in some cases settlement of debts became a major function of the fair, with money changers and bankers joining the throng of merchants. There were two major advantages, quite apart from access to the merchants' own trusted legal system.

First, a clearing house could be set up within the fair. Debts due could be netted off. Coin need only be transported (a perilous activity) to meet any trade deficit or surplus between areas. Merchant A from Venice, owes money for imports, while B is owed for exports. They can be brought together, and settle cash back home. To begin with, physical presence at the fair, in person or through an agent, was needed but in due course correspondent networks could achieve the same end. It became apparent that payments from one place to another could be made more simply quickly and cheaply by sending bills of exchange, rather than coin. This saved the expense of heavily armed escorts, of reminting to local currency (at about 2 per cent, this was not quite as steep as what the banks charge today for retail foreign exchange transactions) and of delay itself. The bills could in due course be netted off and cleared through the trade fair system, and meanwhile constituted an acceptable store of value. The Church used the system for collecting St Peter's Pence (the contributions of the faithful) and disseminating its funds: this core business helped establish the pre-eminence of the Italian merchant bankers of this time (O'Sullivan 1962; de Roover 1948). Although it was eventually necessary to settle differences with coin (there were regular trade flows) transport could often be associated with a visit by a king or an ambassador who in any case needed an armed guard.

Second, properly drawn trade bills in a foreign currency could bypass the usury laws. Today, if a banker is offered a bill of exchange for $10,000 due in three months, and is asked for immediate sterling, he will first convert the value into sterling using not the spot, but the 'forward' exchange rate. He will then 'discount' this amount to allow for three months' interest. A medieval banker might, indeed almost certainly would, make this two stage calculation, but would quote only a 'forward exchange rate' which would include a carefully concealed element of interest. A great deal of trouble would be taken to disguise the true nature of the transaction and to placate the theologians.

In some cases, the main purpose of the fair became to exchange bills, often bills created for the sole purpose of arranging a commercial loan outside the scope of the usury laws. Genoa bankers found it advisable to carry on operations through bills on the Besançon market, while the Florentines used Lyons. For a time, the foreign exchange markets of London and Bruges were dominated by Italians, who needed to carry on their money lending business in a foreign currency. The 'fair' period therefore ushered in a revolution in methods of money transmission between countries, and of the use of (concealed) debt instruments. It was the foundation on which the future history of banking was to be based.

15

THE DEVELOPMENT OF BANKING AND FINANCE

INTRODUCTION

The trade fairs described in Chapter 14 led in their turn to more sophisticated financial arrangements which made it less necessary for merchants to travel. Although the Black Death of 1348 brought a check to economic development, financial techniques continued to improve. The commercial revolution of the fourteenth century had already seen the development of Bills of Exchange, and of banking houses in Italy and elsewhere which lent money to finance both the commercial needs of merchants and the political follies of the crowned heads of Europe.

> . . . the fourteenth century, especially, was one of continuous progress, innovation and experimentation. The draft form of a bill of exchange, for example, although known before 1350, did not come into general use until after that date. The same applies to marine insurance. Mercantile bookkeeping too did not reach full maturity until 1400. . . . Another innovation introduced after 1375 was a combination of partnerships similar to the modern holding company. The best example of this are the Medici Banking Houses founded in 1397.
>
> (de Roover 1971: 44)

These developments started in the great Italian trading cities such as Florence and Venice. German cities followed, but Amsterdam and London were eventually to become the most important financial centres. These operations oiled the wheels of commerce. They reduced the size of the 'convenience' balances of precious metals merchants would otherwise have to maintain to be able to take advantage of opportunities in the market. By enabling merchants to settle accounts by Bills of Exchange they reduced the need for the metals to be transported backwards and forwards between countries and cities. They thus helped the stock of metallic money to work harder, increasing its effective velocity of circulation, without creating any new paper instrument that we would recognise as constituting 'money'.

This chapter summarises developments over a long period, until the outbreak of the Napoleonic Wars. This period is covered, in far more detail, in histories of banking, and of particular banks (notably the Bank of England) as institutions. The South Sea Bubble is covered in more detail in Chapter 16: the present chapter gives a selection of events relevant to the history of money as such.

THE BANK OF AMSTERDAM

Arguably the first real bank, as we understand the term, was the Bank of Amsterdam, founded in 1609 and described in Adam Smith's 'Digression concerning Banks of Deposit' in the *Wealth of Nations*. Before 1609

> ... the great quantity of clipt and worn foreign coin, which the extensive trade of Amsterdam brought from all parts of Europe, reduced the value of its currency about nine per cent below that of good money fresh from the mint. ... In order to remedy this inconvenience, a bank was established in 1609 under the guarantee of the city. The bank received both foreign coin, and the light and worn coin of the country at its real intrinsic value in good standard money of the country deducting only so much as was necessary for defraying the expense of coinage, and the other necessary expense of management.

If that was the end of the story it would in concept have been nothing more or less than a 'mint' operating in the way discussed in Part I. However, Adam Smith continued,

> For the value which remained ... it gave a credit in its books. This credit was called bank money, which as it represented money exactly according to the standard of the mint, was always of the same real value and intrinsically worth more than current money.

Merchants were required to settle all bills in excess of 600 florins in bank money and in practice they kept accounts with the bank to pay foreign bills of exchange. In addition to its 'intrinsic superiority to currency' (although, surely, only to clipped currency) it had other advantages.

> It is secure from fire, robbery and other accidents. The City of Amsterdam is bound for it; it can be paid away by a simple transfer without the trouble of counting, or the risk of transporting it from one place to another.
>
> (Adam Smith 1776/1950: 444–55)

Melon states 'every Person who hath an Account opened in a Bank, must pay ten Florins for it, and one Styver for every transfer afterwards made in the Account' (20 styvers = 1 florin). It actually commanded a premium or agio even over a fully valued coin, and the quick witted could profit from variations in this.

To prevent the stock-jobbing tricks . . . the bank has of late years come to the resolution to sell at all times bank money for currency at five per cent agio and to buy it again at four per cent agio. In consequence of this resolution the agio can never either rise above five or sink below four per cent.

(Melon translated Bindon 1738: 343)

According to Adam Smith 'the Bank of Amsterdam professes to lend out no part of what is deposited with it (and therefore maintained a 100 per cent reserve ratio). It made its profit, as does a mint on the superior value and convenience of the money it produces over the value of the bullion bought into it.

The bank is under the direction of the four reigning burgermasters who are changed every year. Each new set of burgermasters visited the treasure, compares it with the books, receives it up on oath, and delivers it over with the same awful solemnity to the set which succeeds; and in that sober and religious country oaths are not yet disregarded.

(Adam Smith)

Melon, however states.

. . . it cannot be supposed that the State suffers such immense Treasures to remain intirely useless in their Vaults. . . . it is not amiss to take notice, that the Bank supplieth the Lombard Houses with Money to lend out upon pledges.

(Melon)

The Bank charged depositors as a 'sort of warehouse rent', depositors paying a quarter per cent per six months for depositing silver and half per cent for depositing gold (the distinction puzzled Adam Smith as well as us). Other charges are made on transactions. The Bank made a profit for its 'box' on the difference between the 4 per cent and 5 per cent agios and was often able to dispose of foreign coin on the market at a profit over the intrinsic value that had been paid.

The Amsterdam precedent was quickly followed by other major cities. The Bank of Hamburg was formed in 1619 and the Bank of Sweden in 1656 (Melon 1738: 347). The Bank of Sweden made the first issue of actual bank notes in Europe, in 1661. Heckscher (van Dillen 1964: 169) admits that 'the certificates issued before that time by the Italian banks had some of the qualities of bank notes', but differed first, in that they were not even in form issued against deposits and second 'their amounts were in round numbers, given on printed forms'. They were issued as an emergency measure and were withdrawn in 1664. They went to a premium, perhaps because Sweden was on a copper standard.

Adam Smith notes with approval how the Bank of Amsterdam survived the emergency of 1672 when the French armies were closing in Amsterdam. However, shortly after the publication of the *Wealth of Nations*, trouble of a different type hit those responsible for the direction of the bank, many of whom were also directors of the Dutch East India Company. It will hardly surprise readers to learn that, in these circumstances, the bank began making loans to the latter, and in 1780, under pressure of the war with England, to the City of Amsterdam itself. The Bank was eventually wound up in 1819. The other two fared better. The Bank of Hamburg survived to be absorbed into the German Reichsbank. The Bank of Sweden was taken over by the State in 1668, becoming the world's first central bank. It celebrated its third centenary as such (in 1968) by founding the Nobel Prize in Economics. There was a reminder of Dutch pre-eminence when, in 1947, the Bank of England was nationalised. A surprising number of holders receiving compensation proved to be the Dutch descendants of original subscribers in 1694.

BANKING IN ENGLAND

Banking was relatively slow to develop in London. Until 1640 the Tower of London had in effect provided merchants and others with a reliable safe deposit service. Other banking services, notably money transmission and accounting, were provided by scriveners, to whom merchants delegated their day to day financial dealings. These scriveners were professional agents, who kept books, transferred money and organised investments for one or more merchants and generally acted for their clients in the same way that the steward or 'man of business' of a landowner would act for his employer. These simple, and at first workable, arrangements were to change. The first step towards the development of 'goldsmith bankers' came when the goldsmiths persuaded the scriveners to 'deposit' cash with them in return for a small payment, which amounted to interest. The object, at that stage, was not to make a turn by relending the money, but simply to take the opportunity to pick over the coins. The goldsmiths were already developing a lucrative business in foreign exchange. They had the skill and the equipment to weigh, assay, and determine the precious metal content of the coins passing through their hands. The better ones (those where the specie value exceeded the tale value) were culled out and went straight into the melting pot to be sold as bullion for a very useful extra profit. The higher the turnover the greater the profit, and it was worthwhile to pay to borrow the cash passing through the hands of a scrivener or merchant.

Subsequent developments were intimately tied up with the financial problems of Charles I and Charles II. There had been monetary difficulties between 1618 and 1622. The average annual output of the mint now exceeded the whole amount struck during Elizabeth's recoinage:

There was thrown upon a depreciated currency an enormous amount of full-weight coin. Between 1630 and 1640 something like 7 millions of good silver must have issued from the Tower. There was a profit to be made upon the export of every penny of it.

(Feaveryear 1931: 92)

Whatever the cause, there was certainly a deflationary shortage of specie. In 1625 it was proposed to reduce the silver content to stop the bimetallic outflow. In 1626 a proposal to issue £300,000 of debased shillings was opposed in a speech by Sir Thomas Roe (1626). 'In the discussions of 1625–6 the culling and bullion trades had been severely criticised. It has now been proposed to re-establish the Royal Exchequer with a monopoly of dealings in foreign coin and bullion' (Supple 1959: 191; see also Ruding 1840: 382).

There had been a rejected proposal to issue debased shillings to raise money for the Crown. Charles went to the goldsmiths, asked for a loan of £300,000 in return for not debasing the currency. This was refused, and in 1640 he seized assets deposited in the Tower. This is generally thought to have been the incident which destroyed the Tower's credibility as a safe deposit and led to the development of banking, although Feaveryear (1931: 95) in a footnote, takes a different view. Eventually the bullion was returned in exchange for loans secured on tax revenues (his successor was to default on these) but confidence in the Tower as a safe deposit was shaken. Merchants began depositing money directly with goldsmiths on their reputation as men of substance at a rate of interest and presumably in the knowledge that they would deploy this money profitably. The scriveners, as professional men, held money in trust and were guilty of a criminal offence if they applied it in any way for their own purposes. (It is not clear whether they were acting legally in accepting money from the goldsmiths in return for the right to cull coins.) Goldsmiths were under no such professional duty. The only remedy against them, if they failed to repay, was a civil one. The cynic's definition of a banker as 'a lawyer, who can speculate with his clients' account without going to jail' has some basis in history.

The goldsmiths had become bankers, providing the services of a 'running cash'; that is a current account. Not only merchants but also landowners looked to them for safe keeping during the upheavals of the civil war.

Tax policy

A little later Charles I ran into tax problems. He had been brought up in the tradition of absolute ruler and tried to rule without Parliament. The period of 'personal rule' dates from the removal of the Duke of Buckingham in 1628: no Parliaments were called from 1629 to 1640 and the King resorted to several expedients to raise money including the sale of monopolies and of baronetcies. This is not a history of taxation, and still less of the constitutional issues which precipitated the English Revolution and the King's execution. However, tax measures and disputes do go a long way to explain this stage in the development of banking. Having failed to secure Parliamentary subsidies in 1628 and 1629 Charles, and his advisers Weston (Lord Treasurer) and Cottington (Chancellor) resorted to a number of expedients (Coward 1980: 142).

Resistance to tonnage and poundage collapsed in 1629 and customs duties became an important part of the Royal revenues in the 1630s. Commissioners were appointed in 1630 to fine anyone holding land worth at least £40 per annum who had not been knighted. This was upheld by the exchequer barons. Ship money was intended to become a permanent land tax, and was extended to inland counties from June 1635. This 'met with more disapproval than meets most new tax demands' (Coward 1980: 144). John Hampden of Yorkshire refused to pay. He was tried in 1637 and was convicted by a seven to five majority of judges. This 'moral victory' stiffened the resolve of the objectors but it seems that in fact 90 per cent of the tax due was paid (see St John 1640 and Parker 1640).

The Commonwealth

Commercial business continued to develop during the Commonwealth, when, after the Civil War and the execution of Charles I, Cromwell became Lord Protector. During this period Andreades places great stress on Cromwell's tolerance of the Jews, many of whom came from Amsterdam and elsewhere to develop banking businesses.

'The Stop of the Exchequer'

Charles II was restored to the throne in 1660. His financial needs were pressing and, like his father, he raised finance by assigning the yield of certain taxes to the goldsmiths as security for loans. In 1672 'The Stop of the Exchequer', the security was in effect removed. The loans were frozen and converted into 5 per cent perpetual annuities. It was hoped that those to whom the goldsmiths owed money would accept assignment. In 1683 the king stopped paying interest. Ming-Hsun Li asks

> . . . were the goldsmiths prosperous after 1672? Some writers main-
> tained that despite the episode the position of goldsmiths had improved
> steadily afterwards for the 'stoppage' was no more than a partial
> suspension of payment of interest by the Exchequer on its loans.
>
> (Li 1963: 33)

However, it certainly seems that interest was paid during the reign of James II. There were 44 goldsmiths in 1677, but only 12 or 14 in 1695. This cannot be explained by mergers. There were runs on the goldsmiths in 1674, 1678, 1682, and 1688.

The rights and wrongs of the goldsmiths's position were much discussed, some important points of constitutional law. It was argued that 'the letters patent by which Charles had recognised his debt to each of the goldsmiths had been ratified by the House of Lords but had never been presented to the House of Commons and had not passed into law' (Andreades 1909: 41). The goldsmiths brought an action before the Exchequer Court in 1689 (won in 1691). Lord Sommers declared the exchequer court was not competent (Sommers 1733).

Foundation of the Bank of England

In 1694 the country was at war. The immediate problem (again) was public finance. The private banking system was developing nicely, spurred on in part by the justified suspicion of anything that related to the public sector, or the King, and there was no public demand for a public bank. Clapham's famous History opens with these words

> The establishment of the Bank of England can be treated, like many historical events great and small, either as curiously accidental or as all but inevitable. Had the country not been at war in 1694 the government would hardly have been disposed to offer a favourable charter to a corporation which proposed to lend it money. Had Charles Montague, Chancellor of the Exchequer, not thought that out of several scores of financial schemes submitted to him this was the most promising, there would again have been no charter or, perhaps, a different one.
>
> (Clapham 1970 vol. i: 1)

Various attempts were made at this time to set up 'land banks', based on the security of land. These represent a different (and abortive) potential trend, and are discussed in Chapter 22.

Development of stock markets

Stock markets were already established (Morgan and Thomas 1962) as is confirmed by the following extract from a 1695 Act of Parliament 'to Restrain the Number and Ill Practice of Brokers and Stockjobbers'.

> And for the further Preventing the Mischiefs and Inconveniencies that do daily arise to Trade, . . . be itt further enacted . . . That every Policy, Contract, Bargain or Agreement Made and Entred into . . . upon which any *Proemium* already is or . . . shall be Given or Paid, for liberly to Put upon, or to Deliver, Receive, Accept or Refute any Share

or Interest in any Joint Stock, Talleys, Orders, Exchequer Bills, Exchequer Tickets, or Bank Bills whatsoever . . . shall be utterly null and void . . .

Option dealing was becoming a scandal and must be stopped – in 1697! There were also penalties and transitional provisions. However it was provided that 'no Person for Buying any Cattel, Corn or any other Provisions, or Coal, shall be Esteemed a Broker'. Option dealings were not invented in the Twentieth Century. By about 1700, therefore, many of the mechanisms of banking and finance, but not paper money, were in place.

After the South Sea Bubble

For half a century after the events of 1720, there were no major dramas – until 1776 and the events associated with the American and French Revolutions. The currency was stably based on the UK recoinage of 1696 and its equivalents elsewhere. Paper money was used, but still as a convenient means of money transmission, rather than a major component of money supply. The period was also a great age of European music and drama and (more relevant) of economic thought. Tidily, the seminal work on economics, Adam Smith's *Wealth of Nations* was published in 1776, also the year of the American Revolution and the start of another exciting period of financial upheaval. Smith's main concern was with trade: David Hume (1752) in a few succinct essays, probably had more influence on monetary thought.

The development of a permanent National Debt had been a major factor in the birth of the Bank of England – and of the South Sea Bubble. Walpole had begun the 'funding' of the Debt in 1717. The South Sea Bubble having burst, the company still remained the intermediary for much of the Debt. Robert Walpole, later first Earl of Orford, was again Prime Minister from 1721–44. His first financial task was to deal with the collapse of the South Sea Bubble, but his Ministry was noted for its (fairly successful) attempt to reduce the National Debt by means of a Sinking Fund and to negotiate downwards the rate of interest on this debt (Dowell 1884 vol. ii: 9).

There was a fiercely fought battle of the pamphlets beginning with Nathaniel Gould's *Essay on the Public Debts* (1727). Gould had been elected Governor of the Bank in 1711, defying a hard fought Tory challenge to the established Whig order. Little is recorded about Gould's policies and achievements in office. Pulteney's several pamphlets, appear to concentrate on attacking the figures. Gould himself replies as does Walpole himself anonymously in 1835. Sir John Barnard (he of the Jobbing Act) was a 'dry' critic of Walpole, who he did not think had gone far enough in reducing the burden of public debt. In 1737 he proposed that the debt should be put on a 3 per cent basis, and that this should be a condition of the renewal of the Bank of England's Charter in 1742 (Clapham 1970 vol. i: 93–4).

The crisis of 1763

The crisis in 1763 had its roots on the Continent (Hoppit 1986: 49 ff. and Clapham 1970 vol. i: 236 ff.). This coincided with the end of the Seven Years War, (1756–63) the raising of Prussian loans for post-war reconstruction and a financial crash in Amsterdam. In England, according to Clapham, there had been 'no acute banking pressure' during the War although the Government had borrowed heavily. 'The British coin in the Vault is first recorded as dangerously low in the statement for 31st August 1763, six months after peace was signed'. The 'delicate' situation was 'worth careful examination because the year 1763 was one of great international tension. There was no true crisis and no collapse' in London 'although the Bank's August statement showed' what a nice thing it had been with metal reserves (including till money and other earmarked amounts) down to £367,000 against a note circulation of £5,315,000. There was a disruption of international monetary links, and it was perhaps the first case of a crisis largely involved with the private rather than public finance.

The crisis of 1772

'What distinguishes financial crises after 1770 from those before is that they were in a large part caused by economic growth'. They were also no longer based on problems with public credit: private business credit played its part (Hoppit 1986: 51). He points out that businessmen now needed a greater financial freedom to raise funds. They created credit by 'raising money by circulation', drawing and redrawing accommodation bills and notes on each without actually having traded goods at all. This is the technique that we would refer to as 'cheque kiting'. However, this worked only for projects offering a quick return and not for long gestation projects. Such crises 'can all be seen as the early growing pains of the first industrialising nation'.

By the end of the century public finance and private trade were inextricably linked while banking was a commonplace. The story of Part II is now interrupted, in much of the world, by a period of inconvertible money, the subject of Part III.

16

THE SOUTH SEA BUBBLE: 1720

One of the most extraordinary events in British financial history, the South Sea Bubble of 1720 has many parallels with John Law, the Mississippi scheme and his remarkable attempts to create a new financial and monetary system in France. This also collapsed in 1720. Although in terms of speculative mania the two incidents are remarkably similar, the political background is quite different. In France, developments were masterminded by a Scottish adventurer in a despotic, inefficient, and corrupt state. In England, the bubble developed in a democratic and financially sophisticated society: the events had their roots in the political rivalries between whigs and tories. There is another difference, which is why the two incidents are dealt with in different parts of this book. John Law created one of the earlier attempts at inconvertible paper money: in England the monetary system, as such, was never seriously threatened. Public finance, though, was transformed. The period marked:

> ... the advance of stock-jobbing from a private commerce to a public menace, of corruption from an urbane traffic to a scandalous conspiracy ... of company promoting from a dull industry to a fine art ... Noblemen pawned their estates and booksellers endowed hospitals.
> (Erleigh 1933: 2)

THE EARLY HISTORY

By 1710 public life in England had settled down under the Protestant Succession. The country had had a sound coinage since 1696 while the Bank of England, founded in 1694, was closely allied to the whig government, and regarded itself as indispensable to its financial operations of the Exchequer. Britain's finances had been strained by the War of the Spanish Succession (1702–14) and the government had a floating debt of some £9 million. Total debt had increased from £664,000 in 1688 to £36 million by 1714.

The tory, Robert Harley, (later the Earl of Oxford) toppled the whig ministry of Marlborough and Godolphin in August 1710, becoming

138

Chancellor of the Exchequer, and after an election in October, Chief Minister. According to Erleigh p.15 in 1710 Harley published two pamphlets, on Credit and on Loans, ghosted by Defoe. One of his first tasks was to deal with the finances, and with the alleged corruption and profiteering in the provisioning of the forces, by the type of 'moneyed men' his allies in the October Club wished to exclude from Parliament. An expert committee was set up, mainly of Harley's cronies but including John Aislabie, the Member for Ripon. The Bank of England was under the control of the whigs, and had calculated on them remaining in power. Harley could expect little help from them with his financial problems. Meanwhile, a rival financial group was waiting in the wings, hoping that a change of government would give them the opportunity to challenge the Bank's virtual monopoly.

The Sword Blade Company's original sword business became unprofitable and was closed down. John Blunt, a scrivener, had taken over the charter in 1700 (as what we would regard as a 'shell' company) and proceeded to use it for the financial operations of his syndicate, including George Caswell, Elias Turner and Jacob Sawbridge. Daniel Defoe, by far the best of what we would call 'investigative financial journalists' of the day, referred to them as the 'three capital sharpers of England ... together a complete triumvirate of thieving' (Carswell 1960: 34). In 1707, when the Bank of England's charter came up for renewal, the Sword Blade Company attempted unsuccessfully to challenge its monopoly of public finance. The Bank, in turn, succeeded for a time in having the company banned from banking business. Not for long. The Sword Blade Company went on to become the Sword Blade Bank, official banker to the South Sea Company. In 1711 its directors, Caswell, Blunt and Crowley, together with Prime Minister Harley, devised a proposal to form a new chartered company, the South Sea Company to fund the floating debt. Those who were owed money by the government had the opportunity of exchanging this debt for shares in the South Sea Company. Alternatively, shares could be sold for cash subscriptions which would be used to pay off this debt.

How was the government meant to gain by this? An accumulation of short term liabilities, totalling £9 million, would be replaced by a single long term obligation carrying interest totalling £576,532 per annum: 6 per cent plus management charges. This removed the day-to-day problem of treasury management and restored the government's creditworthiness. Much of the short term debt at that time took the form of extended credit provided, not altogether willingly, by suppliers to the navy. More puzzlingly, what was in it for the investors? They exchanged a short term debt due from the government for shares in the South Sea Company which, they expected, would then pay dividends. At this stage of the operation, the only source of income to the company was the interest to be paid by the government. Even if one took the view (which Daniel Defoe for one most emphatically did not) that the promoters of the company were honest and public spirited gentlemen, management expenses and director's fees were bound to nibble into the cash flow. Why, therefore, did the investors not simply lend money to the government and cut out these middle-men?

The answer is in two parts. First, shares in a joint stock company were, in those days, more marketable than government debt. The investor was exchanging an illiquid asset for one that could more readily be realised. British governments up to that date had seen successive debts as a temporary problem, generally caused by some war or other. With hindsight we can see that the need for government to develop a permanent method of long term funding goes back, certainly to 1688 and arguably to 1660, but it was to be another 100 years before anything approaching today's sophisticated market in gilt edged securities would develop. The second inducement offered to the investor was that the government granted a monopoly right or trading privilege (in this case the right to trade in the South Seas) as a sweetener to the company. Investors therefore hoped for profits over and above those earned from the interest on the debt.

The South Sea proposals were not particularly original and were based on what was by then an established practice. The Bank of England itself had been granted its charter in 1694 in return for providing a loan of £1.2 million, and in 1696 the 'ingrafting of tallies' had converted another £1 million. The East India Company had been chartered in 1698 in return for a loan of £2 million, and the Sword Blade Company had itself undertaken a similar operation in 1702. The distinguishing feature of the 1711 South Sea proposal was not its originality, but its size. In one operation it would convert rather more government debt than the total converted over 10 years by the Bank of England and the East India Company together.

The South Sea Company was granted by charter a monopoly of trade to the east coast of South America, south of the Orinoco, together with the whole of the west coast. These privileges were of little use so long as Spain effectively controlled the area. The hawks of the day (typically whigs and 'moneyed men') enthused over the prospect of an aggressive challenge to Spain's trading position but the war with Spain was not popular and most people (Tories, the landed, and the general population) found, to echo Lord Chesterfield 'the expense damnable'. Politics, diplomacy, war and the trading future of the South Sea Company were inextricably intermingled. The story is well summarised in Sperling's essay (1962), and told at more length by Carswell (1960). The failure of the Darien scheme to plant a British (in fact predominantly Scottish) colony on the Isthmus of Panama, had coloured thinking to some extent. The South Sea Company's trading position would have been viable had the Spaniards surrendered the 'security ports' to enable the British navy to police trade with the area. This was never achieved, and the company had to make do with the assignment of the Asiento trading agreement. Its trading achievements, never substantial, were less important than the company's role in public finance.

The Asiento assignment did have some financial consequences. The treaty provided that 28 per cent of the profits were to go to the King of Spain (understandable, expected and acceptable) but there was also a surprising provision reserving 22.5 per cent of the profits to Queen Anne and 7.5 per cent to one Menesers Gilligum, doubtless a front for various fixers and courtiers who had intermediated in the transaction. The South Sea Company directors argued that the Queen and Mr Gilligum should be required to put up their due proportion of the capital and eventually succeeded, after a parliamentary row, in getting these profit shares assigned to themselves. The financial activities were another matter. Subscriptions of £3.1 million were received by the end of July 1711, and nearly £9.2 million by the end of the year. The company did not at first have an unencumbered first charge on the government revenues and interest was sometimes received in arrears.

On average the open market value of the government securities which were exchanged into South Sea stock was £68, i.e. a discount of 32 per cent from par. Thus, although the nominal subscription price was £100, the effective price was only £68. Some historians say that it was not until October 1716 that the stock reached par, i.e. £100, but this is misleading: this would represent a capital gain on the real subscription price of nearly 50 per cent and an annual rate of capital appreciation (in addition to the dividends) of 7.5 per cent. These were very attractive returns in a period of relative price stability, although they pale into insignificance when compared with later events.

Modern readers will hardly be surprised to learn that the funding did not finally clear up the government's borrowing requirements. During the next 3 years a further £6 million was raised, mostly in the form of exchequer bills, but by September 1714, the long term debt had risen to a total of some £40 million. Some £9 million was owed to the South Sea Company, and over £3 million each to the Bank of England and the East India Company. The Government now began to be systematic about modernising and reorganising the national debt. Stock transfer provisions were streamlined and there was a sinking fund to pay off the principal. One disadvantage of the old annuities was that although the holder received £5 per annum for (typically) ninety-nine years, he did not receive a return of his principal at the end of that period. Anyone with a pocket calculator can today demonstrate the promise of a return of the original £100 investment at the end of a ninety-nine year period adds less than 1 per cent to the present value of the annuity, but it could be a vitally important point to investors who, then as now, made a clear distinction between the need to preserve capital and the desire to enjoy income as a return on that capital.

Interest rates had fallen, and the government wanted to 'convert' old loans into new ones at lower rate of interest. Modern public finance was in the making and the transition could (it was thought) be eased with the help of a joint stock company. At this stage the South Sea Company

... was properly seen as nothing more than a society of government annuitants. . . . The financial community judged the value of the stock on the security of the 6% annuity. Profits from trade had properly been discounted at nil.

(Sperling 1962: 16)

There were further, relatively modest, funding operations. In October 1715 Walpole became First Lord, but under Townshend. The national debt was about £37 million: the rate of interest since 1714 had been 5 per cent, but many loans carried interest at between 6 per cent and 8 per cent. In that year, the South Sea Company rounded up its capital to £10 million by, in effect, capitalizing arrears of government debt. In 1717 Walpole introduced his Conversion plan to reduce interest on the national debt, and to form a sinking fund. Both the South Sea Company, and the Bank of England, accepted a reduction in interest rates from 6 per cent to 5 per cent. This conversion excited the speculators, who began to perceive some interesting possibilities. Walpole resigned shortly afterwards in the course of the whig schism. His plans were carried through by Stanhope.

The fun begins

So far the operations had been fairly orthodox. They were on a larger scale than those of the Bank of England and the East India Company, but still only represented a proportion of the government's floating debt. In 1719 Parliament agreed that £135,000 per annum of lottery annuities should be converted into South Sea stock at 11½ years purchase plus 1¼ years of interest. These annuities were due to expire at various dates between 1742 and 1807. (The price would give a yield between 6.77 per cent and 8.69 per cent depending on maturity.) The operations were carried through on the assumption of par value, but as the stock then stood at £114 there was an immediate paper profit to the proprietors. The stock ('paper') being worth more than asset value any share exchange acquisition of assets would give a potential profit to all parties – at least so long as the illusion lasted.

The difference between par and £114 accrued in two ways. The £1,202,702 stock issued in exchange for the annuities 'was delivered to the proprietors, who profited from the fact that stock received at par was worth £114 on the market. The Company's profit arose in the same way' (Sperling 1962: 26). There was an actual sale of £520,000 stock again at £114 to raise £592,800, which on the terms of the arrangement was to be lent to the state at 5 per cent. The proceeds included a premium of £72,800, which we would treat as a non-distributable capital reserve or paid-in surplus: at that time shareholders perceived it as a profit. The scheme had many opponents in Parliament: it would enrich a few and impoverish many. Sir Robert Walpole referred to the dangerous practice of stock jobbing which might divert men's minds from industry and tempt them into ruin.

Although there were parallels with the original 1711 operation there was one difference which was to prove significant for future developments. In 1711 an investor might have been holding £100 nominal of government debt which (although he probably considered that it ought to be worth par) was in fact only marketable at a 32 per cent discount. If he converted into South Sea stock standing (say) at £85 he had converted an unrealised, and probably only grudgingly admitted book loss into a more marketable piece of paper which could be sold immediately for a rather smaller loss and with a reasonable hope of recovering the loss altogether within the next few years. To a sophisticated financial analyst of today there is no difference between such an operation (1711) and the 1719 transaction which involved converting a government security worth £100 into stock of a corporation trading at £114.

There is an important psychological difference between a transaction which limits an existing loss and one which, as if by magic, appears to generate an immediate profit. It is hardly surprising that the investing public wanted more of this magic treatment. London had heard of all the exciting goings on in Paris:

> John Law had apparently successfully carried out a grand conversion of consolidation of the national debt which had greatly reduced the financial burden on the state and opened possibilities for enormous financial and economic expansion.
>
> (Sperling 1962: 26)

It is not surprising that the British government wished to share the advantages which such a great scheme could apparently offer. The King's Speech opening Parliament in November 1719 proposed that this be done. John Blunt lost no time in approaching Aislabie, the Chancellor of the Exchequer, with a scheme by which the South Sea Company would take over the whole of the national debt. Indeed he originally proposed to acquire debt owed to the Bank of England and the East India Company, and to take over the privileges of these corporations. This, not surprisingly, was opposed by these bodies. Under the modified proposals, the rest of the national debt was to be converted into South Sea stock. The scheme was presented to the House of Commons on 22 January 1720.

The proposal involved debts estimated at £30,981,712 with long annuities (96–99 years) capitalized at twenty years' purchase and short annuities at fourteen years. Interest would be reduced from 5 per cent to 4 per cent after 1727. The operation would, after that, save the State £305,030 per annum interest, and the South Sea Company was to pay £3 million for the privilege. Aislabie told the House that, adding the savings to the sinking fund would enable the debt to be paid off in twenty-five years.

The Bank of England submitted an alternative proposal: £5 million and an earlier reduction in interest. Both parties vigorously refused to agree to a parliamentary suggestion that they should prepare a joint scheme. 'No, Sir, we will never divide the child' asserted Blunt. The nation was now virtually on the auction block. The South Sea Company had to make a better and more complex offer which was accepted by Parliament (Scott 1968 (iii): 306).

The reference to the events as a 'bubble' is not based on hindsight. The term was certainly used in the *Weekly Journal* for 9 January 1720: (Erleigh 1933: 60). Scott makes the important distinction between the scheme's 'two different histories. The one was open to men of intelligence, while the other was profoundly secret until the end of 1720' (Scott 1968 (iii): 303). There was certainly a rational element in the exercise, even if the real aim was fraudulent. There is a capital gain in converting unmarketable paper yielding say 8 per cent into marketable securities trading on a 6 per cent basis. However, the company was now taking on obligations it could only meet if the South Sea stock remained above par. Indeed part of the profit of the scheme arose from exploiting the amount of hot air included in the market capitalization of South Sea stock. Certainly nothing in the earnings record of the South Sea Company could underwrite the figure of £7.5 million promised to the government.

The possibility of effective objections from ministerial and Court circles was reduced by purporting to issue £574,000 in what we would call 'letter stock' at par to the right people. (This, of course was not known to investors at the time: Scott's 'secret history'.) These included the King's mistresses, and, it was to be alleged, Aislabie the Chancellor. Erleigh points out that, given the price of the stock, the effective bribes totalled £1,250,000, and explains how the profits were created by book entries and paid over in cash. (There are remarkable similarities with the Japanese Recruit scandal of 1989.) The market price had risen from 128 at the beginning of the year, and by this time (late March 1720) was £210. In due course the difference was distributed as a 'capital gain' to the parties concerned. Needless to say the latter never subscribed cash and never took any risk. Indeed it does not appear that the stock was ever issued, except as a book entry. For the next few months the name of the game was stock manipulation. The higher the price the stock achieved the more justification there was in terms of real assets – an operation that has been repeated many times in the centuries which followed.

Archibald Hutcheson, a leading critic of public debt, gave a succinct example of how inflated stock can be used to generate real values for early participants: all that matters is not to be left with the parcel when the music stops. The technique has been repeated many times in the centuries which have followed. Paraphrasing somewhat, he said:

A, owning shares worth £100, gives out that they are worth £300. B relying on A's great wisdom and integrity puts up £300 new money for shares giving a half interest. Later C comes in at £500, and D at £1,100. Each then has a quarter interest in a business worth £2,000. . . . At that point A has gained £400 while the unfortunate thoughtless D paid the piper and lost £600.

(Beacon, Anon 1825: 108)

The Duchess of Ormond wrote to Jonathan Swift on 18 April 1720.

You remember, as I do, when the South Sea was said to be my Lord Oxford's brat, and must be starved at birth. Now the King has adopted it, and calls it his beloved child . . . he loves it as well as he does the Duchess (of Kendal) and that is saying a good deal. I wish it may thrive, for many of my friends are deep in it: I wish you were so too!

For all the excitement, the 'bubble' was widely satirised as such even as it developed. This is illustrated by the famous collection of cartoons and verse – Het Groote Tafereel Der Dwaashied, or the Great Mirror of Folly (Cole 1949). The Dutch term windnegotie (wind trade) is even more evocative than 'bubble'. The party might have lasted longer except for the need to raise 'money subscriptions' (to pay off what amounted to cash bribes) and the actions of the individual directors in trying to add to their collective reward by private stock manipulation. These subscriptions were typically 'partly paid' which gave considerable leverage to speculators. The price of the stocks had begun to rise in late January 1720. When the Bill received the Royal Assent on 7 April 1720, the stock actually fell from £310 to £290 but was quickly massaged up and on 14 April the first 'money subscription' was issued at £300; 20 per cent down, balance in 10 per cent instalments at intervals of two months. £2,250,000 nominal was subscribed; equivalent to £6,750,000 fully paid. Only £1,350,000 was actually paid up. The stock quickly rose to £340, making the '£60 paid' stock worth £100. (Scott 1912 iii: 308 comments on the irregularity of the over-subscription.)

The directors resolved on 21 April to pay a dividend of 10 per cent, presumably from capital reserves. On 28 April the Company, in accordance with its arrangements issued stock against £427,849 in long annuities and £64,126 in short annuities. This increased the company's nominal capital by £9,454,744. Subscribers were offered thirty-two years' purchase (valued by the agreement at twenty years) for long annuities and seventeen years' purchase (fourteen years) for short annuities; the stock was issued at £375, but part of the consideration was in cash. The arrangement was favourable to all parties.

On 29 April, following the success of the 14 April issues, the directors launched a second 'money subscription' at £400; 10 per cent down and balance in 10 per cent instalments at intervals of 3 months; £1,500,000 nominal subscribed (£6,000,000 fully paid but only £600,000 cash).

On 17 June the third money subscription was issued at £1,000. Terms were again 10 per cent down and balance in 10 per cent instalments at intervals of six months from 2 July, 1721: £5,000,000 nominal was subscribed (equal to £50,000,000 fully paid). The stock rose to a peak of £1050 on 24 June, the highest price ever reached: apart from the 10 per cent down, no further instalments were paid.

On 14 July stock was offered against the redeemable government securities, £11,240,145 converted which increased the company's nominal capital by the same amount. There were created 112,401 shares of £100 par stock; 14,050 shares of stock at £800 were assigned to subscribers, the company retained 98,351 shares surplus. There was a second subscription for both redeemables and irredeemables on 4 August: £2,755,265 of redeemables were converted, which increased the company's nominal capital by the same amount (27,553 shares of £100 par stock); 3,444 shares of stock at £800 were assigned to subscribers and the company retained 24,109 shares surplus stock. On 24 August there was the fourth money subscription, at £1,000; 20 per cent down and balance in 20 per cent instalments at intervals of nine months. £1,250,000 nominal (£12,500,000 fully paid) was subscribed.

It is sometimes said that the South Sea Bubble burst. This is not correct: to begin with, it merely deflated. By 18 August, it slipped back to around £900. On that day that directors issued writs of *scire facias* against the New York Building Company and several rival companies, holding them in breach of the Bubble Act. This Act, which had received the Royal Assent on the 11 June 1720, was not directed against the South Sea Company, but was intended to protect it against the formation of rival Joint Stock Companies.

> There was good reason to believe that the Act resulted from the lobbying of the South Sea directors who wished to cut off speculation in these companies because it drew money out of the market in South Sea stock. The Act incidentally confirmed the incorporation of the Royal Exchange Assurance and London Assurance companies both of which survive today. It was to inhibit commercial development for many years.
>
> (Sperling 1962: 31)

By this time the flood of minor Bubbles was distracting attention from the South Sea Company. The directors needed to maintain the price to secure their subscriptions. The price was maintained at this level until 1 August by the company making loans even on partly paid stocks. These reached £11.2 million. Some of the figures need a little interpretation because of the prevalence of partly paid stock. At this time the company appeared to have a nominal capital of £40 million, a market capitalization of £400 million – a vast sum of money in those days. The greater part of this represented the sudden accretion of 'wealth' to speculators which, with hindsight, we can see hardly existed except on paper.

When such vast fortunes were apparently to be made by speculation and company promotion, it was hardly surprising that others wanted a piece of the action. Some 150 other companies were promoted during this period, – the greatest speculative mania that the United Kingdom has ever seen. An unnamed observer is quoted as saying that, in gaming style:

> The South Sea Stock must be allowed the honour of being the gold table; the better sort of these bubbles, the silver table, and the lower sort, the farthing tables for the footmen. [But (he adds)] some of the footmen soon aspired to the gold table, and many of the big gamblers condescended to compete . . . with the footmen.
>
> (Erleigh 1933: 74)

The most appealing of the promoters was a simple soul who was not too greedy and who did not allow himself to be taken in by his own prospectus. He announced his intention to form 'a company for carrying on an undertaking of great advantage but no one to know what it is'. The company was to have a capital of £500,000 in 5,000 shares of £100 each. He did not expect the public to be so naïve as to put up this money sight unseen, nor did he adopt the device used by the South Sea Company and others of '20 per cent paid'. He merely asked for £2 per share by way of option money in return for which the fortunate subscribers would in due course receive a copy of the full prospectus and the opportunity to pay up the balance of £98. By the standards of more ambitious promoters, the issue was not a success. He rented an office in Cornhill and opened for business at 9 a.m. By 2 p.m. 'only' 1,000 subscriptions (one-fifth of the issue on offer) had been subscribed. The sensible man then closed his office, disappeared a modest but comfortable £2,000 better off, and was never heard of (in that capacity) again.

The South Sea Bubble was an exercise in corporate finance. That aspect is analysed in detail in Neal (1990) 'The Rise of Financial Capitalism' and Dickson (1967). There is also a wealth of information in Scott (1912). The superficially similar 'bubble' at the same time in France had far more important implications for the development of money, and is discussed in Chapter 23.

The aftermath

Inevitably, there was a major political row. Sir Robert Walpole and Lord Stanhope wanted to repair the damage as quickly as possible in the national interest. So, for more personal reasons, did Aislabie, Croggs senior and Sunderland. Against them ranged Archibald Hutcheson, Sir Joseph Jekyll and Lord Molesworth who proposed vigorous action against the plunderers of the nation. On 20 December 1720 the Commons resolved that the conversions should be final and that no contracts would be voided. On 9 January 1721 a Secret Committee of the Commons was appointed to investigate the entire episode.

17

DEPOSIT BANKING IN ENGLAND

BANKING AFTER THE NAPOLEONIC WARS

From 1797–1821 the UK had had an inconvertible paper currency, the 'Suspension of Payments' described in Part III (Chapter 26), and a classic period of monetary debate. After the war, bank notes again became convertible into gold, and the United Kingdom was on a formally constituted gold standard (Chapter 7). The discussions and pamphleteering which had begun before the Bullion Committee report of 1810 continued, but while the earlier debates had focused attention on the monetary role of paper money (bank *notes*) the discussion now had to be extended to accept the reality that bank *deposits* were becoming an increasingly important, and eventually were to be the dominant, component of the money supply. The problems of regulating banks had to be faced up to by those who, only too often, had not come to terms even with the concept of paper money, who did not grasp the intellectual content of the Bullion Report, and who were still bemused by the fallacy of the Real Bills doctrine.

WHAT IS MEANT BY 'MONEY'?

The crises of 1825, 1837 and 1847 played a major part in concentrating minds, and in forming the nature of the English banking system. The period, to about 1860, is one of continuous development and dispute, described in Fetter's (1965) *The Development of British Monetary Orthodoxy, 1797–1875* and discussed in Horsefield (1941). Banking had developed to the point that anyone of some means (and not only merchants and bankers) would generally now hold his immediately available funds in the form not of coin, not of paper bank notes, but as simple bank deposits. He could order his banker to settle his debt by a transfer to another depositor, a procedure which was to become standardised in the form of cheques. Were these deposits 'money?'. Keynes (1913: 12) regarded gold coin as being necessary only 'for certain kinds of out-of-pocket expenditure, such as that on railway travelling, for which custom requires cash payment' and for the payment of wages to servants. A gentleman would, by implication, meet other expenses by cheque, often in settlement of a tradesman's credit account. There were disputes between the currency school and the banking school, which continued well into the nineteenth century and which were to shape subsequent developments. The terms appear to have been coined by George Warde Norman in his evidence to the 1840 Committee of the House of Commons on Banks of Issue (but see Clapham 1970 vol. ii: 181).

The chief proponents of the Currency School were Samuel Jones Loyd (later Lord Overstone), George Warde Norman and Robert Torrens. They held that money derived, and should derive, its value from metal. Paper money should be issued purely for convenience and the amount of paper in circulation should not exceed the value of the bullion held in reserve. Under such a scheme, the paper circulation would be 100 per cent gold backed. (The principle would work equally well on a silver standard, but this was not then an issue in England.)

Although it is an over-simplification to equate the currency school with modern day monetarism and with the hard money men in the United States in the 1890s, they all shared an underlying belief that regulation of the money supply is the foundation of economic management. They had a deep distrust of the wisdom of governments, and a strong preference for formal rules, binding on the political and monetary authorities, over administrative discretion: a regulation that depended on principle, rather than panic. They can be regarded as the successors of the Bullionist school which had had an intellectual victory in 1810 where their opponents had sought (inevitably in vain) to deny any connection between the extension of the money supply, in a period where convertibility into gold was suspended, and 'the High Price of Gold Bullion', meant a depreciation in the currency.

The Banking School, led by Thomas Tooke, had during the first half of the nineteenth century developed an intellectual coherence far removed from the crude and nonsensical denial that printing money had anything to do with the level of prices or the strength of the currency. They did tend to cling to the naïvety of the 'real bills' doctrine, according to which the extension of credit could do no harm provided that it was associated with the genuine needs of trade and provided that accommodation bills were avoided. Thomas Tooke, had supported the findings of the Bullion Committee on the connection between the issue of inconvertible notes and the rise in prices but went on to argue that other means of credit are equally important. Other prominent writers were John Fullarton (1844) and James Wilson (1847). Fullarton developed the idea of a self-regulating note issue – 'the theory of the reflux'.

A modern writer, Lawrence White (1984), identifies a separate 'Free Banking School' out of those more commonly aligned with the Currency School, and which believed in unrestricted and competitive issues of notes convertible into specie. He claims for this persuasion Sir Henry Parnell,

Samuel Bailey, James William Gilbart, Alexander Mundell, Robert Musket and others, and regards James Wilson as a 'fellow traveller'.

The dispute between the banking and currency schools was on how to regulate the banks but there continued to be disputes over the coinage. These have been discussed in Part I (Chapter 7) but in practice the central problem of the coinage had been solved in 1819. The gold standard, though vigorously disputed, was to hold sway in England for the rest of the century. The real issue was what constituted 'money'. The country had to adjust to the idea of 'broad money' constituting not just coin, or even just coin and notes, but also bank deposits.

The main issues

Otherwise the main issues argued between 1819 and 1844 were

- Do the banks cause fluctuations and how, if at all, should money supply be regulated?

- Hence, should the Bank of England have a monopoly of note issues and/or should Joint Stock Banking be encouraged in England?

These were coupled with the analytical questions:

- Can banks create money, and are 'deposits' money?

- What effects does the quantity of money (however defined) have on prices?

- How does (should) the banking system respond to bullion movements, i.e. payments surpluses or deficits?

- Given that issuing banks should contract the note issue under foreign pressure, how should they react to commercial distress?

The currency school asserted, and the banking school denied, that money supply was an immediate cause of fluctuations. They wanted 'a regulation that depended upon principle instead of ... on panic ... that could be measured or regulated by a fixed rule' (Loyd's evidence to 1840 Committee, Q2726). They worried about controlling country note issues.

The level of general public discussion during this period was far higher than at the time of the Bullion Committee.

During the period of the suspension of cash payments, the public was in a state of very imperfect information upon the subject of currency. The doctrines of the Bullionists, it is true had been propounded; but had not then succeeded in making any effectual impression on the community at large. Silent contempt in some quarters, and jealously and suspicion amount almost to animosity in others, was the reception

150

which they generally met with . . . the self styled practical men rather than the abstract reasoners were the popular heroes of the day.

(Loyd 1837: 44–5)

By 1819 though: 'Here terminates the dark age of currency; and we now enter a period characterised by more enlightened views'(Loyd 1837: 53–4). Maybe.

The effects of resumption

Peel's Act of 1819 had provided for a gradual resumption of payments. The effective gold price at which notes could be redeemed was to be reduced in stages and, from 1 May 1823 full convertibility would be restored. The ban on the melting of and exporting of gold was repealed: the effect of this, coupled with the plans for the repayment of £10 million by the government to the bank, was deflationary. The gold price fell, and full convertibility was resumed on 1 May 1821, two years ahead of schedule.

Under the Act of 1822, notes of less than £5 were to continue in circulation until 5 January 1833. This proposal did not follow the recommendation of Ricardo, who had proposed that one pound notes issued by the Bank of England should be circulated in the place of gold. The Bank of England continued to withdraw one pound notes from circulation but country banks took advantage of the opportunity to expand their issues once more.

The company promotion boom

There was a speculative boom between 1824 and 1825, when over 600 new companies were floated, together with a number of South American loans. In 1825 Thomas Boys published *The South Sea Bubble – a Beacon to the Unwary*. In his appendix, he quotes extracts from newspapers of 1719–20 which, he said, 'require only an alteration of dates to render them appropriate to the present period'.

At first the country banks had followed the lead of the Bank in curtailing the issue of small notes. In 1822, Parliament 'scared by the price fall and influenced by a widespread agitation against Peel's Act' (Clapham 1970 vol. ii: 76) extended their note issuing powers until 1833. Such notes began to be used for the payment of wages in certain parts of the country. Issues of country bank notes rose from an average £4 million in 1821–3 to £6 million in 1824 and £8 million in 1825, a major factor fuelling the boom. This enlarged circulation was in principle payable in gold. During the restriction period the public had become accustomed to accept Bank of England notes in redemption of country bank notes. This was now often impossible because the Bank of England stopped issuing notes of less than £5. The country banks actively discouraged the redemption of their notes for gold but a successful petition against a Bristol bank in June 1825 brought home to the public their right to demand redemption.

The crisis of 1825

The Prime Minister, Lord Liverpool, had in March 1825 already warned that there would be a collapse, and that the Government did not propose to bail the banks out by the issue of Exchequer Bills. The balance of payments had deteriorated. We would have recognized this as a warning signal, as indeed would the mercantilists. However, the Bank of England, with its huge reserves, saw no cause for alarm and indeed expanded its own note issue for the purpose of loans to the Government. There was the inevitable collapse, and the Bank of England did cut back on credit by limiting the volume of bills discounted, rationing and sending back a proportion of the bills sent in by City of London banks. There were runs on several country banks. In November Elford and Company, Plymouth, failed. The Bank of England did nothing. In the words of *The Times* (The Thunderer):

> As for relief from the King's Government, we can tell the speculating people and their great foster-mother in Threadneedle Street that they would meet with none – no, not a particle – of the species of relief which they look for. The King's ministers know very well the causes of the evil, and the extent of it, and its natural and appropriate remedy, and we venture to forewarn the men of paper no such help as they are seeking will be contributed by the State.
>
> (Fetter and Gregory 1973: 229)

On the 1 December there was a panic rush to discount at the Bank, said to be like that for 'the pit of a theatre on the night of a popular performance' (*The Times* 2 December 1825, quoted by Clapham 1970 vol. ii: 98).

However on 5 December a large London bank, Pole, Thornton and Company (agent for forty-four country banks) asked the Bank for assistance. They were lent £300,000 but even so did not open for business on Monday 12 December 1825. Six London and sixty-one country banks ceased payment. The problem was discussed at a meeting of the Bank directors on 15 December. It was suggested that the State issue Exchequer bills – or even authorising them, by Order in Council, to stop payment. The Government pointed out that the first solution would be useless now that Exchequer bills no longer circulated as currency. The second course was unthinkable – the Bank would be expected to pay out in full.

On Tuesday, 20 December, the Bank tried to help the market by buying £500,000 of Exchequer Bills, and raised Bank Rate from 4 per cent to 5 per cent: in the event not enough. This increase did not discourage business. On

Thursday 22 it agreed to lend against long bills (over ninety-five days) and approved securities (Clapham 1970 vol. ii: 100). By now

> The ordinary, non-discounting, public was clamouring . . . for money, Bank notes or gold. Neither notes nor sovereigns could be made fast enough: it was the literal physical limit that impeded, for gold was below Mint price, and the Mint was working furiously. By the evening of Saturday 17th the Bank had run out of £5 and £10 notes. However, a supply came from the printers on the Sunday morning.
>
> (Clapham 1970 vol. ii: 100)

The situation was partly saved when a famous 'box of £1 notes' was discovered locked away.

Clapham says that many of the Bank's advances were not actually on goods but on personal security and that the bank was not 'over nice' in its choice of that security. On page 98 he quotes Liverpool, Baring and McCulloch's warnings and suggests

> . . . not only did it do no good, it actually contributed to the crisis. In the crash and panic of December 1825 Lord Liverpool who nine months earlier had specifically stated that the government would not bring relief to speculators, felt committed not to come to the rescue.

The bank now employed Rothschilds to purchase whatever gold it could find. The purchases cost the bank £100,000 more than the mint price. The Mint worked night and day turning the bars into coin. The bank now lent freely:

> Government securities, Exchequer bills, commercial bills, other securities which the bank normally would never have dreamt of taking were purchased or held as collateral. The actual discounts increased from £5 to £15 millions in a few weeks. Commissioners were appointed to go to the provinces and advance money on the security of goods to merchants in difficulties. Bank notes were still signed by hand, the clerks of the Bank could not keep pace with the issues although they worked feverishly far into the night.
>
> (Fetter and Gregory 1973: 222)

With the new year (1826) the gold price came back to the mint price. By the time Parliament met in February 'everyone felt that the crisis was over'.

Lord Bentinck commented that the country had come within twenty-four hours of barter. Although the Bank of England blamed the country banks for the crisis, and vice versa, there was no Parliamentary enquiry as it was fairly clear already what had happened. As William Cobbett said:

> The Bank is blamed for putting out paper and causing high prices; and blamed at the same time for not putting out paper to accommodate merchants and keep them from breaking. It cannot be to blame for

both, and indeed it is blamable for neither. It is the fellows that put out the paper and then break that do the mischief.

(Cobbett 1828 vol. ii: 25)

Lord Liverpool, with the near unanimous backing of Parliament, resolved that all notes under £5, including those of the Bank England, should go. On 13 January he and the Chancellor F. J. Robinson wrote to the Bank at length about the steps to be taken to prevent a repetition of the crisis (Palmer 1837a).

Another twist to the problem was that because of the prohibition of joint stock banks, the country banks were all too small; 'any small tradesman, a cheesemonger a butcher or shoemaker may open a country bank, but a set of persons with a fortune sufficient to carry on the concern with security are not permitted to do so'. Liverpool wanted the Bank to open branches, and to 'give up its exclusive privilege as to the number of partners engaged in banking, except within a certain distance of the metropolis'. These, he said, were the only ways to improve the country circulation:

> With respect to the extension of the term of their exclusive privileges in the Metropolis and its neighbourhood, it is obvious that Parliament will never agree to it. . . . Such privileges are out of fashion, and what expectation can the Bank under present circumstances entertain that theirs will be renewed. But there is no reason why the Bank of England should look at this consequence with dismay.
>
> (Palmer 1837a: 59)

The Bank responded with a short sharp resolution effectively refusing to give up its privileges. Further letters of 23 and 28 January were more peremptory in tone, and the Government took unilateral action.

The proposals were implemented by two Acts. One, (22 March 1826 7 Geo IV & 6) prohibited the issue of new notes of less than £5 in England and Wales and provided for the redemption of existing ones within three years. The other (25 May 1826 7 Geo IV & 46) permitted joint stock companies to carry on the business of banking and issuing notes in any place more than sixty-five miles from London. An attempt to extend the ban on small notes to Scotland was for the present, defeated. Walter Scott (1826), writing as 'Malachi Malagrowther' can claim much of the credit.

Fetter suggests that

> In the situation of late 1825 and early 1826 the Bank of England, albeit reluctantly and belatedly, had acted much as Walter Bagehot might have recommended. But the issue was never squarely faced in any parliamentary investigation and within the Bank Court itself there seems to have been, for the next half century, considerable difference of opinion as to just what the Bank's responsibilities were.

The events of 1825 and 1826 had led to widespread opinion that the bank, then subject to no legal reserve requirements of any kind, had brought on the crisis by its expansive credit policy. No well formulated proposals emerged, but there began to develop a public opinion which would be receptive to specific proposals. As early as 1827 James Pennington prepared a memorandum urging what was the basis of a bank of 1844 – tying fluctuations of the Bank's notes to fluctuations in its specie reserve.

(Fetter and Gregory 1973: 22)

THE BANK CHARTER ACT OF 1833

In 1833, the year after the Great Reform Act, the Bank of England's charter was due for renewal. On 22 May 1832, a Secret Committee of the House of Commons was appointed, on the motion of Lord Althorp (later Earl Spencer), to look into the question. 'Since the members ... had been specially selected with the idea of representing all points of view, it is not surprising that their Report is a somewhat disappointing document' (Gregory 1929: xiii). Thomas Attwood was a strong advocate of inconvertible paper money and a managed currency. Carr Glyn and George Grote spoke for the London bankers. Thomas Tooke gave evidence. 'Nathan Rothschild believed that neither the Bank nor anyone else could really control the exchanges: the balance of demand was their all-powerful regulator' (Clapham 1970 vol. ii: 122–3).

Evidence to the committee

The Act owes much to the influence of Thomas Joplin, a Newcastle stockbroker. He had published a pamphlet in 1822 'An Essay on the General Principles and Present Practice of Banking etc,' praising the stability of the Scottish banking system and also pointing out that the law did not in fact prohibit the formation of joint stock banks provided that they did not issue notes (Clapham 1970 vol. ii: 92–3). In 1824 he had helped to promote the Provincial Bank of Ireland and in 1826 drew up a plan for a 'Provincial Bank of England' and later became a director of the National Provincial Bank of England, one of the constituents of the present National Westminster. In 1832 he published 'An Analysis and History of the Currency Question' which sums up his account of developments to that time.

John Horsley Palmer, who had become Governor in 1830, was responsible for a provision which freed the discount rate from the operation of the usury law. It was provided that such law would not apply to any bill of exchange or promissory note payable within three months. So long as the Bank should maintain convertibility with notes into gold, Bank of England notes would be legal tender as such for all purposes, except by the Bank of England. This it was suggested could make it possible in future panics, for notes to be

155

settled by the issue by the country bank in Bank of England notes rather than gold coin. However, to soothe doubts of the farmers, the act was reworded to provide that the Bank of England notes were only legal tender for amounts 'over' £5. The presenter of a single £5 note (or a succession of such notes) could therefore insist on receiving gold.

Palmer had become a director of the Bank in 1811 and must have followed closely the debates on the Bullion Report. He gave authoritative evidence before the 1832 Committee. Of this, Feaveryear says 'Palmer's conception in 1832 of the proper relationship of the Bank to the money market . . . is of the utmost importance. No one had ever before worked out so complete a scheme of management' (Feaveryear 1931: 230).

His most important contribution was to formulate 'the Palmer Rule': that the Bank should keep one-third of its assets in bullion and two-thirds in interest bearing securities (Q72). This would effectively govern the circulation of the whole country (Q73) and would apply as a reserve against deposits as well as notes (Q74), although he regarded the liabilities against deposits to be the less dangerous (Q77). Although the Bank had the power to extend or diminish the circulation on its own initiative (Q81) it would normally react to an unfavourable exchange rate not on its own initiative but by letting the public act on the Bank (Q82–3). (If there was an outflow of gold, the public would redeem notes for gold forcing an automatic contraction in the issue) (Fetter 1965: 145–6, and Clapham 1970 vol. ii: 162).

In response to a comment that the one-third ratio had remained virtually unchanged for four years he said that he kept it 'as nearly the same as can be managed' (Q84). (Faced with an outflow of gold, the Bank would sell securities to restore the balance: there would be a multiplier effect on the circulation.) He did add (Q85) that the Bank would not necessarily respond to a temporary influx of gold by increasing its holdings of securities. His replies on the response of the Bank to drains arising from other causes, such as a commercial panic, were less convincing (Q92–6). Palmer also held that the Bank should normally compete in the discount market, but should be prepared to discount at a penalty rate – the 'lender of last resort' (Feaveryear 1931: 231; see Q178–88).

The Palmer rule has at times been honoured in the breach. Dowd (1991: 170) has asked why the Bank's management chose to submit themselves to this discipline. Did they genuinely believe that optimal policy was to follow the right simple rule, or did they hope that a rule would give them some protection from a criticism of their policies?

In 1819 the Bank had passed a 'hostile Resolution' denying that there was any evidence that its notes had had any influence on the foreign exchanges: as a body, it was unconvinced by Ricardian economics. Its emergence from the Dark Ages was signalled in 1827 when the hostile Resolution was rescinded (Feaveryear 1931: 230; Gregory 1929: x). This was on the motion of William Ward, a foreign exchange dealer who had been elected to the

Court of the Bank in 1817. He had given evidence to the 1819 Committee in opposition to the views of the then governor, Harman, was a strong supporter of Palmer in 1832, and may have invented the term 'currency school.'

The 1833 Committee Report

The Committee never formally reported, although the evidence was published. All except for the free trader, Henry Parnell, agreed the Bank's charter should be renewed. There was 'a rather fatuous motion of Cobbett's that it should be read this day six months because the legal tender clause 'usurped the King's prerogative'. This was 'brushed aside as it deserved' (see Clapham 1970 ii: 127–30).

The Act (Bank Charter Act 1833, for text see Gregory 1929 vol i: 19–27) provided that the Bank's charter be renewed until 1855. This was subject to the government's option to terminate on twelve month's notice being given in the six month period from 1 August 1844 (v). Bank notes were legal tender, except at the Bank itself (vi). The monopoly of note issuing within sixty-five miles of London (ii) but there was a declaratory clause (iii) 'whereas Doubts have arisen [it declared and enacted] That any Body Politic . . . although consisting of more than six persons may carry on the Trade or Business of Banking in London, or within sixty five miles thereof provided they did not issue notes' – Joplin's point. The parties mainly interested in this provision were a group of 'Noblemen and Gentlemen', mainly Scottish: Bute, Lord Stuart de Rothesay, a Stewart, an Arbuthnot and a Douglas. They wanted to start a stock bank in London, which was duly formed as 'The London and Westminster Bank'. The Bank felt 'very bitterly' about this provision (Clapham 1970 vol. ii: 128).

Defects of the Currency School

The Currency School were on less strong ground, from a modern perspective, in assuming that 'money' and 'currency' were defined only by the total of bank notes and coin in circulation and that 'it was the fluctuation of the quantity of these two taken together which alone affected the value of the pound' (Feaveryear 1931: 245). Norman (1841) argued whether notes should be regarded as an auxiliary currency or as a means of economising the use of money. If bank notes are withdrawn they must be replaced by coin; but the abolition of arrangements for dispensing with the use of money will not need the introduction in their place of an equal amount of coin or bank notes.

This, of course, is really a question of 'velocity'. The school was therefore faced with discussing what measures need to be taken actually to regulate bank notes. There are two problems. First there were the independent issuers of bank notes. Norman had written: 'a single issuer might be easy to deal with but how are we to deal with 500?' (Norman 1841: 84). The answer was gradually to extinguish the issuing rights of all banks save the Bank of England. The second problem concerned the Bank of England itself which was, until the Bank Charter Act of 1844, totally mixing its issues and banking business. Fetter quotes Palmer as having fallen into the error of regarding notes and deposits as liabilities of the same kind to which the reserve might be applied discriminately. Other commentators of the time commented on the conflict between the Bank's public and private business (Fetter 1965: 146 says that Palmer's answer to Q.77 'could easily suggest to those who wanted to translate ideas into legislation that a distinction between notes and deposits had a solid pragmatic basis').

18

MONEY AND BANKING IN THE UNITED STATES

INTRODUCTION

Continental currency issued during the Revolution had lost its value by 1781 (Chapter 24). Events during the 'critical period' between then and 1789, when the Constitution came into force were to have a profound influence on the shape of American currency and finance. During the period discussed in this chapter an American banking system of sorts emerged, but the new nation emerged with remarkably primitive monetary arrangements.

In the early years, the dominant political view in the new nation was conservative, favouring sound currency and distrusting paper money. However, populist left wing influences at the time of Jackson added to the mix, and helped determine the structure of the US banking system which persisted into the late twentieth century. On 17 September 1787, the Constitution was adopted. The relevant provisions clearly gave the exclusive power of coinage to Congress and prohibited the States from issuing legal tender bills. Did it also prevent the States issuing currency of any kind? If economics is an inexact science so is law. The interpretation of the Constitution, beautifully drafted as it is, has kept lawyers in fees for two centuries. The key provisions were:

SEC. 8. The Congress shall have power –

To coin money, regulate the value thereof, and of foreign coin, and fix the standard of weights and measures;

To provide for the punishment of counterfeiting the securities and current coin of the United States; . . .

To make all laws which shall be necessary and proper for carrying into execution the foregoing powers, and all other powers vested by this Constitution in the government of the United States, or in any department or officer thereof . . .

SEC. 10. No State shall . . . coin money; emit bills of credit; make any thing but gold and silver coin a tender in payment of debts.

(Doc. Hist. vol. i: 91)

159

BANKING

Nothing recognisable as a bank appears to have survived the Revolution. The gap was soon filled. The Bank of Pennsylvania was established in June 1780 and raised £300,000 including £10,000 from the ubiquitous Robert Morris. It was essentially an instrument of government finance but was not long lived. Myers (1970:41) quotes Thomas Paine as saying that 'by means of this bank the army was supplied throughout the campaign and being at the same time recruited was enabled to maintain its ground'.

The Bank of North America

The Bank of North America was formed on the initiative of Robert Morris, and a Federal charter was granted (by a narrow majority) in May 1781. It had a capital of $400,000, was limited to assets of $10 million, and commenced operations in January 1782. It was also granted charters in Massachusetts and Pennsylvania although the latter rescinded the charter in 1785. Thomas Willing was the first president. When

> ... the pressure of the times was over there were not wanting those who viewed the prosperous state of the affairs of the bank with a jealous eye [and various fears were spread abroad] as if ... the bare possibility of abuse could ever furnish a good argument against the decided utility of a thing; or if a benefit were to be relinquished because all cannot be benefitted alike.
>
> (Goddard 1831: 50)

The Charter of the Bank of North America was renewed on 7 March 1787 for fourteen years, the pro bank party having regained the ascendancy after a year of disputes (Hildreth 1837: 49). It was renewed again in 1799 and was still flourishing when Goddard wrote in 1831. It continued into relatively modern times, and was absorbed into the East Pennsylvania Banking and Trust Company in 1929.

Two other banks followed: the Bank of New York, promoted by Alexander Hamilton and the Bank of Massachusetts in Boston, both in 1784. The Bank of New York still survives as an independent entity, while the Bank of Massachusetts merged with the First National Bank of Boston in 1903. These three banks were all incorporated as companies, a matter of great dispute in England and Scotland, and indeed pioneered the 'incorporated form' of business which was to prove so important in the development of the United States. These three were the only banks established when the Federal Constitution came into operation in 1787, but were joined by the Bank of Maryland in 1791.

FROM 1787 TO THE WAR OF 1812

Alexander Hamilton and the First Bank of the United States

Alexander Hamilton was appointed first Secretary to the Treasury, established by Act of Congress on 2 September 1789. The Treasurer had a duty to 'receive, keep and disburse the money of the United States' but lacked the physical means of doing this except through collecting agents and the three (soon to be four) banks. Hamilton wrote his 'Report on the Public Credit' in January 1790 (Birley 1944 vol. i: 150–70) and in December that year he presented to Congress his 'Report on a National Bank' (Goddard 1831: 51–94) recommending the formation of a bank on the lines of the Bank of England. Congress he believed had the right to promote such a bank. (He ruled out The Bank of North America, an obvious alternative, as it now had a Pennsylvania charter.)

Hamilton belonged to the Federalist party which believed in a strong central government, and they supported him in Congress. He was opposed by Jefferson and Madison on 'States Rights' grounds, but the Bill incorporating the bank passed the House of Senate. President Washington rejected the advice of the Attorney General and the Secretary of State that the Act was unconstitutional, and signed the bill into law on 25 February 1791.

The Bill did not define the 'business of banking' but the bank was forbidden to trade in anything except bills of exchange, gold or silver bullion, or goods pledged for loans and not redeemed. The capital of the bank was $10 million, one-fifth of which was subscribed by the Federal Government of the United States. The other subscribers could pay three quarters of their subscription in government securities and the rest in specie. The notes were legal tender. It was prohibited from paying interest of more than 6 per cent and (surprisingly) from purchasing public debt, or lending more than $100,000 to the United States or to any State, unless authorised by Congress. The total debt of the bank was not to exceed the capital plus (making a loophole) the 'monies then actually deposited in the bank for safekeeping'. There was no requirement for specie redemption of its notes or for a specie reserve against this deposit. The issue was promptly over-subscribed. The demands of growing cities for branches over-ruled Hamilton's wishes. Eight branches were opened by 1805.

Hildreth discusses the arguments for and against the bank. The latter:

> ... finally settled down upon the constitutional question. ... That question has nothing to do with the theory of banking ... the letter of the constitution is on one side, while there is arrayed upon the other, the practice of all political parties ... the solemn decisions of the Supreme Court and the opinions of every leading statesman with the single exception of Mr Jefferson.

The establishment of the bank:

> ... caused deep concern amongst four banks which up to that time
> had been holding Treasury deposits and conducting foreign exchange
> operations for the government – the Bank of North America, the Bank
> of New York, the Bank of Massachusetts, and the Bank of Maryland.
>
> (Hildreth 1837: 52–3)

Hamilton tried to reassure them, promising the Bank of New York that he
would so conduct the transfer as not to embarrass or distress them, and
deposits were, in fact, run down gradually.

In 1811, the bank's charter came up for renewal. The large banks, but not
the by now numerous small ones, supported it. Amongst its sympathizers
were Madison, and Gallatin who, as Secretary to the Treasury, had found
its operations convenient and helpful. Many original opponents who had
since been profitably involved with State banks, ceased to feel that vehement
dislike towards all banking institutions which they had evinced in 1790
(Hildreth 1837: 55). Its main crime was its association with the Federalist
party, and as usual personality played its part. Two opponents were John
Jacob Astor, apparently for personal reasons, and Henry Clay, leader of the
opposition to the bank in the Senate. To anticipate the Duke of Wellington
by four years, 'it was a near run thing'; re-charter lost by one vote in the
House and was lost in the Senate by the casting vote of 'Vice President
George Clinton of New York who had never forgiven Gallatin and Madison
for opposing his nomination to the presidency' (Myers 1970: 72). So ended
what is known to history as the 'First' Bank of the United States.

The country was now without a national bank, and the Treasury had to
look for other banks in which to deposit its funds and through which to
make foreign payments. The difficulties of the Treasury, and the uncontrolled proliferation of small, unsound, State banks is now generally blamed
on the ending of the Government's relationship with an expert source of
financial guidance. Hildreth, though, took a different view:

> The admirers and advocates of national banks, with the usual logic of
> practical men, have ascribed all the disturbances in the currency ...
> to the non existence of a national bank. These things *followed* the
> winding up of the Bank therefore they were *produced* by it.

[He has other explanations and suggests that the First Bank was lucky that]
by ceasing to exist [it] escaped temptations to which others succumbed.

> Since the purpose for which banks had been incorporated was to earn
> interest on loans which were largely extended in the form of notes, the
> volume in circulation inevitably increased ... few of the bank charters
> contained any requirement that the issuing bank redeemed its notes on
> demand, or that a specie reserve be maintained in order to ensure
> redemption.
>
> (Hildreth 1837: 56)

Banking on these terms was literally 'a licence to print money' with no effective limit unless and until there were net redemptions of notes and if then (as was almost inevitable) the underlying security for the loans proved difficult to realise. Nemesis was soon to follow.

THE WAR OF 1812 AND SUSPENSION

The war of 1812 was an attempt by the fledgling United States to take advantage of the diversions of the Napoleonic wars and drive the British out of Canada. It was expensive, bloody and, in the end, unsuccessful. When it was ended by the Treaty of Ghent, (December 1814) nothing had been achieved and the parties simply agreed to restore the *status quo ante bellum*. Brogan describes the war as 'one of the most unnecessary in history, and reflects as little credit on Britain as any she has ever fought . . . its greatest battle (New Orleans) was fought just after peace was signed' (Brogan 1985: 259). (General Andrew Jackson fought the battle of New Orleans in January 1815: he was later to fight a financial 'war' with Nicholas Biddle with dramatic consequences for the future of the American banking system. The federalist party which opposed the war effectively sank without a trace.)

Leaving aside the issues and the outcome of the war, how was it financed? The European capital markets were closed to Americans, and 'at home a large proportion of the moneyed men were opposed to the war, and not well inclined to furnish the means of carrying it on' (Hildreth 1837: 57). High interest rates had to be offered. The collapse of trade, and the embargo, had reduced customs revenue (Myers 1970: 65). The Federal government had no direct taxing powers and could raise revenue only by placing a levy on the States. That old cynic Hildreth says that the government refrained from levying taxes 'out of tenderness for the people or a tender regard for their own popularity, perhaps a mixture of both'.

The war was more popular in the Middle and Southern states, and banks there provided, directly or indirectly, most of the funds. In March 1812 attempts were made to raise $11 million in 6 per cent twelve year bonds. Even though only 12.5 per cent of the subscription price was payable on application only half the issue was sold. A later 6 per cent loan could only be sold at a price of $88. Nominal debt was $150 million by the end of 1815. An Act of 30 June 1812 authorised the issue of $5 million of one year treasury notes in denominations of $20 or greater bearing interest at 5.4 per cent. An interesting feature was that these were legal tender for debts due to the government but it is doubtful whether this feature had any useful effect: they did not really circulate and were used mainly to pay taxes or to subscribe for bonds.

The number of banks in the United States increased from ninety in 1811 to 250 in 1816. In the three years 1810–12 alone, forty-one new State banks were chartered with an aggregate capital of $736 million making a total of

120 banks with a nominal capital (perhaps not real) of about $76 million. The banks mainly extended loans in the form of notes and there was a substantial increase in effective circulation. In 1814, Thomas Jefferson wrote to John Quincy Adams predicting a breakdown of the banking system. In August that year the British attacked Washington. Banks there and in Baltimore suspended payments immediately, Philadelphia and New York followed soon after. Gallatin suggested that if the Bank of the United States had still existed the suspension might have been avoided.

By the middle of 1814 the government desperately needed money. The banks could not help: there were too many notes in circulation. One infers that they had already put a greater proportion of the proceeds of their note issues into long term loans than was prudent. Outside New England, suspension was general, with the honourable exception of the Bank of Nashville. There was the inevitable rise in prices, and a rush of new bank incorporations. An unfortunate side effect was that trade was diverted from honest money Boston to other ports where duty could be paid in depreciated bank notes: an example of monetary virtue being unrewarded.

Was the suspension of specie payments by the banks a reaction to emergency or was it, as Hildreth suggested, a cynical and pre-arranged fraud? On his version the successful operation required

> the tacit approbation of the government; for if the government would consent to go on receiving their notes in payment of public dues, it would give them a credit which would sustain their circulation. [This actually happened:] the government were at the mercy of the banks . . . they had no power to refuse for if the banks did not supply them with money where were they to get it?
>
> Examples of successful fraud seldom lack imitators. In this exigency the bank directors bethought themselves of what the Bank of England had done and was still doing. They already knew how profitable a speculation it had proved to that Bank – it was suggested among them, and the resolution was presently adopted, *to suspend specie payments.*

They therefore, he said, deliberately lent money to the government with the tacit agreement that there would be a suspension: not a fair description of the Bank of England's motives or behaviour. This stricture did not extend to New England:

> the bank directors there, did not choose to become parties to this scheme for enriching themselves, and assisting the government at the expense of honesty and their creditors; . . . but south and west of New England every bank in the country became a party to this fraud, with the sole exception of the Bank of Nashville, the sturdy honesty of whose directors amidst such general knavery, is not less praiseworthy than it is remarkable.

Although the war was over in another five months suspension continued for two or three years.

> The years 1815, 1816 may be well marked on the calendar as the jubilee of swindlers and the Saturnalia of non-specie paying banks. Through-out the whole country, New England excepted, it required no capital to set up a bank. All that was wanted was a charter; and influential politicians easily obtained charters from the blind party confidence, or interested votes in the state legislatures.
>
> (Hildreth 1837: 57 ff.)

Specie payment was only renewed when, following the formation of the second Bank of the United States, Congress resolved that nothing should be received in payment of the public dues except specie or notes of specie paying banks (Hildreth 1837: 62).

New England was a special case, discussed by Felt. In March 1812, the government of Massachusetts decided to resort again to treasury notes. 'They were the more needed from the fact that the National Bank which had conducted the moneyed operations of the union was to have its charter repealed in a few days'(Felt 1839: 216). The General Court of the Commonwealth of Massachusetts, put a tax on the stock of banks at 0.5 per cent half yearly and provided that the charters of some banks in the state should not be renewed. Felt praises the formation of the New England Bank which took steps to do something about the discount between 3 per cent and 5 per cent applying to 'bills called foreign because not issued in Boston'. Because of this, he says, 'scarcely a dollar of Boston paper could be seen, being laid aside for profitable speculation' a classic example of Gresham's law resulting in good money being hoarded while bad money circulates.

The New England Bank announced that it would handle the collection of foreign bills for expenses only: by so doing it brought down the discount to one half per cent. There were some problems. The Bank sent certain bills on New York to be collected and exchanged for specie. The three cart loads of silver were 'seized by the order of the Collector of New York and the money was deposited in the vaults of the Manhattan Bank' of which the collector was a director (Felt 1839: 218). He argued that he had acted because he suspected the cash was going to Canada. The money was restored after court action and after the matter had been laid before the President of the United States.

In the New England states, banks were liable to a penalty of 12 per cent per annum on the non-payment of their notes (Gouge 1842: 254), a measure apparently to ensure sound banking in New England, and an example of how a 'tax' can act as a substitute for 'regulation.' Gouge contrasts UK experience. After the Bank of England suspended payments, its notes remained at par for some time and 'when they began to depreciate the notes of all the other banks experienced an equal depreciation because they were exchangeable for those of the Bank of England'. The depreciation was thus uniform throughout the country. The American suspension was not universal and the scale of depreciation varied across the country. The cost was passed on.

> The paper, however, still served as a medium of commerce. The merchant of Pittsburgh put an additional price on his goods equivalent to the depreciation of the currency in that quarter: and, as he had obtained ten or twenty per cent more on his sales, he was enabled to spend ten or twenty per cent more on his purchases. A loss was sustained by individuals when the paper underwent an additional depreciation while remaining in their hands; but their indignation, instead of falling on the banks, was vented on the innocent and useful exchange merchants.
>
> (Gouge 1842: 256)

THE SECOND BANK OF THE UNITED STATES

Although, after peace was signed the financial pressure was off the Government, public finance was greatly complicated by the problem of the inconvertible notes. The Secretary of the Treasury (A. J. Dallas) was prohibited by law from accepting depreciated bank notes, and was effectively therefore unable to withdraw funds from some of the many banks in which he had to keep accounts.

In 1816 The Second Bank of the United States was granted a twenty-year charter and was founded with a capital of $35 million, compared with the $10 million of its predecessor. Of this, the government was to subscribe one-fifth and to appoint five of the twenty-five directors. The bank had the privilege of receiving *deposites* (a term, and spelling, which was to become very important) of public funds free of interest, and had effectively unlimited note issuing powers. In return the Bank paid a bonus of $1.5 million, and handled government banking business without charge.

To secure support, the State banks had to be reassured that there would be no pressure on them for a sudden resumption of specie payments. Public balances were withdrawn only gradually from other banks and aid was promised to any that ran into difficulty. Three-quarters of the capital of the new Bank could be subscribed in Government stock. Demand by would-be subscribers brought these stocks to par. Of this stock, the Bank then redeemed $13 million against notes of non-specie paying banks held by the Government. This may well have been a cosmetic fudge.

It has been argued that the formation of the Second Bank was the only way in which convertibility could have been restored. Hildreth disagrees:

> ... it was only necessary to pass a resolution that nothing should be received in payment of the public dues, but specie or the notes of

specie paying banks. Such a resolution was passed, to take effect a few days before the Bank commenced its regular operations; and it was that resolution, and that resolution alone, which compelled the resumption of specie payments.

(Hildreth 1837: 62)

Such a measure was both necessary and sufficient to ensure the banks would resume payment, or face bankruptcy if they could not meet their notes.

'The power to destroy'

Shortly after its formation, in 1819, the bank was involved in a classic law suit, *McCullough* v *Maryland* (Birley 1944 vol. ii: 2–18; Clarke and Hall 1832: 782). The State of Maryland imposed an annual tax of $15,000 on any bank operating within the State without a Maryland charter. The Bank of the United States refused to pay and the State's position was (not surprisingly) upheld by the State Court. The bank appealed to the Supreme Court, and Chief Justice Marshall found for them, in words often quoted out of context: 'the power to tax is the power to destroy'. The issue was not the iniquity of taxation as such, but the more subtle constitutional one of the power of a State government to tax a creature of the Federal government. Marshall had from the start striven to make the Supreme Court, previously dismissed by Hamilton as 'beyond comparison the weakest of the three departments', the active ally of the Federalists. In this case his key points were:

(1) That a power to create implies a power to preserve.
(2) That a power to destroy, if wielded by a different hand, is hostile to and incompatible with, the powers to create and preserve.
(3) That where this repugnancy exists, that authority which is supreme must control, not yield to that over which it is supreme.

Therefore, he concluded:

The power to tax involves the power to destroy; that the power to destroy may defeat and render useless the power to create.

The State could not, therefore, tax a Federal entity.

The panic of 1819

The stock of the new Bank rose rapidly, apparently in the mistaken belief that honest banking would prove as profitable as the issue of inconvertible notes had been. It began lending liberally, at a time when other banks were contracting or going out of business. There was a sharp price fall, in terms of notes. Debts contracted in depreciated currency continued to be payable at par. A general contraction in trade resulted in notes being presented for payment. The Bank itself was threatened, and many private banks failed (Hildreth 1837: ch. xvi). Following the 1819 crisis, Thomas Ellicott and William Meredith, as a 'committee of inspection and investigation' reported to the shareholders of the Bank in October 1822 (Goddard 1831: 99–106). This was supplemented by Langdon Cheves' report on the Bank in October 1822 also reprinted in Goddard (1831: 106–28) which explains the difficulties. The Bank had received notes 'without reference to the places where they were payable'. Notes were returned to the southern and western offices on an enormous scale. Goddard explains that when he became President of the Bank on 6 March 1819 he secured approval of some obvious steps such as forbidding these offices from issuing notes when the exchanges were against them, and to claim of the government the time necessary to transfer funds from one office to another (the banks were already on to the key idea of securing for themselves the profit from delays in money transmission), and to pay debentures in the same money as the duties on which they were secured were paid.

Nicholas Biddle, Andrew Jackson and the Bank Wars

Nicholas Biddle (then aged 37) was appointed President of the Bank in 1823 and dominated it for the rest of its existence. From the start he had treated the Board of Directors, including the five Government appointees, as a cipher and as early as 1824 had written a letter (Schlesinger 1945: 75–6) to the head of the Washington branch saying his sole duty was to execute the orders of the Board (i.e. Biddle himself) 'in direct opposition, if need be, to the personal interests and wishes of the President and every officer of the Government.' The Bank expanded. The only limit on its note issues was that they were required to be signed personally by the President and the cashier. In 1827, Biddle side-stepped this limitation, and the risk of writer's cramp, by the device of 'branch drafts'. Although similar in appearance to, and in practice accepted as bank notes, they were actually bills of exchange (Schlesinger 1945: 74). (Biddle was a Jeffersonian Republican, and a man of the world. An English traveller remarked on his 'exemption from national characteristics', meaning it as high praise (J. S. Buckingham, quoted by Schlesinger 1945: 82). He was undoubtedly a skilled political operator.)

Political background

Although the Second Bank was born with a majority of political support, its future and ultimate end was dominated by politics. One of the dilemmas facing the new Republic, particularly after the external threat had receded, was how to reconcile universal democracy with the perceived need to retain political power in sound, responsible (for which read propertied) hands.

Jefferson's ideal had been a 'paradise of small farms, each man secure on his own freehold' (Schlesinger 1945: 8) and to preserve this he would have been happy for his country to remain the farm of the Europeans, a role which was later explicitly to be rejected by Australia. Better he felt, to import manufactured goods than to import working men 'and with them their manners and principles'. By the 1820s, a decade of discontent, urban manufacturers were a significant factor in the wealth of the nation. There were serious fears of violence and rebellion, and the franchise became a central issue.

Daniel Webster and the Federalists had argued that it was 'political wisdom to found government on property' and that 'universal manhood suffrage could not long exist in a community where there was great inequality of property'. Inexorably, the vote spread to those whom Biddle characterised as 'men with no property to assess and no character to lose'.

Schlesinger (1945: 35) describes how John Quincy Adams had become aware of the problem of popular discontent. His election in 1824 gave the business community its last chance but he failed to meet the challenge, and in 1828 he was defeated by Andrew Jackson.

General Jackson, the military hero of the Battle of New Orleans, was the first President to be elected on a populist vote. He was to serve two terms and to be succeeded by the Vice President of his second term, Martin van Buren, who carried on his traditions. This background, and the general political situation made inevitable the clash with 'finance capitalism' which was to shape the development of the United States banking and monetary system. In this he was aided by a 'Kitchen Cabinet' (the origin of the term) of his confidential allies 'an influence, at Washington, unknown to the constitution and to the country' (Schlesinger, 1945: 67).

The chief allies of John Quincy Adams were John Clay and Daniel Webster. (Van Deusen says that they, with Postmaster General Barry and Amos Kendall, had borrowed from the bank.) Clay, in opposing the economic policy of Jackson, drew on the support of the Bank. It was a 'mammoth monopoly' but according to van Deusen (1959: 62) in 1830 it had only one-fifth of the country's bank loans and had about one-fifth of the total note issue. In the run-up to the election of 1832, when Jackson was seeking re-election for his second term, it became clear that in spite of Biddle's efforts to cooperate with the government a head-on clash with Jackson was inevitable. Jackson was opposed to the re-chartering of the bank and wanted to replace it by a more limited bank, under Treasury control, which could issue no notes, and make no loans. The charter was, in fact, renewed, but with some amendments. 'Clay and Webster pushed the measure through. It had passed the Senate by a vote of 28 to 20 in the House of Representatives three weeks later by a vote of 107 to 85' (van Deusen 1959: 65).

The Bill was sent to Jackson on 3 July 1832. Taney had already drafted

169

a memorandum recommending veto. He, Jackson and Amos Kendall set to work on his veto message. It was a masterly document, stressing the constitutional aspects, playing down the 'hard money' element and seeking to reassure the West. He knew the veto would be over-ruled, but its publication on 10 July changed the whole tone of the political debate (Birley 1944: 84–90). The battle lines between 'the enlightened classes' and the common man were now drawn. The issue secured a landslide re-election for Jackson, but the 'Bank War' had begun.

Opposition to the Bank came from two quarters – unlikely allies. Politically, the Bank was regarded as the natural ally of property against the growing conviction that sovereignty belonged to the people. Chartered companies in general, and banks in particular, had unacceptable privileges, and did not hesitate to use influence, lobbying, control of the press and even old fashioned bribery to protect and extend them (Schlesinger 1945: 125). From the point of view of such as 'Old Bullion Benton, the doughty Senator from Missouri, who honestly disapproved of all paper money and the banks which issued it' (Myers 1970: 90) the more specific evil was the power to issue bank notes. These encouraged speculation and benefitted the business class at the expense of 'the planter, the farmer, the mechanic and the labourer'. This was a 'hard money' argument one normally associates with the right in politics, and indeed, odd as it may seem to the modern reader, Jackson's populist left wing government was (once the Bank War was over) to pursue an active conservative sound money policy worthy of the staunchest English bullionists of the time.

Jackson had to play off this group against the West, and the States Rights activists. They had no objection to bank notes and actually favoured cheap money, provided that the issuers were under State rather than Federal control. The Bank, by its policy of presenting the notes of other banks for redemption as soon as possible after they received them, had restrained their issue. This was a particularly sensitive issue in Kentucky following the 'Relief War'. Banking had expanded, under the lead of the Bank in Kentucky and other States. The 1819 contraction (see above) had produced a wave of bankruptcies, to prevent which 'relief' legislation was passed. This made matters worse, and the legislation was declared unconstitutional by the Kentucky Court of Appeals. This decision was based on Marshall's judgment in *Sturges* v *Crowinshield* (1819). The Relief Party won the State election in 1824 and tried to remove the Court. This row rumbled on: one of its pamphleteers was Amos Kendall, later a prominent member of the Kitchen Cabinet.

'The Removal of the Deposites'

Jackson, having been re-elected, was more than ever determined to oppose the Bank.

The general was moved by dislike and distrust of an institution which he did not understand and which had sought to thwart his will and the arguments of Taney and Kendall, fortified his determination to deprive it of its remaining power in the financial and political community.

(van Deusen 1959: 80)

He wanted to press his offensive against 'America's Nobility System' led, as he thought, by the Bank (Schlesinger 1945: 97). He quotes Kendall as saying that Americans 'have their *young* Nobility system. Its head is the Bank of the United States; its right arm, a protecting Tariff and Manufacturing Monopolies; its left, growing State debts and State incorporations'. He also feared that the Bank could engineer a financial panic before the 1836 election. Taney thought the bank had made loans in return for political support, and still believed it to be unconstitutional. According to Myers: 'Jackson himself knew little of banks and he confessed to Biddle on one occasion that he had been suspicious of banks ever since he had read about the South Sea Bubble' (Myers 1970: 90).

What could be done? The Charter had three years to run. There was only one lever: the Secretary of the Treasury had power to remove the Government 'deposites' and this Jackson determined to do. In November 1832 Jackson told a Cabinet meeting that he was convinced the bank was insolvent and suggested withdrawing the deposits in it which had been made by the government. Supported by Roger Taney, the Attorney General, he asked Congress to investigate the bank. A Treasury investigation found the Bank sound, and Congress resolved that the government deposits were safe in its hands. After a triumphant post election tour of the United States. Jackson instructed Amos Kendall to seek alternative depository banks. Kendall reported that the banks would be more than glad to have the funds (van Deusen 1959: 81) and Jackson presented this report to the Cabinet on 10 September. Nicholas Biddle told Daniel Webster that this would be 'a declaration of war'.

The then Secretary of the Treasury, Louis McLane did not favour the removal, and was supported in Cabinet by Cass and Duane. In, the course of reshuffle McLane was moved to the State Department (the previous incumbent became Ambassador to France) and was replaced by William Duane (Schlesinger 1945: 99–100).

> Jackson took it for granted that Duane would remove the deposits but he soon discovered that he had caught a tartar. Duane had no more love for state banks than he had for the Bank of the United States and he, too, refused to do the President's bidding. He told the President ... that a change to local banks as depositories would shake public confidence; that local banks already had an over-inflated currency of better than six dollars in paper to one in silver. [The implication being

171

that deposit in local banks would inevitably result in further inflation of the currency.]

(van Deusen 1959: 81)

Duane was therefore dismissed (no ambassadorship for him, although Schlesinger suggests he had refused the offer of Moscow as an inducement to resign) and was replaced by the reliable Roger Taney, whose later reward was appointment to the Supreme Court. The Washington Post carried an announcement on 20 September that the deposites would be withdrawn on 1 October. The government had told the Second Bank that the deposites would not be immediately withdrawn. The general strategy was to draw down these deposites for current expenditure while putting new receipts into various other banks, including six associated with Jackson's friends and advisers and which were popularly referred to as the 'pet banks'.

Taney had given certain of the state banks a series of drafts drawn on the Bank of the United States to be used if necessary in retaliation against any hostile moves by the bank. One of the pet banks, the Union Bank of Maryland faced with financial difficulties caused by the speculations of its head and Taney's friend, Thomas Ellicott, jumped the gun and presented two of these drafts. Biddle had not been told how many such drafts were outstanding and according to his party's version of events, thought it prudent to reduce its loans more rapidly than it had originally planned. This sharp contraction of loans by the Second Bank before the new depositories were in a position to expand, caused a short sharp recession. Schlesinger explains events differently, suggesting Biddle deliberately engineered the recession to bring the government to heel (Schlesinger 1945: ch. ix).

In August 1833 the Bank began to call in loans, reduce discounts and present the notes of State banks for redemption. Merchants, forced into bankruptcy, at first blamed government policy. Taney fought back, arguing that if the Bank won on this point, democracy was dead. From August 1833 to 1 November 1834, the Bank reduced its loans by $18 million. The recession was made worse by other factors. A provision in the 1833 tariff required customs duties to be paid at the time of importation. 'New York merchants who sent a delegation to Washington to appeal for relief were told by Jackson that the fault lay entirely with the bank and that nothing would induce him to restore the government deposits to it' (Myers 1970: 93).

Van Deusen has the President 'trembling with rage and with the intensity of his convictions' telling one deputation of businessmen: 'go to the monster, go to Nicholas Biddle. I never will restore the deposits. I never will recharter the United States Bank or sign a charter for any other bank so long as my name is Andrew Jackson' (van Deusen 1959: 83) and another group, from Baltimore: 'the failures that are now taking place are amongst the stockjobbers, brokers and gamblers and would to God they were all swept from the land! It would be a happy thing for the country'.

172

The charter of the Second Bank was not renewed, but it was re-chartered under State law as the United States Bank of Pennsylvania 'by means that would not bear a critical examination according to the standards of either business or political integrity' (Kinley 1910: 24). It ceased trading for a time in October 1839, and finally went bankrupt in 1841. Galbraith is somewhat snide about Biddle, who was charged with fraud, indicted by a grand jury, but acquitted. 'His fate was that of nearly all who have dealt in innovative fashion with money' (Galbraith 1975: 82). This is hardly fair. Biddle was a conservative and competent banker. Maybe he was a megalomaniac, certainly a single minded political opportunist, but hardly even an innovator. In terms of public choice theory he was a 'rent seeker' par excellence.

19

AFTER THE BANK WARS: THE UK/US CRISES OF 1836 TO 1839

As we saw in Chapter 18, Hildreth had ended his History on an optimistic note looking ahead to 'a new era in the commercial history of America . . . the science and industry of the present age will accumulate stores of wealth, and the means of comfort and pleasure, hitherto unknown'. Shortly after these words were written, the 1837 crash hit the country. This involved both the United States and the United Kingdom, and this chapter is relevant to the history of both.

There had been a short sharp financial crisis in the United Kingdom in 1825. That, and indeed those of 1847, 1857 and 1866 can be dated precisely and unambiguously. The one dated 1836, (or was it 1837 or 1839?) cannot be pinned down easily. From the point of view of the history of money this period was very important. It was the first Anglo-American crisis, with knock-on effects in both countries, but also involved the Continent of Europe. It was partly precipitated by the aftermath of the American Bank Wars, while in the United Kingdom it brought home dramatically the weaknesses of the rules governing the Bank of England's role as an issuing bank and led directly to the Bank Charter Act of 1844. Given that events were not fully synchronised, it might be better to regard the period as a recession, including several periods of bank failure.

THE UNITED STATES AFTER THE BANK WARS

President Jackson having killed the Second Bank the United States, by now a major economic power, was without a Central Bank, without any proper banking legislation, and with a Constitution which, for all its merits, was to make it difficult to fill these gaps. Not only was there no Central Bank, the Federal government did not even have a bank account. There was no Federal banking law, and bank regulation was entirely a matter for the States. When the government terminated its special relationship with the Second Bank in 1833, it had transferred deposits to Jackson's pet banks. This arbitrary transfer of 'high powered money' from an established bank to others unable quickly to find good outlets for loans had already caused a sharp

174

contraction. It was compounded by two other measures. The sale of public lands and the 'distribution of the surplus' to the States in 1837 resulted in an arbitrary distribution of funds amongst the States. A radical government committed to a hard money policy, and distrusting finance capitalism did not wish to be dependent on a suspect system. The *Specie Circular* also affected monetary changes.

The distribution of the surplus

The 'distribution of the surplus' arose from the sale of Federal lands. The Federal government had a vast surplus and the national debt was paid off. It was difficult to find suitable banks into which Federal money could be deposited. In June 1836 a law was passed by which the surplus (then $50 million) could be distributed to the states. By January 1837, when the first distribution of $9 million was made the figure had fallen to $37 million. The second distribution was made in April 1837 which helped precipitate a crisis: in April:

> ... the serious nature of the crisis became apparent. A public meeting in New York ... appointed a committee of fifty, with Gallatin at its head to appeal to the administration to abandon a policy which threatened the destruction of the material interests of the nation.
>
> (Hepburn 1903: 123)

There had already been 250 failures. Nevertheless the third instalment of $9.3 million was made in July. It was to be the last.

The Specie Circular

In 1832 the government rescinded the Resolution of 30 April 1816 by which the Government accepted bank notes (including 'notes of banks which are payable and paid on demand in the said legal currency of the United States' which was capable of broad or narrow interpretation). The situation thus paralleled England after resumption. It was still desirable to check the abundance of paper money, even convertible paper, and to restore a specie circulation. This meant discouraging paper, except for mercantile transactions, and bringing gold back into circulation. Benton's bill to revise the bimetallic ratio to sixteen passed Congress in June 1834 (Doc Hist vol. ii: 116). It was supported by Adams, Webster and Calhoun, old enemies of the 'depositites', but opposed by Clay and Binney. Gold immediately returned to the mint. The Specie Circular was published on 11 July 1836 (Doc Hist vol. ii: 117).

The other leg of the policy was to outlaw 'shinplasters', as the small denomination notes (some for as little as 12.5 cents) were known. A Treasury circular of April 1836 prohibited the acceptance of notes under $5, by the Treasury, and forbade banks holding US deposits from issuing such notes. In February 1836 the prohibited figure was raised to $10. An Act of April 1836 raised it again to $20, and imposed other controls on banks. Jackson, with some success, persuaded the States to bring in similar rules.

By the time Van Buren succeeded Jackson the government was, as a result of these policies, in serious trouble. Hepburn puts the situation in early 1837 brutally. The Second Bank, which 'had acted as regulator . . . of state banks by refusing the notes of doubtful concerns and requiring the redemption of others' had lost its Federal charter and ceased to perform that function.

> This check upon the state bank issues having been removed and the enticing prospect of obtaining public deposits being held out . . . resulted . . . in a large increase in the number of state banks and . . . inflation of both notes and discounts. Many banks were conducting business without a dollar of actual capital being paid in, and a majority were subject to no legal restriction.
>
> (Hepburn 1903: 122)

The UK political background to the crisis

Buxton, gives the political background but he is more interested in taxes than in money:

> If the Government could not boast of doing much for fiscal reform at least they deserve credit for economy . . . the years between 1825 and 1840 were the halcyon days of economy and finance – a period to which Mr Gladstone has more than once adverted in fond reminiscence to point of moral against more modern extravagance as the time when Tory and Whig alike strove and strove successfully to reduce the public expenditure. . . .
>
> (Buxton 1888: 28)

In 1830 'while revolution raged abroad and reform was largely demanded at home' the Duke of Wellington, Prime Minister, had declared 'that the existing system of representation was as perfect as the wit of man could devise'. Buxton says in a footnote that the Funds fell from eighty-four to seventy-seven and a half 'this is probably the only speech of a Minister on a purely domestic subject which has ever seriously affected the price of the public securities'. The Government fell, and the whigs were to rule, with one short break, for eleven years until 1841. There is a lot of comment on Althorp's budget (but nothing on his actions on funding). There was a break in whig rule in 1834, precipitated by Althorp going to the House of Lords as Earl Spencer on the death of his father. The King 'exercising, for the last time in English history his constitutional right, himself dismissed the Ministry'.

176

Kindleberger says that President Jackson considered the responsibility for the crisis should be divided equally between Britain and the United States. British speculation was in cotton, cotton textile, and railroads and American speculation in cotton and land. The Commons preferred cotton. On timing

> ... it broke out in England in 1836 and 1837, spread to the United States and then in May 1838 when England was quietly recuperating erupted in Belgium, France and Germany to spread back again to England and the United States in 1839.
>
> (Kindleberger 1984: 125–6)

THE CRISIS

The crisis proper, though, began in the United Kingdom. Recovery from the crash of 1825 had it seemed been slow, but from 1831 to 1835 good harvests made the country almost self-sufficient in grain, and prices fell. A classic boom developed. One factor was that the East India Company lost its monopoly in the China market, realised assets and built up its balance in the Bank of England. When this reached £3 million they 'persuaded' the Bank against all precedents, to pay interest. At its peak there was a deposit of £4.7 million at 3 per cent on which the Bank itself felt it had to earn a return. This it did in the form of advances to Bill Brokers (Clapham 1970 vol. ii: 146–8).

Tooke criticises the Bank for its role in redeploying the East India Company deposits, apparently thinking they could have been sterilised. He quotes figures to show how far the Palmer rule had been breached.

> It is utterly impossible ... to explain away the glaring inconsistency which the above comparison exhibits between the state of the circulation as it was administered and that which *ought to have been* its state, if it had been administered according to any recognised rule for the administration of a convertible paper currency.
>
> Tooke 1838 vol. ii: 300).

Some capital was also moving into the United States, where for reasons discussed above money was flowing into the unregulated and chaotic banking system. Easy money domestically was compounded by the inflow of capital, and there was a speculative boom.

In June 1836 (Clapham 1970 vol. ii: 151) the Bank of England found its reserves were falling, as the gold flow to the West was partly stimulated by the revaluing of the gold dollar, and they had a substantial amount of acceptances from seven houses with Anglo-American business. These included the notorious 'Three W's', Wilson's, Wiggins, and Wildes. Browns (later Brown Shipley) 'were expert in the sterling dollar exchange and in the troublesome effects of the recent alteration in the American bimetallic currency system.'

177

Bank Rate which had been steady at 4 per cent for nearly a decade was raised to 4.5 per cent on 21 July 1836 (too little and too late) and 5 per cent on 1 September. In November 1836 Irish banks began to fail and a pushy joint stock bank, Northern and Central Bank of England, proved to be in difficulties. It closed in December and came effectively under the control of the Bank of England. It was eventually wound up without loss to the depositors or the Bank of England. 'Directors and directors' friends who owed the company large sums when sued from the ranks put in the plea that one partner cannot sue another for debt – and as the law then stood, they got away with it' (Clapham 1970 vol. ii: 156). Otherwise the worst of the 'American crisis' passed without a real panic in the United Kingdom.

Tooke also criticises the late rise in bank rate and again on the late subsequent increase to 5 per cent. He suggests that 'if the Northern and Central Bank had been suffered to undergo the penalty which the gross mismanagement of its direction so amply merited and the benefit of examples so strongly required the Bank of England would not have experienced any great additional drain.' However the Bank's reserves were 'at that time so low so culpably low as to give grave concern as to what might have happened had there been a further spread of the state of discredit.'

The sharp rises in prices at the end of 1836 were accentuated by the change of the parity of the pound against the dollar from $4.44 to $4.87 which tended to encourage the export of gold. The problems of Northern and Central where there were gross irregularities have to be contrasted with those of Esdailes where there was no suspicion of dishonesty. In that case, the Bank organised what we would now call a lifeboat. A recession, with high level of bankruptcies, continued during the first quarter of 1837 and in April it became clear that there were serious problems with cotton related business on both sides of the Atlantic. The Three W's sought, and eventually obtained, help from the Bank. American payments were suspended on 20 May 1837 and on 30 May (news had to cross by sea by boat) Wilsons and Wiggins announced they could not meet their liabilities as a result of the 'almost universal suspension of credit throughout the principal commercial banks of the United States'.

Tooke comments that after February 1837 'there appears to have been a slow but progressive influx of bullion. The circulation of the Bank underwent comparatively very little alteration during the remainder of the year. The state of commercial discredit was however very great throughout the first six months of 1837.' He says that the week beginning 1 June 1837 was the main period of panic but uneasiness persisted for the rest of the month. The situation was then relieved. 'The great mass of doubtful paper and credit having been removed or much reduced the circulation was restored to a healthy state'. Trade revived, confidence came back

> ... and as only twelve months ago the bank was encumbered with
> securities and drained of its treasure so it has recently become bearer

of securities and its coffers overflowing. The Bank having scrambled through its difficulties into a position of safety may naturally claim credit from the event . . .

But Tooke does not think they deserve it:

> In the subsequent recriminations the Bank of England blamed the country banks, and especially the new joint stock banks, while they, and many others, blamed the Bank of England. The case against the Bank is that it had not followed the Palmer rule and that it delayed raising interest rates and restricting its lending until far too late.
>
> (Feaveryear 1931: 254)

Feaveryear gives summary figures (Tooke gives more detail). He points out that certain country banks had surrendered their note circulation to the bank in return for a right to discount up to the limit at a special rate of 3 per cent regardless apparently of bank rate. He stresses the role of loans and subscribers of the £15 million government loan to compensate West Indian planters for the emancipation of slaves and is more critical than Clapham about the Bank's role in offering facilities to gold brokers.

Feaveryear says that the crisis of 1839 was more serious in its effects on the Bank's reserve than that of 1836 and contrasts the two events. There was a substantial demand for gold from the Continent following failures during 1838. The 'crisis' seemed to have taken the form of a threat to the Bank's reserve position and 'was not followed by any extraordinary commercial or banking failures. Trade however remained dull for another two years'. He comments on criticisms of the Bank which had accepted the obligation of 'lender of last resort' and had accepted the principle that its liability should be reduced as bullion was drawn for export.

> On the other hand it is true that either through faulty judgment or from the desire to maintain its income restrictive action was too long delayed and securities were, contrary to the Palmer principle, allowed to rise and the reserves were falling.
>
> (Feaveryear 1931: 257)

From the point of view of monetary history we are concerned not with a post mortem but with the fact that the events described were sufficient to precipitate a complete re-examination of the Bank of England's role as a Bank of Issue.

Hyndman (1892) (described by his biographer as 'Prophet of Socialism') blames the speculators 'each successive generation of ten years produces its fresh crop of needy adventurers and credulous premium-hunters'. In 1836, forty-two new banks of issue were formed. In the spring of 1836 the drain of gold to America forced the Bank of England to raise its discount rate and reduce its note issue. The private banks 'instead of following the . . . lead, issued fifty per cent more notes than before'. There was 'a great failure in Ireland', presumably the Agricultural Bank (Barrow 1975: 136).

The Independent Treasury

The United States government was still without proper banking arrangements. President Van Buren summoned Congress on 4 September 1837 and stated:

> it is apparent that the events of the last few months have greatly Augmented the desire, long existing among the people of the United States, to separate the fiscal operations of the Government from those of individuals and corporations.

Congress considered three schemes, a new National Bank, continuing the deposit system established on 23 June 1836, and the Independent Treasury. This had originally been proposed by Senator Gordon in 1834 and was revived by Senator Silas Wright of New York. It was supported by Gouge (1837) who reckoned that thirty-six depositories would be needed, and that the cost would be $101,600, less than the banks were charging. He put forward in support of his case two decidedly odd and unconvincing arguments: there was less risk from robbery, as thieves would be able to carry little of the heavy metal, and that the system would decrease executive patronage! (Kinley 1910: 38–9).

Daniel Webster and Albert Gallatin opposed the plan. It was impossible, they said, to separate public and private finance. To insist on specie payment while the government hoarded gold and silver would be a deflationary attack on the credit system. As Webster said on 12 March 1838 'The use of money is in the exchange. It is designed to circulate, not to be hoarded. . . . To keep it that is to detain it . . . is a conception belonging to barbarous times and barbarous governments' (Webster Senate speech 1838).

After a long political battle the Bill to introduce the Independent Treasury was passed on 30 June 1840 (Doc. Hist. vol. ii: 177). From that date, one quarter of government dues had to be paid in specie, increasing by a quarter each year until full specie payment was due from 1843. Public money was already largely held by collecting officers. The sub-Treasury Act was repealed on 13 August 1841 (Doc. Hist. vol. ii: 189) and state banks were once more to be used as depositaries. The banks were now (it was said) safer. It seems that government agents continued to act as depositaries.

There were later developments. The Democrats regained office in 1845, with the extreme anti-bank 'Loco Foco' faction dominant. A new sub-Treasury Bill was pased in 1846. Secretary of the Treasury Walker instructed all government offices to accept only gold and silver coin and treasury notes, but Congress had made no provision for the extra costs (Myers 1970: 132). In 1847 the government issued 20 million of treasury notes to finance the Mexican war, and in May 1854 the ubiquitous William Gouge was appointed special agent to examine the condition of the sub-treasurers.

20

PRIVATE BANKING IN THE
EARLY UNITED STATES

PRIVATE BANKING BEFORE 1837

Chapter 18 concluded with the demise of the Second Bank. This was the
end of a series of attempts to set up a public banking system in the United
States. Meanwhile, what of the private banks? Most of this chapter is
concerned with the period after 1837, but the earlier history is also relevant.
The Panic of 1819

> placed great strains on the US banking and financial system. The crisis
> exposed a basic inconsistency between two goals . . . specie converti-
> bility . . . and liberal extension of farm credit . . . Economists since the
> time of Adam Smith had understood that banks which issued conver-
> tible notes . . . could not safely lend to farmers . . . loans were typically
> long term, illiquid and relatively risky.
>
> (Russell 1991: 49)

This led, in the agrarian South and West, to experiments with the issue of
inconvertible notes. The banks could only stop runs by suspending payments. Notes continued to circulate, but at varying discounts leaving the
holders with financial losses.

The Western States (for this purpose, essentially Kentucky, Tennessee,
Indiana, Illinois and Missouri: Pennsylvania and Ohio were also sometimes
counted as 'Western') had large numbers of small banks, most of which
were, following the Panic, insolvent. The States reacted by revoking their
charters, and their role was taken over by State controlled 'relief banks'.
Their inconvertible notes were given a constitutionally dubious quasi-legal
tender status. Their history was 'brief, controversial and generally undis-
tinguished' (Russell 1991: 50) and most collapsed after court challenges,
some orchestrated by the Second Bank.

In the South (mainly North Carolina, South Carolina and Georgia, but
also perhaps Virginia and Alabama) banks were typically larger and better
capitalized, with branch networks. Although they suspended payment, they
continued to operate and the discounts were much smaller. Russell argues

that this was a successful experiment, with noteholders carrying part of the portfolio risk. The Second Bank eventually forced resumption: Virginia and South Carolina in 1823, and the others during the following five years. In 1828 Georgia established a Central Bank to deal with the problem of short term bank credit. The southern States were actively to oppose the renewal of the charter of the Second Bank.

The demise of the Second Bank also had substantial consequences for the future of private banking. Standard works on American financial history tend to concentrate on the big public banks and have relatively little to say on the private banks which were proliferating during the period. Contemporary sources give much more information, and it has proved well worth the effort of tracking them down. There is in fact a long and complicated history of State chartered banking, and the issues were now brought into sharp focus. After 1834 there was no longer anything of the nature of a Central Bank – and indeed it was not until 1913 that the Federal Reserve took up this role. Bank regulation was a State matter, but the mood of the country favoured hard money and treated all banks, and all paper money, with suspicion. Three methods of bank control were adopted at different times and in different places. All have their parallels in Europe, and all have lessons for the modern world: The Safety Fund system; The Suffolk Bank system; and 'Free Banking'.

William Gouge and other writers

One of the classic works on the private note issuing banks at this period is *The Curse of Paper Money and Banking, or a Short History of Banking in the United States of America* published by William Gouge of Philadelphia in 1833. (The full text was also reprinted in the successive issues of The Journal of Banking edited, and probably mainly written, by Gouge. These appeared in Philadelphia from July 1841 to July 1842, and is the version referred to in subsequent notes.) It was republished a few months later in England by William Cobbett, M.P., a determined opponent of paper money. In his introduction he says:

> The following history is the work of an apparently exceedingly dull and awkward man: the arrangement of the matter is as confused as it can well be made, the statement of facts is feeble and there is as little of clearness as can well be imagined in anything coming from the pen of a being in its senses. There was a 'FIRST PART' consisting of the moral and philosophical and economical . . . lucubrations of the author; but I am very sure that if my reader could see these he would thank me for leaving them out, especially as the omission is attended with a deduction from the price of the book.
>
> (Cobbett 1833: ix)

Cobbett was wrong. The first part is, at least to a modern reader, more readable than the second, which, as an accumulation of facts, is rather heavy going. Van Deusen (1959) quotes from it with approval, claiming that his own paragraphs are based on a careful study of the book, and regarding Gouge as the principal economic theorist of Jacksonian democracy.

Gouge thought that gold and silver were natural money, but that bank notes constituted an artificial and dangerous inflation of the currency. He argued that this caused booms and panics (an argument reflected in the English discussions of the time) and that it gave bankers an unfair opportunity for making profits. Gouge disliked banks both because they made inflationary issues of paper money and because they were corporations. Corporations, he said,

> ... are unfavorable to the progress of national wealth. As the Argus eyes of private interest do not watch over their concerns their affairs are much more carelessly and much more expensively conducted than those of individuals. Corporations are obliged to trust everything to stipendiaries, who are often less than the clerks of the merchant ...
>
> (Gouge 1841–2: 80)

He quotes 'A celebrated English writer' (in fact Lord Thurlow) as saying 'corporations have neither bodies to be kicked, nor souls to be damned'.

Various sources give figures for the number of banks at various dates. Goddard lists, with details of paid up capital and dividend record, 137 banks operating in twenty-four cities in 1831, but does not give incorporation dates from which a pattern could have been derived. Gouge gives a table (Cobbett 1833: 184–5) showing the number of banks in the various states at different dates. He comments 'While so much uncertainty hangs over Bank accounts, the reader will be content with an abstract of the tables and statements of Mr Gallatin'.

Some figures from various sources are given in Table 20.1

These figures do not include banks which had failed by the date given. Gouge mentions 165 'broken banks' by 1830. There was, by any test, a huge

Table 20.1 Growth of US Banks and circulation of US $: 1792 to 1813

Date	Number of banks	Circulation ($ million)	Source
1792	8		(Hildreth)
1794	18		(Myers)
1810	80		(Hildreth)
1811	88	28.1	(Gouge)
1815	208	45.5	(Hildreth)
1816	246	68.0	(Gouge)
1820	307	44.8	(Gouge)
1830	330	61.3	(Gouge)

expansion after 1812. Many of these new banks were in the South and West, and these were formed mainly to give credit to farmers (Russell 1991: 49). This was important for later developments.

Gouge also summarises information on banks in existence and bank notes in circulation, but cautions his readers about the sources of his information. His list of banks by states, shows fifteen were in Massachusetts and thirteen in Rhode Island in 1811. His rather tedious and repetitive discussions of the histories of different banks, indicates a lot of activity. Many banks failed and the notes of others which were probably solvent circulated at a discount.

New charters in this period had to be granted individually by the State legislatures and, said Myers, 'obtaining a charter from an unfriendly legislature was sometimes difficult if not impossible'. Banks typically extended loans as notes and these were used even for small payments. 'Not until 1813 did the law of New York forbid the issues of notes of less than $1 in value' (Myers 1970: 69–70).

Robert Tucker's (1839) *The Theory of Money and Banks Investigated* is much more readable, but is more in the tradition of the learned tracts then being published in England. Tucker was born in Bermuda (The family is one of the 'Forty Thieves' said to run the island). He became successively an American lawyer, Professor of Moral Philosophy and Political Economy in the University of Virginia, and chairman of the East India Company.

Thomas Goddard (1831), in spite of his title, deals only briefly with European banks, and reproduces at length key documents from the history of the Second Bank. He wrote just before the Bank War. He appends considerable information on the capital and dividend of a long list of banks as at 1831, and on insurance companies and other institutions.

McCullough's contribution on 'Money' to the eighth edition (1858) of the Encylopaedia Britannica contains a few pages on banking in the United States.

> It has been the uniform practice of the different States of the union to allow banks to be established for the issue of notes payable in specie on demand. In cases where the liability of shareholders in banks was to be limited to the amount of their shares, they had, previously to 1838, to be established by acts of local legislatures. But in general, these were easily obtained, and down to a comparatively late period, it may be said that banking was quite free and that practically all individuals or associations might issue notes provided they abided by the rules laid down for their guidance and engaged to pay them when presented. Under this system the changes in the amount and value of the paper currency of the United States have been greater than in any other country and it has produced an unprecedented amount of bankruptcy and ruin.
>
> (McCullough 1858: 491)

Hildreth (1837), begins with a brief and readable account of John Law, English and Scottish banking and of the 'suspension' during 'Pitt's anti Jacobin war'. It is interesting as an expert American view in 1837. He argues that the Bank of Amsterdam was needed because of a depreciated circulating medium. Hildreth's History ends on an optimistic note:

> since which time [1831, the beginning of his fourth period] we may reckon a new era in the commercial history of America. It is not to be supposed that business will continue to go on with the same rapid progression for which the last six years have been distinguished. But though its progress will not be so rapid still business will go on; and unless war returns again to curse the earth and barbarize its inhabitants, the science and industry of the present age will accumulate stores of wealth, and the means of comfort and pleasure, hitherto unknown.
>
> (Hildreth 1837: 91)

As so, eventually, it was. Weeks after the words were written, the 1837 crash, already described in Chapter 19, hit the country.

Jackson's second term

Jackson's veto message had been deliberately ambiguous, as he feared that too much emphasis on the hard money aspect of opposition to the Bank might alienate some of his supporters. In 1833, re-elected with strong Western backing, he had the confidence to embark on his real programme, or rather that of Taney and Benson. The motives were partly political 'Democracy implies a government by the people . . . aristocracy implies a government of the rich'. In his view this meant destroying the Bank:

> . . . the centre and the citadel of the moneyed power . . . A national bank is the bulwark of the aristocracy, its outpost and its rallying point. It is the bond of union for those who hold that Government should rest on property.
>
> (Schlesinger 1945: 125)

There was also a coherent economic policy, largely set out by Gouge, whose book circulated widely. He was to work for a time for the Treasury from 1835 and felt the need to explain, in his 1841–2 'Journal' version, that it had been written before he was a public servant. The economic arguments divided into two. Honest money benefited the working man, who had often been cheated by being paid in depreciating bank notes. Excessive paper issues may have stimulated trade, but by profiting the moneyed classes at the expense of the others. The other argument appears to have been based on a primitive, but broadly sound, theory of the trade cycle.

New York safety fund system

All banks chartered by New York had, since 1829 subject to certain regulations, to subscribe to a 'safety fund' out of which the notes of failed banks could be redeemed: 'it does not level the root of the evil; and has the obvious defect of taxing the honest for the sins of the fraudulent' (Hildreth 1837: 75).

The early history of private banks, as described above, parallels the attempts to develop an official 'Bank of the United States'; attempts defeated by Andrew Jackson during the dramas of the Bank Wars. The system is also discussed at length in a paper by Robert Chaddock, prepared for and published by the National Monetary Commission. New York, not surprisingly, had a long tradition of private banking, which goes back certainly to 1800. 'Sound banking develops slowly out of experience. The charters from 1800 to 1825 show certain common provisions to which others were added as experience dictated' (National Monetary Commission, Chaddock 1910: 243). There was, for instance, an innovation in 1811 by which the State legislature in chartering the Union Bank and two others retained the right to appoint the first directors. In the same year another bank, the Middle District, had Commissioners appointed mainly by the legislature to distribute the stock and arrange the first election of directors. 'This latter method by commissioners, continued to be followed under the safety fund system for several years and was the source of much complaint and abuse.'

Other specific provisions are discussed on the following pages. There was a debate on the renewal of bank charters in 1827 in which the Speaker of the House said that the profits of City banks 'do not depend upon the circulation of their bills but arise from the discount of notes', distinguishing their activities from those of the country banks. Chaddock's chapter 2 discusses the idea of the Safety Fund which had been first mooted in 1829. Martin van Buren (at that time Governor of New York) pointed out that, of the forty banks operating in the state, the charters of thirty-one expired within four years and that it was necessary either to arrange promptly for the renewal of the charters of the sound banks or 'to anticipate the winding up of their concerns by the incorporation of new institutions'. He rejects in a sentence the prospect of living without banks or relying only on Federal ones and in a few more words, the idea of a state bank.

> If by a state bank it is intended an institution to be owned by the state and conducted by its officers it would not seem to require much knowledge of the subject to satisfy us that the experiment would probably fail here as it has elsewhere.
>
> (Doc. Hist. vol. i: 319)

Successful and beneficial banking 'must be conducted by private men upon their own account'.

Van Buren goes on to expand on the right basis for renewing charters and granting new ones. 'The policy . . . of requiring the payment of a large bonus to the state for performance of some special service as the price of bank charters is condemned by experience'. The conditions for the grant should therefore 'refer exclusively to the safety and stability of the institution'. The legislature must ensure that the citizen when he exchanges his 'property or services for bank paper may rest contented as to its value'. The plan he himself puts forward with real or pretended dividends to the independent legislators is intended 'to make all the banks responsible for any loss the public may sustain by a failure of any one or more of them' (collective responsibility).

A few days later he goes into more detail and the Act itself, the New York Safety Fund Act, was passed on 2 April 1829 (Doc. Hist. vol. i: 325 ff). According to Chaddock (1910: 259) Joshua Foreman had devised the safety fund proposals. The banks, he argued 'had the exclusive privilege of furnishing a paper currency by which they made a profit. Therefore the state would lack a guarantee for the soundness of that paper. The banks should in common be answerable for it'. Foreman had also argued that public injury caused by the management of solvent banks in lending excessively and then suddenly calling in their loans to the inconvenience and sometimes ruin of their customers were greater than the losses from bank failures. (Chaddock comments that the discussion assumed that banking was identified with note issue, rather than deposit banking.)

Under the proposals subsequently enacted each bank was required to pay in a sum equal to one half per cent of its capital each year into a safety fund, such payments to continue for as long as the assets of the fund did not exceed 3 per cent of such capital. The interest on the fund after expenses was to be paid to the banks and the fund itself was to be used to meet debts (but not the capital stock) of failed banks. The administration was in the hands of three bank Commissioners, one appointed by the governor of the state and two by the banks. They required to visit each bank quarterly and more often if requested by any three other banks.

A 'monied corporation' as the Act referred to banks, could by Section 28, be wound up if it was three months in arrears with its sinking fund contribution if it should have lost half its capital stock, suspended payment of its bills in specie for ninety days or refused access to the commissioners. A rejected proposal was that all bank notes should be countersigned by a central agent to prevent fraudulent over issues. This caused problems, of which more later. There continued to be provisions by which capital had to be paid up before a bank could open: the officers of the bank had to declare on oath that no arrangements had been made to finance the purchase of stock with money borrowed from the bank. In 1829 sixteen charters were renewed and eleven new ones granted. There was some resistance from the New York City banks who argued that they were less profitable because of competition with the Bank of the United States.

There was little provision for debts other than bank notes. The City banks actually had a substantial deposit business and there were some arguments in 1841 as to whether the deposits were effectively covered by the guarantee. A free banking system was inaugurated in 1838 but the safety fund system appears to have continued. The later appears to have worked well until 1838. It had to deal with five cases of insolvency but most of the losses were eventually recovered. There was a procedural meeting in 1837 involving three Buffalo banks. It was found that the fund intervened after the liquidation was completed and the final deficit known. This could result in loss to note holders and an Act of May 1837 enabled the authorities to take measures to pay the notes of failed banks at once out of the fund and thus prevent depreciation and loss to note holders' (Chaddock 1910: 302).

After the crash of 1837

The 1837 law, while bringing forward the date at which the safety fund could intervene did not permit it to top up its funds until liquidation of the insolvent bank was complete. An 1841 law repealed this and permitted calls at a rate of one half per cent per annum to top up the fund. This was construed to mean that banks which had not yet paid up their full 3 per cent would have to contribute at the rate of 1 per cent per annum. There were also provisions for permitting banks to make their contributions in the notes of failed banks.

During 1840–2 there were eleven bank failures in New York State, listed in Chaddock (1910: 309) and described individually on his following pages. In 1842, when it was discovered that failed banks had debts other than notes of over $1 million the law was changed to relieve the safety fund of responsibility for deposits or any debts other than notes. The table in Chaddock (1910: 383) shows how between 1836 and 1860 the character of banking had changed because of the growth and eventual dominance of deposits and the decrease in the use of bank notes. He comments 'evidently banks did not realise until the panic of 1857 that deposits now constituted the danger point in banking and must be covered by a reserve as well as notes'. See also Rockoff (1991: 91).

Free banking

In New England, where the monopoly of banking privileges had always been least complete, and where the banks had been well managed the number of banks had gone on increasing. In 1830 Hildreth says there were 230 banks in the United States, of which 170 were in New England. The safety Fund proved inadequate to cope with the 1837 crisis, and Free Banking legislation was introduced in 1838.

[In principle, anyone could obtain a charter for a bank, which granted] the necessary powers to carry on the business of banking by discounting bills, notes and other evidences of debt; by receiving deposits; by buying and selling gold and silver bullion, and foreign coins; by buying and selling bills of exchange and by issuing bills, notes and other evidences of debt; and *no* other powers whatsoever except as are expressly granted by this act.

(Free Banking Act 1838)

This was by no means laissez faire. There were many restrictions. First, there were strict reserve requirements. The bank was required to hold a 100 per cent reserve against its notes in the form of mortgages or state bonds and an additional 12.5 per cent in specie. (The specie requirement was repealed in 1840.) These were really quite strict: a bank could not raise funds for commercial lending by issuing notes, although there was undoubtedly a profit from the operation. Indeed the issue of $100,000 of notes required the commitment of $12,500 of own funds as capital. One problem was that the value of the state bonds held as security could fluctuate with interest rates and the perceived quality of the issuer. The 'reserve requirement' was therefore technically imperfect.

Another weakness is that, at least in New York, there was no reserve requirement for deposit liabilities. Of eighteen states which adopted free banking by the 1850s, some took deposits into account, while others permitted part of the reserves to be held as deposits in other banks. Second, convertibility was into the US specie dollar, which at this time was essentially gold. Technically, there was a bimetallic standard but the ratio favoured gold. Third, many states had usury laws, restricting the rate of interest that banks could charge.

White and Seglin (1989) discuss how a Free Banking system can evolve, mentioning the case of the Boston banks in establishing the concept of 'par acceptance'; the strategy of one bank accepting the notes of another at par. Why should private banks, assumed to be acting in their self-interest, do this? The profit of a note-issuing bank is a function of 'the face value of its outstanding note issue the proportion of that issue which it may safely lend at any time [i.e. after maintaining a prudent reserve for withdrawals] and the rate of interest earned on its loans'. Clearly it wants the highest proportion of its loans outstanding, and benefits from making its own notes more attractive. Superficially, this argues against making those of its rivals more acceptable but, it is suggested, there is an even greater benefit from making notes in general more widely held. Mutual acceptance widens the circulation, and may be a more attractive strategy than 'note duelling'. This involves a bank building up a stock of the notes of a rival bank, and then presenting them for redemption. The dangers, to both parties, are obvious. The practice reduces collective profits by forcing banks to maintain higher specie reserves (White and Seglin 1989: 228).

New York Free Banking is discussed by McCullough (1856: 49), who says:

> It is objectionable because, 1st, A longer or shorter, but always a considerable period necessary elapses after a bank stops before its notes can be retired and 2nd, Because the securities lodged for the notes are necessarily . . . of uncertain and fluctuating value; while, in periods of panic or general distrust, they become all but inconvertible.

He quotes a letter from the sub-secretary of the (Federal) Treasury, supporting his view, and lists six banks operating under the system which had failed. Time would elapse before the notes would be redeemed. Only one bank would (eventually) redeem at par. In other cases the pay-off was between 77 and 94 cents.

Jevons (1875) says of the Free Banking system under which a banker has discretion over the reserves kept against the notes issued:

> As a general rule, no doubt, notes thus issued will be paid; but, having regard to the great fluctuations of commerce . . . [there will be periods of pressure and experience shows] that a certain number of individuals will calculate too confidently on their good fortune
>
> (Jevons 1875: 230–1)

He later implies that the pre-1845 Scottish system would work admirably, 'if we were all Scotchmen, and had only 11 great banks.' The system had no lender of last resort: Did this matter? Rockoff (1991) discusses the effect of the 1857 crisis, which resulted in a suspension of specie payments. He also discusses wild cat banking. One method of generating a multiplier effect was to deposit State bonds purchased at a discount: the State insisted that its bonds be valued at par.

By the Civil War, some semblance of order had taken the place of the chaos of early unregulated wild cat banking. There was still no national banking system, no central bank and no Federal banking law, but some States at least seem to have filled the gap remarkably well. Soon, though, there was to be a major upheaval, described in Chapter 27.

THE BANK CHARTER ACT OF 1844 AND THE CRISIS OF 1847

THE BANK CHARTER

In 1837 Colonel Robert Torrens had put forward a proposal to separate the Bank of England into two departments. He followed Ricardo on wanting, eventually to go one step further and 'to withdraw the right of issue from the Bank altogether'. He was supported by two fellow members of the Currency School, Loyd and Norman. A new Parliamentary Committee was set up in 1839 but when Parliament was dissolved in 1841 it simply published the evidence without a report. Peel, in opposition, had been a member of the committee but did not attend for any of the evidence given by Tooke, the only representative of the Banking School.

In 1841 Peel became Prime Minister but took no immediate action. There was a provision by which the government could terminate the charter of the Bank of England in 1844, which provided a convenient opportunity for introducing the Bank Charter Act. This, perhaps the most important single piece of legislation in nineteenth century financial history, received surprisingly little debate. The Chancellor, Henry Goulburn, wrote formally to the Bank on 26 April. He hinted that if separation of functions was not agreed, the right of issue could be taken over by the Treasury. The Bank replied on 30 April, accepting separation without comment but raising a number of questions affecting its income (Clapham 1970 vol. ii: 180).

The Bank Charter Act of 1844 ('Peel's Act') was not pure 'Currency Principle' but was a compromise. A newly created issue department took over £14 million of securities from the banking department in return for the issue of notes. This 'fiduciary issue' was not backed by gold but was intended to be a fixed amount – only to be increased by an amount equal to two-thirds of the amount of lapsed country bank note issues. It was actually increased to £19,700,000 by 1923 when the last of the country banks of issue (Fox Fowler and Company) was absorbed by Lloyds Bank.

Apart from the fiduciary issue, all notes issued by the Bank had to be backed 100 per cent by gold or silver, not more than one-fifth of the total being silver. The Bank was required (Sections III and IV) to issue notes and exchange all gold bullion offered to it at the rate of £3.17s.9d. per ounce of standard gold (Equivalent to £4.4s.10d. per ounce of fine gold). (This had in fact been the practice of the bank since 1829.) Section VI of the act required the Bank to publish a weekly return of its position. The form of this return remained unchanged until 1959 even though the historic fiduciary issue, shown as a separate item, was swamped by other issues.

Other provisions of the Act were designed gradually to extinguish the country note issues. Only banks issuing notes on 6 May 1844 were in future to have the right to issue notes, the right being limited to the bank's average circulation for the preceding twelve weeks. The rights would lapse if a bank (other than an existing joint stock bank) acquired more than six partners by amalgamation or otherwise. Where the right of issue lapsed the Bank of England might apply for an Order in Council adding two-thirds of the relevant amount to the Fiduciary issue. Separate acts in 1845 extended these measures to Scotland and Ireland. Joint Stock Banks within the sixty-five mile radius of London may 'draw, accept, or endorse Bills of Exchange, not being payable to a Bearer on Demand'. The Bank was released from the payment of stamp duty on its notes but was required to pay £180,000 (£120,000 as in the 1833 Act plus £60,000 in lieu of stamp duty).

There were criticisms. John Stuart Mill suggested that, as gold exports were likely to come from deposits, 'the deposit department might have no alternative but to stop payment' even though 'the circulating department was still abundantly supplied with gold'. James Wilson, founder of the Economist said that if Peel's object had been to increase the intensity of a crisis, he could not have adopted a more certain plan (Clapham 1970 vol. ii: 195; and see also Thomas Tooke, 'Inquiry into Currency Principles'). These were soon to be proved right but on 2 September 1844, for better or for worse, there came into force what Clapham called 'a law which was to stand for eighty years, but not always upright' (see Wilson 1847).

THE CRISIS OF 1847

The Bank Charter Act came into force in 1844. It principles were soon to be tested and its key defect became apparent. The Crisis of 1847 was the first based on excessive credit (i.e. 'deposits' as part of the 'money supply') rather than on the over-issue of bank notes. The best contemporary account is in D. Morier Evans (1848), himself extensively quoted in Clapham. Evans divides his book into three parts – the Railway Mania (1845), the Food and Money Panic (1847 the 'crisis' proper) and the French Revolution (that of 1848). These events were, however simply the climax. The commercial and financial structure of England (and Scotland, whose story is significantly different) was changing, and changing fast. The successive crises were, arguably, a necessary if uncomfortable part of the process of change.

Background to the Crisis

Trading companies had to finance goods which were four months or more in transit. Initially traders operated with their own capital, but became increasingly keen to obtain credit from the banks. This was normally done by discounting bills and the competitive efforts of the joint stock banks made it easier to raise finance on bills of six months or even longer. The entry of the Bank of England into this market is very significant for what was to follow.

From 1832 until the middle of 1836, the total of bills held by the bank was generally below £3 million (though rising exceptionally to over £11 million during the pressure of 1837–9). In 1844 the bank had held about £15 million of gold against a note issue of £21 million. After the transfer of gold to the issuing department as required by the Bank Charter Act, it was found that the banking department held bullion equal to 60 per cent of deposit liabilities. Its 'earning assets' were only 40 per cent. A Committee on 'the present state of the Discount Department', reporting in advance of the operative date of Peel's Act, recommended that discount rates should be fixed in line with market rates. This was intended to ensure that sufficient good borrowers were at all times attracted to the Bank. In line with this policy in September 1844 the bank rate was reduced from 4 per cent to 2.5 per cent. The Bank then began to lend aggressively. Total discounts reached £9.5 million by end 1845 and £12 million by March 1846. Although the Bank did not discount bills with a longer date than ninety-five days it started advancing money (in form for three months at a time) on much longer eastern trade bills. Arguably the intention of the authors of the 1844 Act were defeated. The directors of the Bank appeared to think that provided they kept to the rules governing the issue department, the banking department could lend indiscriminately.

The Crisis at its height

The railway mania was a prelude to the full crisis of 1847, which really developed from the price of corn (i.e. wheat). In 1845–6 the failure of the Irish potato crop led to a rise in the price of corn. Given the mood of the time there was the inevitable speculation and the Bank of England was called upon to discount 'an inordinate number of corn bills'. The cost of importing corn

> ... coming at a time when so much of the country's savings were sunk in unfinished and as yet unwanted railways, caused serious drain on gold. The Bank of England who supplied the market with £7–10 million of floating funds by discounts and by market loans was in a bad position both for curbing speculation and for checking the drain. As soon as it attempted to do so there was bound to be shrinkage of credit [and a risk of panic]. As a matter of fact however the leading

directors for some time came to the believe that they need do nothing. They waited for the Currency Principle to work and complacently watched their banking reserve dwindle away without taking any effective measures to protect it.

(Feaveryear 1931: 261)

Contrary to the predictions of the Currency School there was no shrinkage in the note issue and the outflow was entirely at the expense of the reserve ratios of the banking department. The bank action was too little too late. Bank rate was raised in stages from 2.5 per cent to 5 per cent by 10 April 1847. In late April the Bank announced that it would cut by half the value of bills discounted. There was a temporary lull in the crisis and an inflow of gold.

Later in the year the prospect of good harvest brought down the price of wheat from 110 shillings to 60 shillings a quarter and there were failures in the corn trade. On 21 August a firm of corn dealers, whose senior partner, W.R. Robinson, had recently been elected as Governor of the Bank of England, failed. Robinson formally disqualified himself by selling his bank stock. Two other directors, Gower and Reid, went in September, disqualified because of 'unpaid bills on discount accounts of their respective firms' (Clapham 1970 vol. ii: 203). 'There had never been such commercial slaughter of Directors' (Clapham 1970 vol. ii: 198). In October when the return showed a frighteningly small reserve, the Bank announced that it could no longer lend money on government securities. This led to panic sales on the stock exchange.

The crisis now spread to the banks, who came to the Bank of England for help. This they could not give for technical reasons. Any advance made to a country bank gave that bank the right to withdraw notes from the Bank of England, and the Bank's right to issue notes was limited by the Bank Charter Act of 1844. The directors would not, and arguably could not, accept the undertakings of the banks that they merely wished to settle by cheque and did not require bank notes. The country bankers sought political help, and begged the Chancellor, Sir Charles Wood, to suspend the Act. He refused their request until on 18 October the Bank of Liverpool stopped payment. On 2 October the government instructed the Bank to advance freely promising an Act of Indemnity should this result in an increase in the fiduciary issue above the legal maximum. The text of the Government's letter (Evans 1848) reads:

Gentlemen
Her Majesty's Government have seen with the deepest regret the pressure which has existed for some weeks upon the commercial interests of the country, and that this pressure has been aggravated by a want of that confidence which is necessary for carrying on the ordinary dealings of trade.

They have been in hopes that the check given to transactions of a speculative character, the transfer of capital from other countries, the influx of bullion, and the feeling which a knowledge of these circumstances might have been expected to produce, would have removed the prevailing distrust.

They were encouraged in this expectation by the speedy cessation of a similar state of feeling in the month of April last.

These hopes have, however, been disappointed, and her Majesty's Government have come to the conclusion that the time has arrived when they ought to attempt, by some extraordinary and temporary measure, to restore confidence to the mercantile and manufacturing community. For this purpose, they recommend to the Directors of the Bank of England, in the present emergency, to enlarge the amount of their discounts and advances upon approved security, but that, in order to retain this operation within reasonable limits, a high rate of interest should be charged.

In present circumstances, they would suggest that the rate of interest should not be less than 8 per cent.

If this course should lead to any infringement of the existing law, her Majesty's Government will be prepared to propose to Parliament, on its meeting, a Bill of Indemnity. They will rely upon the discretion of the directors to reduce as soon as possible the amount of their notes, if any extraordinary issue should take place, within the limits prescribed by law.

Her Majesty's Government are of opinion that any extra profit derived from this measure should be carried to the account of the public, but the precise mode of doing so must be left to future arrangement.

Her Majesty's Government are not insensible of the evil of any departure from the law which has placed the currency of this country upon a sound basis; but they feel confident that, in the present circumstances, the measure which they have proposed may be safely adopted, and at the same time the main provisions of that law, and the vital principle of preserving the convertibility of the Bank-note, may be firmly maintained.

We have the honour to be, Gentlemen,

Your obedient number servants,

(Signed) J. Russell,

To the Governor and the Deputy-Governor of the Bank of England.

To this communication the Bank returned the following reply:

Bank of England Oct, 25 1847

Gentlemen

We have the honour to acknowledge your letter of this day's date, which we have submitted to the Court of Directors, and we enclose a copy of the resolutions thereon, and

195

We have the honour to be, Sirs, your most obedient servants,
(Signed)
James Morris, Governor,
H. J. Prescott, Deputy-Governor.

To the First Lord of the Treasury and the Chancellor of the Exchequer.

Resolved – That this Court do accede to the recommendation contained in the letter from the First Lord of the Treasury and the Chancellor of the Exchequer, dated this day, and addressed to the Governor and Deputy- Governor of the Bank of England, which has just been read.

That the minimum rate of discount on bills not having more than 95 days to run be 8 per cent.

That advances be made on bills of exchange, on stock, on Exchequer-bills and other approved securities, in sums of not less than £2,000, and for periods to be fixed by the Governors, at the rate of 8 per cent, per annum.

The effect of the Government letter is described in the evidence of Mr. Glyn thus:

It produced the same effect as if the Bank of England has made an issue; because it brought out the hoards of notes, and they went into circulation of the country, and it removed the cause of the panic, which is stated to have arisen from the act of 1844.

Samuel Gurney illustrated this statement by his own case. He observes:

We required about £200,000 and had it at 9 per cent. On the Monday morning we had again a very heavy demand upon us; and we applied to the Governor, and said that, to supply Lombard Street with what was wanted, we should require £200,000 more. It was a case of difficulty for the Bank under its reduced reserve, and under the limitations of the act. The Governor postponed a decision on our application till two o'clock. At one o'clock, however, the letter from the Government authorising relaxation was announced. The effect was immediate. Those who had sent notice for their money in the morning sent us word that they did not want it – that they only ordered payment by way of precaution. And after the notice we only required about £100,000 instead of £200,000. From that day we had a market of comparative ease.

(Evans 1848: 87)

The Bank did in fact make substantial advances at 8 or 9 per cent but there was (as promised) little actual demand for notes. The fiduciary issue was not in fact exceeded and the bill of indemnity was unnecessary. As the country bankers had pointed out the demand was not in fact for notes but for facilities against which cheques might be drawn. The problem was not in the issue department but in the banking department the reserves of which were so thin that there was a grave danger that any increases in advances would spill over into the potential right for depositors to call for more bank notes than the issue department could legally issue. The Bank Charter Act had been designed to avoid repetition of past crises based as they were on over issue of bank notes (Hawtrey 1932: 125; Bagehot 1915: 193).

The Currency School had become preoccupied with this point and had unintentionally paved the way for a new type of crisis based on the extension of bank advances. John Palmer had in fact written to Sir Robert Peel when the Bank Charter Act was before the House of Commons, pointing out that the strict rules might make it impossible for the Bank to render assistance during a crisis. Henry Bosanquet (1810) had also written to Peel about the same time, drawing attention to the same problem and suggesting that during the first five years of the new system whenever the bank rate should rise to 8 per cent the issue department should be permitted to make advances at that rate or the deposit of Exchequer bills. In such circumstances the Bank would have the option of making a special issue of notes which would have been receivable in the payment of taxes but not convertible into gold. Peel, while admitting that the Bank would find it difficult to help in a crisis such as that of 1825 or 1839, said he was convinced that such a crisis would henceforth be most unlikely.

> Not the least remarkable thing about the Currency theorists was their simple faith that the mere separation of the Bank into two departments and the fixing of the fiduciary note issue at the perfectly arbitrary figure of 14 millions would banish forever the risk of commercial panic. Torrens had said that the adoption by the legislative of his plan would effactually prevent a recurrence of those commercial revulsions those cycles of excitement and depression which resulted from the alternative expansion and contraction of an ill regulated currency.
>
> (Feaveryear 1931: 256–7)

The crisis was over, but 33 major firms had failed. The inevitable Committee of Enquiry was set up. The Bank Charter Act had faced up to its first test and suffered the first of the several suspensions. The general structure of UK banking law and practice was, from a monetary point of view, now in place.

Part III

INCONVERTIBLE
PAPER MONEY

22

INTRODUCTION – LAND BANKS

INTRODUCTION

This Part deals with inconvertible paper, the most 'modern' form of money. Part I dealt with money as coin which, as Part II has shown, gradually came to be supplemented and substituted for by various forms of paper credit instruments and bank deposits. By the late nineteenth century, and the end of our main period, bank money of one form or another constituted the greater part of the money supply in most countries, although all these other forms of money were directly or indirectly convertible into gold (or silver).

In the Middle Ages, and indeed in the ancient world, we had to make a distinction between the value of money in tale or in specie. Coins backed by strong royal authority could acquire a fiat value in excess of the value of their metal content. This raises an interesting question. If the King's authority can result in a coin containing 8 pence worth of silver being accepted in trade for 10 pence, why not reduce the silver content to 6 pence or 2 pence, or dispense with it altogether and substitute a piece of paper? This, of course, is what we have today: paper money and base metal coins of little or no intrinsic value universally accepted in trade.

As one might expect, the normal order of events was for a country first to become familiar with convertible bank notes, and that then, under the pressure of a crisis (usually a war) these should be declared inconvertible. This is indeed what happened during the American Revolution (Chapter 24) and again during the American Civil War (Chapter 27). During the Napoleonic Wars the United Kingdom 'suspended payment' in this way (Chapter 26). However, the French, with a less sophisticated banking system, actually introduced a new system of inconvertible paper money 'the Assignats' (Chapter 25). In two of these five examples the United Kingdom, and the winning side in the American Civil War, convertibility was later restored at par. In the other three, the American Revolution, France and the Confederate States, the paper money became worthless. Apart from these five major examples, discussed in detail, there were other, early cases, some of which are mentioned briefly in Chapter 28. In many of these, when the crisis was over, bank notes had some residual value on a currency reconstruction.

During the twentieth century inconvertible paper money became universal. There have been dozens, indeed hundreds, of cases of the complete collapse of a currency, and no country has been free from periods of inflation. (These were chronicled, in the early post War period, in the annual volumes of Pick's Currency Year Book. Indeed an early acquaintance with Frans Pick helped give this author a taste for the more off-beat cases of monetary chaos.) The first European experiment, that of John Law discussed in Chapter 23, was in one sense a precursor of these other experiments but it was different in an important and interesting respect. The late seventeenth century is a turning point in the history of money and the history could, had Law succeeded, have taken a different course.

Credit instruments had for long made it unnecessary for transactions, particularly international transactions, to be settled by the immediate payment of gold and silver, and generally these instruments economised in the use of metal money. Deposit bankers who provided a safe custody service were beginning to learn the techniques of lending out a proportion of the money entrusted to them. These arrangements were still just 'money substitutes' and did not yet have the quality of 'money'. The next step was for the public to perceive bankers' deposit receipts as 'bank notes', and as a perfectly adequate and acceptable form of money. At the end of the seventeenth century the Western world was ready for this step. In England and elsewhere the coinage was inadequate and in a bad state, while in any case expanding trade called for a more efficient means of payment. As we have seen in Part II, the way forward, at least in the United Kingdom, was the development of a system of bank notes and bank deposits backed by fractional reserves in gold. Some theorists of the time thought that was not radical enough: gold and silver could not provide an adequate currency and we needed 'a new species of money'.

LAND BANKS

One concept was that of the Land Bank which would issue notes in exchange for land, their value being based on the value of that land. This was perceived as a conservative concept. The value of land was thought to be more stable than the value of gold and silver, subject as they were to the vagaries of discovery. Indeed, the history of gold discoveries had some influence on the timing of these developments. 'Money supply' in the form of newly mined gold and silver had expanded rapidly until about 1650, and had met the needs of expanding trade. After that money supply grew more slowly, while the real economy continued to expand.

John Law had contributed to the debate on land banks and his early theoretical work can conveniently be discussed here alongside that of his contemporaries. Law's early prejudices appear to have been in the direction of sound money even though his actual experiments were very quickly to result in inconvertible and eventually worthless paper money. One interesting aspect of his thinking was that securities such as shares in the Bank of England constituted 'liquid assets' and could, with proper institutional arrangements, actually serve as money. Indeed Chapter 16 showed how the shares of the South Sea Company were much more liquid, at that time, than Government debt. Sir William Petty, in Quantulumcunque (McCullough 1856), had suggested in 1682 that banks could be used to remedy a shortage of money: he argued against restrictions on interest, saying that Sir Josiah Child (who argued for lower rates) was confusing cause and effect.

Hugh Chamberlen, an obstetrician, proposed a Bank of Credit on Land Rents in 1695 (Scott 1912 iii: 246ff). The owner of land could mortgage it for 150 years, receiving for every £150 of rent, £8,000 in notes of the bank, paying 0.25 per cent interest and 1 per cent capital redemption for the privilege. Alternatively he could sell outright for 80 years' purchase, payable in notes of the bank. Scott describes the operation in detail, saying that 'the schemes of Barbon and Briscoe . . . were much less unsound [and although Chamberlen has been given the main credit for the proposal] his promotion was in reality the extreme extravagance of the movement, not its natural outcome.' It was not successful.

Another English projector of a land bank was John Asgill who wrote a commentary on the legislation and also a tract called *Several Assertions Proved in Order to Create Another Species of Money than Gold and Silver* (Asgill 1696, Second Edition, 1720). This asserts the need for more money, dismisses the idea of making bills of credit legal tender, and argues that land held has the qualities of money and is capable of being turned into money. The operation would lower the rate of interest and raise the price of land (eventually he suggests, to 100 years' purchase). In a postscript to the second edition (1720) he refers to 'Money and Trade Considered' and says of Mr Law

> it now seems that his late successes abroad have enrolled him amongst the prophets as not without honour save in his own country. [Somewhat cryptically, he goes on to say] his extraordinary Advances and supernatural Productions, Making and calling Things that are not, as though they were, being a Conviction (to them that believe it).
>
> (Asgill 1720)

It is quite clear from his commentary on the Bill that the desire of landowners to raise money on their land and indeed to increase its price was as much a motive as the need to augment the coinage which was at that time being reformed by Isaac Newton.

> The landed gentlemen of the House of Commons . . . did not take kindly to arguments about the difference between a bill and a

mortgage. A land bank that among other things might satisfy these longings eventually became a Tory plank when the foundation of the Bank of England was in the offing. At the right time (1693) an intellectual, Hugh Chamberlen, an obstetrician by profession presented a plan of a land bank where landowners would get loans at 4 per cent and the governor would get more money than it got from the Bank of England.

(Schumpeter 1954: 294)

The Asgill/Barbon scheme would allow the bank to make loans on landed property up to 'the value of the register', i.e. three-quarters of the actual value, ('the value of the auditor') the difference representing 'the equity of redemption'. Loans were made in 'bills of charge' carrying interest at 3.5 per cent paid quarterly or 4 per cent paid half-yearly (Scott 1912 iii: 249–50). Briscoe's (1694) National Land Bank was to purchase agricultural land at 20 years' purchase, and ground rents at 22 years. Interest was 2 pence per £100 per day, or just over 3 per cent per annum. Schumpeter (1954) says that John Briscoe 'claimed to have been plagiarised by Barbon and Asgill and was himself accused of having plagiarised Chamberlen'. Barbon, he says, renounced theoretical metallism on the grounds that 'money is a value made by law' to which the value of the material is not essential'.

In late 1695 Briscoe proposed a scheme to help finance the war, based on legislative approval for his land bank. Asgill and Briscoe were originally rivals, but in early 1696 they amalgamated and submitted revised joint proposals. The House of Commons resolved on 5 March 1696 that a National Land Bank should be set up, and the Bill received the Royal Assent on 21 April 1696. The bank was to raise a loan of £2,564,000 to the government at 7 per cent, and would be authorised to lend a similar sum on the security of land. The subscription list opened on 25 May, but by 11 June only £40,000 (only £7,700 according to one source) had been subscribed: the promoters were reduced to announcing that they were ready to accept 'old clipped money that cannot be passed away without loss' The scheme collapsed on 1 August. (The threat of a rival may have helped precipitate a run on the Bank of England: Scott (1912) says that it was the run which caused the failure of the subscription.)

John Law and the shortage of money

A curious manuscript (once in the possession of the present author and later traded to Antoin Murphy, who now ascribes it to Law) describes the case for a land-mint which would issue notes on the security of land instead of on silver. It is unsigned and undated, and a gap in the middle suggests it may be a fair copy rather than the original. One of the few references is to Locke 'Considerations' (1691: 7) so it must be later. References to the guinea 'now' being worth £1.1s.6d. and to gold having increased in value to 15½ times that of silver suggest a date no later than 1695, when there was a sharp rise in the gold/silver ratio and in the silver price of the guinea, an event that could hardly have been ignored by a writer on money. It must also have been before the National Land Bank legislation of 1696.

Money and Trade Considered

The above apart, John Law's first pamphlet *Proposals and Reasons for Constituting a Council of Trade* was published in Edinburgh in 1701. This was followed by *Money and Trade Considered* (1705). His Land Bank proposals were sent to and discussed, but eventually rejected, by the Scottish Parliament. *Money and Trade Considered with a Proposal for Supplying the Nation with Money* is a general tract on economics with a strong bias towards suggesting that the problems of Scotland are those of a shortage of money. Chapter V discusses land banks and points out the fall in the value of money over 200 years. Chapter VI examines a proposal by 'Dr H. C.' (i.e. Hugh Chamberlen) to issue notes on land. Chapter VII gives the actual Proposal, which was, in summary as follows

> To Supply the Nation with Money, it is humbly propos'd. That 40 Commissioners be appointed by Parliament [who shall] have Power to Coin Notes which Notes to be received in Payments where offered [i.e. to be legal tender. He sets out details of where and when they should meet and to whom they should be answerable and suggests three ways in which Parliament might authorize them to issue notes.]
>
> (1) To authorise the Commission to lend Notes on Land Security, the Debt not exceeding one half, or two Thirds the Value and at the ordinary Interest.
> (2) To give out the full Price of Land as it is valued 20 years' purchase more or less according to what it would have given in Silver-money. The Commission entering into Possession of such Lands, by Wadset granted to the Commission or Assigneys; and redeemable betwixt and the expiring of a term of years.
> (3) To give the full price of Land upon Sale made as such Lands, and disponed to the Commission or Assigneys irredeemably.

The Commission would hand over its land (or charges on or interest in land) against the redemption of its notes but the notes would not be redeemable in silver or gold. He also proposed that Scots money be reduced to the English standard: this was to be done about two years later. He argues for the superior quality of paper money.

Schumpeter (1954: 294–6) speaks highly of Law, who 'worked out the economics of his project with brilliance and, yes, profundity which places him in the front rank of monetary theorists of all time . . .'

205

23

JOHN LAW, RICHARD CANTILLON, AND THE MISSISSIPPI SCHEME

INTRODUCTION

John Law, a Scotsman, became effectively Finance Minister and virtually Prime Minister, of France and was responsible for the earliest European experiment in inconvertible paper money. This collapsed in 1720, the year of the South Sea Bubble, (Chapter 16) but although there are many parallels between the two speculative manias, they fit logically into different sections of this book. This chapter begins with a brief early history of John Law, and goes on to discuss the dramatic events in France, concludes with a note on Law's lower profile but perhaps in the end more successful contemporary – the Irishman Richard Cantillon. Law's theoretical writings, and earlier experiments with Land Banks, have been covered in Chapter 22. For a definitive account of this period we must await work in progress by Antoin Murphy.

The early history of John Law

John Law was born in April 1671, the son of William Law, an Edinburgh goldsmith and banker. He showed a precocious talent for mathematics, for extravagance, and for charming ladies. There are several accounts of his life, mutually contradictory but good stories all. His father died when he was young, leaving him well provided for financially, but without the wise guidance and discipline he might have had if his father had lived. He went to London, described by Mackay (1852) as 'very young, very vain, good-looking, tolerably rich, and uncontrolled'. He became a great and apparently successful gambler. Contrary to the old adage, he was equally lucky in love: 'Ladies of the first rank smiled graciously upon the handsome Scotsman – the young, the rich, the witty, and the obliging'.

Some years later his luck turned. He fell into the classic gambler's trap of playing for higher stakes to recoup earlier losses and eventually had to mortgage the family estates in Scotland to his mother. About this time, in 1695, he fought a duel and killed Edward Wilson (Beau Wilson), was convicted of murder and condemned to death. The sentence was commuted to a fine, but Wilson's family appealed against the commutation. He was detained again, but managed to escape to the Continent (Oudard 1928).

Although John Law devoted his evenings to gambling, and to the activity referred to by writers of that time as 'gallantry', he appears to have found time in the mornings to study banking, finance and trade. He lived in Holland around 1696 and was very impressed with the Bank of Amsterdam, which had been founded to deal with the poor state of local coinage, and whose bank notes and Bills of Exchange payable in bullion at the bank, actually commanded a small 'convenience' premium over coin and bullion (Chapter 15).

Adventures in Europe

Law having tried unsuccessfully to obtain a pardon for his English crime, returned to the Continent, first to Paris where he had many friends. Given his influential connections, he tried to introduce his land bank proposals to the French Government. His approaches to Desmarets, the Comptroller General, were rejected, apparently by Louis XIV. Law then proposed his scheme to Victor Amadeus, King of Sardinia who replied that his dominions were too small for the execution of so great a design. He added that 'he was by far too poor a potentate to be ruined, and advised Law to return to France. 'If I know the disposition of the people of that kingdom, I am sure they will relish your schemes' (Mackay 1851). Montgomery Hyde (1948) regards this interpretation as too cynical. The scheme was for a sound bank which would always keep a cash reserve of 75 per cent. In his version, the king was impressed, and remained on good terms with Law.

Law is said, while in Turin, to have opened an account at the Bank of Amsterdam, and to have a personal fortune of £109,000. In 1712 he bought a house at the Hague, and promoted a state lottery. He left for France, with his share of the takings, a year later. On 1 September 1715 Louis XIV died, his son and grandson having both died shortly before. His heir and great-grandson Louis XV being a minor, the Duke of Orleans, Law's patron, became Regent. During the next five years of the Regency, Law was to leave an indelible mark on financial history.

The splendours of the reign of Louis XIV (Le Roi Soleil) proved to have been on a very shaky foundation. Corruption was rife at all levels, with sufficient incentives for the private sector's 'invisible hand' to gravitate towards the public purse. The national debt was 2,000 million livres, with interest at 80 million livres per annum. Revenue was 145 million and expenses (before interest) were 142 million livres. Law moved quickly after the King's death. Within two months he had had detailed discussions with the Duke of Orleans and others likely to be concerned. However, at a decisive meeting on 24 October his project was rejected in spite of the Regent's support. Shortly afterwards Law is reported to have remarked that the secret of the philosopher's stone was to make gold out of paper. 'When shall we see this masterpiece?' asked the Abbé Dubois. 'Within three or four years' (Montgomery Hyde 1948: 73).

In 1716 there was a recoinage by which the currency was depreciated by a fifth and the Chambre de Justice initiated an extensive purge of corrupt tax farmers. In most cases 'confiscation' effectively amounted to a fine, as much of the wealth was effectively concealed. In many cases a bribe to a courtier could be substituted for a fine and MacKay suggests (without giving any authority) that of the 180 million livres collected, only 80 million went towards the debt (3,000 million on his figure) and 100 million found its way into the pockets of the courtiers. This did not satisfy the people who 'did not see the justice of robbing one set of rogues to fatten another'. The purge continued and rewards to informers were so attractive that many honest tradesmen were harassed and put to considerable trouble and expense to prove their innocence. This was Law's opportunity. He made proposals on paper money and banking. The Duke of Orleans, the Regent, canvassed the Council for support and obtained it, only Saint-Simon dissenting, on 1 May.

The Banque Génerále

By edict of 5 May 1716 a bank, Law & Company, (later the Banque Générale) was formed with a capital of 6 million livres in 1,200 shares of 5000 livres each. As with the Bank of England, it received privileges in return for taking over part of the National Debt. One quarter of the subscription for shares had to be made in specie, the balance in Billets d'Etat. As Billets were trading at about 40 the effective capital was only 3.3 million livres, with 1.5 million cash actually paid up. Shareholders would have one vote for five shares, with a maximum of 30 votes per holder. The Abbé Dubois was given 30 shares as a gift for services rendered: 'become my partner and in three years you will be able to buy the whole of Paris' . . . 'No', he replied 'I have too much to lose'. The notes issued by the bank were acceptable in payment of taxes: a classic 'definition' of legal tender status. The initial concept was a good one. The notes were backed by specie, were to be redeemable on demand and in coin current at the time they were issued. MacKay described this as a 'masterstroke of policy' making them proof against the debasement of the coinage.

The Banque Générale notes, none of which are known to have survived (Lafaurie 1952), read 'promet payer au Porteur à vue . . . livres Tournois en Especes du poids du titre de ce jour, valeur reçue'. Later those of the Banque Royale read merely 'en Especes d'Argent', effectively removing this guarantee, and a few, dated 1 January 1720, omit even these words. Under the impact of Law's notes, commerce quickly recovered. The notes themselves rose to 15 per cent premium while the billets issued by the government were at a discount of some 60–70 per cent. John Law expressed himself very strongly both at this time and in his earlier writings about the need for a bank to have adequate security. It is not clear what Law & Company had in the way of earning assets in its balance sheet, nor what would have happened had the story stopped there – but these stories never do.

The Mississippi scheme

The Mississippi Company, the Company of the West (Compagnie d' Occident) was incorporated in August 1717 with a capital of 100 million livres in 200,000 shares of 500 livres each. The whole of this was payable in Billets d'Etat at nominal value. These were currently at a discount to specie: (Murphy gives a range of 68–72) so that the effective cost per share was about 140–160 livres. A substantial part of the assets comprised government obligations rather than trading assets. According to Murphy, the initial impetus came from Crozat, who wanted to surrender his Louisiana lease in lieu of Visa taxes. (Visas involved the conversion of floating debt into the new billets d'état.) He operated through Le Gendre d'Arminy, his brother-in-law and front man. Until 1719 the operations were closely modelled on those of the South Sea Company: after that the fortunes of the company were closely linked with those of Law's bank.

In May 1719 the Mississippi Company merged with the Company of the East Indies, and took over the exclusive privilege of trading to the East Indies, China and the South Seas. Renamed 'The Company of the Indies' it created 50,000 new shares, 'filles' in contrast with the original shares, now known as 'mères' for a nominal value of 500 livres each payable in full in Billets d'Etat at face value. These shares promised a yearly dividend of 200 livres. The shares were six times over-subscribed and there was a delay of several weeks before the subscription list was published. There was a crazy scramble to obtain shares.

The Banque Royale

Meanwhile in 1718 'the Duc d'Orleans, observing the uncommon advantages resulting from that establishment [Banque Générale], resolved to take it into His Majesty's hands. . . . This resolution . . . could not be relished by Mr. Law – but they knew the inutility of opposition to the will of the Regent' (Wood 1824: 30–1; Montgomery Hyde 1948: 98). By decree ('Declaration du Roy, pour convertir la Banque Générale en Banque Royale' 14 December 1718) the public was informed that the bank was renamed the Banque Royale that the king had reimbursed the former proprietors (in specie, giving them a profit) and had himself become answerable for the note issue. Initially, these were to be reimbursed in current coin – subject to arbitrary debasement – and were therefore capable of being rendered effectively inconvertible. This was by then 59 million livres. 'By subsequent edict' the King undertook that the notes 'should not be subject to such diminutions as might be made on the specie but would always be paid in full': Law's original principle (Wood 1824: 3; Montgomery Hyde 1948: 99). Law was named Director-General and continued to be in charge.

According to Wood (an apologist for Law) 'the bank . . . departed from the principles of private and mercantile credit . . . and proceeded upon those of public credit, which in an absolute monarchy, as France then was . . . cannot be depended upon'. Wood was writing in 1824, too early to form any views on the financial integrity of a modern liberal democracy! Whether because of, or in spite of, Law the bank issued notes to the amount of 1,000 million livres between 5 January and 20 December 1719. A further 1696 million were issued by 1 May 1720.

The Bank was of course by now totally over extended. When the Regent became Minister of Finance after a further depreciation of coin, the public were offered the right to exchange 4,000 livres in specie and 1,000 in Billets d'Etat in return for 5,000 livres of new coins. Parliament saw the folly of this. Remonstrances having failed, they took the unusual step of passing an edict that only the old money should have legal tender providing that the bank should keep within its charter and that 'foreigners' (whether naturalised or not) should cease meddling in its affairs. The Regent annulled this, but Parliament passed another edict dated 12 August 1718. The Regent supported Law when he was summoned before Parliament. The serious setback proved temporary.

The affairs of the Bank and the Company were now inter-linked. What now happened of course was that the Mississippi Company stock continued to rise in price, purchases being financed by inflated notes issued by the Bank. There was a bureau d'achat et de vente which supported the price of Mississippi stock at 9,000. The parallel English story of the South Sea Company was different: the Bank of England remained independent, successfully resisted a take-over attempt and its notes remained convertible. Another difference was that in France there were no competing 'bubble' companies, everything being centralised under Law's effective control (Murphy 1986: 73). The only problem was that note holders still had a right to demand payment in specie. In early 1720 the Prince de Conti presented notes on such a scale that it is said that three wagons were required to transport the gold. The Prince acted not from financial prudence, but out of spite at not getting the allocation he wanted in new issues of Mississippi stock. Although the claim was met, the transaction alarmed Law, and he complained to the Regent. The latter ordered the Prince to refund two-thirds of the specie. There was no run on the Bank but some of the wiser jobbers and speculators quietly converted some of their profits into specie and spirited it away from France.

All payments were now made in paper, and between February and May 1720 1,500 million livres of notes were printed. These were of course inconvertible. The notes were guaranteed by the State but the profits of the bank were transferred to The Company of the Indies. There remained enough credulous citizens at large for this transaction to raise the value of the shares of the company. In May 1720 it was calculated that there were 2,600 million of Law's notes in circulation, more than twice the amount of coins. By Edict of 21 May both the shares of the company and the notes of the bank were to diminish in value until the end of the year when they would only have one half their nominal value. This nearly caused a revolution and was rescinded. But on 27 May the bankers stopped payment in specie. D'Aeguesseau, dismissed in 1718 was recalled as Minister of France and on 1 June the 'exchange controls' were reimposed. Nearly 25 million new notes were created and on 10 June the bank was re-opened. The system finally collapsed in November.

Law returned to England for a time after receiving a pardon, but died in Venice in 1729.

His epitaph sums up his life:

> Ci git cet Ecossois célèbre,
> Ce calculateur sans égal
> Qui, par les règles de L'algèbre,
> A mis la France à l'hôpital

Richard Cantillon

In striking contrast to the flamboyant Scotsman John Law, his Irish-born contemporary Richard Cantillon, kept a low profile. There are no tales of high life, gambling, duels or sexual intrigue. Law's various biographies are bespattered with famous names. Cantillon's is not one of them. Yet, as his activities become better documented, they reveal him as in many respects the more interesting man of the two.

In 1755 there was published posthumously Richard Cantillon's 'Essaie sur la Nature du Commerce en Général'. This was rediscovered in 1881 by Stanley Jevons and is now recognised as one of the greatest of the early tracts on modern economics. Part II, on money, and part III, on international trade are particularly good and reflect the views of a man of experience as well as depth of thought. Cantillon's 'Monetarism' has been contrasted with Law's 'Keynesianism' and while this is perhaps an over simplification, his work, closely followed by that of David Hume, is perhaps the first in a tradition which continued, through Ricardo, to modern monetary economics. Certainly Jevons refers to the essay as 'the veritable cradle of political economy' and asks 'What is the nationality of the economic science?' He concludes that

> The first systematic Treatise on Economics was probably written by a banker of Spanish name, born from an Irish family of the County

Kerry, bred we know not where, carrying on business in Paris but clearly murdered in Albemarle Street. The treatise was written either in English or French, it is not known which; it was first printed in Paris in the guise of a French translation, purporting to be published by Fletcher Gyles over against Gray's Inn in Holborn; was damned in England by a base garbled English retranslation, erroneously attributed to a merchant later of the City of London, perhaps the brother [actually the cousin] of the author. Except that it was once mistakenly quoted by Adam Smith it has remained to the present unknown or entirely misinterpreted in England, while in France it has been explicitly acknowledged as the source of the leading ideas of the great French school.

(Jevons 1881)

Richard Cantillon was born in Ireland, probably in or around 1680. He applied for French nationality in 1708, this then being regarded as a routine precaution for foreign merchants trading within France. He was one of the 'wild geese', Irish Catholic gentry who fled Ireland after the Battle of the Boyne in 1690. They added much to the commerce of France, just as the Protestant Huguenots, driven out of France were making their impact in England and elsewhere. During the War of the Spanish Succession he served as assistant to James Brydges, who made a fortune as Paymaster General and became Duke of Chandos, Handel's patron. During the next ten years he was to become associated in various ways with John Law and his system.

In 1715, his uncle and namesake, already banking in Paris, went bankrupt. The nephew was able to repay the creditors and to take over the business. He must by then already have been a man of substance and the records available show that, as a banker, he was capable of handling large transactions. He appears to have operated successfully in accordance with the sound principles he was later to write about. On 19 December 1718, Cantillon entered into a joint venture with John Law and Joseph Edward Gage. The object was to take a concession from John Law's Mississippi company and set up a colony in Louisiana. An expedition led by his brother set out in 1719. A little later Gage, seeing a substantial paper gain on his Mississippi stock and wishing to speculate in foreign exchange, 'borrowed £53,000 from Cantillon's bank on the security of the shares'. In the spring of 1720 foreigners sold Mississippi shares but, according to Murphy (1986: 106), not all the funds were repatriated. Some were used to take up positions in French currency.

Cantillon distrusted Law's scheme, particularly in its later stages, and had accurately prophesied in private correspondence that it would collapse in the latter half of 1720. Earlier that year everything was riding high and many speculators who had accumulated a huge fortune on paper were to try their luck in London and the South Sea Bubble as well as in foreign exchange. They were not willing to sell what they already had, but wished to borrow on their stock in order to make yet further speculations. Cantillon was happy to oblige them. His bank then appears to have sold the securities deposited with it as security. This of course would represent a 'short sale' with the danger that if and when the borrowers repaid their loans and wanted their security back he might have to buy shares back at a higher price. In the event his belief that he would be able to buy them in at a lower price was justified.

Cantillon's Essay, Part Three chapter VIII, discusses the Bank of England 'la Banque nationale de Londres' and refers to the South Sea Bubble, and is well worth quoting at length.

> If a Minister of State in England, seeking to lower the rate of interest or for other reasons, forces up the price of public stock in London and if he had enough credit with the Directors of the Bank (under the obligation indemnifying them in case of loss) to get them to issue a quantity of bank notes without backing, begging them to use these notes themselves and buy several blocks and capitals of the public stock, this stock will not fail to rise in price through these operations. And those who have sold stock, seeing the high price continue, will perhaps decide (so as not to leave the bank notes idle and thinking from the rumours spread about that the rate of interest will fall and the stock will go up further in price) to buy it back at a higher price than they sold it for. If several people seeing the agents of the Bank buy this stock step in and do likewise, thinking to profit like them, the public funds will increase in price to the point which the Minister wishes and it may happen that the Bank will cleverly resell at a higher price all the stock it has purchased at the Minister's request, and will not only make a larger profit on it but will retire and cancel all the extraordinary bank notes which it has issued.
>
> If the Bank alone raises the price of public stock by buying it, it will by so much depress it when it resells to cancel its excess issue of notes. But it always happens that many people wishing to follow the Agents of the Bank in their operations help to keep up the price. Some of them get caught for want of understanding these operations, which they enter infinite refinements or rather trickery which lie outside my subject.
>
> It is then undoubted that a Bank with the complicity of a Minister is able to raise and support the price of public stock and to lower the rate of interest in the State at the pleasure of this Minister when the steps are taken discreetly, and thus pay out the state debt. But these refinements which open the door to making large fortunes are really carried out for the sole advantage of the State and those who take part in them are generally corrupted. But if some panic or unforeseen crisis drove the holders to demand silver from the Bank the Bomb would burst and it would be seen that these are dangerous operations.
>
> (Cantillon 1931: 321–3)

This can now be seen as a brilliant analysis of the techniques of the market operations undertaken by governments throughout the ages, and still attempted by the Government Broker and the US Federal Reserve. However, as we saw in the operations of the Henry VIII, we now know that every time such a trick is tried (at least within the fairly short memory of market players) it becomes less effective. We can also see, from a historical perspective, how such an insight was derived from first hand experience of the activities of John Law.

24

THE AMERICAN REVOLUTION AND THE BIRTH OF THE DOLLAR

INTRODUCTION

The two great revolutions of the late eighteenth century, in America and France, and the Napoleonic wars which followed the latter, are a major turning point in the history of the Western world. They are also associated with three experiments with inconvertible paper currency, which are, between them, a turning point in the history of money.

In France, as in the United States, the imperative was the need to finance a revolution and to defend it from its enemies, within and without. There are some similarities (but more differences) between the two experiences, both of which ended with the collapse of the revolutionary currency. Europe and America emerged from the drama and the rather different British events with a considerably extended paper money and banking system, but one again (for a time) to be based on convertibility into the precious metals.

The American War of Independence was the first war, at least in the West, to be financed with depreciating paper money. The method of finance (and the war itself) were successful. The paper issues, and their unfortunate holders, were not. Following Independence, the new nation had to face the problem of building a monetary system. A series of extraordinary accidents and apparently random decisions resulted in the birth throes of what was to become the world's leading currency – the United States dollar.

WORLD MONEY BEFORE 1776

For about fifty years most of the world had enjoyed stable prices and a sound currency system. It was possible to publish 'hardback' ready reckoners for calculating the exchange between the major countries without the fear that they would become out of date. The figures were based on the bullion values of the various national coins and the assumption of a stable bimetallic ratio. The introduction of 'milled' (machine made) coins defeated the efforts of the (private enterprise) clippers. No debasements (the public sector

215

equivalent) were attempted. Such paper money as existed was at this stage fully convertible into coin (for two brief exceptions see Chapter 28), and still played a subsidiary role. Each of the major nations of Europe had its distinctive national currency, but merchants (aided by the ready reckoners) had few difficulties in exchanging one currency for another.

International trade, with the East, the Americas and elsewhere, was mainly conducted in one of the European currencies. Inevitably, certain national coins became more widely accepted than others for this purpose, notably the British gold guinea, the French louis d'or and the Austrian silver thaler, the latter being, via the Spanish rial or 'piece of eight' the ancestor of the American dollar. This is a classic period during which 'good money drove out bad' as Gresham's Law, properly understood, permits.

Money in the American Colonies before 1776

The thirteen Continental Colonies, which were to become the first States of the USA, developed separate currency systems which were not at par either with the British system or with each other. McCusker (1978) give comprehensive information on systems and exchange rates. A key problem was a shortage of coin. As with Ireland, the problem of money in the colonies was largely ignored by the British Government. Mercantilist principles then in vogue (Adam Smith's *Wealth of Nations*, the classic refutation of mercantilism, was to be published in the year of the American Revolution) discouraged the transfer of gold and silver to the colonies. Wampum, an Amerindian 'Primitive Money' based on strings of cowrie shells (Quiggin 1949: 305–8) was declared legal tender in Massachusetts from 1637 to 1661 for debts up to 12 pence (10 pence from 1641) but 'depreciated' in value from '4 a penny' for the white 'and blueu at 2 a penny' to '6 a penny'. On 26 May 1652 that colony set up its own mint to strike Pine Tree shillings, but was forced in 1665 to retreat from this breach of Royal Prerogative (Doc. Hist. vol. i: 5–7).

In 1690 Massachusetts pioneered the use of Bills of Credit which, as the term implies, were issued for a specific purpose and designed to by-pass the issue of 'money' by the Colonies. South Carolina followed in 1703 and by 1730 (following a paper by Benjamin Franklin) these Bills had become the principal currency of all the colonies (Doc. Hist. vol. i: 9–27). The various Treasuries issued paper money, sometimes in very small denominations such as 6 pence, 8 pence, or 12 pence. Massachusetts scored another 'first': its Proclamation Money has been afforded 'the dubious distinction of having had the first depreciation in value of publicly issued paper money' (Newman 1976:9). Issued in 1702 at a rate of 133 shillings to 100 shillings sterling, it depreciated to 150 in 1713, and slid down to 1100 by 1749. It thus had the edge on Louisiana, then a French colony, which experienced the collapse of the Law system in 1720. An act (1707) of Queen Anne 'for Ascertaining the Rates of Foreign Coin in Her Majesty's Plantations in America' was designed to enforce a proclamation of 18 June 1704. Another act (1751) of George II

> ... to regulate and restrain Paper Bills of Credit in His Majesty's Colonies or Plantations of Rhode Island and Providence Plantations, Connecticut, Massachusetts Bay, and New Hampshire in America and to prevent the same being legal Tender in Payment of Money.
>
> (24 Geo. II, Cap. 53)

Background to the revolution

Colonies were regarded as an essential feature of British trade policy. The Navigation Acts sought to maintain colonies as markets for British exports. This followed then current mercantilist theories: the *Wealth of Nations* had yet to be published. The London government had traditionally not interfered much with the internal affairs of communities of fellow country-men who had settled abroad. The 'Continental Colonies' in particular had strong elected assemblies and regarded themselves as self-governing. The Seven Years War (1756–63) between Britain and France (known in North America as 'the French and Indian war'), was fought over North American possessions. It ended with the Peace of Paris by which France was obliged to concede Quebec, a number of forts including Detroit and 'all territory east of the Mississippi except New Orleans'. Victory was expensive, as was the consequent need to maintain a British army in the acquired territories. The national debt had risen to £140 million, and Parliament now became acutely conscious of the financial cost (as opposed to the trade gains) of the Colonies.

George III had come to the throne in 1760, and attempts were now made to make the Colonies self supporting: the Government needed to collect from them in taxation at least enough to cover its costs. This first meant strengthening the hand of the governors, the King's representatives appointed from London. Previously a law passed by the colonists had been valid unless the Privy Council exercised a rare veto. Governors were now instructed not to sign legislation unless it included a clause, 'the suspension clause' suspending it until positive approval from the Privy Council had been obtained. This caused a great deal of resentment, and was the second criticism of the King made in the Declaration of Independence. 'He has forbidden his Governors to pass laws of immediate and pressing importance, unless suspended in their operation till his assent should be obtained; and when so suspended, he has utterly neglected to attend to them'. The first taxing measure, the Stamp Act, was passed by Parliament in February 1765 and nearly precipitated the Revolution ten years early. There were riots and protests and the provisions were never successfully enforced.

The government of Granville fell, to be succeeded by that of Rockingham, which, giving way to mercantile pressures, repealed the Stamp Act, but tried to save face with a Declaratory Act. Although the immediate crisis was averted the battle of taxing powers was not over. The Declaratory Act was interpreted by the London Parliament as authority to tax: the Colonists took the opposite view. Dowell (1884: 145), the historian of taxation, has this to say of Granville.

> A legal education, which quickens and invigorates the understanding but is not apt to open and liberalize the mind exactly in the same proportion, and a long course of official training, which gives knowledge that is valuable but fixes the mind upon form and precedent; these, in combination, had led him to conceive that the flourishing trade of this country was greatly owing to law and institution and not quite so much to liberty, and to believe regulation to be commerce, and taxes to be revenue.

Townshend, the Chancellor introduced duties (including the tea duty which led to the Boston Tea Party) budgeted to produce £400,000. We know that the cost of collection was £15,000; the most optimistic estimate of the gross yield was £16,000, a 'profit' of £1,000 and in practice it is doubtful that costs were covered. For such sums were the colonies lost. In 1770 New York *legally* imported 147 pounds of tea: Philadelphia imported 65 pounds.

The Revolution begins

The first Continental Congress met in Philadelphia in September 1774 but the discussion was of economic boycott rather than political independence. It soon became clear that the colonies were in a state of rebellion, and the Declaration of Independence was approved on 4 July 1776. The first action of the second Continental Congress was to create an army. Armies have to be paid for and the Congress had no taxing powers. It therefore arranged for the issue of $2 million of Bills of Credit in June, and another $1 million in July. It also sought to allot taxes between the colonies to be collected by the colonies and to be paid into the newly created Continental treasury. Needless to say the Bills of Credit were not 'as good as gold' but moral persuasion was used to induce people to accept them.

> Any person who shall hereafter be so lost to all virtue and regard for his country as to refuse the Bills or obstruct and discourage their currency or circulation shall be deemed published and treated as an enemy of the country and precluded from all trade and intercourse with its inhabitants.
>
> (Resolution of 11 January 1776)

A year later Congress said that:

... the Continental money ought to be supported at the full value expressed in the respective Bills by the people of the States who stand bound to redeem them according to the like value and to guard against the artifices of the enemies of liberty who impair the credit of the Bills by raising the nominal value of gold and silver.

(This view foreshadowed the issues to be discussed by the Bullion Committee in England some years later.)

The Bills were made legal tender as 'Treasury Notes'. During 1777 some $13 million of paper were issued – these were valued at about two to the silver dollar at the beginning of the year but depreciated to four by its end. Private enterprise joined in the fun, and many counterfeit Bills were issued. By the end of 1779 a total of $241 million of Bills had been issued. This, of course, was not the only method of finance used. Loans were raised, and the various States sought to confiscate the property of the loyalists. Foreign aid was also obtained. The French in particular came to the aid of the struggling new Republic (the French Revolution was yet to come) but the desire to aid England's enemies was tempered by diplomatic prudence. Losers, after all have to live with victors, particularly when near neighbours have been squabbling over what were after all distant possessions. By October 1779, Congress had to resolve that gold and silver should be received in payment of taxes at the rate of 1 Spanish gold dollar for 40 dollars of bills. By the end of 1780 the of exchange rate was 75 for 1, the depreciation being aided by issues by the States as well as the Congress. Eventually, there was a complete default. Thomas Jefferson said that the public feared that this would shake the Confederacy to its very centre, but instead

... their annihilation was not only unattended by tumult but was everywhere a matter of rejoicing and congratulation. Their great services as a support of the War were known and felt by all and all knew and felt their destruction was a certain public good. . . . In Rhode Island – an obstreperous little commonwealth – some Continental bills were buried with the honours of war. They were enclosed in a special repository, and over this a eulogy was pronounced as over the remains of a departed friend and benefactor.

(Schuckers 1874: 90)

Continental currency was eventually exchanged into US Treasury Bonds at 1 per cent of face value.

THE BIRTH OF THE DOLLAR – A CURRENCY FOR THE NEW NATION

After these early attempts at finance, culminating in default, the new nation was still without a real currency of its own. However foreign coins appear to have been a major part of the circulating medium. On 19 April 1776 a tariff was published rating various foreign gold and silver coins in terms of the Spanish dollar or piece of eight. The English guinea for instance was valued at 4 and two-third dollars. The implied bimetallic ratio was 15.21:1, as in England. (The word 'dollar' is a corruption of 'thaler', itself a shortened version of 'Joachimsthaler' from Joachimsthal, the Bohemian valley which was the source of the silver for the first major issue of these large coins in 1519.)

The War of Independence formally ended in 1783, and the Continental Currency had lost its value by 1781. The States had also issued inconvertible paper money, but these eventually ceased following a 1777 request by Congress. These too lost their value. There was a short 'critical period' between then and 1789, when the Constitution came into force. Events during this period were to have a profound influence on the shape of American currency and finance. Some States issued Bills of Credit and others considered so doing. Men of property were opposed to this: they 'came to view paper currency as a device by which popularly elected governments sought to permit the common people to escape the burdens of their public and private debts'. At the time the Constitution was born conservative opinion, favouring sound currency and distrusting paper money, was politically dominant: 'Thus the peculiar historical circumstances of the post-revolutionary critical period had a profound and lasting effect on the nature of the US monetary system' (Russell 1991: 46–7). (We have seen in Chapter 18 that left wing influences at the time of Jackson added to the mix, and helped determine features of the US banking system which, even today, seem odd to the European observer.)

When Continental currency was effectively discredited in 1780, some States moved to fill the gap. There was a rush of issues, particularly in 1785 when Rhode Island, New York, Pennsylvania New Jersey, North Carolina, South Carolina and Georgia all made issues. These were all, in principle, based on convertibility into specie. All, except those of Rhode Island, were eventually redeemed in full (Newman 1976: 14). Newman says that Massachusetts was an exception where 'the refusal of the State to authorise paper money caused Shay's Rebellion'. He also describes the Rhode Island Bills. The original Bills were issued under an Act of 2 July 1780 authorising the issue of $130,000. They were later convertible into Bills authorised at various dates from May–August 1788. The law declared that the legal tender provision was to be enforced summarily without jury trial. This was challenged in the case of *Trevitt* v. *Weedon*, in which a butcher appealed against his conviction for refusing to accept a Bill. This case is noted in legal history as the first to establish the right to jury trial in the United States. The illegal feature of the issue were removed by an Act of December 1788: the issue depreciated 10 per cent of face and the Bill ceased to be legal tender in September 1789. Meanwhile, these experiments in paper money apart, the new nation was still without a real currency of its own.

THE BIRTH OF THE DOLLAR

Robert Morris

The country's first Superintendent of Finance was Robert Morris. Brought from England at the age of 13, he was apprenticed to Charles Willing, a Philadelphia merchant, with whom he became a partner ten years later, and was a Signatory of the Declaration of Independence. As Superintendent of Finance from 1781–4 he set the public finance of the new Republic onto as sound a footing as was, in the circumstances, possible. He was to play a role, with Alexander Hamilton, in establishing a banking system. Asked by Congress to prepare a scheme for national coinage, he submitted a report on 15 January 1782. This was quickly approved by Congress, which instructed Morris to prepare a plan for a mint. On 6 July 1785 Congress resolved to adopt the dollar unit on a decimal system. A second, unsuccessful, attempt was made to start a mint, if only to replace the Birmingham copper coins in circulation.

On 17 September 1787, the Constitution was adopted, giving the exclusive power of coinage to Congress. The Mint itself was not established until the Mint Act of 2 April 1792 – sixteen years after the Declaration of Independence (Evans 1894 and Stewart 1924). The Federal government had a monopoly of coinage, but the States, in practice, had the right to charter note issuing banks. There was the inevitable corruption, fraud, and 'wild cat banking', and, in response to the problems, experiments in regulation, in 'free banking' and the 'safety fund system' of mutual guarantees. Attempts to set up a Federal bank collapsed in the 'Bank War' between President Andrew Jackson and Nicholas Biddle of the Second Bank of the United States. This explains why the United States lacked a nation-wide banking system for so long, and why retail banking practices have seemed so primitive by English, never mind Scottish, standards. Modern phenomena have their roots in history.

25

THE FRENCH REVOLUTION AND THE ASSIGNATS

MONEY IN PRE-REVOLUTIONARY FRANCE

John Law's experiment set back the development of money, other than coin, in France. The story of the country's experiments in public finance is told by one of its great practitioners, the Finance Minister, Jacques Necker (Necker 1786; see also Bailly 1830). In the period before the Revolution the French unit of currency was the livre, divided into 20 sols or sous, each of 12 deniers. This was the same Carolingian system operating in England but the more rapid decline of the French currency meant that the UK pound was worth about 24 French livres. The major circulating coins were the gold louis, worth 24 livres (together with the double louis and half louis) and the silver ecu of three livres. There were smaller silver coins of 24, 12 and 6 sols; and for small change copper sols, halves (6 deniers) and quarters (liards, of 3 deniers).

Prior to the recoinage of 1785, the gold/silver ratio was 14.5:1 compared with 15:1 in England. The recoinage changed the mint ratio to 15.5 and doubled the seigniorage on gold to 2 per cent. A mark of gold was actually coined into 768 livres and the mark of silver into 49 livres 16 sou. There was the inevitable outflow of silver.

THE FRENCH REVOLUTION

The immediate cause of the French (as of the American) Revolution was taxation. France had effectively been driven out of her American colonies by the British, and (though itself an absolute monarchy) had supported the American revolutionaries against the old enemy. Revenge was sweet, but expensive, and the French king, Louis XVI, needed money. In France, the nobility and clergy were effectively exempt from tax. The Finance Minister, Necker, decided that this must end, as the burden was simply too high for the rest of the nation. The Court party opposed him, and he resigned. The king's only resort was to borrow – at ruinous rates of interest. His attempts to raise taxes were opposed by the Parlement (a toothless body) and there was a demand for the recall of the Estates General, a more representative body, which had not met for over a century.

The King agreed, and also restored Necker. The Estates General had three Chambers or Houses, for the Nobles, the Clergy and for the people 'the Third Estate'. The people claimed the right to as many representatives as the other two combined. The King, on Necker's advice and against fierce Court opposition, agreed. Fine, but how were they to vote? If by Chamber, the Nobility and Clergy would outvote the Third Estate two to one. If by representatives the people, who could expect support from some of the clergy, would prevail. No agreement could be reached, and in June 1789 the Third Estate unilaterally declared themselves the National Assembly. Led by Mirabeau, a noble who had joined them, they defied the King. Yielding to pressure from the Court, Louis called up the army and dismissed Necker. On 14 July 1789, the Paris mob stormed the Bastille.

The Assignats

Although the King was not deposed for another three years (he was executed in January 1794), the National Assembly (or Constituent Assembly as it now styled itself) became the *de facto* government of France. One of its early tasks was to come to grips with the country's financial problems. After some months of detailed and urgent discussion a new paper currency, the Assignats, was introduced in December 1789. (A proposal to issue (interest bearing) paper currency had been made on 16 August 1788, still under the Monarchy. This was for temporary purposes but public protests, based on memories of John Law, resulted in the edict being revoked on 14 September.)

In January 1789, Parlement bitterly opposed any suggestion for a new form of money, one argument being:

> . . . above all we will not countenance the introduction of a paper money or a national bank, either of which can only produce a great evil and of which the memories alone are capable of frightening us because of the abuse and speculation that they occasioned in the past. . . . [However] then came the Revolution, and with it a remarkable change in the attitude towards paper money. Expediency demanded paper money; the success of the people's Revolution was impossible without it. . . . A comprehensive system of education, that purported to demonstrate the uniqueness of the new paper money – especially as regards the peculiar land security that emphatically differentiated the Assignat from Law's paper – aided in the complete transformation of public opinion.
>
> (Harris 1930: 8)

The classic English language account is still 'The Assignats' by Harris (1930), his Ph.D. thesis of 1926. Harris explains how the idea of a land bank was floated. On 10 October 1789 Talleyrand formally proposed that the possessions of the church should be confiscated. However, mere ownership of the land, and the revenue that it would eventually produce, was not enough to finance the revolution. The obvious step was to sell at least part of it and this was indeed proposed and discussed. There was strong support for the issue of paper money. This was criticised by Necker who did, however, want to see an increase of note issues to finance the anticipated deficit of 170 million livres. He was accused of inconsistency, and the debate continued. Most of the discussion was based on alternative suggestions for issuing notes on the direct or indirect security of church lands. Talleyrand favoured the creation of a new national bank and this plan was examined in association with Necker. On 5 December it was pointed out by d'Angely, and generally accepted, that there would have to be a sale of church lands as a guarantee for the issues of paper money. He then made the key suggestion that the paper money should be redeemable against the purchase of the lands. The Commission reported on 19 December and their proposals which drew on various features of earlier discussions were approved and the issue of paper money was authorised on the same day.

The first issue of *Assignats* which amounted to 400 million livres, was to bear interest and it would be used partly to repay the existing debt to the Caisse d'Escompte. The Assignats would be supported by the eventual sale of lands to this value and the proceeds of these sales were used to redeem the Assignats within five years. The Assignats would have special rights for the purchase of lands but were not (at this stage) legal tender.

The subsequent history and depreciation of the Assignat is divided by Harris into six periods. What is remarkable is that for the first five of these (a period of four years) the system seems to have worked well, and to have been a major source of profit to the government. However, Harris (1930: 53) discusses the difficulties attached to the 'statistics of circulation, emissions, burnings and exchange of Assignats'. During the first period the figures suggest about 1,500 million livres of notes in circulation. There was also still some gold and silver circulating, but these had gradually been hoarded or exported. This compares with a total figure of about 2,000 million livres for the money in circulation before the Revolution so that there was little net change in money supply. There is no evidence of any general increase in prices, although the Assignat fell to a price of 77 per cent in terms of gold and silver.

A feature of the initial issue (the interest bearing one) was that the smallest denomination was 200 livres, (about £8 English), and coins were still needed for small payments. The second issue included denominations of 50, 60, 70, 80, 90 and 100 livres: those issued on 6 May 1791 comprised only notes of 5 livres known as 'corsets' after the signatory. Harris points out that

> . . . this absence of depreciation in a country which still remembered the disturbances caused by Law is worthy of comment. . . . Probably

the most satisfactory explanation of the stability of this period is to be found in the general belief that the Assignat with its land security was anything but a replica of Law's dreaded paper.

(Harris 1930: 169)

Later he comments that the relative stability 'is the more remarkable in the light of the many attacks upon it. The numerous attacks of the pamphleteers emphasised in particular the weakness and fictitiousness of the security'. Antoin Murphy has suggested that one of the difficulties of studying this period is in fact the shortage of pamphlets. What was fair comment in England could be treason in France. In any case, so far, the experiment had been a success both in the terms of public acceptability and as a method of public finance. The proceeds of the issue had provided the government with the equivalent of two years of ordinary revenue.

During the second period, January to May 1792, there were substantial new issues of notes, and an effective increase in circulation increased to 2,250 million livres. The issues included even small denomination notes of 10,15, 25 and 50 sous or sols, there being 20 sous to the livre. Confidence began to wane. Assignats were no longer regarded as a store of value and there was a rush to hoard commodities and (in the case of merchants and farmers) to withhold supplies from the market. Velocity must have increased. The 'explanation for the apparent higher depreciation in terms of gold and silver' quoted by Harris on page 174 is unconvincing: 'The premium on the metals for export purposes should have made them redundant abroad; but moved by fear people everywhere hoard gold and silver' said Laffon-Ladebat. The silver ecu stood at a premium of 70 per cent, and the gold louis at 90 per cent.

During the third period, June to December 1792, there was a revival of confidence and the opportunity was taken to issue more notes. The first two issues were of 5 livre 'corsets': later in the period larger and smaller denominations were issued, including 400 livre notes with mechanical numbering. There was often said to be an increase in their value but close examination by Harris suggests that commodity prices actually continued to increase. 'A speculative fall in the price of gold and silver is the explanation of the apparent rise'. There were important military victories but political and economic conditions were unsound. War with England became inevitable. Against this, tax revenues actually seem to have improved.

The fourth period (January to August 1793) began with the execution of the King in January, the February bread riots and the start of war with England. The period was one of external military defeat culminating with the surrender of Toulon and much of the French fleet. The Reign of Terror, with the guillotines working round the clock, began in July. During the period nearly 5 billion livres of mainly small denomination notes were emitted (the total pre-revolution money supply was 2 billion) and the value of the Assignats fell to about a quarter of their face value in bullion. The Law of Maximum was hardly effective during this period. There was considerable hoarding and farmers were concealing their supplies. Because of lack of confidence land sales fell making it difficult to absorb the surplus Assignats. Exchange controls prohibited private contracts to be settled in gold and silver of which the government was desperately short.

During the fifth period (September 1793 to July 1794) the notes circulation rose to 7.2 billion livres. In spite of this further increase in money supply the value appears to have recovered. This may be a misinterpretation of the statistics (Harris 1930: 181–2). However we interpret the statistics, the government certainly had a remarkable success in putting so much new paper into circulation without a sharp fall in value. The explanation is, of course, in the remarkable power of the central government led by the Committee of Public Safety in enforcing its dictates through the Reign of Terror. A contemporary writer describes how

> Robespierre . . . seized all the specie . . . and paid for it with assignats. He then imposed the Law of the Maximum, and that of requisitions; measures which . . . gave this new money a forced circulation, and a pretended value. . . . The assignats issued were but a sort of bills of exchange, drawn on the Revolutionary Tribunal, and paid for with the Guillotine, which Robespierre is said to have called an engine for coining money.
>
> (D'Ivernois, September 6 1795: 3–4)

He went on to predict disaster.

The sixth period (August 1794 to December 1795) 'is the period of spectacular depreciation. It aroused the legislatures to a rather sustained interest in the financial situation. The fall of the Assignat was virtually uninterrupted from August 1794 to March 1796 when the Mandat was substituted'. The period began with the fall of Robespierre on 28 July 1794. The Maximum system became ineffective even though it was not repealed until December. The notes were now denominated in francs, between 100 and 10,000 francs. Some 30 billion francs of notes were printed and there were some 20 billion in circulation at the end of the period. According to the local tables, the value fell from 32 per cent in November 1794 to 0.8 per cent in November 1795. This implies a rate of inflation of 36 per cent per month, falling rather short of the classic (50 per cent per month) definition (Cagan 1956) of hyperinflation.

Harris mentions the 'au cours' payments (payments adjusted according to the changing value of paper money, or what we would call indexation) as contributing to the depreciation, although surely the volume of note issues is a sufficient explanation. He discusses the details in a later chapter. The point is relevant in determining how profitable the operation was to

Government, which was now forced, to some extent, to suffer the effects of its own depreciation and as we found with the final stages of the Tudor debasement, this stage caused the most dramatic price fall, but is the least profitable and effective.

Another factor was that the discussion of the 'indexation' was itself 'disconcerting to the public . . . Even an official recognition of a depreciation that everyone was aware of, made the public doubt the Assignats more . . . success never came of any of these plans before the Assignat was beyond saving' (Harris 1930: 187–8).

Harris summarises his conclusions on the causes of depreciation:

> Why stop to explain the depreciation of a paper money issued to excess? An uninterrupted fall, in the opinion of some was inevitable. Hawtrey's emphasis on speculation is helpful, although he does not consider speculation in all its ramifications. The most serious deficiency in Hawtrey's treatment – to be expected in a brief essay – is his failure to consider the many forces that affected depreciation.
>
> (Harris 1930: 201)

He suggests that the allegiance of the economists to the quantity theory 'often explains a neglect to inquire further into the process of depreciation. As has been indicated, however, the writers and thinkers of the Revolution found much that was not explicable in terms of quantity'.

Is it in fact so surprising that contemporaries with little history to guide them (Law could be dismissed as a special aberration) had not developed an adequate monetary theory? Certainly as we shall see in Chapter 26, most of those who gave an opinion in the United Kingdom (where there was no restraint on an exuberantly exercised freedom of discussion) failed to spot what we today would regard as a simple and obvious relationship. They, too, persisted in inventing and putting forward complex and irrelevant theories even though a minority of thinkers, notably including Thornton and Ricardo, were expounding, in simple, lucid, English prose, a straightforward and surprisingly modern monetary explanation.

The government's gain from its money operations

It would be interesting to compute how much 'profit' the French government made from the operation. This could be calculated by the amount of the emissions calculated at 'stable value' and net of any paper that had to be accepted back by the government at face value. From this we would have to deduct redemptions at 'stable value'. Some part of the issues would, of course, simply become worthless in private hands leaving the whole 'profit to the government'. The government had certainly financed the revolution (so far) with the printing press. The amount in circulation was, in nominal value, about 20 times the pre-revolution money supply but was at best worth much less. About 7 billion was in circulation by end 1794, perhaps at an average value of 40 in gold francs: say 2.8 billion. 1795 added perhaps 35 billion, at about 20: another 7 billion. After that, the game was over. What came next?

There are also profits and losses between private debtors and creditors of which more below. From a 'public policy' point of view Ramel said of the Assignats in January 1796 'they have led to the destruction of class and privilege; they have destroyed the monarchy and established the Republic. They have armed and equipped those formidable columns which have carried the tricolors beyond the Alps and the Pyrenees'.

However White (1876: 92–3) says the loss fell on 'the working classes, employees and men of small means, whose property was not large enough to invest in stores of goods or national lands'. The better off fled to real values, while 'the heartless, debauched, luxurious, speculator, contractor and stock-gambling class' did very well indeed. Whereas a few years before, French society ladies 'showed a nobility of character and simplicity in dress worthy of Roman matrons' they were replaced by a different and vulgar breed 'demanding of their husbands and lovers vast sums to array them and feed their whims'.

The final failures of the Assignats, and their successors, the Mandats

How did it all end? The most interesting, and the most neglected, aspect of major depreciations such as this is the way in which a sound currency is restored: unfortunately Harris does not cover this period. There was a last fling, under the Directory, in December 1795 when it was decreed that issues of Assignats should be limited to 40 billion. The paper was already virtually worthless.

> On February 18 1796, at nine o'clock in the morning in the presence of a great crowd, the machinery, plates, and paper for printing assignats were brought to the Place Vendome and there . . . these were solemnly broken and burned . . . a report by Camus [said] that the entire amount issued in less than six years . . . had been over forty-five thousand millions of francs . . . and that at the final catastrophe there were in circulation close upon forty thousand millions.
>
> (White 1876: 92–3)

This method of finance being no longer available, the Directory tried unsuccessfully to raise a forced loan of 600 million (gold) francs, and to promote a bank. There had been an attempt to issue 'Promesses de Rescriptions' early in 1796 but this appears to have been a failure. They then

... bethought themselves of another expedient. This was by no means new. It had been fully tried out on our continent [America] ... and here, as elsewhere, always in vain. But experience yielded to theory. ... It was determined to issue a new paper which should be 'fully secured' and 'as good as gold' ... under the name of 'mandats'.

(White 1876: 95–6)

This time few were fooled, in spite of propaganda and harsh penalties against those who refused to accept or 'who by their discourse or writing shall decry [Mandats]'. Their history was, predictably, shorter. They were first issued in February 1796, allegedly convertible into choice public land at an agreed valuation, but fell to 35 per cent of face value before they could come off the printing press. Five months later, on 16 July, it was decreed that both mandats and assignats could exchange at valuation – by then about 2 per cent. In February 1797 the mandat presses were destroyed and they ceased to be legal tender. The experiment had lasted a year, and, unlike the assignats, the mandats profited the government hardly at all.

Finally in September 1797 it was ordered that two-thirds of national debts should be paid in bonds 'which could be used in purchasing confiscated real estate' (these fell to 3 per cent of face value) while the remaining 'Consolidated Third' 'was placed on the "Great Book" to be paid ... as the government should think best' (White 1876: 99).

The aftermath

Histories tend to be disappointingly thin on the aftermath of monetary disasters. In spite of 'great fears were felt as to a want of circulating medium between the time when paper should go out and coin should come in' there seem to have been few problems; 'coin came in gradually as it was wanted'. However while the acute suffering lasted nearly ten years, 'it required fully forty years to bring capital, industry and credit up to their condition when the Revolution began' (White 1876: 104, quoting Thibaudeau). White concludes that the lessons were learnt: Napoleon conducted the rest of the war on a specie basis, and the much later Franco-Prussian War was financed without the aid of the printing press. White contrasts this favourably with the American Civil War, an obvious stimulus to his interest, a few years after that event, in the history of monetary depreciation.

A retrospect: money confusion

From the point of view of private contracts, what was the official currency of France? Was it the Assignat which, during its last year may or may not (depending on definition) have suffered hyperinflation? Was it the gold (or silver) livre (or franc)? Debtors took advantage of the low value of the paper money to pay off long term debts, but at one stage debtors were barred by law from paying their capital debts. Harris goes on to discuss 'a more careful definition of the concept, scarcity of currency', but his analysis seems a little unsound. The lawyer, Dr F. A. Mann, makes some reference to this problem. We need not agree with his economic history when he says:

> During the early period of monetary history, when money was given and taken by weight rather than tale, when the names nowadays employed to designate a unit of account originated and in terms described a certain weight ('pound', 'livre', 'peso', 'mark') no other conception was possible.
>
> (Mann 1982: 43)

He refers to American and British legal cases involving Assignats. The American case *Searight* v. *Calbraith* (1796) 4 US 325 concerned an action on a bill of exchange for '150,000 livres tournois' payable in Paris. The plaintiff refused to accept Assignats. Mr Justice Peters of the Supreme Court said:

> The decision depends entirely on the intention of the parties of which the jury must judge. If a specie payment was meant, a tender of assignats was unavailing. But if the current money of France was in view, a tender in assignats was lawfully made.
>
> (Mann 1982: 85)

Dr Mann does not say what the jury (it would be a lower court) decided on the facts.

In England, the problem was discussed (obiter) by the Privy Council in *Pilkington* v *Commissioners for Claims on France*. If the wrongdoer 'has received the assignats at the value of 50d., he does not make compensation by returning an assignat which is only worth 20d.; he must make up the difference between the value of the assignats at different dates' (Mann 1982: 289). This, however, is merely an early statement of the principle (only recently abandoned) that English courts assess damages only in sterling and not in foreign currencies.

APPENDIX

Table 25.1 Value of Assignats: 1789 to 1796 (as percentage of initial value in 1789)

Month	Year 1789	1790	1791	1792	1793	1794	1795	1796
January		96	91	72	51	40	18	0.46
February		95	91	61	52	41	17	0.36
March		94	90	59	51	36	13.28	
April		94	89	68	43	36	10.71	
May		94	85	58	52	34	1.52	
June		95	85	57	36	30	3.38	
July		95	87	61	23 .	34	3.09	
August	98	92	79	61	22	31	2.72	
September	98	91	82	72	27	28	2.08	
October	97	91	84	71	28	28	1.36	
November	96	90	82	73	33	24	0.77	
December	95	92	77	72	48	20	0.52	

Source: Henri Seé, *Histoire Economique de la France*, in Capie (1991: 11).

26

THE SUSPENSION OF PAYMENTS, 1797 TO 1821

In the United Kingdom the second Great Debate on money was occasioned by the Napoleonic Wars and the 'suspension of payments' (1797–1821) during which the United Kingdom effectively had an inconvertible paper currency. The climax of the debate was the Bullion Report of 1810, and the whole period is a happy hunting ground for book and pamphlet collectors, and for connoisseurs of economic sense and nonsense.

Monetary matters, in England at least, had been relatively tranquil during the middle of the eighteenth century. There were no major dramas between the South Sea Bubble and the American and French Revolutions. There were some coinage adjustments (Chapter 7) and some crises, notably in 1763 and 1772 and a lot going on in public finance. The development of a permanent National Debt had been a major factor in the birth of the Bank of England – and of the South Sea Bubble. Walpole had begun the funding of the Debt in 1717. The South Sea Bubble having burst, the company remained the intermediary for much of the Debt. Robert Walpole, Prime Minister from 1721–44 had to deal with the collapse of the South Sea Bubble, but his Ministry was noted for its (fairly successful) attempt to reduce the National Debt by means of a Sinking Fund and to negotiate downwards the rate of interest on this debt.

THE STATE OF THE BRITISH COINAGE IN 1797

Since Newton's recoinage in 1696, England had had a stable system, with a plentiful gold coinage based on the guinea (21 shillings) and its halves and thirds. The price of 22 carat gold was fixed at £3.17s.10½d. per ounce. The United Kingdom (as it was by now) was technically on a silver standard, with the guinea fixed at 21 shillings of silver, giving a bimetallic ratio of 1 to 15.21. This slightly overvalued gold as compared with Continental markets. The small differential was enough to make it unprofitable to coin silver, but there was also little profit in actually melting it down. The routine operation of clippers and normal wear and tear meant that the silver content of coins actually circulating was worth less than their face value. De facto, the silver coinage had already become a subsidiary coinage. It was in a fairly poor state, and in short supply, but the situation was not regarded as urgent.

Paper money was used, but still as a convenient means of money transmission, rather than a major component of money supply. The Bank of England issued £10 and £20 notes, and although these circulated freely amongst merchants in the London area, they were little used further afield. 'Country banks' (unincorporated banks with no more than six partners) continued to issue £5 notes for local circulation. Merchants were familiar with banking, bills of exchange and with bank notes, but the latter were of relatively limited importance. £10 in those days had a purchasing power of over £200 or $300 of 1993 money.

WAR WITH FRANCE

War with France broke out in February 1793. About this time there was a banking crisis, caused by excessive note issues by country banks. The increase had been gradual over a number of years rather than the result of a sudden excess of speculation. Confidence was shaken by the declaration of war. A Newcastle bank was the first to collapse, followed by scores of others. Following an examination by a Select Committee, the crisis was checked by an offer by the government to lend up to £5 million to merchants in difficulty. In the event only £2.2 million was actually needed (Feaveryear 1931:165–6).

Heavy government borrowing to finance the war put a strain on the Bank of England.

> The crisis came in 1797 – the black year of the Mutiny of the Nore – when the gold balance of the Bank of England was reduced to £1,272,000 and a panic was commencing which threatened to result in a run which could not possibly have been met.
>
> (Oman 1967: 539)

There were invasion rumours, and 1200 French convicts in uniform were actually landed in Wales. They were soon rounded up, and it appears to have been a ruse to cause a panic rather than a serious raid.

On Saturday 18 February the farmers of Newcastle (again), moved by some local (unspecified) rumour, sold cattle for what they could get and descended on the banks to cash their notes for gold. On Monday all the Newcastle banks agreed to stop payment. Bankers in other districts appealed to the Bank of England for help. (Feaveryear 1931: 168. Neither Clapham nor Oman mention this incident, nor give any real explanation of what precipitated suspension. Tooke, 1838, vol. i: 203 gives a quotation from the 1797 Lords Committee of Secrecy referring to it.)

The Suspension of Payments

The directors of the Bank of England now regarded the situation as desperate. On Sunday morning 26 February 1797, Pitt convened a meeting of the Privy Council, at which were present the King, (summoned from Windsor) the Lord Chancellor, the Lord President, the Duke of Portland, Marquis Cornwallis, Earl Spencer, the Earl of Liverpool, Lord Grenville and himself. This meeting

> ... passed and communicated at once to the Bank a resolution which declared the unanimous opinion of the Board that it was indispensably necessary for the public service that the Directors of the Bank of England should forebear issuing any cash in payment until the sense of Parliament can be taken on that subject and the proper measures adopted thereupon for maintaining the means of circulation and supporting the public and commercial credit of the Kingdom at this important conjuncture [and] required that the directors on the grounds of the exigency of the case to conform thereto until the sense of Parliament can be taken as aforesaid.
>
> (quoted in Cannan 1919: x–xi)

This was the famous 'suspension of payments' which seems to have been accepted remarkably coolly. On Monday midday there was a meeting of merchants and bankers at the Mansion House. This passed unanimously a resolution that they would not refuse to accept bank notes. This was published, bearing 4,000 signatures. The directors also published a notice assuring the public that the Bank's condition was sound. (Text in Andreades 1931 vol. i: 277).

The order was confirmed by the 'Bank Restriction Act' of 3 May 1797 (37 George III C.45.) passed as a temporary measure intended to continue only until 24 June of the same year. Sir William Pulteney's Third Reading speech on 7 April moved to amend 'so distant a date as the 24 of June' in favour of 6 May 1797; 'National and commercial credit might be re-established within a month' (Pulteney 1797:6). He asked 'whether there was ... any instance where a monopoly had ever conducted its affairs well' and suggested the Bank's problems 'had been occasioned by their own misconduct'. He said that his object was 'merely to divest the Bank of its monopoly' and not of its right to act as a corporation. He did not want to injure shareholders nor 'to deprive the directors of their salaries' but only 'the dangerous part of their present powers'. He denied that he 'intended to propose the establishment of an opposition bank', but a month later, however, he was defeated, by 50 votes to 15, on a motion for leave to bring in a Bill for a rival bank.

One month or two? It was an academic argument. In the event specie payments remained suspended for twenty-four years until the 'resumption' in 1821 and during that period 'the most important single topic of parliamentary debate and of parliamentary investigation in the monetary field was the causes of the suspension of payments by the banks and the actions necessary to maintain exchange rate stability' (Fetter and Gregory 1973: 10).

The early years of suspension

Suspension, like income tax, was introduced as a temporary measure although it was to persist for twenty-four years. For the first few years, in spite of fears by Fox and others that the notes would go the way of the assignats (Chapter 25) the Bank appears to have conducted its business as if its notes were convertible. There was, at this stage, relatively little over-issue. It is interesting to speculate on what would have happened had the Bank been Pitt's 'creature'. Would the government have adopted a soft option like its successors (and like its enemy across the Channel) – of printing notes to finance a war?

Exchange rates remained stable for some six years, apart from a brief period in 1800 when there was a depreciation in the Hamburg exchange and a rise in commodity prices. There was at first little public discussion of the problems of paper currency (except for Tom Paine's 1796 pamphlet) in spite of the awful warning of the collapse of the Assignats in France. In 1801 Walter Boyd wrote 'a letter to Right Honourable William Pitt on the influence of the stoppage of issues and specie at the Bank of England on the prices of provisions and other commodities' (Boyd 1801; see also Cope 1983). This adopted a monetary explanation. Henry Thornton's classic work appeared in 1802: those of Wheatley and King in 1803. By this time exchange rates had recovered to pre-suspension levels, and the public interest waned.

The Irish pound and the 1804 Report

There were problems in Ireland. There was a sharp depreciation in the Irish pound in 1803, and the debate, which had been initiated by Boyd and Thornton, now focused on the Irish pound. Lord King raised the issue in Parliament on 3 May 1803 (Fetter 1955: 25; King 1803). On 2 March 1804 John Foster, Secretary of State for Ireland, moved for the appointment of a committee to investigate the condition of the Irish currency. Its report, published in 1804 (reproduced in Fetter 1955), rehearsed many of the arguments that were subsequently to be discussed by the Bullion Committee of 1810.

Ireland had for long had 'currency problems'. In 1701 the English silver shilling had been proclaimed to be worth 13 pence Irish. Another proclamation, of 1737, correspondingly declared the gold guinea to be worth 22 shillings and 9 pence Irish. £100 English was nominally equivalent to £108

6s. 8d. (£108.33) Irish. The actual exchange rate was referred to both by market custom and in contemporary literature, as a percentage premium. A premium of 8.33 per cent represented par: the actual premium fluctuated within a narrow range in accordance with the direction of bullion flows. For practical purposes Ireland was on a 'sterling exchange' standard. The Bank of Ireland had been incorporated in 1783. It shared note issuing rights with private Dublin and country banks. In 1797 it was estimated that notes amounted to £1.4 million, compared with £5 million of gold in circulation. There was no foreign exchange market except with London and (occasionally) Lisbon.

The Irish Parliament had approved an Irish Bank Restriction on 20 April 1797 and this became law on 3 July 1797. The two Restrictions were assimilated by a provision in the Act of Union on 1 January 1801. The Bank of Ireland was a little less circumspect, and by 1802 the circulation of Irish bank notes had increased fourfold.

The witnesses divided into two groups. The 'balance of payments' explanation favoured by the Bank of Ireland suggested that monetary policy had no influence on exchange rates, which were entirely determined by changes in the country's balance of payments and caused by issues other than monetary policy.

To support their case they brought into argument the 'real bills' doctrine, an important concept in the history of bank money. The bankers argued that so long as a bank granted credit only on the basis of bills representing business transactions, credit expansion could have no effect on prices or on the exchanges.

This fallacy continued to be current amongst practical bankers well into the nineteenth century, long after it had been universally discredited amongst economists.

The other view, which in the end prevailed mainly thanks to Henry Thornton, was referred to at the time as the 'bullionist' view. (We might call it monetarist.) The over-issue of money in Ireland had been the prime cause of the depreciation in the exchange. The balance of payments deficit was caused by monetary policy. The correct policy conclusion was that the Bank of Ireland could, by limiting credit, maintain a stable exchange rate.

The Committee reported on 19 June 1804. It divided the problem into three parts:

1. As to the Fact of an unfavourable Exchange existing, and to what Extent;
2. As to the Causes which have created it;
3. As to the Remedies which can be resorted to for either removing or alleviating the Inconveniences arising from it.

The report received relatively little attention, mainly because the Dublin/London exchange rate did, shortly afterwards, return to par. It was not until

1809 and the collapse of the (English) pound on the Hamburg exchange that the debate was once more opened. Fetter suggests that

> ... monetary transactions, and particularly foreign exchange operations ... affected directly the economic fortunes of only a small part of the population of Ireland ... For only two groups, the absentee landlords and merchants dealing between England and Ireland, would the Dublin-London exchange fluctuations appear as a major problem.
>
> (Fetter 1955: 26)

The 1810 Royal Commission

The next stage of the debate centred on England. The first shot was fired by David Ricardo who wrote three letters to the Morning Chronicle on 'The Price of Gold'. Following this, on the motion of Francis Horner, (whig) The House of Commons appointed the 'Select Committee on the High Price of Gold Bullion' the report of which now ranks as one of the great classics of economic literature. (The best modern edition of this, with an introduction by Edwin Cannan, was published in 1919 as 'The Paper Pound of 1791–1821'. Page references are to the 1925 second edition.)

They were an expert rather than a political committee. Three men dominated it and can be presumed to have drafted the report. Francis Horner was at the time a young barrister of 32. In 1802 he had helped found The Edinburgh Review, the great whig journal which was the first to treat the book review as an art form, actually paying distinguished reviewers generously to write vigorous, in depth and independent comments on the books and issues of the day. Horner actually intended to write up the Report for the Edinburgh Review, rather than risk whom he referred to as 'the odious Milne' (James Mill, father of John Stuart) undertake it. In the event, the task was entrusted to Malthus. William Huskisson (then aged 40) had studied the assignats, and subsequently published his views in a cogently argued pamphlet, while Henry Thornton (50) had of course already published an economic classic on the subject.

A number of witnesses were called and examined. All are named in the Minutes of Evidence except for one described as 'a Continental Merchant' whose evidence was particularly fascinating. He was one of the few 'bullionist' witnesses, and was allowed to remain anonymous. He was often assumed to be Nathan Meyer Rothschild but later research has identified him with John Parish of Hamburg.

The Committee 'began by dealing with the popular explanations ... common at the time amongst severely practical men ... who disdained all theorising' such as Bosanquet (Feaveryear 1931: 182-3). The Bank of England witnesses repeated the fallacies put forward by the Bank of Ireland in 1804, namely that monetary policy had nothing to do with exchange rates and that credit on 'real bills', no matter how extensive, could have no inflationary effect. These arguments were later to be described by Walter Bagehot as 'almost classical by their nonsense'. Other 'practical men' regarded the effect on the exchange as being due merely to increased demand for a commodity (gold) or a by-product of the adverse effect on the balance of trade of Napoleon's Continental System.

Fortunately the members of the Committee having been chosen for their expertise rather than merely for their political standing, had the sense to reject the muddled thinking of the 'practical bankers'. Bullion had not in fact risen in price on the Continent and the balance of trade had been positive. The Committee therefore concluded, correctly, that sound management of the credit policy of the Bank of England was a necessary and sufficient condition for maintaining a stable exchange rate. They also recommended that the convertibility be resumed within two years, even though the war was not at that time over. This last advice was rejected.

The Bullion Report

Much of the Report of the Committee is taking up with the recital of factual evidence, and the conclusions are set out patiently with many repetitions in the hope that they will (to adapt a standard blurb associated with educational primers of the day) be 'capable of being understood by those of the meanest intelligence'. The main conclusions are simple and clear. This is one of the most important documents in the development of sound monetary thought and practice in the United Kingdom. It begins by setting out the problem. The price of gold had risen to about £4.11s.0d. The foreign exchanges on Hamburg and Amsterdam had been 'depressed as low as from 16 to 20 per cent below par'. Straying beyond their original brief 'it appeared [correctly] to your Committee that it might be of use in judging the cause of the high price of gold bullion to be informed also of the prices of silver during the same period'. It will hardly surprise us and certainly will not have surprised Horner, Thornton and his friends that the pattern was much the same. They therefore concluded (p. 5) that

> . . . so extraordinary a rise in the market price of gold in this country coupled with so remarkable a depression of exchange with the Continent very early in the judgment of your committee pointed to something in the state of our own domestic currency as the cause of both appearances.

Nevertheless

> . . . they thought it proper to enquire more particularly into the circumstances connected with each of those two facts and to hear from persons of commercial practice and detail what explanations they had to offer of so unusual a state of things.

Part 1 examines the evidence relating to the gold price. The rise was 'ascribed by most of the witnesses entirely to an alleged scarcity of that article arising out of an unusual demand for it upon the continent of Europe'.

In the Report, they give a fair hearing to this line of argument but are clearly unimpressed by it.

> Your Committee are of the opinion that in the sound natural state of the British currency the foundation of which is gold no increased demand for gold from other parts of the world however great or from whatever causes arising can have the effect of producing here for a considerable period of time a material rise in the market price of gold.

Before expanding on the principle the Committee examined the evidence as to whether there had ever even been a real scarcity of gold. First if there had been an unusual demand for gold on the Continent:

> . . . it would of course influence also, and indeed in the first instance its price in the continental markets; and it was to be expected that those who ascribed the high price here to a great demand abroad, would have been prepared to state that there were corresponding high prices abroad. Your Committee did not find that they grounded their inference upon any such information . . . it does not appear that during the period when the price of Gold bullion was rising here as valued in our paper there was any corresponding rise in the price of Gold Bullion in the market of the Continent as valued in their respective currencies.

It is clear from the report and even clearer from the minutes of evidence that they gave the witnesses a pretty hard time on this point. The Committee observed

> . . . that both at Hamburgh and Amsterdam where the measure of value is not Gold as in this Country but Silver, an unusual demand for Gold would affect its money price, that is its price in silver and that as it does not appear that there has been any considerable rise in the price of gold as valued in silver at those places in the last year the inference is, that there was not any considerable increase in the demand for Gold.

They drew attention to the shift in the bimetallic ratio in favour of gold and pointed out that this took place before the increase in paper currency.

Referring to the 'alleged demand for Gold upon the Continent for the supply of French Armies' they suggest that it is balanced by another factor. 'The general supply of Europe with gold has been augmented by all that quantity which this great commercial Country [i.e. France] has spared in consequence of the substitution of another medium of circulation' (the assignats). Furthermore there is no evidence that previous similar events,

239

such as the seven years war and the American war had had any effect on the price of gold. The Committee thus dismissed the evidence that there was any shortage of gold, and were satisfied that this was not a sufficient explanation. 'But even if these assumptions were proved – to ascribe the high price of gold in this country to its scarcity seems to your committee to involve misconception on which they think it important to explain'.

They then go on to explain the gold standard mechanism and how, with free minting without seigniorage anyone can send bullion to the mint at no cost other than a 'loss of interest by the detention of their gold in the mint'. They put this loss at a maximum of 1 per cent which is the limit

> . . . of the possible rise of the value of coin above that of Bullion: for to suppose that coin could, through any cause, rise much above this limit would be to assume that there is a high profit on a transaction in which there was no risk and everyone has an opportunity of engaging.

They commented on the 'very questionable policy' which prohibited the melting down or export of gold coin but dismissed this as not being a material factor. (They refer later to 'that ancient but doubtful policy'.)

They then demonstrate conclusively that an increase in the quantity of the circulating medium will raise prices and that 'by means of the increase in the quantity, the value of a given portion of that circulating medium in exchange for other commodities is lowered; in other words the money prices of all other commodities are raised, and that of Bullion with the rest'. They conclude:

> In this manner, a general rise of all prices, a rise in the market price of Gold and a fall of the Foreign Exchanges, will be the effect of an excessive quantity of circulating medium in a country which has adopted a currency not exportable to other countries, or not convertible at will into a coin which is exportable.

> (Report: 17)

They then go on in Part II to look at the state of the exchanges. Much of this section is taken up with an explanation of the mechanism of exchange.

It deals with the concept of the 'par of exchange'. It is the rate at which the precious metal contents of the two currencies are precisely equal. 'If 25 livres of France contained precisely an equal quantity of pure silver with twenty shillings [i.e. £1] sterling, 25 would be said to be the par of Exchange between London and Paris'. They go on to discuss how when one country uses gold and the other uses silver the bimetallic ratio has to be taken into account. The actual exchange rate can fluctuate between what were later to be called specie points. In the last resort trade has to be settled by shipping gold from one centre to another. The physical cost of transporting gold from London to Hamburg was of the order of 1.5 per cent to 2 per cent to which has to be added the cost of insurance. As a result of war-time conditions the insurance rates had risen sharply, making the total cost about 7 per cent. A fluctuation of this magnitude could, they point out, have been explained, away, but not one of 20 per cent. They discussed the effect on change in the parity explaining that the real Par will be altered:

> ... if any change takes place in the currency of one of the two countries, whether that change consists in the wear or debasement of metallic currency below its standard or in the discredit of a forced paper currency or in the excess of a paper currency not convertible into specie.

They conclude Part II by stating:

> From the foregoing reasonings relative to the state of the Exchanges if they are considered apart, Your Committee find it difficult to resist an inference that a portion at least of the great fall which the Exchanges lately suffered must have resulted not from the state of trade but from a change in the relative value of our domestic currency. But when this deduction is joined with that which your Committee have stated respecting the ... market price of Gold, that inference appears to be demonstrated.
>
> (Report: 52)

The committee summarised the real bills 'doctrine' on page 46.

> The Bank Directors ... showed a great anxiety to state to Your Committee a doctrine of the truth of which they professed themselves to be most thoroughly convinced, that there can be no possible excess in the issue of Bank of England paper so long as the advances in which it is issued are made upon the principles which at present guide the conduct of the Directors, that is so long as the discount of mercantile Bills is confined to paper of undoubted solidity arising out of real commercial transactions, and payable at short and fixed periods.

The fallacy of the doctrine of real bills they said 'lies in not distinguishing between an advance of capital to merchants as an additional supply of currency to the general mass of circulating medium' (page 50). The concept

> ... that while the Bank is restrained from paying in specie, there need be no other limit to the issue of paper than what is fixed by such rules of discount and that, during the suspension of cash payment the discount of good Bills falling due to short periods cannot lead to any excess in the amount of Bank paper in circulation, appears to Your Committee to be a *doctrine wholly erroneous in principle and pregnant with dangerous consequences in practice*
>
> (Report: 50–1, emphasis added)

241

The Committee found that the real bills fallacy was

> ... entertained by some of those individuals who had been at the head
> of the affairs of the Bank. The opinions held by those individuals are
> likely to have an important practical influence and appear to Your
> Committee moreover the best evidence of what has constituted the
> actual policy of the establishment in its corporate capacity.
>
> (Report: 51)

> Your committee cannot hesitate to say, that these opinions of the Bank
> must be regarded as in a great measure the operative cause of the
> continuance of the present state of things.
>
> (Report: 54)

The report alludes to several other factors, including the issue of notes by
country banks. They point out that

> ... so long as the cash payments of the Bank are suspended, the whole
> paper of the Country Bankers is a super-structure raised on the
> foundation of the paper of the Bank of England. The same check which
> the convertibility into specie, under a better system, provided against
> the excess of any part of the paper circulation is, during the present
> system provided against an excess of Country Bank paper by its
> convertibility into Bank of England paper.
>
> (Report: 61)

> The amount of paper which should be in circulation would depend on
> the needs of the trade and 'the effective currency of the country
> depends upon the *quickness of circulation and the number of exchanges
> performed at a given time* as well as upon its numerical amount.
> (Report: 57, emphasis added).

This of course is a reference to 'velocity' the second factor in the quantity
theory equation. Velocity was in fact increasing as merchants found ways
of economising in the use of actual money. 'But above all, the same amount
of currency will be more or less adequate in proportion to the skill which
the great money-dealers possess in managing and economising the use of
the circulating medium' (p.58).

This secular increase in velocity occasioned by the development of the
banking system would, they suggest undogmatically, have been more than
enough to take care of the expanding needs of trade. Their conclusion was
clear.

> That there is at present an excess in the paper circulation of this
> country of which the most unequivocal symptom is the very high price
> of Bullion and next to that the low state of the Continental Exchanges;
> that this excess is to be ascribed to the want of a sufficient check and

control in the issues of paper from the Bank of England; and originally to the suspension of cash payments which removed the natural and true control. For upon the general view of the subject Your Committee are of opinion that no safe, certain and consistently adequate provision against an excess of paper currency however occasional or permanent can be found except in the convertibility of all such paper into specie.

(Report: 66)

They therefore

... report it to the House as their Opinion, That the system of the circulating medium of this country ought to be brought back with as much speed as is compatible with a wise and necessary caution to the original principle of cash payments at the option of the holder of bank paper.

(Report: 68)

They also refer to the profits which must have been made by the Bank of England from the operation. 'The addition of between 4 and 5 million sterling to the paper circulation of this country has doubtless been made at a very small expense to the parties issuing it, only about £100,000 having been paid thereupon in stamps to the Revenue'. The Bank:

... had been enabled under the protection of the law which virtually secures them against such demands to create within the last year or 15 months at a very trifling expense and in a manner almost free from all present risk to their respective credits as dealers in paper money, issues of that article to the amount of several millions operating in the first instance and in their hands as capital for their own benefit and when used as such by them, falling into and in succession mixing itself with the mass of circulation of which the value in exchange for all other commodities is greatly lowered as that mass is augmented.

(Report: 65)

If the committee had not been recommending resumption 'they would not hesitate to declare an opinion that some mode ought to be devised of enabling the State to participate much more largely in the profits accruing from the present system'. This part of their advice has at least been noted by future governments!

The Bank of England was unrepentant. The directors resolved and transmitted the resolution to the Commons committee as follows:

That this court cannot refrain from adverting to an opinion strongly insisted on by some that the Bank has only to reduce its issues to obtain a favourable return of the exchanges and a consequent influx of the precious metals; the court conceives it to be its duty to declare that it is unable to discover any solid foundation for such a sentiment.

(Fetter and Gregory 1973: 13–14)

Meanwhile the government was still having difficulty with its finances. A proposed Property Tax was rejected by Parliament, comprised mainly of landowners. For the first (but by no means the last) time, the Government was a net borrower in time of peace, to meet current expenses. It was suggested that the Bank increase its capital and make a loan to the state of £3 million at 3 per cent to be repayable in 1833. During this period bank notes would continue to be accepted in payment of taxes. As 'three per cents' then stood at 60 to yield 5 per cent this did not appeal.

Towards resumption

In February 1818 Vansittart told the House that resumption was again to be postponed. His Bank Restriction Continuance Act (68 Geo. III c.37) postponed resumption until 5 July.

> The debates took place in a fog of ignorance about essential matters that it is hard for those who live in an age of public statistics to picture. . . . No Member of Parliament, unless he were a Director, had any accurate information, except what the Bank told Vansittart and Vansittart told the House.
>
> (Clapham 1970 vol. ii: 65)

A Commons Secret Committee recommended another postponement. The Bank of England published a memorandum, arguing that restriction was not their fault. They made snide remarks about 'the System of Finance which it had been thought proper to adopt' – a reference to Parliament's failure to balance the Budget.

The day after the first report (5 April 1819) Parliament forbade the Bank to make further gold payments. The second report (6 May 1819) led directly to Peel's Act (59 Geo. III c.49) which became law on 2 July 1819. This provided for a gradual resumption of payments. Suspension was to continue until 31 January 1820. From then until 1 October 1820 notes could be cashed for gold bars of a minimum weight of 60 oz, at £4.10s.0d. per standard ounce (that is a premium of 2.7 per cent). This price was to be reduced in stages and, from 1 May 1823 full convertibility at the old parity would be restored. The ban on the melting and exporting of gold was repealed: the effect of this, coupled with the plans for the repayment of £10 million by the government to the bank, was deflationary.

The gold price fell, and full convertibility was actually resumed on 1 May 1821, two years ahead of schedule. In the words of Feaveryear:

> Peel's Act had left the pound upon a basis which approached more nearly to a completely automatic metallic standard than at any other time before or since. The seigniorage and other mint charges had long been abolished. Charles II had established a free and open mint. . . .

244

Peel had abolished the restriction upon the melting and export of coin. The old bullionist laws had long fallen into abeyance. Mercantilism was dying. No one now thought that the government should make laws to secure the country's treasure. No one cared much whether gold came in or went out.

(Feaveryear 1931: 211)

The Government, acting upon the recommendations of the theorists, clumsily extinguished a large amount of credit, and the acute depression which followed gave rise to the agitation of Cobbett and the farmers and to the repeated efforts of Western to upset the settlement; and although the latter was unsuccessful in securing an enquiry into a working of Peel's Act, his efforts were not without result.

(Feaveryear 1931: 216)

In preparation for resumption, the Bank had accumulated a considerable reserve of bullion. Lord Overstone questioned whether this was appropriate:

The man who, because he had accumulated an unusual quantity of water, thought he could therefore fill with it a tub which had lost its bottom was not more absurd than the Bank, in thinking that the accumulation of specie put it in a position to make some effectual progress towards a return to cash payments, without any previous or accompanying measures for putting a bottom to its tub by regulating the exchanges.

27

THE AMERICAN CIVIL WAR
AND THE GREENBACKS

BACKGROUND TO THE WAR AND THE FINANCING
OF IT

After the resumption of gold payments in 1821 the United Kingdom, and much of Europe, had an active paper circulation fully and freely convertible into bullion. This regime was to continue for the rest of the century and indeed until the 1914–18 Great War.

Across the Atlantic there was another upheaval. In 1861, soon after the outbreak of the Civil War, both sides resorted to inconvertible paper as a method of financing the emergency. The Union's greenbacks at one time fell to a third of their gold value, but were eventually redeemed at par. Confederate paper, like the French Assignats and the earlier American Continental currency, sank without a trace. The total cost of the war, has been estimated (O'Brien 1988), at almost $5 billion, including the destruction of capital in the South, but excluding the human cost of 600,000 dead and 475,000 wounded. This was vastly greater than the cost of the Wars of Independence, and was undoubtedly the greatest social and financial upheaval of the century.

The War, was of course, about slavery. The practice, regarded by the cotton growing Southern States as the foundation of their economy, had become increasingly repugnant to the majority of the country. The Constitution gave the Federal government inadequate power to force abolition: the fifteen pro-slavery states could easily block the three-quarters majority needed to secure a constitutional amendment. The problems really came to a head between Lincoln's election in November 1860 and his inauguration the following March. The lame duck outgoing President, Buchanan, was too weak to cope. The 'Confederated States of America' declared themselves independent on 4 February 1861. The siege and surrender of Fort Sumter in April made war inevitable.

Lincoln had inherited from Buchanan a financial as well as a political problem. He appointed Senator Salmon P. Chase, former governor of Ohio, as Secretary of the Treasury. Chase represented the conservative wing of the party, and his appointment was partly to balance that of the more radical Seward as Secretary of State. He was a hard money man and a supporter of the Independent Treasury, but believed he should be President. In February 1861, Congress had authorised the issue of $25 million 20-year bonds at 6 per cent. Of these, $18 million were sold at a discount of 11 per cent. On 2 March, a further issue of $10 million was authorised, but Congress decreed a maximum interest rate of 6 per cent, and that bonds could not be sold below par.

Chase, having inherited this unrealistic proviso, had to go through the motions of making a formal offer of 20-year 6 per cent bonds at par. As similar bonds were trading in the market at 84 there were obviously no real takers (there were in fact three applications for a total of $12,000, but these were withdrawn). This cleared the way for Chase to issue interest bearing treasury notes (Mitchell 1903: 12). In his first three months of office Chase found that the receipts of the treasury were $5.8 million and its expenditures $23.5 million. He was forced to borrow. The Congress met in special session on 4 July 1861. President Lincoln's message asked for at least 400,000 men and $400 million to fight the war. To meet the needs of the next twelve months it was proposed to raise $80 million by taxation and $240 million as loans. Bonds could be issued at 7 per cent, notes at 7.3 per cent. In retrospect Wesley Clair Mitchell, the historian of the period, suggests that the country and Congress were willing to submit to a high level of taxation.

Chase now began a policy of issuing non interest bearing treasury notes, payable on demand in gold and receivable for the payment of taxes and customs. These were not readily accepted and the banks, fearing competition for their own notes, objected. They said that they would submit for redemption any notes received by them. Chase apparently put pressure on the banks by refusing to allow the proceeds of the loan to remain on deposit with them (Mitchell 1903: 26–8).

The annual report of the Treasury published on 10 December 1861, showed a dramatic increase in expenditure. On 16 December it was learnt that the British government was in effect threatening war unless two Confederate prisoners, seized by force from a British ship, were released. There was a panic on the markets and government securities fell 2½ per cent (Mitchell 1903: 38). The banks had to pay out coin to government contractors, but the normal flow back of coin ceased as the contractors became reluctant to deposit their receipts. The banks themselves had much of their assets locked up in government securities which had become relatively unmarketable. In the report, Chase had proposed a form of 'bond-secured currency similar to that issued by New York banks under the Free Banking Act 1838'. This 'fell on deaf ears'. The New York banks suspended payment on 30 December 1861. This 'although largely due to his own intransigence, was an unexpected blow' to Secretary Chase (Myers 1970: 153). Inevitably this forced the Treasury itself to suspend payments. The treasury notes issued by Chase were now effectively inconvertible.

The Greenbacks

There then began the debates on the first Legal Tender Act. Chase made two proposals. One would require all banks to purchase US government securities as backing for their note issue, 'a proposal out of which the national banking system developed some two years later' (Mitchell 1903: 44–5). A sub-committee of Ways and Means chaired by Senator Eldridge G. Spaulding considered a proposal that the United States should issue an irredeemable paper currency of legal tender notes.

It was Spaulding rather than Chase who was 'the father of the Greenbacks'. His own account of the period is given in 'History of Legal Tender Paper Money' (Spaulding 1869).

James Gallatin, speaking for the banks, objected to the proposal and suggested the sale of long term bonds at their market value. This would imply a fixed per cent loan at between 60 and 75 per cent of par. Spaulding objected. Was Spaulding inconsistent? Was he advocating

> ... the issue of paper money upon the ground of sheer necessity? To substantiate this argument it was of course necessary to show that no other feasible method of obtaining funds existed. Why, when the bankers declared that there was an alternative ... the only logical answer for the legal tender bill was to show that the bankers were mistaken. But such was not the answer that Mr Spaulding made. He replied that selling bonds below par was more objectionable than issuing paper money.
>
> (Mitchell 1903: 49)

The debate in Congress raised all the objections. Specifically,

> rhetoric was employed to picture in vivid colours the unhappy consequences that had followed the issue of paper money by France during the Revolution, by England in the Napoleonic wars, by Austria and Turkey, by Rhode Island in the colonial days, by the Continental Congress in the War of Independence and finally by the Confederate States, then fairly launched upon the paper money policy.
>
> (Mitchell 1903: 55)

Mitchell himself, in his preface, apologises for making no comparisons between American and foreign experiences as these 'presented too large a subject to be dealt with as a side issue'. He also suspected (wrongly) that insufficient statistical information was available on these foreign experiments. Supporters of the Bill argued away each of these examples. One said that 'the true lesson of experience was that of moderate issues'. Mitchell concludes that 'it was easy to show that one of the striking lessons of experiments of paper money is that such moderation, which the issuer at first intends to observe, has almost invariably been soon forgotten' (Mitchell 1903: 56).

Spaulding and his colleagues, though pleading the necessity of the Act, intended it to be temporary. Mitchell quotes him as saying 'when peace is secured I will be among the first to advocate a speedy return to specie payments' and comments that this promise was kept. There was some analysis of Chase's attitude and an interesting quotation on page 71 on what he said later when he was Chief Justice in 'one of the legal tender cases' (*Hepburn* v. *Griswold* 8 Wallace 603 (1870)). In this case the Supreme Court headed by Chief Justice (as he now was) Chase declared that it was unconstitutional for Congress to make Greenbacks legal tender. 'Not only did he not disqualify himself, but in his capacity as Chief Justice convicted himself of having been responsible for an unconstitutional action in his capacity as Secretary of the Treasury!' (Friedman and Schwartz 1963: 46; see also Galbraith 1975 ch. vii).

The Bill was signed into law by President Lincoln on 25 February 1862. The Bill authorised the issue of $150 million of United States notes in denominations of not less than $5. They were to be 'lawful money and a legal tender in payment of all debts public and private within the United States except duties on imports and interest on the public debt'. They were to be exchangeable at any time for 6 per cent 5/20 bonds (i.e. redeemable in not less than five and not more than 20, years at the option of the government) of which $500 million were to be issued. Holders of notes could also deposit them for a period of not less than 30 days and receive 5 per cent interest.

The proposal to pay debt interest in coin had been hotly contested. The House had originally rejected this Senate amendment.

> To pay the army in depreciated paper money and the money lender
> in coin was unjust to the soldier risking his life on the field of battle:
> it makes two classes of money one for the banks and brokers and
> another for the people.
>
> (Mitchell 1903: 77, quoting Mr Stevens)

The opposing argument was that this would preserve the value of bonds and as the notes were convertible into bonds this would preserve the value of the notes themselves. The matter was eventually resolved by a conference committee. The proposal to require import duties to be paid in coin was part of the deal. The '5/20' bond was a key factor in the rather complex relationship.

As many had predicted, the sums involved were not enough. The second Legal Tender Act was signed into law on 11 July 1862. This authorised the issue of a further $150 million and provided for notes of less than $5. The

Postage Currency Act effectively allowed stamps to be used as small change. Although they were not legal tender, they were acceptable for all dues to the United States of up to $5 and were convertible into greenbacks. The Third Legal Tender Act was approved on 3 March 1863 authorising the issue of yet another $150 million of greenbacks and giving Chase the right to borrow up to $900 million during the next two fiscal years (Myers 1970: 156–7; Mitchell 1903: ch. iii and iv). The rest of the War was financed without further issues.

Inflation

The greater part of Mitchell's book is concerned with the economic consequences. The gold dollar had contained 23.2 grains of fine gold. The greenbacks at all time traded for less, reaching a low of 9 grains in July 1864. His appendix A gives daily figures to the end of 1865, for the nominal gold value of $100 of paper money. For the first six months the value remained above 90 but fell to about 75 by the end of 1862. The low point, 35.09, was reached on 11 July 1864 after which there was a recovery to about 67 in December 1865 when the Civil War ended. The greenbacks were finally made convertible in June 1879, and contrary to prophecies, there was no final repudiation. (Dewey (1931: 376) gives a table for the annual average for the period not covered by Mitchell. Generally, there was a fairly steady recovery from just over 70, in 1866–8, to 97.5 in 1878, just before resumption.) Mitchell also gives very detailed figures of prices and wages. Although there were, as one would expect, substantial changes in relative prices at a time of uncertainty and a modest general increase in prices in gold terms the table on his page 77 shows graphically that the changing value of greenbacks in terms of the gold dollar was by far the most important cause of changes in US price levels. Chapter 1 of Part II summarises the issues in a form which will be familiar to the modern reader. Inflation does not simply cause a steady and parallel upward movement of all wages and prices, and although the operation of free competition will (he suggested) tend to restore 'the relative distribution of wealth between different classes prevailing before the disturbance had occurred' there were obstacles. He lists these

1. At any given time business men are bound to a considerable extent by legal contracts calling for the payment or receipt of specified sums ... whether the purchasing power of dollars rises or falls, such contracts are fulfilled by the payment of the specified number of dollars. Until the termination of the contract there is no alteration in the nominal amount of the money to be paid. In this way the scale of money payment existing before depreciation is legally petrified.

2. Rapid readjustment is further hindered by the fact that the nominal amount of many money payments is a conventional sum. [He mentions] the fee of a boot black, the barber the notary the physician, the price of a newspaper, a cigar, a ride in the street car. [Of course, if inflation persists for too long these payments are in fact adjusted.]

3. Even when legal contracts are not in the way and prices paid are most of the subject of bargaining the change in the amount of payment produces friction . . . at every step the advance in the scale of money payments is impeded.

(Mitchell 1903: 138–40)

Much of this part of his book is taken up with a detailed analysis of the effect of the depreciation of the paper currency on prices and wages.

Were the Greenbacks cheap finance?

Mitchell's final chapter raises, but does not completely answer one central question. Was the issue of the greenbacks the most cost-effective method of financing the Civil War? He points out

> . . . that most of the unfortunate consequences that followed their enactment were foretold in Congress – the decline of real wages, the injury done creditors, the uncertainty of prices that hampered legitimate business and fostered speculation. But a majority of this Congress were ready to subject the community to such ills because they believed that the relief of the treasury from its embarrassments was of more importance than the maintenance of a relatively stable monetary standard. There was little of that confusion between economic and fiscal considerations that has frequently been held responsible for the attempts of government to use its power over currency as a financial resource. Rather, there was a conscious subordination of the interests of the community in a stable monetary standard to the interests of the government in obtaining funds to carry on the war. It is therefore incumbent upon one who would judge the policy from the standpoint of its sponsors to enquire into the financial effects which to them seemed most important.

(Mitchell 1903: 403–4)

Mitchell divided this question into two parts. In part I 'an attempt was made to show how much immediate help the greenbacks afforded Mr Chase. It remains for the present chapter to treat the larger question: what effect had the greenbacks upon the amount of expenditures incurred?'

Contemporary critics declared that the policy 'would increase the cost of waging the war by causing an advance in the prices of articles that the government had to buy'. Simon Newcomb estimated the figure at the end of 1864 at $180 million while Holbert, controller of the currency, reported for 1867 that 'probably not less than 33 per cent of the present indebtedness of the United States is owing to the high prices paid by the government while its disbursements were heaviest'. Professor H. C. Adams has estimated that of the gross receipts from debts created between 1 January 1862 and 30 September 1865 amounting to $2,565 million the gold value was but $1,695 million.

O'Brien's (1988) survey of recent scholarship deals mainly with the broader economic effects: the South clearly lost heavily, but did the North derive any economic benefit from the war? He confirms that Congress lagged prices but queries Mitchell's conclusion that businessmen profited from this at the expense of wage-earners. Prices rose above wages because of indirect taxes and the cost of imports. A substantial part of the redistribution was to the Government. Certainly, real wages fell 30 per cent, necessary to free resources. Could this have been engineered by taxation without the help of the subtler 'tax' of inflation? Did business profit (undoubtedly somewhat higher) help in government funding?

Mitchell found that published accounts were inadequate, particularly for him to break down expenditure between commodities and services. The figures suggest, very tentatively, that higher prices increased expenditure by $791 million, but this must be offset by an increase of receipts by $174 million.

> The public debt reached its maximum amount August 31st 1865 when it stood at $2846 million: of this immense debt the preceding estimates indicate that some $589 million or rather more than a fifth of the whole amount were due to the substitution of United States notes for metallic money. Little as these attempts can pretend to accuracy, it seems safe at least to accept the conclusion that the greenbacks increased the debt incurred during the war by running into some hundreds of millions. If so, it follows that, even from the narrowly financial point of view of their sponsors, the legal tender acts had singularly unfortunate consequences.
>
> (Mitchell 1903: 413)

One question of interest is whether the depreciation of the currency affected the prices paid by the government for commodities as much as it did prices paid by private purchasers. Was the sheer weight of government procurement forcing up relative prices against them? The evidence is thin, and Mitchell does not put much weight on this factor. He showed

> that the dominant factor in determining prices during the war was the fluctuating valuation of the currency. There is no reason why knowledge that it would be paid in greenbacks should affect in different

degrees the prices that a dealer would ask from the government and from private men. Since, then, the fairly satisfactory wholesale price data show a rather close parallelism between prices of commodities and of gold it seems fair to infer that the sums asked of the government for identical goods also arose and fell in rough agreement with the premium. True, prices seem not to have gone up so quickly as did the gold quotation but neither did they fall so quickly. Everything considered then, the most trustworthy index of the increase in the sums expended by the government upon commodities is probably found in the average premium upon gold in the several fiscal years.

(Mitchell: 1903: 410)

Key figures on the funding of the war

According to O'Brien the war cost the North $2.3 billion in 1860 (i.e. gold) dollars. Only 'a small proportion' of this came from taxes. The rest was financed as shown in Table 27.1.

Table 27.1 How the North financed the American
Civil War

Money raised as:	Amount raised	
	$m	(%)
Greenbacks	644	28
Short term notes	759	33
Bonds	897	39
Total	2,300	100

In 1866 total debt was $2,756 billion, presumably at 1866 'paper' prices.

If as a working assumption we can take as given the 'real' level of expenditure of the government and the corresponding 'real' receipts from taxation, we know the real sums that had to be financed by borrowing. It is probably also a fair approximation to use gold dollar values as a proxy for real values. The government could have financed this either as it did, by the issue of depreciated currency, or it could have raised the funds required for the war by bond issues. We can only conjecture at what rate of interest these bonds would then have had to be issued, but market conditions at the beginning of the war suggest that it could hardly have been less than 9 per cent. (In 1861 20-year 6 per cent bonds were trading at 84, implying yield to redemption of 7.58 per cent. A yield of 9 per cent would imply a price of 72.6.) There was in the event no default and ultimately the government's debts were all paid in full in gold dollars.

To take the extreme example, in June 1864 the value of the greenback hit its low of 35.09 per cent in terms of gold dollars. To meet its procurements during that month, the government would have had to have incurred liabilities equal to nearly three times the amount of the gold value of the purchases. This, in Mitchell's terms, would be a substantial increase in debt. However, to the extent to which the government's purchases were funded by the issue of newly printed greenbacks which were then held for the fourteen and a half years until specie payment was resumed, it was effectively financing its expenditure by a 'zero coupon bond'. The cost of this finance works out at 7.94 per cent which represents the maximum outcome cost of greenback finance. This, surely, is less than the rate at which money could have been obtained by bond finance. Generally, finance by 'printing money' was cheap. Borrowing at these rates was expensive.

A note on the real interest rate

Mitchell has a quite modern treatment of the concept of the real interest rate. He says

> ... that the problem is that both lenders and borrowers failed to foresee the changes that would take place in the purchasing power of money between the dates when loans were made and repaid. ... If for instance men arranging for loans in April 1862, to be repaid a year later, had known that the in the meantime the purchasing power of money would decline 30 per cent they would have agreed upon a very high rate of interest. On the assumption that, monetary conditions aside, the rate would have been 6 per cent the lender gifted with second sight would have demanded 50.52 per cent i.e. 6 per cent, plus 42 per cent of both capital and interest to offset the decline of 30 per cent of the purchasing power of the dollars received in repayment as compared with that of the dollars lent. According to the table of relative prices any interest rate less than this would have deprived capitalists of a portion of their ordinary turns and on the other hand the prices of products increased on average 42 per cent between April 1862 and April 1863 borrowers could afford to pay on the average 50.52 per cent of loans quite as well as they could afford to pay 6 per cent in years of stable prices. ... If as the table indicates the rates prevailing in the New York market 1862 to 1863 were less than 7 per cent it must have been because the extraordinary rise of prices was not foreseen by borrowers and lenders.
>
> (Mitchell 1903: 369)

(A 30 per cent decline in the value of money actually represents an increase in prices of 42.86 per cent and the real rate of interest at 6 per cent nominal should be 51.34 per cent. Mitchell uses an approximation in the first stage of his calculation, but does then correctly calculate the second stage to two places of decimals.)

There was in fact little change in nominal interest rates as the table on his page 367 shows. The effect on real interest rates was dramatic. One complication arose of a provision in the Legal Tender Act.

> Interest on many forms of government bonds was paid in gold. Capitalists who invested their means in these securities consequently received an income of unvarying specie value. But even these investors did not escape all the evil consequences of the paper-money system because as has been shown prices rose in the end to a greater height than the premium upon gold.
>
> While persons had purchased bonds as an investment before the war suffered no great loss of income, persons who had sufficient faith in the stability of the federal government to purchase its securities at the low price that had prevailed during the war realised a very high rate of interest.
>
> (Mitchell 1903: 377–8)

He shows the effect of the returns to a foreigner who invested $1,000 worth of gold in January in each of the four relevant years, but these figures are running yields and need to be calculated in terms of redemption yields. An even greater return could presumably have been obtained by selling after the end of hostilities but before 1881.

28

SOME OTHER CASES OF INCONVERTIBLE PAPER MONEY

INTRODUCTION

The previous chapters have discussed six major experiments in inconvertible paper money, ranging from John Law in 1720 to the American Civil War in the 1860s. There were plenty of other examples, some of which deserve at least a brief mention. These include the extraordinary if ill-documented story of China, which experimented with paper money centuries before Europe. Russia and Sweden 'suspended payments' before the Napoleonic Wars (but after John Law) and there were several lapses during the generally stable mid-nineteenth century. Not surprisingly, some of these examples are in Latin America.

China

Paper money was invented in China. China, too had its 'John Law', but much earlier. Also, perhaps typically Chinese, the story, instead of reaching its climax in two or three years, covers much of the life of the Sung Dynasty. There was paper money inflation from about 1190 to 1240 just as the Western European monetary systems were emerging from the dark ages. Mrs Quiggin (1969) discusses the early history of money in China. She gives some intriguing comments on early paper money, although it is strictly outside her subject. In 1877 W. Vissering wrote a thesis on the subject which reveals rather more. The third source is an essay by Kann (1937), citing articles in the Bank of China Quarterly. Volume V of *Science and Civilisation in China* (Tsien Tsuan-Hsuim; editor Joseph Needham, 1985) deals with paper and printing and devotes a few pages (96–102) to paper money. It is presumably more reliable, if less sensational, than the other sources, but its approach is artistic rather than monetary.

There are 'vague reports of paper money as early as 2677 BC (Vissering 1877) while Kann (1937: 366) says there are records of paper money during the T'ang dynasty, (c. 650) but questions their authenticity: Tsuan-Hsuim suggests there may have been paper imitations of coins buried or burnt to propitiate the souls of the dead, but the 809 issues are, he says, 'a well established fact'. It does seem clear that Bills of Exchange were invented in ninth century China in the form of 'flying money' *(fei ch'ein)* as a convenient way to avoid transporting metal coins. This institution was originally a private arrangement between merchants but was taken up by the government in around 812 as a method of forwarding local taxes. Since the 'flying money' was primarily a draft it is generally considered a credit medium rather than true money. It did gradually evolve into a paper currency. Examples are illustrated in Qian Jiaju (1883).

Vissering (1877: Chapter vi) suggests that the use of money bills may have originated in the receipts for government products issued by the State to pay for any purchases. The bills were first issued in 1011 and appear to have been redeemable every three years, but in 1076 after sixty-five years ('the 22nd triennial term') few were presented for payment. At this stage new bills were issued with a seventy-year (twenty-five term) life. There were then two series of bills in circulation. He says that issues were initially limited (to 1,256,340 string) but forgeries appeared in 1068. A total of 1,250,000 string of twenty-five term bills were issued in 1072.

'Fiat money was not only invented in China, but the authorities there grasped the necessity of maintaining metallic reserves. These reserves were originally three-sevenths of the issues' (Kann 1937). Trouble began in 1107. The war with the Tartars put financial pressure on the state, met by a vast supply of paper money. Holders could no longer effectively redeem in specie, but received in exchange a new emission of 'bills of credit notes', in the ratio of one new bill for four of the old. Under the emperor Kas-Tsung (1127–63) 'the issue of paper money was expanded in the most reckless manner' under Tartar pressure (Vissering 1871: 177).

Lui 1983 appears to have more accurate data. This is only summarised in his paper which is mainly concerned to see how the history fits Cagan's (1956) hypothesis. He says that 'in 1161 a new kind of paper money, the *hui-tzu* or "check medium" was issued. The new Emperor . . . soon decided the government should carefully regulate the supply'. By 1178 it was reported that circulation had increased to 45,000,000 string and an official advised against further issues. There were further issues in 1204. Lui shows money supply rising from 224 in 1181–90 to 4,949 in 1240, with a similar movement in prices. The bills were soon reduced to one-tenth of their value – and eventually notes of 1,000 cash fell to the value of 10 cash. Paper money is said to have brought down the Sung dynasty.

Marco Polo visited China in 1271–95 – after the currency collapse. He is said to have described the notes as being worth from half a tornesel to 10 groats Venetian and others from 2 to 10 gold Bezants. 'All these pieces of paper are issued with as much solemnity and authority as if they were pure silver or gold'.

Paper money in Imperial Russia

Two European countries issued inconvertible paper money before the Napoleonic Wars: Russia and Sweden. Russia issued paper money in 1768 and suspended payments in 1786. 'Russia adopted a paper currency during the reign of Catherine the Great – oddly enough she anticipated France in naming the notes assignats' (Einzig 1962: 193). Two note-issuing Assignation Banks were formed in 1768. The Queen 'promised in her message that these notes would be forever redeemable and would never be appropriated by the Government (or lent to it) for its own purposes. This promise was not kept' (National Monetary Commission Report 1909 vol. 18). There was some doubt as to whether payment was to be in silver or copper. 'According to Storch, opinions on that point were still divided when he wrote in 1815. From 1769 till 1787 the amount in circulation was uniform at 40 million' (Walker 1888: 366). It then increased to 50, and then 100, million and much of the proceeds of the issue were handed over to government as an interest free loan.

In 1839 the emperor ordered cash payments in silver 'in the proportion of 3.5:1'. Walker 1888, quoting Seyd, suggests the Imperial government had lost control of its liabilities and was not aware how many notes were in issue. Other evidence suggests that this silver standard actually lasted for many years: certainly, it seems, to 1868 but perhaps not to 1897. The change was made in 1840 in consequence of the Supreme Manifesto of 1 July 1839 'to put an end to the rise in the value of paper money (assignation) which had begun to take place in several parts of Russia, owing to different circumstances' (Royal Commission on Decimal Currency 1857). At the time of the report the Russian unit was the silver rouble, 278 grains of fine silver, and in answer to a question: 'Before the introduction of the present system the money of account was the ruble of assignation, 3.5 times less than the present silver ruble . . . all accounts, contracts and engagements . . . were made, up to the introduction of the silver money of account, in rubles of assignation'. The 1868 (UK) Royal Commission on International Coinage sent out a questionnaire to Russia. The information on page 265 confirms that the silver standard was then still in force. It appears to have collapsed at some later date and that there was a period of inconvertible bank notes until, in 1897 a gold standard was introduced by Count Sergei Witte, the finance minister.

Sweden

The Swedish example is a little earlier. Eagly 1971 (The Swedish Bullionist Controversy) translates, with a commentary, the Pehr Niclas Christiernin's lectures of 1761. Between 1739 and 1772 two political parties 'Hats' and 'Caps' vied for control of the Riksdag. Hats (in power 1739–65, and

1769–71) were protectionist, mercantilist and supportive of local industries, notably textiles. They resorted to the printing press, using the Riksbank to issue inconvertible bank notes. Notes outstanding rose from 6.9 million daler in 1745 to 13.7 in 1754, and a peak of 44.5 in 1762. Inflation and the exchange rate reflected these changes, but the Caps, in power briefly 1765–9 engineered a deflation which brought the currency back to par. (The Caps had another brief period of power in 1771–2 when a coup d'état engineered by the Hats, the nobility and the Crown destroyed democracy.) The Caps representing small industrialists, merchants and importers were more laissez faire in their economic views and took a 'bullionist' approach to money. However Eagly says that their theory of value was based on the assumption that notes 'should always designate the same quantum of precious metal. The notion is simplistic and the economic analysis naive'.

Italy

After the Napoleonic Wars, Europe returned to silver, gold or both, but there were some lapses. Italy had a period of inconvertible lira from 1866 to 1881 'Il Corso Forsoto' or forced currency. Italians were little accustomed to paper money. 'In 1865 only one-tenth of the money in circulation consisted of bank notes. Such notes were said to stay in circulation no longer than ten weeks on average' (Kindleberger 1984: 140). He says the mild inflation may have helped Italian financial development. The period is discussed in more detail by Tito Canovai (National Monetary Commission 1911 vol. 18), although his economic insights are frustratingly thin. State and bank notes circulated, at a discount in the range 10–16 per cent. In 1881 a new government promised to abolish forced currency: the task fell to the finance minister Agostino Magliani. A gold loan, led by Hambro and Baring, was raised for 644 million lire: sufficient to redeem about two-thirds of the outstanding notes. The passing of the bill (which predated the loan) had already brought the discount down to 1.6 per cent, but it rose again with the Paris based crisis of 1882.

Austria

The Bank of Vienna effectively failed after the Napoleonic Wars and a new National Bank was created in 1816. During the crisis of 1869 the government counted foreign bills of exchange as equivalent to specie 'a hint of the gold exchange standard to come' (Kindleberger 1984: 130). Convertibility was suspended in the crisis of 1873, and continued for some years. Silver went to a premium, but this ran off after 1879 'not because the Austrian florin was improving but rather due to the falling price of silver'. Indeed the story is complicated by two other factors, the collapse of bimetallism and the price of silver and the unification of Austria and Hungary. After 1876, arbitrageurs were buying silver abroad, having it coined into Austrian florins which were then exchanged for paper. The unwanted coins piled up in the bank vaults until silver coinage was suspended in 1879. In 1892 Austria-Hungary adopted a gold standard (Zuckerkandl in National Monetary Commission 1911 vol. 18).

Latin America

The Napoleonic Wars precipitated the perhaps already inevitable collapse of Spanish control of Latin America.

> Independence proceeded, *cabildo* by *cabildo*, following the organisa-
> tion of a system that concentrated everything in towns. There was no
> united opposition to imperial taxation, no Continental Congress. . . .
> There were no colonial institutions analogous to the assembly of the
> English colonies that could provide a coherent framework for the
> ordering of conflict. The independence movement rapidly assumed the
> character of a civil war.
>
> (Lang 1975: 99)

Perhaps inevitably, the emerging independent Latin American states had recourse to inconvertible paper money in the nineteenth century, acquiring habits they found hard to break. Typically these experiments were, by twentieth century standards, only modestly inflationary, and unlike the experiences of the American and French revolutionaries, ended with the paper money having some residual value. The implications were discussed in a conference paper by Guillermo Subercaseaux (1909), Professor of Political Economy at the University of Chile. He distinguishes between such money introduced 'as a product of progressive and calm deliberation of monetary institutions' and the results of crises, whether 'a shortage of money by the State' or a 'monetary crisis specially affecting banking institutions' (p.7). There are also brief accounts in Muhleman 1908. Del Mar (1895) has a comprehensive chapter on Argentina, going back to the early monetary history of that country (and making some contribution to the then still smouldering debate on bimetallism), while Deaver (1970) discusses Chile.

Argentina

The Bank of Buenos Aires was formed in 1822, and its bank notes were initially worth a 'slight premium' over gold (Del Mar 1895). His account of the next period is paralleled by that of Subercaseaux (1909). In 1826 its notes were declared inconvertible (war with Brazil) and it was taken over by the government. By 1828 the 'ounce [of gold] of 16 old pesos was quoted at 116 in notes; by 1840 it was 514. In 1867 there was a resumption and a reconstruction on the basis of 25 paper pesos for 1 gold peso. (Del Mar says this level was reached in 1856, after which the exchange was fairly constant until 'resumption'.) On 16 May 1876 the 'resumption' was 'suspended' (Del Mar 1895) and gold went to a 50 per cent premium. By 1891 paper had depreciated so that 230 paper pesos were worth 100 gold pesos. In 1899, when economic circumstances were favourable, the exchange was fixed at 44 centavos gold for 1 paper peso, and new notes were issued on a gold base (Subercaseaux 1909: 36). In 1899 steps were taken to fix the rate for depreciated paper money at this figure but he adds that about half the outstanding 518 million pesos of notes remained unguaranteed: he describes the country as 'emerging from the regime of heavily depreciated paper' (Muhleman 1908: 156). Del Mar (p. 895, pp. 456–7) refers to a Legal Tender law being introduced in October 1863, a formal gold standard in 1875, and a US-style 'National Banking System' in 1881: the latter was liquidated in 1891 and replaced by the Banco de la Nacion Argentina.

Brazil

The situation was broadly similar to that in Argentina. Notes of the Bank of Brazil date from 1808. Gold and silver had disappeared, leaving copper coins as the metal money into which notes could be changed. In 1820 notes had depreciated and the circulation of inconvertible paper as money continued. In 1829 the government took notes under its guarantee, and in 1833 took over the note issue from the Bank. These were given the status of legal tender in 1835. After 1840 the circulation of bank notes was added to the paper money of the State, and in 1846 there was a reform of the metallic money system, diminishing the gold value to take account of the depreciation of paper. The exchange with London, 30 to 32 pence in 1840, was fairly stable, only rarely falling as low as 25 until 1876, when it fell to 20, recovering to 28 in 1889. As a result of over-issue, it fell to 5 in 1898, and there was a reconstruction in 1906 (Subercaseaux 1909: 36). In 1898 the government took exclusive note issuing powers (Muhleman 1908).

Chile

In Chile, commercial banking began in 1860 and developed rapidly. Bank notes became inconvertible during the war with Spain in 1865. In 1878 specie payments were suspended, and there was a policy of forced circulation. In the early period inflation was modest. Subercaseaux refers to issues of 'billets fiscaux' with legal tender status. The system had previously been bimetallic – but in practice exclusively silver. The peso fell on London from its 1879 rate of 42 pence to 12 pence by 1894 (the silver peso by then being 23 pence because of the fall in the relative value of silver). In 1895 a gold standard was adopted on the basis of an 18 pence peso, since when 'this enterprising

261

republic has endeavoured ... to recover from the depreciated paper currency regime but has not yet succeeded' (Muhleman 1908). Gold sovereigns remained legal tender at 13.33 pesos: the premium on gold remained in the range 15 per cent to 70 per cent. Deaver (1970) says that unsuccessful attempts to restore a metallic standard were made in 1879 and 1928. In the 1890s note issuing privileges were withdrawn from the banks and given to the treasury. Subercaseaux says that a new period of paper money began in 1898 which he puts into his second category.

The general pattern in other Latin American countries was broadly similar. There were periods of inconvertible paper, which typically retained some residual value at the end of the period. Most adopted the gold standard at the end of the century. They all do seem to have been determined to manage their own monetary arrangements rather than to adopt the obvious expedients of allowing foreign money to circulate, or organising a 'monetary union' between themselves. (Loyd 1837: 51).

29

POSTSCRIPT – THE EARLY TWENTIETH CENTURY

INTRODUCTION

This book set out to cover the period to 1896, the year which saw the end of 'The Great Depression' and (effectively) of the Silver Wars. This ushered in a period of stable prosperity which, even though it lasted only eighteen years, is looked back on as a Golden Age by those who yearn for the (apparent) simplicities of the gold standard. It fell apart in 1914, and was stable only in comparison with the turmoil which was to follow. The gold standard was eventually to be abandoned and replaced almost universally by inconvertible fiat money. Inflation would become chronic and persistent in many countries, and there would be many cases of hyper-inflation and of complete currency collapse. There is a huge literature on twentieth century monetary history, and this chapter is intended only as a brief postscript to the main work.

Was the 'golden age' even so stable? During the period US wholesale prices rose nearly 50 per cent: an average of 2.5 per cent per annum, the then highest ever peacetime rate. In the United Kingdom, prices rose by 26 per cent (Friedman & Schwartz 1963: 135). All this was without any debasement or other form of monetary cheating. The world had simply found more gold, in South Africa, Alaska and Colorado, so that the supply of monetary gold almost doubled during the period. On the 'demand' side the absorbtion of monetary gold, as countries had switched from a bimetallic to a gold standard, had been completed.

The United States, gold and the Federal Reserve

Bryan having been defeated in 1896, the United States could resolve its monetary question. Commercial interests agreed with Treasury Secretary Carlisle:

> We cannot therefore preserve our trade relationships with the best customers ... unless we maintain a monetary system substantially in accord with theirs ... we ought to continue our adhesion to the gold

standard of value with as large a use of silver as is consistent with the
strict maintenance of that policy.

(quoted in Myers 1970: 220)

A Monetary Commission was set up in January 1897. Its four hundred page
report, was largely the work of Professor D Lawrence Laughlin. The Gold
Standard Act, (Doc. Hist. vol. iii: 19; and National Monetary Commission
1909–10 vol. 33: 610) introduced into the House in December 1899 was
passed into law in March 1900. The Act confirmed the gold dollar as the
standard of value, with silver as a subsidiary coinage. The Treasury was
authorised to issue 2 per cent gold bonds which could be used by banks for
the issue of their currencies. As a sop to the silver interests Section 14 of
the Act states:

> that the provisions of this Act are not intended to preclude the
> accomplishment of international bimetallism wherever conditions shall
> make it expedient and practicable to secure the same by concurrent
> action of the leading commercial nations of the world and at a ratio
> which shall ensure permanence of relative value between gold and
> silver.

Any period of rising prices is likely to generate a boom and bust cycle,
and this was no exception. The panic of 1907 had several causes: Thibaut
de St Phalle (1985: 47) particularly draws attention to 'a lack of a centralised
banking institution able to come to the aid of any bank in difficulty'. There
were also real factors such as the enormous insurance claims following the
San Francisco earthquake in April 1906, and the need to finance an unusually
large harvest. At the end of 1906 London banks refused to discount any
more American paper and:

> there were problems caused by the lack of any central organisation:
> scattered reserves, lack of clearing facilities, absence of any lender of
> last resort. Excessive individual banking independence meant that in
> times of panic each bank acted independently to protect its own liquid
> position. If a run started in one bank all the others would attempt to
> collect large amounts of cash simply to protect themselves against a
> similar run.

The National Bank Act allowed banks to deposit part of their reserve
requirements with other banks in major cities, notably in New York, where
'pyramided reserves' were often used profitably to finance stock market
loans. Prohibition of inter-state banking (a relic of the Bank Wars) made it
difficult to transfer money quickly from one part of the country to another.
The crisis came to a head with the failure on 22 October, 1907, of the
Knickerbocker Trust. Banks, at first in New York and later more generally,
refused to repay depositors in gold, which went to a 4 per cent premium

over deposits. J. P. Morgan successfully organised a pool of banks to support the market (see Friedman and Schwartz 1963: 156–63; de St Phalle 1985: 46–8). Restrictions on cash payments were removed in January 1908.

A National Monetary Commission, comprising nine members of the Senate and nine of the House, was set up to study the banking system in the United States and various other countries and to make recommendations about changes to the banking system. They failed to produce a workable plan. This was not for want of research. As the bibliography shows, their published reports are an invaluable reference source for the student of money and include much material which almost certainly would never have been translated into English but for their efforts.

A group of New York bankers, together with Senator Nelson Aldrich and other congressional supporters met in secret at Jekyll Island and drafted a Banking Bill, 'the Aldrich plan' (Congress was not told that Wall Street bankers had had any part in drafting it). This would have created a National Reserve Association with a single central bank (de St Phalle 1985: 50). There was another delay until the Glass Owen Bill was approved by Congress as the Federal Reserve Act of 1913, a few months after the death of J. P. Morgan who, it was said, had alone saved the situation in 1907. One of the first governors of the Federal Reserve Bank, an important player behind the scenes, and the first historian of the bank (Warburg 1930) was Paul Warburg.

The United Kingdom and the Great War

The 1907 crisis had affected London: a run on the reserves was reversed by a 7 per cent Bank Rate, which had squeezed the domestic economy. Otherwise, these eighteen years had, in the United Kingdom, been stable, with little to interest the monetary historian.

> In the days before the War all who studied the English financial system . . . contemplated it with admiration, mingled a little with awe. London, they said, was the financial centre of the world, the banker of all nations. . . . A mountain of credit of unprecedented size was reared up internally upon the reserve of the Bank of England, and that reserve was amazingly small. . . . Even the big bankers were a little awe-struck in contemplating the system of which their institutions were a part. They had read about the great panics of the nineteenth century . . . and shuddered to think of what would happen in the event of a great European war. They shook their heads at the smallness of the gold stock . . . it is not surprising that when the crisis came, it was they . . . and not the public, who lost their nerve. The credit system was even greater than they thought.
>
> (Feaveryear 1931: 299)

The war showed up the weakness of the system, which was totally transformed in the two weeks beginning with the Austrian ultimatum to Serbia on Sunday 26 July 1914. The stock market collapsed next day with several failures. Bank Rate was raised from 3 per cent to 4 per cent (a routine increase) but many stockbrokers were hammered and the Stock Exchange was closed on the Friday. In the resulting panic interest rates rose to between 8 per cent and 10 per cent while banks, other than the Bank of England, refused to pay out gold. It was time for yet another suspension of the Bank Charter Act, and sure enough on Saturday 1 August, Cunliffe, the Governor of the Bank of England, called on the Treasury. He received a 'Treasury Letter', 'an untidy handwritten letter signed by Asquith and Lloyd George' (Sayers 1976: 74) like those of 1847, 1857 and 1866, giving an indemnity against any excess over the legal fiduciary issue but with (as in 1866) the requirement that Bank Rate be raised to 10 per cent.

Monday was August Bank Holiday and the banks were then closed for a further three days, reopening on Friday 5 August. Prompt action was taken authorising the Bank of England to discount approved Bills without recourse thus restoring the liquidity of the market. On 6 August Parliament passed the Currency and Bank Notes Act, empowering the Treasury to issue currency notes. During the week of the extended 'bank holiday' the printing presses had worked overtime: the £1 note (Waterlow) was issued on 7 August and the 10 shilling note (De la Rue) a week later. The notes were known as 'Bradburys', being signed by John Bradbury, Permanent Secretary to the Treasury. All these events took place in the space of two weeks. Gold ceased to circulate and was replaced by these Treasury notes. Although they were technically convertible, it became regarded as unpatriotic to demand gold. The formal structure of Government/Bank of England relations was maintained but this still left scope for indefinite credit financing. Prices more than doubled by the end of the War. The South Africans were required to sell newly mined gold at the official price, a 1916 order under the Defence of the Realm Act (DORA) prohibited the melting down of gold coin and there were a series of measures, at first voluntary, to requisition US and Canadian securities held by British investors.

There were similar phenomena in other countries and the widespread abandonment of the use of gold for monetary purposes led to a fall in its real value. There was obviously little scope for international arbitrage. Gold was shipped to the United States for UK government account and there was surprisingly little evidence of any widespread hoarding of sovereigns.

AFTER THE WAR: THE RETURN TO GOLD

The War ended in November 1918 and for a time prices actually fell. In the United Kingdom the Cunliffe Committee recommended deflation and the restoration of a sound credit position. Their conclusions are criticised in Feaveryear:

the Committee had no idea of the width of the gap which existed . . . between the value of the pound and the value of the sovereign's weight of gold either in England or elsewhere. In parallel circumstances in 1811 the whole political and financial world had had clearly before its eyes the price of gold bullion and had thrashed the matter out. . . . The history of the period from 1820 to 1830 were written plainly in the pages of Hansard for all to read but nevertheless the Committee recommended deflation.

(Feaveryear, 1931: 318–9)

Arguably, he said, this was because nine of the twelve members were traditional bankers, whose main concern was to get back to doing their old business in their old ways.

There was a post war world-wide boom followed by a major collapse in 1920. UK Wholesale prices (1914 = 100) had risen from 240 at the end of the war to 323 by March 1920. In the following year they fell dramatically to 197. There had been similar booms and busts in 1720 and 1825, which may or may not give some comfort to the long wave theorists. In 1920, UK silver coins began to be struck from silver only 0.500 (instead of 0.925) fine. This was precautionary: the silver had had a bullion value less than fiat (face) value for a century, and in spite of rising prices the 0.925 coins were still not quite worth melting down.

Restrictions on the export of gold and silver were due to expire in 1925, and in 1924, the market assuming that the powers would not be extended, the dollar exchange rate rose quite sharply. In the same year the Treasury had appointed a Committee, ostensibly to consider amalgamating the issue of the Treasury and Bank of England issues, but which in fact spent much of its time discussing the restoration of the gold standard. Winston Churchill, the Chancellor, announced in his Budget Speech on 28 April 1925 that the Bank of England was to have a general license to deliver gold for export against legal tender money. A couple of weeks later the Gold Standard Act of 1925 was passed. This introduced a 'gold exchange standard'. The public would not be entitled to convert bank notes or currency notes into gold coin, and the right to have gold bullion coined at the Mint was reserved exclusively to the Bank of England. The Bank would be required to sell 400 ounce bars of gold (about £1,700) to the public in exchange for notes, a measure sufficient to check the excessive use of the printing press. This was effectively the Ricardo 'Proposals for an Economic and Secure Currency' (Ricardo 1951 vol. iv: 49–142).

The last paragraph of the first edition of Feaveryear (1931: 333) written while the UK was still on gold points out that the history of the pound is continuous from King Offa to 1928 with no real break but with a continuous, if moderate, depreciation. However, the French franc (then 124 to the pound) and the Italian lira (92) were originally at par, while the

German mark had totally collapsed. He concludes his book: 'Against these examples, the history of the English standard appears eminently respectable.'

The hyper-inflations of the 1920s

Some other countries, including Germany, were less lucky. The German inflation began during the War: taking 1913 = 100, prices rose to 217 (average) in 1918, and to 415 (average) in 1919 (Kindleberger, 1984: 310–28). Keynes speculated against the mark too early, with near disastrous consequences. The figure was 7030 in June 1922, a doubling over six months, but still short of the '50% per month' definition of hyper-inflation. From then until November 1923 inflation gathered pace. Eventually, prices were 1400 billion times the pre-war level. Various proposals were put forward for monetary reconstruction, including one for a Roggenmark, linked to a commodity, in this case rye, and another for a Gold Note Bank authorised to issue notes with a 2:1 reserve ratio. These were rejected in favour of a 'land bank'. (Shades of Asgill, Chamberlen and John Law: Chapter 23.) On 20 November 1923 the old reichsmark was demonetised and replaced with the Rentenmark on the basis of 1,000 billion (10^{12}) old for one new. This 'dropping of noughts' as such achieved nothing except a saving in printer's ink: there are many Latin American examples. The Rentenmark was issued by the Deutsche Rentenbank backed by a mortgage of 3.2 billion gold marks on the land and other assets of the Reich. (Part of this operation was effectively a capital levy.)

The decree establishing the Rentenbank (an 'independent central bank') limited the notes that could be issued to the government to 1.2 billion marks, forcing drastic measures to balance the budget. Inflation was immediately checked. The Rentenmark was replaced by the Reichsmark in 1924. There were similar hyper-inflations in Austria, Hungary and Poland. They are all discussed in Sargent, 'The Ends of Four Big Inflations' (in Cagan 1956), which mentions briefly how Czechslovakia avoided the fate.

Russia

The Russian case had some different, and interesting features. The gold standard had been abandoned in 1914. War-time inflation turned into hyper-inflation after the Revolution. Between 1922 and 1928 there was a parallel currency, the chervonetz, which was informally linked to gold (Hanke and Schuler, 1991). During the Civil War the British and other allies supported the northern (anti-communist) provisional government based in Archangel, where they conducted a fascinating experiment in creating an alternative currency. This was devised by Dominick Spring-Rice, attached to the allied forces as a financial adviser, in close liaison with Maynard Keynes, then at the UK Treasury. The provisional government established a new agency, the National Emission Caisse (North Russia), which issued notes at a fixed rate of 40 roubles to the pound sterling guaranteed by all the assets of the government. The notes could only be acquired with foreign currency. The Caisse was required to keep at least 75 per cent of the issue on deposit with the Bank of England. It was permitted to invest the balance of 25 per cent in the bonds of the provisional government. This last point apart, it was a pure seigniorage operation comparable to that used in the Island of Jersey, or currency boards such as the West African currency board.

The war with Germany having ended, the allies decided to pull out of the Russian Civil War. The Caisse was closed on 4 October 1919. Notes held by the army were destroyed (they failed to burn so were dumped at sea) and a book entry credit was made at the Bank of England. The Caisse continued to redeem notes and moved its operations to London.

The Crash of 1929 and the collapse of monetary order

Sweden, 'tired of waiting' had returned to gold in March 1924, one of the pressures leading to the UK action discussed above. Many other countries adopted or re-adopted the gold standard, and by the end of 1928 it was virtually universal (Feaveryear, 1963: 360; Kindleberger, 1984: 339). The terms at which the United Kingdom had returned to gold are said to have implied a pattern of exchange rates which left British industry at a competitive disadvantage compared with Germany, the United States and other countries. There had also been significant changes in the international distribution of gold. In 1913, Britain had held 9 per cent of the world's monetary gold. By 1925 this had fallen to 7 per cent, while the North American share had risen from 24 per cent to 45 per cent. This also put the United Kingdom at a comparative disadvantage, although the Depression of the 1930s was a world-wide phenomenon.

The Wall Street Crash of 1929 and the failure of the Hatry empire were early symptoms of a general collapse of the world monetary order. A generally declining confidence in banks and a move to liquidity (that is gold) reached panic proportions with the failure of the Creditanstalt on 31 May 1931. There was a run on Germany in particular, and following the collapse of the Deutschemark on 13 July speculators, as is their wont, turned their attention to sterling. (The MacMillan Committee Report was published that day, which may or may not have been relevant.) The Labour Party, then in government, split, one wing going into opposition leaving Ramsay MacDonald and Philip Snowden to head a National (coalition) Government. They accepted American loans, the terms of which were criticised as a 'bankers' ramp'.

The Bank of England actually ran out of gold and on 19 September 1931 the gold standard was suspended. The Gold Standard (Amendment) Act 1931 stated that 'until His Majesty by proclamation or otherwise directs sub-section 2 of section 1 of the Gold Standard Act 1925 shall cease to have effect'. Bank Rate was raised but sterling depreciated. The Japanese Yen was the next target: the gold standard was suspended on 14 December (Kindleberger 1984, Chapter 20). The German Left opposed any devaluation, even to follow sterling with the slogan 'no tampering with the currency', an early indication of the fear of inflation which was so valuable to Germany in the post-1945 period.

The Sterling Area

The United States, Canada and some European countries remained on gold. The European 'gold bloc' countries (France, Belgium, Holland, Italy, Poland and Switzerland) entered into an agreement for mutual cooperation but the French franc was devalued in 1936. The other Commonwealth countries, together with Portugal and the Scandinavian countries, constituted themselves informally into the Sterling Area and immediately after the suspension of the gold standard sterling fell reaching a low of $3.457 in February 1932.

On May 12 1933 the Thomas Amendment to the Agricultural Adjustment Act gave the American President power to reduce the gold or silver content of the dollar by up to 50 per cent. The Gold Reserve Act of 1934 completed the process, effectively putting the United States on to a gold exchange standard, and devaluing the dollar from 23.22 grains ($20.67 per oz) to 13.714 grains ($35 per oz) (Doc. Hist. vol. iv: 240). The United States embargo on gold exports raised the price of gold, which eventually stabilised at $35 an ounce (where it remained until the days of President Nixon). The pound appreciated to $5 but fell sharply to $4.03 (where it remained until the days of Sir Stafford Cripps). At the outbreak of the Second World War, exchange controls were imposed (where they remained until the days of Margaret Thatcher).

The original members of Sterling Area (Day, 1953: Ch. IV), Commonwealth apart, were countries whose currencies had tended to fluctuate with sterling in the aftermath of the Great War, and who were in 1931 subject to pressures resulting from the Depression. There was a hard core of countries effectively on a sterling exchange standard and an outer group of those who chose, because of trading or banking connections, to make common cause with the United Kingdom for the defence of their currency. There was no formal membership, but the Scandinavian and Baltic countries, Egypt, Iraq, Portugal and Siam could be regarded as shadowing sterling quite closely, while Japan, Argentina and Greece simply used sterling as their main intervention currency. With the introduction of exchange control, membership became formalised, and limited essentially to the Commonwealth, excluding Canada.

Sterling survived the 1939–45 war relatively well, although after the war monetary arrangements were never the same again. There were two formal devaluations of sterling against the dollar, in 1949 and 1967, and in 1971 attempts to maintain fixed exchange rates (with the US on a gold exchange standard) were abandoned.

The post-war period had everything: formal devaluations, speculative runs, hyper-inflations, currency collapses and reconstruction. There have been plenty of monetary conferences and 'plans', and economic fashion has shifted between the virtues of fixed and floating rates. Governments have sought a recipe for achieving stability with an inconvertible, 'fiat' currency with for some of the time in many countries (and most of the time in Germany), a remarkable degree of success. One feature, for which there are few real precedents in earlier history, has been the prevalence of exchange control. The history of that would, itself, make a fascinating study.

NOTES

1. Any analysis of the bullion content of coins must (or should) distinguish between the 'mint equivalent' (the value of one pound Troy weight of minted coins) and the 'mint price' (the value of the coins paid by the mint for 1 pound Troy of bullion allowing for the deduction, or seigniorage, to cover the cost of minting and to provide a profit for the coin issuing authority.
2. See Feaveryear (1931: 346 and 347) for a summary of the rates in England.
3. See Lane and Mueller (1985: 33).
4. The comment is said to have been made in 1560 when the base Edward coins were cried down; it is not mentioned in Ruding (1840) I, 340.
5. Although the 'pound' and 'shilling' (or their translations) always meant 240 and 12 pence, the meaning of other ghost moneys varied from place to place, depending on the accident of the relationship at some past period of stable prices. For instance the Genoan 'florin of account' was equal to 300 pennies or 25 shillings, while the Venetian 'ducat of account' was 124 shillings.
6. See Spink Coin Auction 55, lot 116.
7. Deputy 1883–5; Governor 1885–7; served on Court with usual breaks between 1853–1900. Created Lord Aldenham in 1896.
8. Deputy 1879–81; Governor 1881–3; served on Court between 1865 and 1902.
9. Presumably 'What is a Pound?' June 1881. Grey's first letter was dated 31st May, Grenfell's reply 9 June and Grey's rejoinder 13 June.
10. Robert Lowe, Chancellor of the Exchequer in 1869 raised to the peerage 1880.
11. presumably Grenfell: Gibbs became Governor in 1885
12. This to some extent seems to have its origins in the coinage systems of the Vandals, Ostrogoths and Visigoths. Del Mar 26–7, having pointed out that 'in the Persian system 20 silver shekels went to one gold daric' gives some evidence for the use of bronze coins in Persia (1 Chron xxix 7) and goes on 'What relation of value such bronze coins bore to the silver one has not been determined positively but should it turn out ... duodecimal, we shall be able to trace the well-known arithmetical proportions of £s.d. to at least the sixth century before our era'. This is little more than conjecture.

BIBLIOGRAPHY AND
BIBLIOGRAPHICAL NOTES

Acres, W. M. (1931) *The Bank of England from within, 1694–1900*, Oxford: Oxford University Press.

ACT to make perpetual an Act made in the Seventh Year of the Reign of His present Majesty, Intituled 'An Act to Prevent the Infamous Practice of Stock-Jobbing' (1737).

ACT for better securing certain Powers and Privileges intended to be granted by His Majesty by Two Charters for Assurance of Ships and Merchandizers at Sea, and for Lending Money upon Bottomry, and for restraining several Extravagant and Unwarrantable Practices as therein mentioned ('The Bubble Act' 1720).

ACT to prevent the Infamous Practice of Stock-Jobbing (1734).

ACT for making several Provision to restore the Publick Credit, which suffers by the Frauds and Mismanagement of the late Directors of the South-Sea Company and others July 31 1721 (Sperling: 308).

ACT for restraining and preventing several unwarrantable Schemes and Undertaking in His Majesty's Colonies and Plantations in America.

ACT to Restrain the Number and ill Practice of Brokers and Stock-Jobbers (1695).

ACT for restraining and preventing several unwarrantable Schemes and Undertaking in His Majesty's Colonies and Plantations in America (extended the Bubble Act 1741).

Aislabie, J. The case of the Right Hon. John Aislabie, Esq., bound with . . . A speech upon the consolidated Bill . . . The speech of . . . upon his defence made in the House of Lords . . . Mr A.'s second speech . . . (All 1721.)

Akerman, J. Y. (1849) *Tradesmen's tokens current in London and its vicinity between the years 1648 & 1672*, London: John Russell Smith.

Andreades, A. (1909 second edition 1924) *History of the Bank of England (1640–1903)*, trans. from the Greek by Christabel Meredith with a preface by H. S. Foxwell, London: P. S. King.

Anon (1696) 'A Review of the Universal remedy for all disease incident to coin with Application to Our present circumstances' in a letter to Mr. Locke.

Anon (1841) 'Dear Sir, I wish to address a few remarks to you. . . .'

Anon (1720) 'Considerations on the present state of the Nation as to publick credit and stocks, the landed and trading interests. With a proposal for the speedy lessening of the publick debts', London.

Anon (1825) 'The South Sea Bubble, A Beacon to the Unwary Against Modern Schemes', London.

Anon (1896) 'Universal Remedy'.

Asgill, J. (1696) 'Remarks on the proceedings of the commisioners for putting into execution the act passed last sessions, for establishing of a land-bank', London.

Asgill, J. (1720) *Several Assertions Proved in order to Create another Species of Money than Gold and Silver*, Second edition. (First edition 1696.)

Ashley, Sir W. (1919) *An introduction to English Economic History and Theory*, London: Longmans Green, (Kelley reprint 1966).

Ashton, T. S. and Sayers, R. S. (eds) (1953) *Papers in English Monetary History*, Oxford: Oxford University Press.

Bagehot, W. (1873) *Lombard Street, a description of the Money Market*, fourteenth edition (1915) London: John Murray.

Bagehot, W. (1877) 'Some articles on the Depreciation of Silver' reprinted from *The Economist*, London: Henry S. King.

Bagehot, W. (1881) *Biographical Studies*, London: Longmans Green.

Bagehot, W. (1898) *Literary Studies*, vol iii, London: Longmans Green.

Bailly, A. (1830) *Histoire Financière de la France depuis l'origine de la monarchie jusqu'à la fin de 1785*, Paris.

Ball, D. B. (1985) 'The Confederate Currency Reform of 1862' paper given at conference 'In America's Currency 1789–1866', the American Numismatic Society.

Banco Central do Brasil, (1979) *Iconografia de valores impressos do Brasil*, Brasilia.

Barbour, Sir D. (1885) *The Theory of Bimetallism*, London: Macmillan. (Barbour was Financial Secretary to the Government of India.)

Barbour, Sir D. (1912) *The Standard of Value*, London: Macmillan.

Baring, Sir Fr. Bt. (1797) *Observations on the Establishment of the Bank of England and on the paper Circulation of the Country*, London.

Baring, Sir Fr. Bt. (1801) *Observations on the Publication of Walter Boyd, Esq., M.O.*, London.

Barrow, G. L. (1975) *The emergence of the Irish banking System 1820–45*, Dublin: Gill and Macmillan.

Batterson, J. G. (1896) *Gold and Silver as currency*, Hartford, Conn. (Opposes free coinage of silver. Author was founder of Travelers Insurance Co . . . and sponsor of the first collected edition of Bagehot.)

Baum, L. F. *The Wizard of Oz* (see Rockoff 1990).

Bautier, R.-H. (1971) *The Economic Development of Medieval Europe*, London: Thames & Hudson.

Bautier, R.-H. (ed.) (1982) 'La France de Philippe Auguste, le temps de mutations', paper read at conference in Paris 1980, CNRS Paris.

Birley, R. (ed,) (1944) *Speeches and Documents in American History*, two volumes, Oxford: Oxford University Press.

Blunt, Sir J. (1722) 'A true state of the South-Sea-Scheme, as it was first formed with the several alterations made in it, before the Act of Parliament passed. And an examination of the conduct of the Directors in the execution of that Act; with an enquiry into some of the causes of the losses which have ensued', London.

Boase, H. (1803) *Guineas an unnecessary and expensive incumbrance on commerce: or, the impolicy of repealing the bank restriction bill considered*, Second edition with appendix, London: W. Bulmer & Co.

Boase, H. (1811) 'Remarks on the New Doctrine concerning the supposed depreciation of our currency' (comments on Huskisson) London.

Bonar, J. (ed.) (1887) *Letters of David Ricardo to Thomas Robert Malthus 1810–1823*, Oxford.

Bosanquet, C. (1810) 'Practical Observations on the Report of the Bullion Committee', 2nd edn, corrected with a supplement, London.

Boyd, W. (1801) 'A letter to the Right Honorable William Pitt on the influence of the stoppage of issues and specie at the Bank of England on the prices or provisions and other commodities'.

Boys, T. (1825) *The South Sea Bubble – a Beacon to the Unwary*, London.

Braudel, F. (1972) *The Mediterranean and the Mediterranean World in the Age of Philip II*, trans. from the French by S. Reynolds, vol. I, London: Collins.

—— (1973) *The Mediterranean and the Mediterranean World in the Age of Philip II*, trans. from the French by S. Reynolds, vol. II, London: Collins.

Briscoe J. (1694) An abstract of the Discourse on the late funds of the Million Act, etc.

Brogan, H. (1985) *The Pelican History of the United States of America*, London: Pelican Books.

Brooke, G.C. (1932) *English Coins*, London: Methuen.

Bubble Act An Act for better securing certain Powers and Privileges intended to be granted by His Majesty by Two Charters for Assurance of Ships and Merchandizers at Sea, and for Lending Money upon Bottomry, and for restraining several Extravagant and Unwarrantable Practices as therein mentioned. ('The Bubble Act' 1720)

Bullion Report (1810) Report together with Minutes of Evidence and Accounts from 'The Select Committee appointed to inquire into the cause of the High Price of Gold Bullion, and to take into consideration the state of the circulating medium and of the exchanges between Great Britain and foreign parts', London.

Burns, A. R. (1927) *Money and Monetary Policy in Early Times*, London: Kegan Paul.

Butchart, M. (1935) *Money, The Views of Three Centuries*, London: Stanley Nott.

Buxton, Sydney, M. P., (1888) *Finance and Politics: an Historical Study. 1783–1885*, two volumes, London: John Murray (ex Marshall Library).

Cagan, P. (1956) 'The Monetary Dynamics of Hyperinflation', in Friedman (ed.) *Studies in the Quantity Theory of Money*, Chicago: University of Chicago Press.

Calhoun J. C. (1834) 'Speech on the motion of Mr Webster Mar 21'.

Callender, G. S. (1965) *Selections from The Economic History of the United States 1765–1860*, New York: Augustus Kelley (reprint).

Calomiris, C.W. (1988) 'Institutional Failure, Monetary Scarcity, and the depreciation of the Continental', *Journal of Economic History*, March.

Cannan, E. (1919) 'The paper Pound of 1797–1821', *The Bullion Report 8th June 1810* edited with an introduction by E. Cannan, first published 1919 (second, 1925, edn reprinted London 1969).

Cantillon, R. (1725) 'Essai sur la Nature du Commerce en Général' edited and with an English translation and other material by Henry Higgs, C. B. (1931), reprinted (1964) New York: Augustus Kelley.

Capie, F. H. (ed.) (1991) *Major Inflations in History*, Aldershot: Edward Elgar.

Capie, F. H. and Wood, G. E. (eds) (1991) *Unregulated Banking: Chaos or Order?*, London: Macmillan.

Carlyon-Brittan, R. (1949–50) 'The coinage of Henry VIII and Edward VI', *Spink Numismatic Circular*.

Carswell, J. (1960) *The South Sea Bubble*, London: Cresset Press.

Carus-Wilson, E.M. (1967) *Medieval Merchant Venturers*, University Paperbacks (first published 1954).

Cazalet, E. (1879) *Bimetallism and its Connection with Commerce*, Second Edition, London.

Cernuschi, H. (1876) *M. Michel Chevalier et le bimetallisme*, Paris.

Cernuschi, H. (1877) *Nomisma or Legal Tender*, New York.

Cernuschi, H. (1878) *The Bland Bill, its grounds, its alleged dishonesty, its imperfections, its future*, Paris.

Cernuschi, H. (1881) 'The Monetary Conference' (questions addressed to the British and Belgian Delegations).

Cernuschi, H. (1886) *Anatomie de la Monnaie*, Paris.

Chaddock, R. (1910) See National Monetary Commission (1910).

Challis, C. E. (1978) *The Tudor Coinage*, Manchester: Manchester University Press. This deals mainly with the coinage but is also a useful counterweight to Gould.

Challis C.E. (ed.) (1992) *A New History of the Royal Mint*, Cambridge: Cambridge University Press.

Charles I (King of England) (1626) 'Instructions which His Maiesties Commissioners for the loane of money to His Maiestie throughout the Kingdome, are exactly and effectually to observe and follow', London.

Chevalier, M. (1859) *On the Probable Fall in the Value of Gold*, trans. R. Cobden, New York.

Chevalier, M. (1839) *Society, Manners and Politics in the United States*, trans. T. G. Bradford, Boston, reprinted Burt Franklin, (see letters lll, IV, V, Vl Vlll, Xlll, XIV, XXIII, XXIV).

Chown, J. F. (1976) 'The Bristol Mint under Henry VIII and Edward VI', *Spink Numismatic Circular*, July/August.

Cipolla, C. M. (1967) *Money, Prices and Civilisation in the Mediterranean World – Fifth to Seventeenth Centuries*, New York: Gordian Press.

Cipolla, C. M. (1970) *The Economic Decline of Empires*, London: Methuen.

Cipolla, C. M. (1976) *Before the Industrial Revolution, European Society and Economy 1000–1700*, London: Methuen.

Citizen of Boston (1837) 'A New System of Paper Money', Boston.

Clapham, Sir J. (1967) *A Concise Economic History of Britain, from the earliest times to 1750*, Cambridge: Cambridge University Press (first published 1949).

Clapham, Sir J. (1970) *The Bank of England. A History*, Cambridge: Cambridge University Press.

Clarke and Hall (1832) *Legislative and Documentary History of the Bank of the United States including the original Bank of North America*, Washington, (Kelley reprint 1967).

Clarke, Sir G. (1946) *The Wealth of England from 1496 to 1760*, Home University Library.

Clement, S. (1718) 'Remarks upon a late ingenious pamphlet entituled "A short . . . real cause . . . scarcity of our Silver Coin"', S. Baker. G5451.

Cobbett, W. (1828) *Paper against Gold or The History and Mystery of the Bank of England, of the Debt, of the Stocks, of the Sinking Fund, and of all the tricks and contrivances, carried on by the means of Paper Money*, London.

Cole, A. H. (1949) *The Great Mirror of Folly*, Cambridge, Mass.: Baker Library, Harvard Business School.

Cope S. R. (1983) *Walter Boyd, A Merchant Banker in the Age of Napoleon*, London: Alan Sutton.

Cotton, Sir R. (1626) Speech on the Alteration of Coyn. Given 1626, published 1651, reprinted in Shaw 1896 and in McCullough 1856.

Coward, B. (1980) *The Stuart Age*, London: Longman.

Cowperthwaite, J. H. (1892) *Money, Silver and Finance*, New York/London.

Craig, Sir J. (1953) *The Mint*, Cambridge: Cambridge University Press.

Crump, A. (1889) *Causes of the Great Fall in Prices which took place coincidentally with the demonetisation of silver by Germany*, London: Longmans Green (Greenwood reprint 1969).

Damalas, B.V. (1946) *Monnaie et Conjuncture, Tome 1 La Monnaie et les Théories Monetaires*, Paris: Presses Universitaires de France.

Day, A. C. L. (1953) *The Future of Sterling*, Oxford: Oxford University Press.

Day, J. (1987) *The Medieval Market Economy*, Oxford: Blackwell.

Deaver, J. V. (1970) 'The Chilean Inflation and the Demand for Money', in Meiselman (*op. cit.*)

de Roover, R. (1948) *Money, Banking and Credit in Medieval Bruges: Italian Merchant-Bankers, Lombards and Money Changers; A Study in the origins if Banking*, Mediaeval Academy of America, Cambridge, Mass.

de Roover, R. (1971) 'The Organisation of Trade', in Economic Organisation and Policies in the Middle Ages 1971,*Cambridge Economic History of Europe*, vol. III, Cambridge: Cambridge University Press

de St Phalle, T. (1985) *The Federal Reserve, an Intentional Mystery*, New York: Praeger.

Decimal Coinage Report (1867) Report of the Royal Commission on Decimal Coinage, London.

Defoe, D. (1719) *The Anatomy of Exchange Alley: or, a system of stock- jobbing*

Defoe, D. (1720) *The Chimera or 'The French Way of Paying National Debts laid open, being an impartial account of the Proceedings in France for raising a PAPER CREDIT and settling the MISSISSIPPI STOCK'* London.

Del Mar, A. (1895) *History of Monetary Systems*, London: Effingham Wilson.

Del Mar, A. (1899) *The History of Money in America* (reprinted Omni Publications, California 1966).

Del Mar, A. (1902) *History of the Precious Metals*. New York: Cambridge Encyclopaedia Co. (Kelly reprint.)

Dewey, D. R. (1931) *Financial History of the United States* (eleventh edn 1931, original edn 1903), New York: Longman.

Dickeson, M. W. (1860) *The American Numismatic Manual of the currency or money of the aborigines, colonial, state, and United States coins*, second edition, Philadelphia.

Dickson, P. G. M. (1967) *The Financial Revolution in England: a Study in the Development of Public Credit, 1688–1756*, London: Macmillan.

Doc. Hist. (1969–83) *Documentary History of Banking and Currency in the United States*, (4 volumes) New York; Chelsea House. (Paula A Samuelson and Herman F. Kross. Gives full text of key documents.)

Dooley, J. H. and Daniel J. W. (1891) 'Payment of Gold Contracts in Silver', Richmond Va.: Hill Printing Co.

Dowd, K. (1991) 'The Evolution of Central Banking in England, 1821–90', in Capie and Wood (1991).

Dowell, S. (1884) *A History of Taxation and Taxes in England*, four volumes, London: Longmans Green.

Eagly, R.V. (1971) 'The Swedish Bullionist Controversy' (translation and commentary on P. N. Christiernin's 'Lectures on the High Price of Foreign Exchange in Sweden' (1761), Philadelphia.

Ede, J. (1808) *A Complete View of the Gold and Silver Coins of all Nations*, London.

Ehrenberg, R. (1928) *Capital and Finance in the Age of the Renaissance, a study of the Fuggers and their connections*, trans. H. M. Lucas, London: Jonathan Cape.

Einzig, P. (1931) *Behind the Scenes of International Finance*, London: Macmillan

Einzig, P. (1962) *The History of Foreign Exchange*, London: Macmillan.

Ellis, H. S. (1941) 'Exchange Control in Central Europe', *Harvard Economic Studies*, 69. Cambridge, Mass.

Engel A. and Serrure, R. (1890) *Traité de Numismatique de Moyen Age*, (3 vols) Bologna: Arnaldo Forni.

Erleigh, Viscount (1933) 'The South Sea Bubble', author's typescript, (published New York 1933).

Evans, D. M. (1848) *The Commercial Crisis 1847–1848*, London: Letts Son & Steer.

Evans, D. M. (1860) *Commercial Crisis, 1857, and the Stock Exchange Panic of 1859*, London, reprinted New York 1969.

Evans, D. M. (1864) *Speculative Notes and Notes on Speculation*, New York: Burt Frankin, reprinted 1968.

Evans, G. G. (1894) *Illustrated History of the United States Mint*, revised edition, Philadelphia.

Evans, Sir J. (1886) 'The Debased Coinage bearing the name of Henry VIII', *Numismatic Chronicle*.

Eyo, E. (1979) *Nigeria and the evolution of Money*, Lagos: Central Bank of Nigeria.

Faure, E. (1977) *La Banqueroute de Law*, Paris: Editions Gallimard.

Feaveryear, A.T. (1931) *The Pound Sterling: A History of English Money*, Oxford: Oxford University Press.

—— *The Pound Sterling A History of English Money*, second edn revised by E. Victor Morgan, Oxford 1963.

Felt, J. B. (1939) *A Historical Account of Massachusetts Currency*, Boston: Perkins and Marvin (also Franklin reprint, nd).

Fetter, F. W. (1955) 'The Irish Pound' A reprint of the Report of the British House of Commons on the Condition of the Irish Currency, with selections from the Minutes of Evidence presented to the Committee, London. (The introduction is important.)

Fetter, F. W. (1965) *The development of British Monetary Orthodoxy 1797– 1875*, Harvard University Press.

Fetter F. W. and Gregory T. E. (1973) *Monetary and Financial Policy in 19th Century Britain*, Dublin: Irish University Press (includes extensive bibliography).

Fisher, I. (1914) *Why the Dollar is Shrinking*, New York: Macmillan. (Dedicated to Sir David Barbour.)

Fisher, I. (1920) *Stabilising the Dollar*, New York: Macmillan.

Fisher, I. (1920) *The Purchasing Power of Money*, New York: Macmillan.

Fisher, I. (1935) *100% Money*, New York: Macmillan.

Fitzgerald, A. L. (1903) *The Thirty Years' War on Silver*, New York: Ainsworth (Reprint 1969).

Fitzmaurice, Lord E. (1895) *The Life of Sir William Petty, 1623–1687*, London: John Murray.

Fleetwood, W. (1694) 'A Sermon against Clipping preached before the Right Honourable the Lord Mayor . . . on December 16 1694'. (Chaplain in Ordinary to Their Majesties, later Bishop of Ely.)

Fleetwood, W. (Bishop of Ely) 'Chronicum Preciosum or An Account of English Money the Price of Corn and other Commodites for the last 600 years' (i.e. 1107–1707).

Flynn, D. O. (1982) 'Use and Misuse of the Quantity Theory of Money in early modern Historiography', in *Munzpragung, Gelumlauf und Wechelkurse* (proceedings of the International Economic History Congress, Budapest).

Folkes, M. (1736) *Tables of English Silver and Gold Coins*.

Foster, J. (1804) 'An essay on the Principle of Commercial Exchanges, and more particularly the exchange between Great Britain and Ireland: with an inquiry into the practical effects of the bank restrictions' – bound for William Downes, Lord Chief Justice of Ireland.

Fournial, E. (1970) *Histoire Monetaire de l'Occident Mediéval*, Paris: FAC.

Friedman, M. (ed.) (1956) *Studies in the Quantity theory of money*, Chicago: University of Chicago Press.

Friedman, M. (1992) *Money Mischief, episodes in Monetary History*, New York: Harcourt Brace.

Friedman, M. and Schwartz, A. (1963) *A Monetary History of the United States, 1868–1960*, New York: Princeton University Press.

Fullarton, J. (1844) *On the Regulation of Currencies*, London: John Murray

Gairdner, C. (1889) 'The Royal Commission on gold and silver – an examination of the report with remarks on bimetallism', Glasgow.

Galbraith, J. K. (1975) *Money. Whence it came, where it went*, Boston: Houghton Mifflin.

Gibbs, H. C. (1894) *A Bimetallic Primer*, London: Effingham Wilson.

Gibbs, H. H., M.P., (1877) 'Correspondence with Professor Bonamy Price on the Reserve of the Bank of England'.

Gibbs, H. H., M.P., (1879) *Silver and Gold*, London: Effingham Wilson.

Gibbs, H. H., M.P., (1883) 'The silver question. Two letters to the Rt Hon G.J. Goschen', London.

Gibbs, H. H., M.P., (1884), 'The scramble for gold', reprinted from the *Bullionist*, 18 March 1882, London: Bank of England.

Gibbs, H. H., M.P. (1884), 'Bimetallic England', reprinted from the *Bullionist*, 24 June 1882, London: Bank of England

Gibbs, H. H., M.P, (1889) *The Value of Money*.

Gibbs, H. H., M.P., (1892) 'International Bimetallism and the Gresham Law. With a rejoinder by Herbert Gibbs', London.

Gibbs, H. H. and Grenfell, H. R. (1886) 'The Bimetallic Controversy', London: Effingham Wilson. A collection of pamphlets, papers, speeches and letters, from 1881–6.

Gies, and Frances (1972) *Merchants and Moneymen, The Commercial Revolution 1000–1500*, London: Arthur Barker.

Giffen, Sir R. (1880) *Essays in Finance*, London, (especially 'Notes on the Depreciation of Silver' (1876) p. 196 and 'The Case against Bimetallism' (1879) p. 286).

Glendining & Co. 'Catalogue of British Coins' (sold Wednesday 4 April 1979), Lots 60–172 were the present author's collection of Tudor coins.

Goddard, T. H. A. (1831) *General History of the most Prominent Banks in Europe*, New York (in fact mainly on the United States).

Goldsmith, R. W. (1987) *Premodern Financial Systems. A historical comparative study*, Cambridge: Cambridge University Press.

Gordon, T. F. (1834) *The War on the Bank of the United States*, Philadelphia.

Goschen, G. J. (1891) 'Speech at Leeds on the Insufficiency of our Cash Reserves and of our Central Stock of Gold', London, (ex Treasury Library).

Gouge, W. M. (1833) *The Curse of Paper – Money and Banking or a short history of banking in the United States of America*, Philadephia. Republished July 1833 in London with an introduction by William Cobbett, M. P., (also facsimile Greenwood New York 1968).

Gouge, W. M. (1837) 'An inquiry into the Expediency of Dispensing with Bank Agency and Bank Paper in the Fiscal concerns of the United States'.

Gouge, W. M. (1841–2) 'The Journal of Banking . . . to which is annexed A Short History of Paper Money and Banking in the United States from 1690 to 1832 together with an inquiry into the Principles of the American Banking System', 26 issues 7 July 1841 to 22 June 1842, Philadelphia.

Gould, J. D. (1970) *The Great Debasement – Currency and the Economy in Mid-Tudor England*, Oxford: Oxford University Press. The best economic analysis, but technical and controversial.

Gould, Sir N. (1727) 'An Essay on the Publick Debts of This Kingdom'. In a Letter to a Member of the House of Commons Fourth Edition London. (Goldsmiths 6549 – for first edition 1726 see 6473).

Gould, Sir N (re) (1727) 'Remarks on a late book entitled, "An essay . . . In which the evil tendency of that book, and the design of its author, are fully detected and exposed"', London, Goldsmith 6554. (Attack on Gould).

Graham, Sir J. (1927) 'Corn and Currency; in an address to the Land Owners', London: James Ridgway.

Gregory, T.E. (1929) *British Banking Statutes and Reports, 1832–1928*, two vols, Oxford: Oxford University Press.

Gregory, T.E. see Fetter and Gregory.

Grenfell, H. R. (1881) 'What is a pound?' Reprinted from the *Nineteenth Century*, June 1881, London: Bank of England, 1884.

Grenfell, H. R. (1879) 'Letters on Mr. Clarmont J. Daniell's pamphlet "Gold in the East", with correspondence in the Economist thereon', London.

Grenfell, H. R. (1882) 'What is a standard?'. Reprinted from the *Nineteenth Century* May 1882: Bank of England.

Grenfell, H. R. (1886) 'Bimetallism'. Address at Memorial Hall, Manchester 16 February.

Grenfell, H. R. see also Gibbs and Grenfell

Grey, E. (1881) 'The double standard, correspondence with H. R. Grenfell, governor of the Bank of England'. Reprinted in Gibbs and Grenfell (*op. cit.*)

Groseclose, E. M. (1934) 'The Human Conflict', Norman, Oklahoma: University of Oklahoma Press.

Hamilton, A. (1790) First Report on Public Credit, 9 January.

Hamilton, A. (1791) Report on the Establishment of the Mint.

Hamilton, A. (1791) Report on Manufacturers, 5 December.

Hamilton, E. J. (1970) *American Treasure and the Price revolution in Spain, 1501–1650*, New York: Odaga Books.

Hamilton, R. (1814) *An Inquiry concerning the rise and progress, the redemption and present state of and the management of the National Debt of Great Britain.* The second edn enlarged, Edinburgh

Hammond, B. (1939). 'The Federal Reserve System, its purposes and functions', Washington Board of the FRS. (D. H. Robertson's copy.)

Hammond, B. (1957) *Banks and Politics in America: from the Revolution to the Civil War*, New York: Princeton University Press.

Hanke, S. H. and Schuler, K. (1991) 'Ruble reform: a lesson from Keynes', *Cato Journal*, 10(3), Winter.

Hanning, W. (1826) 'Proposal for making Country Bank paper equally secure – letter to the Earl of Liverpool', Taunton.

Hargrove, F. (1791) 'The case of the Bankers. With the arguments of Lord Chief Justice Treby, Lord Chief Justice Holt and of the Lord Keeper Somers . . .', Dublin.

Harris, J. (1757) *An Essay upon Money and Coins*, London: Hawkins.

Harris, S. (1930) *The Assignats*, Harvard University Press.

Hart, A. B. (1990) *Salmon P. Chase*, New York: Chelsea House.

Hawtrey, R.G. (1932) *The Art of Central Banking*, London: Longmans Green.

Hawtrey, R.G. (1928) *Currency and Credit* London: Longman.

Hemming, J. (1970) *The Conquest of the Incas*, London: Macmillan.

Hendy, M. (1985) *Studies in the Byzantine Monetary Economy*, Cambridge: Cambridge University Press.

Hepburn, A. B. (1903) *History of Coin and Coinage in the United States*, New York: Macmillan.

Herschell Report (1892) 'Commission appointed to inquire into the Indian Currency, commonly known as the Herschell Report', reprinted Washington, 1893 by order of Congress.

Higgs, H., C. B., see Cantillon.

Hildreth, R. (1837) *The History of Banks, to which is added a demonstration of the advantages and necessary of free competition in the business of banking*, Boston, Mass.

Hollander, J. H. (ed.) (1932) *Minor Papers on the Currency Question*, Johns Hopkins.

Horsefield, J. K. (1941) *The Duties of a Banker. The Eighteenth Century View.* Reprinted in Ashton and Sayers 1953.

Horton, S. D. (1887) *The Silver Pound*, London.

Houldsworth, Sir Wm *et al.* (1892) 'The Bimetallic Question'. Deputation to Salisbury, Goschen and Balfour, 11 May, 1892, London: Effingham Wilson, and Manchester: J. E. Cornish.

Howe, J. B. (1879) *Mono-metalism and Bi-metalism; or, the Science of Monetary Values*, Boston, Mass.

Hume, David (1752) *Philosophical Discourses.* V On the Balance of Trade. Edinburgh.

Huskisson, W. (1819) *The question concerning the Depreciation of our Currency Stated and Examined*, (seventh Edn, London).

Huskisson, W. (1839) *Speeches*, with a biographical memoir, three vols, London: John Murray.

Hutcheson, A. (various dates 1714–19) 'A Collection of Treaties relating to the Publick Debts. (1) COMPUTATIONS relating to the Public Debts, April ll. 1717. (2) A Short State of the same, December, 1717. (3) Some Considerations relating to the Payment of the Public Debts, May 14. 1717. (4) A Proposal for Payment of the Public Debts, and a Letter to His Majesty relating to the same; referred to in the last-mentioned Treaties, January 14 1714.(5) Calculations and Remarks relating to Half-Pay, and the Frugal Management of the Public Money, January 14, and 23 1717. (6) Calculations relating to the Public Debts, and a Proposal for the entire Discharge of the same, July 14. 1718. (7) An answer to Mr Crookshanks's Seasonable Remarks, October the 30th 1719.

Hyde, H. Montgomery (1948) *John Law, the history of an honest adventurer*, Amsterdam: Home and van Thal.

Hyndman, H. M. (1892) *Commercial Crises of the Nineteenth Century*, London, (also Augustus Kelley reprint).

Hynes, H. B. 'Brief Memoires Relating to the Silver and Gold Coins of England', Goldsmith MS 72.

International Currency Report (1868) Royal Commission on International Coinage, London.

Irish Currency Report (1804) Minutes of Evidence and Appendix from the Committee on the Circulating Paper, the Specie, and the Current Coin of Ireland; And also, on the Exchange between that Part of the United Kingdom and Great Britain. May and June 1804, Ordered by the House of Commons to be reprinted 26 May 1826.

D'Ivernois, F. (1795) 'A Cursory View of the Assignats, and remaining resources of French Finance', (6 September 1795), trans. from the French, (specimen assignats bound in), Dublin: P. Byrne.

Jackson, A. (1832) Message at the Commencement of the second session of the 22nd Congress 4 December.

Jevons, W. S. (1875) *Money and the mechanism of exchange*, London: Henry S. King.

Jevons, W. S. (1881) 'Richard Cantillon and the Nationality of Political Economy', *Contemporary Review.* Reprinted in Cantillon 1931.

Jevons, W. S. (1909) *Investigations in Currency and Finance.* Second edn. Includes:
II A serious fall in the value of Gold ascertained
XI Gold and Silver: A letter to M. Wolowski (1869) P278
XII The Silver Question (1877) P282
XIII Bimetallism (1881) Page 292
XIV Sir Isaac Newton and Bimetallism (unfinished fragment) p.304

Jiaju, Q. (1983) *A History of Chinese Currency, 16th Century* BC *to 20th Century A.D*, Xinhua.

Jobbing Acts 1695 An ACT to Restrain the Number and ill Practice of Brokers and Stock-Jobbers.

Jobbing Acts 1734 An ACT to prevent the Infamous Practice of Stock-Jobbing.

Jobbing Acts 1737 An ACT to make perpetual an Act made in the Seventh Year of the Reign of His present Majesty, Intituled 'An Act to Prevent the Infamous Practice of Stock-Jobbing'

Johnson, A. (1867) 'Message from the President of the United States . . . concerning the international monetary conference held at Paris in June 1867', Washington, 17 December.

Jones, A. H. M. (1953) 'Inflation under the Roman Empire', *Economic History Review*.

Jones, W. R. D. (1973) *The Mid Tudor Crisis 1539–1563*, London: Macmillan.

Joplin, T. (1822) 'An Essay on the General Principles and Present Practice of Banking etc.' in Clapham (1970) Vol. ii.

Joplin, T. (1832) *An analysis and history of the Currency Question, together with an account of the origin and growth of joint stock banking in England*, London: James Ridgway.

Kaeuper, R. W. (1973) *Bankers to the Crown, The Riccardi of Lucca and Edward I*, New York: Princeton University Press.

Kann, E. 'The Currencies of China old and new' in Gayer, AD (ed.) *The lessons of Monetary Experience – essays in Honor of Irving Fisher*, New York 1937. (Copy presented by Fisher to Herbert Hoover.) This refers to three articles by himself in the Central Bank of China quarterly, June and October 1936, January 1937.

Kerr, A. W. (1884) *History of Banking in Scotland*, Glasgow: David Bryce & Son.

Kerridge, E. (1988) *Trade and Banking in Early Modern* England, Manchester: Manchester University Press.

Keynes, J. M. (1971–9) *The Collected Writings*. Macmillan for the Royal Economic Society. Citations are to the volumes in this edition.

Kindleberger, C. (1984) *A Financial History of Western Europe*, London: George Allen & Unwin.

King, Lord (1803) Thoughts on the Restriction of Payment in specie at the Banks of England and Ireland (1803). (Henry Thornton's copy bound with Wheatley. The second edition, 1804, was titled 'Thoughts on the Effects of the Bank Restriction'.)

King, W. T. C. (1936) *The History of the London Discount Market*, London: Routledge. Kinley, D. (1904) *Money, A Study of the Theory of the Medium of Exchange*. New York: Macmillan, (Reprinted Greenwood, 1968).

Kinley, D. (1910) 'The Independent Treasury of the United States and its Relations to the Banks of the Country', National Monetary Commission, Washington DC 1910 (facsimile reprint: Augustus Kelley 1970).

Knapp, G. F. (1924) *The State Theory of Money*, abridged and translated by H. M. Lucas and J. Bonar, London: Macmillan.

Lafaurie, J. (1952). 'Les Billets des Banques de Law'. *Bulletin de la Societé de l' Etude pour l'Histoire de Papier Monnaie*. 7 Année 1952.

Lafaurie, J. Les Assignats et les Papiers Monnaies émis par l'état au XVIIIe Siècle, Paris: Le Leopard d'or.

Landry, A. (1969) *Les Mutations de Monnaies dans l'ancienne France*, Philippe le Bel- Charles VII. Paris: Eds Champion.

Lane and Mueller, (1985) *Money and Banking in Medieval and Renaissance Venice*, vol 1, Coins and Moneys of Account, Johns Hopkins.

Lang, J. (1975) *Conquest and Commerce – Spain and England in the Americas*, New York: Academic Press.

Lauderdale, Earl of, (1812) *The Depreciation of the Paper Currency of Great Britain proved*, London: Longman Hurst.

Laughlin, J. L. (1892) *The History of Bimetallism in the United States* 2nd edn, New York (ex Treasury Library).

Law, J. Observations on the new system and finances in France. Particularly on the repurchase or paying off the annuities: and on credit and its use. Translated from the French by Sir J. E. and dedicated to the managers of the South Sea Stock 1720.

Law, J. (1705) *Money and Trade considered with a proposal for supplying the nation with money*

Leake, S. M. (1726) *Nummi Britannici Historia or an Historical Account of English Money*, London: W. Meadows.

Lehfeldt, R. A. (1926) *Money*, Oxford: Oxford University Press.

Lerner, E. M. (1956) 'Inflation in the Confederacy 1861–65', in M. Friedman (ed.) *Studies in the quantity Theory of Money*, Chicago: Chicago University Press.

Lester, R. (1970) 'Chapter VII Retention of the Gold Standard in California and Oregon during the Greenback Inflation' in *Monetary Experiments*, reprinted David & Charles 1970.

Li, M.-H. (1963) *The Great Recoinage of 1696–9*, London: Weidenfeld & Nicolson.

Lindsay, A. M. (1878) 'A Gold Standard without a Gold Coinage in England and India', Edinburgh, 1879 (reprinted with additions from the Calcutta Review of October 1878).

Lipson, E. (1943) *The Economic History of England*, vol. III 'The Age of Mercantilism' 3rd edn, London: A. & C. Black. (First edn 1931.)

Liverpool, 1st Earl, (1805) 'A Treatise on the Coins of the Realm; in a Letter to The King', 1st edn.

Liverpool, 1st Earl, (1879) 'A Treatise on the Coins of the Realm; in a Letter to The King', reprinted, with an introduction and dedication to Sir Stafford Northcote, Chancellor of the Exchequer by J. W. Birch and H. R. Grenfell, Governors of the Bank of England 1879.

Locke, J. (1691) 'Some Consideration of the Consequences of the Lowering of Interest and Raising the Value of Money' second edition bound with Locke, J. (1695) 'Further Considerations Concerning Raising the Value of Money', London: A. & J. Churchill.

Locke, J. (1696) (reply) 'Short observations on a printed paper, "Further Considerations concerning Raising the Value of Money"'.

Lopez, R. S. (1976) *The Commercial Revolution of the Middle Ages, 950–1350*, Cambridge: Cambridge University Press.

Lopez, R. S. (1986) 'The shape of Medieval Monetary History', London: Variorum Reprints (useful collected articles in English, French and Italian).

Lowndes, W. (1695) An Essay for Amending the Silver Coins.

Loyd, S. J. (1837) 'Reflections suggested by a perusal of Mr J. Horsley Palmer's Pamphlet . . .', London.

Loyd, S. J. (Lord Overstone) (1857) Tracts etc, on Metallic and Paper Currency, facsimile reprint 1972.

Lui, F. T. (1983) 'Cagan's Hypothesis and the First Nationwide Inflation of Paper Money in World History', *Journal of Political Economy*. Reprinted in Capie (ed.) 1991.

Mackay, C. (1841) *Memoirs of Extraordinary Popular Delusions and The Madness of Crowds*, London 1852 (1st edn, 1841).

MacLeod, H. D. (1894) *Bimetalism*, 2nd edn London. (Anti; "by a pioneer in modern credit theory".)

McCullough, J. R. (1845) *A Treatise on the Principles and Practical Influence of Taxation and the Funding System*, edited by D. P. O'Brien, Scottish Economic Society 1975.

McCullough, J. R. (ed.) (1856) *A Select Collection of Scarce and Valuable Tracts on Money*, Political Economy Club.

McCullough, J. R. (1858) Encyclopaedia Britannica 8th edn.

McCusker, J. J. (1978) *Money and Exchange in Europe and America 1600–1775, A Handbook*, University of North Carolina (Macmillan UK).

Malagrowther, M. see Sir Walter Scott.

Mandeville, B. de, The Fable of the Bees, or Private Vices, Publick Benefits. 6th edn J. Tonson 1732 (Part 2, 2nd edn 1733).

Mann, F. A. (1938) *The Legal Aspect of Money*, 4th edn, Oxford 1982.

Marshall, A. (1923) *Money Credit and Commerce*, London: Macmillan.

Meiselman, D. (ed.) (1970) *Varieties of Monetary Experience*, Chicago: University of Chicago Press.

Melon, J. F. (1734) 'A Political Essay upon Commerce', translated by David Bindon, Dublin 1738. ('Essai politique sur le commerce'.)

Miskimin, H. A. (1963) *Money, Prices and Foreign Exchange in Fourteenth Century France*, Yale, (Maxwell Reprint Company 1970).

Miskimin, H. A. (1969) *The Economy of Early Renaissance Europe, 1300–1460*, London: Prentice Hall.

Miskimin, H. A. (1989) 'Cash, Credit and Crises in Europe, 1300–1600'. Variorum Reprints, London (collected essays, mostly in English but one in French).

Mitchell, W. C. (1903) A History of Greenbacks, Chicago: University of Chicago Press.

Monroe, A. E. (1927) *Early Economic Thought*, Harvard University Press (notably extracts from Aristotle and Aquinas).

Moran, C. (1863) *Money*, New York.

Morgan, E. V. and A. D., (1976) 'Gold or Paper?', *Hobart Paper 67*, London: Institute of Economic Affairs.

Morgan, E. V. and Thomas, W. A. (1962) *The Stock Exchange: Its History and Functions*, London: Elek.

Muhleman, Maurice M. (1908) *Monetary and banking Systems . . .*, New York: Monetary Publishing Co.

Munn, C. W. (1981) *The Scottish Provincial Banking Companies, 1747–1864* Edinburgh: John Donald.

Munro, J. H. (1982) 'Mint Outputs, Money and Prices in late Medieval England and the Low Countries', in Munzpragung, Gelumlauf und Wechelkurse (proc. of International Economic History Congress, Budapest).

Munro, N. (1928) *The History of the Royal Bank of Scotland 1727–1927*, privately printed Edinburgh: R & R Clark.

Murphy, A. E. (1983) 'Richard Cantillon – an Irish Banker in Paris', in *Economists and the Irish Economy*, Hermathena Trinity College Dublin, Winter.

Murphy, A. E. (1986) *Richard Cantillon: Entrepreneur and Economist*, Oxford: Oxford University Press.

Murphy, A. E. (1991) *The evolution of John Law's theories and policies 1707–15*, Elsevier 1991.

Murphy, A. E., John Law's Essay on a Land Bank. Unpublished.

Murphy, A. E., 'John Law and the Mississippi System', in *The Economic Theories and Policies of John Law*, Oxford: Oxford University Press, (forthcoming).

Murphy, A. E. (1990), 'John Law and the Assignats', in G. Faccarello and P. Steines (eds) *La Pensée Economique pendant la Révolution Française*, Grenoble: Presses Universitaires Grenoble.

Myers, M. G. (1970) *A Financial History of the United States*, New York: Columbia University Press.

National Monetary Commission (1910) 'State Banking before the Civil War', (Davis

R. Dewey) and 'The Safety Fund Banking System in New York 1829–1866', (Robert E. Chaddock), Washington.

National Monetary Commission Vol. 10 (1911) 'The Reichsbank and the Renewal of its charter', Washington 1911.

National Monetary Commission Vols 12 and 13. The German Bank Enquiry of 1908.

National Monetary Commission (1911) Vol. 17. 'Banking in Sweden and Switzerland' (A. W. Flux and Julius Landmann), Washington.

National Monetary Commission (1910) 'The Independent Treasury of the United States and its Relations to the Banks of the Country', (David Kinley), Washington (facsimile reprint: Augustus M. Kelley 1970.)

National Monetary Commission (1910) 'Laws of the United States Concerning Money, Banking and Loans, 1778–1909'. (A.T. Huntington and Robert J. Mawhinney), Washington

National Monetary Commission Vol. 18 (1911) 'Banking in Italy, Russia, Austro-Hungary and Japan', Washington.

Neal, L. (1990) The Rise of Financial Capitalism. International capital markets in the Age of Reason, Cambridge: Cambridge University Press.

Necker, J. (1786) Oeuvres de M. Necker. First collected edition. 4 vols, Lausanne.

Nelson, B. N. (1949) The Idea of Usury from tribal brotherhood to universal otherhood, New York: Princeton University Press.

Newman, E. P. (1976) The Early Paper Money of America, Bicentennial Edition, Racine Wis.: Western Publishing Company.

Nicholson, J. S. (1887) The stability of a fixed ratio between gold and silver under international bimetallism, London.

Nicholson, J. S. (1895a) Bankers Money.

Nicholson, J. S. (1895b) Money and Monetary Problems.

Norman, G. W. (1841) Letter to Charles Wood, M.P., on Money and the Means of Economising the use of it, London.

Norman, J. H. 'A Colloquy upon the Science of Money, with Norman's single grain system for determining the par values of all moneys' . . . and 'The exchanges upon a scientific basis' and 'The coming debate on bimetallism', all London 1889, bound together, ex Treasury Library.

North, J. J. (1960) English Hammered Coinage. Volume 2 1272–1662, London: Spink, 3rd edn, 1992.

O'Brien, P. (1988) The Economic Effects of the American Civil War, Macmillan for Economic History Society.

O'Kelly, E. (1959) The old private banks and bankers of Munster, Cork: Cork University Press.

O'Sullivan, M. D. (1962) Italian Merchant Bankers in Ireland in the Thirteenth Century, Dublin: Allen Figgis.

Oman, Sir C. (1967) The Coinage of England, London: H. Pordes. (First published 1931. Page references are to 1967 edition.)

Oudard, G. (1928) John Law A Fantastic Financier 1671–1729 (trans. from the French by G. C. E. Masse) London: Jonathan Cape.

Outhwaite, R. B. (1969) Inflation in Tudor and Early Stuart England, Economic History Society.

Paine, T. (1796) The Decline and Fall of the English System of Finance, Paris, reprinted London 1796. Note: this copy has 16 pages and is said to be the first edition printed in London. Goldsmith lists seven editions in Paris in 1796, (32–46 pages) plus a New York edition (56 pages) 'from a London copy, taken from the first edition' and a French translation. This edition is not included.

Palmer, J. H. (1837a) The Causes and Consequences of the Pressure upon the Money Market, London.

Palmer, J. H. (1837b) 'Reply to the Reflections, etc of Mr. Samuel Jones Loyd on the Pamphlett . . .' London.

Panic, M. (1992) *European Monetary Union – Lessons of the classical gold standard*, London: Macmillan.

Parker, H. (1640) The Case of Shipmony briefly discoursed according to the Grounds of Law, Policy and Conscience and most humbly presented to the Censure and Correction of the High Court of Parliament, 3 November 1640.

Patterson and Shearer (1982) 'Canada and the US Greenback Inflation', in Munzpragung, Gelumlauf und Wechelkurse (proc. of the International Economic History Congress, Budapest).

Perlin, F. (1982) 'Changes in the production and circulation of money in 17th and 18th century India', in Munzpragung, Gelumlauf und Wechelkurse (proc. of International Economic History Congress, Budapest).

Petty, Sir (1682) W. 'Quantumcunque', in McCullough, J.R. (ed.), 1856.

Petty, Sir W. see Fitzmaurice.

Pick, A. (1990) standard catalog of World Paper Money, vol 1, specialised issues. 6th edn, Iola Wis.: Krause.

Pick, F. (1965) *Pick's Currency Yearbook 1964–5*, New York.

Pirenne, H. (1936) *Economic and Social History of Medieval Europe*, trans. by I. E. Clegg, London: Routledge (refs are to 1978 paperback edition).

Pirenne, H. (1969) *Histoire Economique et Sociale du Moyen Age*, Paris: Presses Universitaires de France.

Poor, Henry V. (1878) 'Resumption and the Silver Question', New York (Reprint 1969).

Porteous, J. R. (1969) *Coins in History*, London: Weidenfeld & Nicolson.

Postan, M. M. (1973) Medieval Trade and Finance, Cambridge: Cambridge University Press.

Postan, M. M., Rich, E. E. and Miller, E. (1971) 'Economic Organisation and Policies in the Middle Ages', *Cambridge Economic History of Europe, vol. III*, Cambridge: Cambridge University Press.

Probyn, J. W. (ed). (1877) 'Correspondence relative to the Budgets of Various Countries', (compiled for the Cobden Club) Cassell Petter & Galpin

Pulteney, W. (1727) 'The State of the National Debt as it stood December the 24th 1716 compared with the Debt at Michaelmas 1725', London.

Pulteney, W. (1735) 'The Case of the Sinking Fund . . . being a Defence of an Enquiry into the CONDUCT of our Domestic Affairs and a full Reply to 'Some Considerations', London.

Pulteney, W. (Earl of Bath) (no date) 'The State of the National Debt as it stood at December the 24th 1716 with the payments made towards the Discharge of it out of the Sinking Fund 20 etc compared with The Debt at Michaelmas 1725'.

Pulteney, W. (1797) Substance of the Speech of Sir William Pulteney, Bart, on his Motion 7th April 1797 for shortening the time during which the Bank of England should be restrained from issuing cash for its debts and demands, London.

Quiggin, E. H. (1949) *A Survey of Primitive Money: the beginnings of currency*, London: Methuen.

Rae, G. (1886) *The Country Banker*, American edition with a preface by Brayton Ives, New York: Charles Scribner.

Ramsey, P. (1972) *Tudor Economic Problems*, London: Gollancz.

Remini, R. V. (1970) *Martin Van Buren and the Making of the Democratic Party*, New York: Norton.

Report of the Indian Currency Committee (1892).

Ricardo, D. (1811) 'Reply to Mr Bosanquet's Practical Observations on the Report of the Bullion Committee', London.

Ricardo, D. (1951) *The Works and Correspondence*, edited by Piero Sraffa, Vol III Pamphlets and papers 1809–11, Cambridge for Royal Economic Society.

Richards, R. D. (1929) *The early History of Banking in England*, London: P. S. King & Son.

Rist, C. (1938) 'History of Monetary and Credit theory from John Law to the present day', orig. Paris 1938, trans. Jane Degras, London: George Allen & Unwin (1940).

Rockoff, H. (1990) 'The Wizard of Oz as a Monetary Allegory', *Journal of Political Economy*, August.

Rodney, Hon. R. S. (1928) *Colonial Finances in Delaware*, Wilmington Del.: Wilmington Trust Company.

Roe, Sir T. His Speech in Parliament 1640. Printed 1641.

Roll, E. (1971) *History of Economic Thought*, new and revised edn, London: Faber & Faber.

Rothwell, W. T. (1897) *Bimetallism Explained*, London: Chapman & Hall.

Royal Commission on International Coinage Report (1868).

Royal Mint (?) (1848) The Currency of the British Colonies, W. Clowes for HMSO.

Royal Mint (1915) Coinage of the British Empire: Statutes and statutory rules and orders etc. relating to the Coinage & c, HMSO (ex Treasury Library).

Ruding, R. (1840) *Annals of the coinage of Great Britain and its dependencies*, three vols, London: John Hearne.

Ruelle, J. R. (1775) Opérations Des Changes Des Principales Places De L'Europe.

Ruggles, S. B. Letter from SBR in behalf of the New York Chamber of Commerce to the Director of the Mint of the United States. November 28th 1876. (Vital necessity of Preliminary Monetary Conference for establishing relative legal values of gold and silver coins.)

Russell, H. B. (1898) *International Monetary Conferences, their Purposes, Character and Results, with a study of the conditions of currency and finance in Europe and America during intervening periods, and their relations to international action*, New York and London: Harper Brothers.

Russell, S. (1991) 'The US Currency System: A Historical Perspective', *Federal Reserve Bank of St Louis Review*, September/October.

St John, O. 'Mr. St. John's Speech to the Lords in the Upper House of Parliament, January 7 1640, concerning SHIP MONEY'.

S. R. (no date) A Letter to a Member of Parliament from his Friend at OXFORD concerning the Settling of Gold and Silver.

Samuelson, P. A. and Kross, H. F. (1969–83) *Documentary History of Banking and Currency in the United States*, New York (4 vols.), cited as 'Doc. Hist'.

Saul, S. R. (1985) *The Myth of the Great Depression 1873–1896*, Macmillan for Economic History Society, 2nd edn.

Say, L. Les Finances de France; 15 December 1881 to 20 December 1882, Paris: Guillaumin (nd but near contemporary)

Sayers, R. S. (1976) *The Bank of England 1891–1944*, three vols. Cambridge: Cambridge University Press.

Schlesinger, A. M., Jr (1945) *The Age of Jackson*, Boston: Little Brown.

Schuckers, J. W. (1874) *A Brief Account of the Finances and Paper Money of the Revolutionary War*, Philadelphia, reprinted Sanford J. Durst 1978.

Schumpeter, J. A. (1954) *History of Economic Analysis*, London: George Allen & Unwin.

Scott, Sir W. (1826) ('Malachi Malagrowther') Thoughts on the proposed change in currency.

Scott, W. R. (1912) *The Constitution and Finance of English, Scottish and Irish Joint-Stock Companies to 1720*, 3 vols., Cambridge (reprinted Peter Smith 1968).

BIBLIOGRAPHY AND BIBLIOGRAPHICAL NOTES

Seaby, *Seaby's Standard Catalogue of British Coins* (annual).

Senior, N. (1830) 'Three lectures on the cost of obtaining money . . . London 1830' (Lectures delivered at Oxford, Trinity Term 1829).

Senlecq, C. M. (1895) L'or et l'argent dans le circulation mónetaire. Le Monometallisme Or, cause prépondérante de la ruine agricole et industrielle, Paris.

Seyd, E. Bullion and Foreign Exchanges 52–3.

Shaw, W. A. *The History of Currency 1252–1894*, London: Wilson and Milne nd (c1896?).

Shaw, W. A. (ed.) (1896) *Select Tracts and Documents illustrative of English Monetary History 1626–1730*, George Harding.

Shepherd, E. M. (1880) *Martin Van Buren* reprinted with an introduction by Robert V. Remini (1983), New York: Norton.

Sherbrooke, Viscount (1882) 'What is money?' Reprinted from the *Nineteenth Century*, April 1882. (Bank of England 1884.)

Shortt, A. (1974) *Canadian Currency and Exchange under French Rule*, Montreal: Osiris.

Slater, R. (1855) *Inquiry into the principles involved in the Decimalisation of the Weights, Measures and Monies of the United Kingdom*, London.

Smith, A. (1776) *An Inquiry into the Nature and Causes of The Wealth of Nations* (Refs are to the sixth Cannan edition, 1950.)

Smith, T. 'An Essay on the Theory of Money and Exchange' 2nd edn with considerable additions including an examination of the report of the Bullion Committee, London, 1811, with inserted review of the first edition from the Edinburgh Review October 1808 (James Mill). See Ricardo III, 9.

Sommers. (1733) The Argument of the Lord Keeper Sommers on his giving Judgement in the Banker's Case: Delivered in the Exchequer-Chamber, June 23 1696.

South Sea Bubble Het Groote *Tafereel* Der Dwaasheid, Amsterdam 1720, see Cole (1949).

Spaulding, E.G. (1869) *History of the Legal Tender Paper Money issued during the Great Rebellion, being a loan without interest and a national currency*, Buffalo.

Sperling, J. G. (1962) The South Sea Company. An historical Essay and Bibliographical Finding List. Kress Library of Business and Economics No 17. Harvard.

Spiegel, H. W. (1983) *The Growth of Economic Thought*, 2nd edn Durham NC.: Duke University.

Spufford, P. (1988) *Money and its use in Medieval Europe*, Cambridge: Cambridge University Press.

Stern, Fritz. (1977) *Gold and Iron. Bismarck, Bleichroder and the Building of the German Empire*, New York: Knopf.

Stewart, F. H. (1924) *History of the First United States Mint its People and its Operations*, privately printed.

Stewart, I. H. (1955) *The Scottish Coinage*, Spink & Son London (2nd edn with supplement 1967).

Subercaseaux, G. (1909) 'Essai sur la Nature du Papier Monnaie envisage sous son aspect historique et économico-monétaire' (paper presented to a conference in Chile).

Suess, E. (1893) *The Future of Silver* (trans. Robert Stein) Washington: Government Printing Office.

Supple, B. L. (1959) *Commercial Crisis and Change in England, 1600–1642*, Cambridge: Cambridge University Press.

Symonds, H. 'The English Coinage of Edward VI', British Numismatic Journal XI.

Taussig, F. W. (1893) *The Silver Situation in the United States*, 3 edn 1990 New York: Putnam.

288

Thornton, Henry, M. P. (1802) *An enquiry into the nature and effects of The Paper Credit of Great Britain*, London: Hatchard.

Tooke, T. (1838) *A History of Prices and of the State of the Circulation from 1793 to 1837*, vols I and II, London.

Tooke, T. (1840) *A History of Prices and of the State of the Circulation in 1838 and 1839*, vol. III, London.

Tooke, T. (1844) *An Inquiry into the Currency Principle*, London, (LSE reprint 1959).

Tooke T. and Newmarch (1857) *A History of Prices and of the State of the Circulation during the nine years 1848–1856*, vols. V and VI, London.

Tsien T.-H. (1985) *Science and Civilisation in China*, ed. Joseph Needham, vol. 5:1 Paper and Printing, Cambridge: Cambridge University Press.

Tucker, G. (1839) *The Theory of Money and Banks Investigated*, Boston.

Turnor, T., The Case of the Bankers . . . 1674 (First edition Goldsmith 2088, later edition revealed the author as Thomas Turnor).

Ullmann, W. (1965) *Medieval Political Thought*, London: Pelican.

Unwin, G. (ed.) (1918) *Finance and Trade under Edward III*, London: Longmans Green.

van Dillen, J. G. (1964) *History of the Principal Public Banks*, London: Frank Cass.

Van Deusen, G. G. (1959) *The Jacksonian Era, 1828–1848*, New York: Harper & Row.

Viner, J. (no date) 'Religious thought and Economic Society' (four chapters of an unfinished work, edited by Jaques Melitz and Donald Winch).

Vissering, W. (1877) *On Chinese Currency, coin and paper money*, Leiden, reprinted Taipeh 1968.

Vlack, R. (1985) 'Currency in Crisis: America's Money 1830–1845', in Coinage of the Americas Conference, American Numismatic Society.

Walker, F. A. (1888) *Money*, London: Macmillan.

Walpole, R., (1st Earl of Orford) (1735) 'Some Considerations Concerning The Publick Funds, The Publick Revenues, and Annual Supplies, Granted by Parliament. Occasion'd by a late Pamphlet, intitled An Enquiry into the Conduct of our Domestic Affairs, from the Year 1721 to Christmas 1733. London 1735'. (Reply to Pulteney.)

Warburg, P. M. (1930) *The Federal Reserve System, its origins and growth*, 2 vols, New York: Macmillan (presentation copy to Kurt Hahn).

Webster, D. (1834) Leave to introduce a Bill to continue the Bank of the United States for another six years. Senate speech 18 March 1834.

Webster, D. (1834) Remarks on the Removal of the Deposites and on the subject of a National Bank. Senate speech January 1834.

Wentworth, F. L. (1896) *A Silver Baron*, Iowa City: Mercer Printing Co, 1932 (first published 1896).

Wheatley, J. (1803) Remarks on Currency and Commerce, (Henry Thornton's copy, bound with King 1803).

White, A. D. (1876) *Fiat Money Inflation in France* in Capie (ed.) (1991).

White, L. H. (1984) *Free Banking in Britain: Theory, experience and debate, 1800–1845*, Cambridge: Cambridge University Press.

White, L. H. (1989) *Competition and Currency. Essays on free banking and money*, New York: New York University Press.

White, L. H. and Seglin, G. A. (1989) 'The Evolution of a Free Banking System' in White, L. H. (1989) *op. cit.*

Wilson, James, M. P. (1847) 'Capital, Currency and Banking . . .', *Economist*, London. (Articles in the journal which Wilson founded.)

Wolowski, M. (1870) *L'or et l'argent*, Paris.
Wood, J. P. (1824) *Memoirs of the life of John Law of Lauriston*, Edinburgh.
  Appendix is translation of Henri Storch, Cours d'Economie Politique, Paris
  1823.

INDEX

Notes: 1. Sub-entries are generally in chronological order; 2. US is used as an abbreviation for United States and UK for United Kingdom

Eadgar, King of England 25, 41
Eagly, R. V. 258–9
East India Company (Dutch) 132
East India Company (England) 99, 140, 141, 142–3, 177
Eastern Europe 3, 268, 270; coinage in 24, 35, 86
Edinburgh mint 28
Edward I, King of England 27, 28, 30, 37, 63
Edward III, King of England 36, 38–9
Edward IV, King of England 39
Edward VI, King of England 23, 29, 41, 45–6, 52, 54, 55–9
Edwy, King 25
Egypt 110, 270
Einzig, P. 258
electrum 4, 107, 112
Elford and Company (bank) 152
Elizabeth I, Queen of England 16, 20, 52, 56–7, 59, 63
Ellicott, Thomas 168, 172
Emery, Philip 25
Engel, A. 24
England: banking and finance in 132–7, 230, 235 (see also deposit banking and Napoleonic Wars and South Sea Bubble); land banks 203–5; after 1801 see United Kingdom; see also England, coinage in
England, coinage in: before 1250 (including Anglo-Saxon period) 13, 16, 23, 24–8; commercial revolution (13th to 15th centuries) 15, 20–1, 32, 34, 36–9, 125–6, 127; 16th to 18th centuries 11, 13, 15, 17–18, 115, 116–17, 232–3 (see also recoinage of 1696)
Erleigh, Viscount 138–9, 144, 147
Esdailes (bank) 178
Europe, banking and finance in 129–37, 174, 211–13, 217, 219; see also Law, John
Europe, coinage in: ancient world 107–12; before 1250 4–5, 23–30 (see also Carolingian system); commercial revolution (13th to 15th centuries) see commercial revolution and trade fairs; 16th to 18th centuries 15, 18; 19th century 15, 67, 71–2, 75–82, 83–92, 102; 20th century 270; bimetallism 67, 75–82, 90–1, 102; gold standard 67,

71–2, 270; monetary unions 3, 8, 83–92; see also individual countries in particular France; Germany; Italy; Spain
European Monetary Union (EMU) 3, 8
Evans, D. Morier 192, 194, 196, 197
Evans, G. G. 221
Evans, Sir John 54
exchange rates 7, 60, 72; 19th century 127, 177, 219, 235–7, 240–1; 20th century 3, 267–8, 269; Bretton Woods system 7, 103; Exchange Rate Mechanism (ERM) 3
Exchequer Bills 152, 196, 197

failures, bank 186–8, 190; see also crises
fair wear and tear 9, 13–14
Feaveryear, A. T. 272; on War with France (1793) 233; on banking, development of 133; on Royal Commission (1810) 237; on Bank Charter Act (1833) 156, 157, 244–5; on crisis of 1836 179; on crisis of 1847 193–4, 197; on gold standard 68; on Great War 265; on interwar years 267–8, 269
Federal Reserve Bank (US) 117, 182, 214, 265
Felt, J. B. 165
Fetter, F. W.: on Bank Charter Act (1833) 156, 158; on banking, development of 148; on crisis of 1825 152–5; on gold standard 70; on suspension of payments 235, 237, 243
fiat value see tale
'fiduciary issue' 191–2
First Bank of United States 161–3, 165
First National Bank of Boston 160
Fisher, Irving 99, 100, 118
Flanders 38, 50, 61; trade fairs 124
Fleetwood, William 62
Florence: banking and finance in 129; coinage in 18, 19, 22, 32, 33, 34, 35, 125, 127
foreign bills and currency (US) 165, 216, 220
foreign exchange 5; see also exchange rates
Foreman, Joshua 187
forward exchange rate 127
Foster, John 235
Fox, Charles 235

Montgomery Hyde, H. 207, 209–10
Morgan, E. V. 135
Morgan, J. P. 265
Morris, James 196
Morris, Robert 160, 221
Mueller 12, 32–3, 35, 40, 272
Muhleman, Maurice M. 260–1, 262
Mundell, Alexander 150
Murphy, Antoin E. 204, 206, 209, 210, 212, 225
Musket, Robert 150
Myers, M. G.: on United States: banking 160, 162, 163, 171, 172, 183, 184; bimetallism 75, 97; gold standard 264; greenbacks 247, 250; Independent treasury 180

Naples 12
Napoleon Bonaparte 77, 238
Napoleon, Prince Jerome 88
Napoleon, Louis 86
Napoleonic Wars 68, 115, 260; and suspension of payments (1797–1821) 226, 230, 232–45
National Assembly (France) 224; see also French Revolution
National Bank (Austria) 259
National Bank Act (US) 264
National Bimetallism 101–2
National Debt (France) 208
National Debt (UK) 61, 136, 232; and joint stock company see South Sea Bubble
National Debt (US) 175, 252–3
National Emission Caisse (Russia) 269
National Land Bank (England) 204–5
National Monetary Commission (US) 101, 186, 264, 265; on inconvertible paper money 258, 259, 260
National Provincial (later National Westminster) Bank (UK) 155
Navigation Acts (England) 217
Neal, L. 147
Necker, Jacques 222–4
Needham, Joseph 256
Nelson, B. N. 122
Netherlands: banking and finance in 6, 129, 130–2, 137 (see also Amsterdam); coinage in 67, 85, 270 (see also Low Countries)
New England banks 160, 162, 164–5, 184, 188, 216, 247

New Jersey banks 220
New York 218; banks 160, 162, 164, 165, 184, 186–90, 220, 264–5; Building Company 146; safety fund system 186–8
Newcastle 27, 155, 233
Newcomb, Simon 252
Newman, E. P. 216, 220
Newton, Sir Isaac: recoinage of 1696 6, 17, 52, 61, 62, 64–7, 77, 203
Nicea, Council of (325) 120
nickel in coinage 14
nineteenth century see banking and finance; bimetallism; gold standard; monetary union
Norman, George Warde 149, 157–8, 191
North and South Carolina banks 181–2, 216, 220
Northern and Central Bank of England 178
Northumberland, Protector 41
Norway see Scandinavia

O'Brien, P. 246, 252, 253
Offa, King of Mercia 23, 24, 267
offsetting/clearing balances 116
Ohio banks 181
Oman, Sir C. 24, 37–8, 41, 67, 233
options trading 117, 136
Oresme, Nicholas 16
Orford, First Earl of see Walpole
Orleans, Duke of see Louis XV
Ormond, Duchess of 145
O'Sullivan, M. D. 127
Ottonian Empire 24
Oudard, G. 206
Overstone, Lord see Loyd
Oxford, Herbert Asquith, Earl of 266
Oxford, Robert Harley, Earl of 138–9

Paine, Thomas 160, 235
Palmer, John Horsley 154, 155–6, 157, 158, 197; 'Palmer Rule' 156
Panic, M. 67, 72, 73
panics see crises
Parieu (France) 90
Paris mint 29
Parish, John 237
Parker, H. 134
Parnell, Sir Henry 149, 157
Peel, Sir Robert 71, 151, 191–2, 197, 244–5

and concepts of money 7, 15–16, 17, 19
silver trade *see* bullion trade
sinking fund 141, 232
small change *see* petty coins
Smith, Adam 68, 106, 130–2, 136, 212, 216
Snowden, Philip 269
Solon of Athens 4, 108
Somerset, Protector 41
Sommers, Lord 135
South African gold 263, 266
South America *see* Latin America
South Sea Bubble (1720) 6, 115, 117, 136, 138–47, 151, 203, 210, 212, 232; early history 138–42; and Bank of England 138–9, 140, 141–4, 210, 213; operation 142–7; aftermath 147
Southwark mint 45
Spain 261; banking and finance in 138, 140–1; coinage in 5–6, 15, 34, 216
Spanish Succession, War of 138, 140, 212
Spaulding, Eldridge G. 248–9
specie 9, 12, 18; backing notes *see* converibility; Specie Circular in US 175–6; *see also* bullion; gold; silver
speculation: and banking and finance 170, 177, 179; *see also* fraud and corruption; South Sea Bubble
Speiser, Johann Jakob 84–5
Spencer, Earl (Lord Althorp) 155, 176, 234
Sperling, J. G. 140, 142, 143, 146
Spinks Numismatic Circular 54
Spring-Rice, Dominick 268
Stamp Act (England, 1765) 217–18
stamp duty 192
Stanhope, Lord 147
state banks in US *see* local banking
Stefan I, King of Hungary 24
Stephen, King of England 25
Sterling Area of 20th century 269–71
Stern, F. 90
Steuart, Sir James 99
Stevens, Mr 249
Stewart, F. H. 221
Stewart, Ian (*now* Lord Stewartby) 28
stock markets: development of 135–6
'Stop of the Exchequer' (England, 1672) 134–5
Storch (1815) 258
Stuart de Rothesay, Lord 157

Subercaseaux, Guillermo 260–1
Sunderland, Lord 147
Supple, B. L. 133
surplus distributed in US 175–6
suspension of payments: 1672 (England) 134–5; 1814–16 (US) 164–5, 166; 1861 (US) 247; 1914 (UK) 266; and War of 1812 (US) 163–6; *see also* resumption
suspension of payments in 1797–1821 (UK) 69, 149, 150–1, 232–45; coinage 232–3; resumption, towards 244–5; and war with France 233–45
'sweating coins' 13
Sweden: banking and finance in 131–2; coinage in *see under* Scandinavia; inconvertible paper money 258–9
Swift, Jonathan 21, 145
Switzerland 8; coinage in 82, 83, 84–5, 90, 270
Sword Blade Company (later Bank) 139–40

tale 9, 11, 12, 16–17, 18, 108
Talleyrand-Périgord, Charles 224
Taney, Roger 169–70, 171–2, 185
tax: and American Civil War 247, 252, 253; on American colonies 217–18, 219; on bullion trade 66; and costs of mint 11; and French revolution 222; land 134; policy and banking and finance 133–4; on US banks 165, 167
Tennessee banks 164, 181
Thibaudeau 230
Thomas, George Henry 270
Thomas, St 121
Thomas, W. A. 135
Thornton, Henry 227, 235, 236, 237, 238
Thurlow, Lord 183
Tooke, Thomas 70, 149, 155, 177–9, 191, 192, 233
Torrens, Colonel Robert 149, 191, 197
Tours mint 28–9
Tower of London mint 45, 132–3; Tower Pound 42
Townshend, Charles 142, 218
trade: and banking and finance 169, 172; in coins 74, 75–6, 78–80; and inconvertible paper money 216–17; tokens 20; trading companies 209, 210 (*see also* South Sea Bubble); *see also* bullion trade; trade fairs and credit
trade fairs 31–2, 116, 123–8; history and

weight reduction in coinage 27, 28; 13th
  to 18th centuries 38–9, 63, 65; 19th
  century 69, 74, 75; *see also* clipping;
  debasement
Wellington, Arthur Wellesley, Duke of
  Westminster 71, 162, 176
Weston (Lord Treasurer) 134
Wheatley, J. 235
White, A. D. 229–30
White, Lawrence H. 149, 189–90
William I, King of England 23, 25
William IV, King of England 176
William de Gloucester 37
William the Lion, King of Scotland
  26
William of Orange, King of England 21,
  60
Willing, Charles 221
Willing, Thomas 160
Wilson, Edward (Beau) 206

Wilson, James 149–50, 192
Wilson, Rivers 88
Witte, Count Sergei 258
Wolsey, Cardinal 42
Wood, Sir Charles 194
Wood, J. P. 209–10
Wood, William 21
World Wars: First 265–6, 268, 269;
  Second 270
Wren, Sir Christopher 61
Wright, Silas 180
Wriothesley, Thomas 44, 49
'W's, Three' (Wilson's, Wiggins and
  Wildes) 177–8

York mint 45, 46

Ziani, Sebastiano 33
Zuckerkandl 260
Zwilchenbart, Mr 85